THE TREASURE
WITHIN THE
KINGDOM OF GOD

TERRY E. LURSEN

**366 Daily Readings
According to the Gospel of
Jesus Christ
The Kingdom of God**

TEL Publishing

For further information please go to
www.perspectivesintruth.com
Or email at terrylursen@gmail.com

Copyright © 2014 by Terry E. Lursen
Cover Design: Stephen Lursen Art
Licensed by: Terry E. Lursen
Published by: TEL Publishing

ISBN: 978-0-9910989-0-3
ebook isbn: 978-0-9910989-1-0

All rights reserved. No part of this publication may be reproduced, stored in a retrieval system or transmitted in any form or by any means, electronic, mechanical, photocopying, recording or otherwise, without the prior written permission of the copyright owner.

Scripture taken from the New American Standard Bible unless otherwise noted.

Scripture taken from the NEW AMERICAN STANDARD BIBLE, © 1960, 1962, 1963, 1968, 1971, 1973, 1975, 1977, by The Lockman Foundation. Used by permission.

Scripture taken from the New King James Version®. Copyright © 1982 by Thomas Nelson, Inc. Used by permission. All rights reserved.

Scripture quotations are from the Holy Bible, English Standard Version® (ESV®) Copyright © 2001 by Crossway, a publishing ministry of Good News Publishers. Used by permission. All rights reserved.

Scripture quotations marked (NIV) are taken from the Holy Bible, New International Version®, NIV®. Copyright © 1973, 1978, 1884, 2011 by Biblica Inc.,™. Used by permission of Zonderan. All rights reserved worldwide. www.zondervan.com The "NIV" and "The New International Version" are Trademarks registered in the United States Patent and Trademark Office by Biblica, Inc. ™

Scripture quotations marked (NLT) are taken from the Holy Bible, New Living Translation, copyright © 1996, 2004, 2007 by Tyndale House Foundation. Used by permission of Tyndale House Publishers, Inc., Carol Stream, Ill. 60188. All rights reserved.

Scripture taken from the Revised Standard Version of the Bible, copyright 1952 [second edition 1971, by the Division of Christian Education of the National Council of the Churches of Christ in the United States of America. Used by permission. All rights reserved.

Library of Congress Cataloging-in-Publication Data
Lursen, Terry E., 1957 -
The treasure within the kingdom of God : 366 Daily readings according to the gospel of Jesus Christ the kingdom of God

Library of Congress Control Number: 2013918749

Preface

A life lived is a life lived with purpose, otherwise, it's not really living. Our purposes in living are as varietal as there are people, for each person has a purpose under heaven and it is up to the individual to discover, at some point in their lives, what their purpose in living truly is. To everything there is a season and to every person there is a purpose. My purpose is found and lived out in Jesus Christ. I trust that you have, or will, discover your purpose in the earth as the Lord has purposed for you in Him.

Through the years, my life has taken its turns for the good, for the worse and back again. I have lived in plenty and I have lived in want. I have lived for the Lord and I have lived solely for my own selfish desires. In and through the last 56 years, there have been many discoveries along the way, but none as impactful as the progression of mature discovery in purpose. I have played sports, sang songs, led worship, led people, worked in education and operations, preached to thousands and preached to myself, written writings, cleaned, started and ran my own businesses, built buildings, built people, prayed, praised the Lord, married, raised three fantastic children, built up lives and in my own pitiful way, tore down a few lives along the way. In that, there is regret. In all of this, I have continued to strive to do one thing and that is to do the will of my Father in heaven. I can honestly say that I was not very good at it...that is, doing the will of my Father in heaven. My transition came when I learned to be in Him as opposed to doing something for Him.

I have come to realize that real maturity in Christ comes at my own expense and not at the expense of another. In jest, I have been accused of maintaining the 'deny thyself ministries'. Real maturity is progressing, growing and always learning. Real maturity is seeing Him and Him alone. I have re-read the scriptures over and over again. I have been led to different cultures than what I grew up in, which was the white Southern Baptist denomination. I married a Catholic who is no longer Catholic, but is known as a Holy Spirit filled believer. Our family progressed through the Baptist church, the Church of God, back to the Baptists, the Four-Square, to the African-American Missionary Baptist, studied different spiritual movements and cultures, moved on to the non-denominational and now, I have become quite free from denominational religion. Yes, I said denominational religion, for it is denominational religion that has become a system unto itself with its own set of rules, guidelines, structures and policies as how to become a Christian and how to live that life out, if one chooses to take the Christian life that seriously. Oswald Chambers stated that, "the institutions of Churchianity are not Christianity. An institution is a good thing if it is second; immediately an institution recognizes itself it becomes the dominating factor."[1]

The church of today has become an isolated entity and system unto itself and preaches its own religion according to its fathers in their respective denominations. American religion, particularly, is not Christianity as Jesus Christ ushered in the Kingdom of God.

I have had to go back to the scriptures, particularly Jesus' words in the four Gospels, and re-read them for myself with only the Holy Spirit as my guide. He is the One true guide into the Word of God. Then, I continually examined my own past education and upbringing. I questioned just about everything I had been taught regarding the preaching of the scriptures and relearned the Word according to what Jesus was really saying and not what some other man said He was saying. I went back to re-reading Billy Graham, Dietrich Bonhoeffer, Watchman Nee, Andrew Murray and Oswald Chambers. I read Tolstoy and his beliefs regarding the Gospel and the doctrine of non-resistance to evil by force. I have continued in the faith with other believers and have continued to listen to other preachers, writers and commentaries to see if they actually know what they're saying in the Spirit. I have employed constant examination of words in the Hebrew and Greek, even though I do not know either language, there are too many books already written that have the interpretations, definitions, and translations, that the majority of the detailed work has already been done. What we have to do is to put it together to make sense of it all in the Spirit, who is the real Author of the Word.

I have arrived at some inconclusive conclusions as a result of my journey. I say inconclusive conclusions because I am still learning and growing in my walk with the Lord and only He is the great conclusion regarding anything in His Word. I am dialectic, in the sense that I desire the truth and will continue to examine my own thoughts and interpretations in the supreme desire for the truth to be made known. The discoveries that I have made have been in regards to the specificity of the Gospel of Jesus Christ, which is the Kingdom of God. Over the last two thousand years, many theologians and preachers have said the Gospel is many different things or phrases. All of this is thoroughly discussed in this work. Suffice it to say, I have come to the conclusion that the traditional religious church beliefs regarding what the gospel of Jesus Christ is and has been, for the most part, so diverse that the systematic church has become divisive and erroneous. Systematic religion repels people. The only people that Jesus Christ repelled were the systematic religionists. Not much has changed in two thousand years. There seems to be something very wrong with a system that repels people when the very heart of its founder died for the sin of the very people that the system attempts to control, manipulate and rob from through self-postulation. Denominational religion and its leaders have become the supreme authority in place of our Lord Jesus Christ.

My discovery has led me to relying solely on Him and not a man. Since becoming a new creation in Him, I have always been able to worship God. My worship was always about Him. My offerings and tithes were always given to Him. However, man, using systematized religion takes the focus off of Jesus Christ and puts it on the preacher, the pope, the bishop, the priest, the worship leader, the building, the class, the future, the baptisms, the statistics, the offerings, the finances, the debt and the myriads upon myriads of obstacles that the leaders for God put in the way of God. Idols and idol worship are preeminent in many houses of worship. It is time to seek the Kingdom of God and His righteousness and give Him His honor now and forevermore.

The purpose of this book of readings is to lead the reader to a maturing relationship with Jesus Christ. All glory is His and His alone. I pray that you will desire to be with Him, not to please Him or serve Him, but to be with Him. There is a difference as you will grow to understand. Secondly, as we learn to be with Him, we will learn to become a true disciple of Jesus Christ. Jesus never told us to go and save people, He told us to make disciples and that takes time and effort. Contemporary evangelism is about the quick conversion, the notch in the belt, the quick buck, building a building or a denomination or adding to the statistics. Preachers and evangelists bragging about their baptisms is a perversion of Jesus Christ's intent. Again, Jesus was never about any of this and He never told us to become this way, but systematized religion has to support itself with new money and warm bodies. It has to pay for its buildings under the guise of evangelization. It is time to obey our Lord in making disciples and stop the madness of perverting the Gospel of Jesus Christ with religion's own brand of desire.

The disciple of Jesus Christ desires Him first and only; has learned the concept of denying himself before His Lord; has taken up his own cross and is learning to follow Jesus Christ in the power of the Holy Spirit. This is the purpose of this book and the purpose of my life today. As you progress through these readings, re-read the scriptures yourself, again and again, with the mindset of the Gospel of the Kingdom of God and the Holy Spirit will reveal Himself to you unlike you've ever known. Get back to Jesus and what He taught. Learn to abide, which is to really live, in Him. Be and remain in Him. The Gospel of Jesus Christ is the Kingdom of God. Journey with Him and we will journey together, in His Life, in His Kingdom now and forevermore.

I want to acknowledge and thank my lovely wife of 31 years, Jane. I love you, Jane. She has been a blessing of magnanimous proportions in so many countless ways. My three children, whom I tirelessly love, Jessica, Stephen and Christian have been the Lord's blessing for me throughout the last 30 years. You all have been my life and my heart, I love you all! Thank you all for your support and encouragement in my life and in this work. We are growing and learning, maturing and loving better and better with each new day. You all have made the difference in me in practicing my theories into reality. Because of you, I know that what I have written can be accomplished in Spirit and in Truth.

Thank you to Ben Goins for being a real friend. As our friendship has grown, I have seen you grow with your family and with our Lord into a maturing disciple of our Lord. Thank you and Emily for reading through this work and for participating and contributing to the work as you both have.

To Chris Thompson, Jerel Law, Dennis Benton and Robert Whitlow…thank you for reading my work, supplying the needed input and encouragement and for being the spiritual unction in me to persevere with these writings. Without your necessary encouragement, this would not only have been a more arduous task, I would have been left in reserved doubt. Your input made the difference in me getting this done on time, so thank you!

Thanks to Beth Bray and Linda Cochran for their reading through portions of this work and for all of the encouragement.

I pray that you, as the reader, will pray through these writings and learn to submit to our Lord, not the writngs, through desiring Him, denying the self throughout the day, taking up your cross and seriously, lovingly following our Lord by resting in Him. He is our peace. He is our rest. He is our joy. Be found in Him and remain in Him all the days of your life in this life and in the life forevermore!

Terry Lursen

November, 2013

Dedication

To Jesus…you already know…I love You! I pray that this work has been what You have desired. You are my life.

To Oswald and his beloved Biddy Chambers, to Watchman Nee, Dietrich Bonhoeffer and Andrew Murray, to the Reverend Billy Graham and to Mr. Leo Tolstoy…you have been my teachers for many years. I have come to know you all personally by your writings and your gifts and my thankfulness for your lives and your gifts goes before our Father as glory unto Him. You lived lives that were pleasing to the Lord and your writings have been left to the world as a witness to our Lord. The inspiration that you continue to give through your works is incalculable and only the Lord knows all that has been done in Him.

I find myself surrounded by a wonderful cloud of witnesses that goes beyond these people of faith who were gifted writers because they were obedient to our Lord in His purposes for their respective lives. Your writings continue to change the world one person at a time. I pray that as the Lord leads me, the writings that I write will be a continuance of the allegiance and fervor that you all displayed and with respect to the Rev. Billy Graham, continue to display, in your lives and in your work.

January 1ˢᵗ

The Words of Jesus Christ are Spirit

In John 6:63, Jesus said, "It is the Spirit who gives life; the flesh profits nothing. The words that I speak to you are spirit, and they are life." (NKJV)

The older I have become, the more I have come to realize that many of my ideas of God and the Word of God have come from the dwelling place of men's minds. Jesus said that His words are 'spirit' and in my submission to Him, I acknowledge that within myself dwells no good thing, but 'in Him', the Spirit gives life. I have to move away from my own understanding of the things of God and move 'into' Him through abiding, living, in Him.

Daily, in the each and every moment, I must submit to Him, giving up the right to myself in order to dwell in His Spirit. It is only then that the words of Jesus Christ come alive and breathe life into me. His words are Spirit and can only be understood in the Spirit.

I have failed so many times, but now I know I don't have to.

Dwell in His Spirit today and see that the Kingdom of God is nearer than you think.

For He whom God has sent speaks the words of God, for God does not give the Spirit by measure. The Father loves the Son, and has given all things into His hand. He who believes in the Son has everlasting life; and he who does not believe the Son shall not see life, but the wrath of God abides on Him.
(John 3:34-36, NKJV)

January 2ⁿᵈ

The Challenge of the Christ-like Life

"...whoever drinks of this water will thirst again, but whoever drinks of the water that I shall give him shall never thirst. But the water that I shall give him will become in him a fountain of water springing up into everlasting life."
(John 4:13b-14, NKJV)

Was it ever in His plan that we should do what Jesus would do? Trying to imitate God in the earth is only a notion that men who lack understanding try to do.

Jesus said that we must be 'born again'. That is to say, we must become a totally new and regenerated being. Jesus said to His disciples, "Whoever desires to come after Me, let Him deny himself, and take up his cross, and follow Me. For whoever desires to save his life will lose it, but whoever loses his life for My sake will find it." (Matthew 16:24-25).

It is in the losing and the loosing of our selves that we find the true 'born again' self that Christ has called his disciples to be. It is the work of the Holy Spirit to make us a new creation. In the desiring of Him and in the denying of myself, I see that it is not I who lives, but that it is the Christ Who lives in me. So, no longer do I think that I can be like Him, but it is Him being Himself in me. This is the mystery of the gospel of the Kingdom that Jesus prayed about in John 17:23, "I in them, and You in Me; that they may be made perfect in one, and that the world may know that You have sent Me, and have loved them as You have loved Me."

Being born again into His Kingdom of grace is the losing of my life for His sake and the finding of His life in me. Then, and only then, do I find the inescapable reality of Truth abiding in me. Paul said, "…to fulfill the word of God, the mystery which was hidden from ages and generations, but now has been revealed to His saints. To them God willed to make known what are the riches of the glory of this mystery among the Gentiles: which is Christ in you, the hope of glory."   (Colossians 1:25b-27, NKJV)

January 3rd

Breathing the Breath of Life

"And the Lord God formed man of the dust of the ground, and breathed into his nostrils the breath of life; and man became a living being."
(Genesis 2:7, NKJV)

Jesus Christ talked about the life, the abundant life, "…I have come that they may have life, and that they may have it more abundantly." (John 10:10b). We continually, in our day by day moments, need to acknowledge that the true life in Him is the life breathing breath of God in the vessel that bears our name.

Without Him, I understand that I am nothing, but in Him, He is everything. Daily submission to Him in His will is the first, the second, and the last thing that I need to do. I have lived a life in want and in need. I have heard the old, old stories of traditional mindsets and traditional ways of searching over the scriptures and then trying to live out His life in service only making me tired, weary, and in greater need. Some conventional thinking requires service to God above all. I have seen the plight of the religious and understand why it doesn't work.

In Him, I find Truth. In the denying of the totality of my self, I find His life. This denying of self is not the denying of things, nor the part and partial giving up of what I choose to give up. This denying of self is not just giving up of the bad and the worst of me, but it is the giving up of all that is me, the bad, the good, and the best of me.

If He has chosen me to be His disciple, then I must submit myself to Him and become the new creation that He has chosen me to be. He, then, by the power of His Holy Spirit, breathes his new life into me. The breath of God is True Life and True Living.

Breathe Him in, and breathe out the breath of Life!

January 4th

Living the Life

"But God, who is rich in mercy, because of His great love which He loved us, even when we were dead in trespasses, made us alive together with Christ (by grace you have been saved), and raised us up together, and made us sit together in the heavenly place in Christ Jesus, that in the ages to come He might show the exceeding riches of His grace in His kindness toward us in Christ Jesus."
(Ephesians 2:4-7, NKJV)

Being in Christ is what He has called His disciples to be and to do. Abiding in, which is living in Him, is the doing. It was His blood shed on Calvary that paid the price for you and me to inherit the grace that abides in Him. And because of that grace, He calls us to Himself as His disciples, to sit with Him in the heavenly places. We are to sit above the fray of the world. To that extent He told us to seek first the kingdom of God and His righteousness. He is His righteousness; He is His kingdom. We are to be with Him in the dwelling place of the Most High.

We are to get out of ourselves and into Him; pray, brother, pray. Intercede for others in the secret place. Our frivolous needs are always met in Him, but when we lose sight of Him and begin to focus on our stuff, we forget where we have been allowed to sit. When we are in Him, in His kingdom, we have been afforded to be in the Presence of the Almighty. Do not take that for granted.

The Truth of the life lived in Him is the exciting, God-breathed type of life as in Ezekiel when God breathed over the dry bones and they came to life! Paul stated, "…in whom we have boldness and access with confidence through faith in Him". (Ephesians 3:12, NKJV).

In all of the Kingdom of God, He shows us the riches of His grace, His kindness… He shows us Himself. That is something to shout about! We have been allowed entrance into His kingdom and have been allowed to sit with Him in His heavenly places. Hallelujah! Be glad that the Creator of all of the universe loves you with such a great and magnanimous love that even while we were yet sinners, He loved us enough to fulfill His plan to die for us. He paid the price for our eternal life with Him. That life is not just for your time after time, but it is for your time today.

Today, live in Him and know where He has placed you with Him in the heavenly places. It is by His wonderful grace that He loves you and is willing to love through you to a lost and hurting world.

January 5th

Daily Submission

"But what things were gain to me, these I have counted loss for Christ. Yet indeed I also count all things loss for the excellence of the knowledge of Christ Jesus my Lord, for whom I have suffered the loss of all things, and count them as rubbish, that I may gain Christ, and be found in Him, not having my own righteousness, which is from the law, but that which is through faith in Christ, the righteousness which is from God by faith;"   (Philippians 3:7-9, NKJV)

It is in the daily dying to self that we realize all that we gain by being in Him. Paul counted all things as loss and we are to follow that example. The greatest example, however, of daily submission and the dying to self was the life and breath of our Lord Jesus Christ.

He denied Himself when no one else even thought of doing such a thing. He left His throne in heaven to fulfill the divine purpose of paying the ultimate sacrifice that needed to be paid for the sin of the world. He lived a life of total denial. And so, must we. We have to learn to deny ourselves even when we are the only one in the room doing it. That is our test. He denied Himself when He was the only one in the world doing it. He has been the Supreme leader.

We cannot describe how wonderful it is when we let go of ourselves and let God have His way. We have to will to let go of our will so that His will is accomplished in and through the life that He lives through us. This is a far different teaching than the over simplification of 'inviting' Jesus into your heart. We cannot take a piece of God for ourselves to use as we please. Total submission to Jesus Christ recognizes Him as our Lord and Master, as well as, our Savior.

In 1 Corinthians 15, Paul stated that he died daily. I am learning to do the same. It truly is in the each and every moment that God has allowed me to breathe His breath that being found in Him is the only place to be. I really do not desire to be any place else. He is His righteousness and it is only by His righteousness that a Holy God provides such an opportunity for us to be in His all-sufficient grace.

January 6th

The Power to Obey and Love

"Jesus answered and said to him, 'If anyone loves Me, he will keep My word; and My Father will love him, and We will come to him and make Our home with him."   (John 14:23, NKJV)

Have you ever tried and tried to obey the word of the Lord and found yourself failing miserably in the process? "I just can't love that person. I just can't forgive him. I just can't seem to find it in my heart to listen anymore because my heart is full of…" And on and on, our excuses endlessly fall to the ground with our hearts wondering, "Why can't I love and be loved?"

If we are honest with ourselves, we have to admit that we fail and fail often in loving, in forgiving, and in being the Christ-like person that we were told that we would be by becoming a Christian. Many, many people have left the faith believing that this thing just doesn't work because they haven't seen any real change in their lives, or more particularly, they haven't seen any change in the lives of others that profess to be Christians.

Many folk who have been led down the paths of religion have been told things that simply are not in the scriptures. We have to look to the scriptures to see what Jesus said about Himself and His Way. He said that if you desire to come after Him, deny yourself, take up your cross, and follow Him. He said that you must be born again. Jesus talked about seeds falling into the ground and dying in order to have the life that they were meant to have. Jesus spoke, but only a few have listened to Him. He also said that if you loved Him, you would obey His word.

To be honest, we are powerless to obey all that Jesus has told us to obey. But, He provided for us the way in which we should go that if we would not depart from it, we would have life, and that, more abundantly. This way is His Way of the unbecoming of ourselves, and becoming an entirely new creation in Him. It is only by His grace that any obedience can ever take place. It is His grace working in us and through us that enables us to submit in obedience to His Words.

Our believing in Him and confessing Him is the total giving of the self in Him for His glory. When we abide in Him and obey His word, He has promised to abide in us and make His home in us. Here is the key…the power to obey, live and breathe out His life is His Holy Spirit power living in you to witness to Himself of a life lived in agreement with Him. He does the work in you and ultimately through you for out of you will flow rivers of living water. (John 7:38) Draw near to the Lord and obey His word and you will see and know the power of His life living through you for His glory and majesty. His Presence is all that we need in us for His purposes to be fulfilled in Him.

January 7th

Abiding in Grace

"Jesus said to him, 'I am the way, the truth, and the life. No one comes to the Father except through Me.'"   *(John 14:6, NKJV)*

It is for certain that no man has testified of the truth that Jesus spoke of Himself, that being – He is the way, He is the truth, and He is the life. It is 'in' Him that we are able to see His way. It is in the power of the cross of Christ that a door is opened to us to enter into the grace that He has afforded us.

Jesus said that He is the door, but the door to what? See it like this…the door, being Jesus Christ, is in the shape of a cross. This door has the shed blood of Jesus Christ poured across the mantel and the doorposts. When we enter in through this door, we stretch out our arms and enter as He did, relinquishing ourselves, our flesh, and submitting to Him.

In the regenerating process of our submitting to Him through His cross, He makes us a new creation in Him; old things pass away, and, behold, all things become new. We take that step through the Door into Him…into His Kingdom.

And, it is in His Kingdom, His Life that we find our abiding place in Him. The abiding place of His grace is the place and person of Jesus Christ. He is our peace and our rest. When the entire world goes into discontent, we don't have to, we can be in Him.

Draw near to Him, submit to Him, and abide in His grace today. His grace does the work and the works that we think we do, He is doing them through us. Remain in Him and His life will exude gloriously through you today!

January 8th

Alone With God

"May my meditation be sweet to Him; I will be glad in the Lord."
(Psalm 104:34, NKJV)

It is to His good pleasure to be alone with Him. The perfect union of a man and a woman as husband and wife united together in love is His example of the shadow of things that are and are to be. It is good to be alone with Him. The work of the Holy Spirit in our lives is to draw us to Him, not just closer to Him that is not close enough. As Jesus said and as the Psalmist said, 'in the Lord'.

May my meditation be sweet to Him in that I know that He knows me and we can be together, alone, and I know that He is sufficient. How could we ever be content without Him? We always want more of whatever we are wanting more of at any given time. We are hardly ever content with what we have or who we are with. But in Him, our wants and desires fade away as darkness fades with the morning light.

Walk in the light as He is in the light and have true fellowship today. Submit to Him in love. Be glad in Him, it is the immediate reciprocation of adoration. When we find ourselves found in Him, gladness of heart is overwhelming. Be glad in Him today!

January 9th

Get Through the Door

"Then Jesus said to them again, 'Most assuredly, I say to you, I am the door of the sheep...I am the door. If anyone enters by Me, he will be saved, and will go in and out and find pasture.'"   (John 10:7, 9, NKJV)

Jesus Christ told his disciples that He was many things. He said He was the way, the truth, and the life. He said he was the bread, the living water; He talked about new wine and us becoming born again and being a new creation. Here, He states that He is the door.

The door represents a passageway that is guarded by an obstacle, that being the door itself. Most doors have locks and can be opened, as well as, closed. Jesus says that He is the 'door of the sheep'. If we have been called to be His disciples, then we are His sheep and the sheep of His pasture. If we know that we enter into the Kingdom of God, we enter into the Kingdom by the door...He is the door, the gateway to His Kingdom.

We enter into Him by and through Him. All of the redemption of man is done in Him. He is the one who saves, and it is He Who keeps us saved in His Kingdom. Abiding in Him is to know that we have the opportunity to get to the door, Jesus Christ. His blood shed on Calvary was the entrance payment for us to get through the door into Him.

Come to know Him as Savior, yes, and come to know Him as Lord, as you come to know Him personally by walking into what He has provided for us. He has provided His rest in His holy Presence.

Behold, Lord, I come to You and find peace and rest in You. It is in You, alone, Lord, that I see and know that You have provided the way and You show us the way by the being the Door into your Kingdom. Thank You, Lord for all that You have done and are doing in my life!

January 10th

The Good Shepherd

"I am the good shepherd; and I know My sheep and am known by My own. As the Father knows Me, even so I know the Father; and I lay down My life for the sheep."   (John 10:14-15, NKJV)

Is it possible for us to know the height and the depth of the love of God by the life giving blood of Jesus Christ? Is it possible for us to fully understand the mystery of His abounding grace that even while we, as the world, were still sinners, Christ died for us on Calvary?

He came to this earth to live and to die for us so that we might have Life in Him. He is the Good Shepherd who knows His sheep and His sheep know Him and know His voice. Do you know His voice? Do you know Him in the fullness of His Kingdom?

Come to know Him, abide in Him, live in Him, speak often with Him, and get to know His voice. It is a pleasure to know that we can know the difference between the Holy voice of God in Christ and the voices of the world that call us and attempt to influence us to our demise.

Jesus, I thank You that You care for me as my guide and my protector, my deliverer and my provider. I pray today, in the each and every moment, that I listen to You as my Shepherd and know that it is You that I follow and not the way of the world. I submit to You, Lord; I submit to You!

January 11th

On True Discipleship

"My sheep hear My voice, and I know them, and they follow Me. And I give them eternal life, and they shall never perish; neither shall anyone snatch them out of My hand."   *(John 10:27-28, NKJV)*

As we come to know Jesus Christ as our great Shepherd, we come to know His voice in listening to Him and obeying what He has said. This is how we know His voice…we read His Word, pray with Him and listen and obey. He has sent His Holy Spirit to guide us in His Word for He speaks to us in His Word.

Jesus said that His sheep hear His voice and He also said that His sheep follow Him. Many times I have seen and heard so-called Christians wanting to claim their right to eternal heaven by saying they know Jesus, but they do not follow Him at all…they follow themselves in the way of the world. Jesus said explicitly that His sheep, His disciples, hear His voice; that is to say, they know what His voice sounds like and they follow what He has to say. He knows who His disciples are. He knows His sheep.

The promise of eternal life is for those who know Him; He knows them, they hear Him, and they follow Him. These are the ones who shall never perish or ever be out of His Presence.

Those who worship Him, worship Him in Spirit and in Truth. Abide in the Truth of His grace. Hear and follow Him. He knows the way in which you should go.

Submit to Him now. Listen to His Holy Spirit and follow Him today!

January 12th

The Living Resurrection

"Jesus said to her, 'I am the resurrection and the life. He who believes in Me, though he may die, he shall live. And whoever lives and believes in Me shall never die. Do you believe this?'" (John 11:25-26, NKJV)

When we are confronted with the idea of Jesus Christ, we are confronted with a choice, to believe, or not to believe. In the instance of the New Testament, the belief, or the confession, was in the regards of the totality of the being. That is to say, I do not simply believe with my mind alone, but I believe with every corpuscle of my being. I would choose to believe that Jesus Christ was and is Who He said He is and in my belief, I lay down what I previously knew to be true and choose His Truth over everything. I believe with my mind, my heart, my soul, and my body follows in obedience to that belief. This is true confession. This is true discipleship.

There has been some evangelistic preaching and praying that says you can pray an eight second prayer and you will be "saved". Their gospel is as though you can speak a magic formula of words and be saved forever and there isn't any mention of a submitted or 'born again' life. Is that Jesus' gospel, or man's? Bonhoeffer referred to that as cheap grace,[1] offering salvation without repentance. This in no way negates the power of the Holy Spirit at work in a person for the power of the Holy Spirit can accomplish any work, but are we sharing His gospel, or some man's idea, just to make it simple and ultimately not tell people the whole truth?

Jesus said that you must be born again. Do you believe that? Do you believe that His resurrection is our resurrection of being born into Him and being born into a totally new creation? He is the resurrection and the life and no man comes to the Father except though Him. The life that He gives is for today and forevermore. He has taught us that by His death, burial, and resurrection, we, too, can be made new from the death of our old man and be resurrected into new life in Him. But we have to die and give up the old to have this new life. The old has to die just as the seed falls into the ground and dies in order to become its purposed fruit. What most men fear most is letting go of control. His perfect love casts out all fear and raises us up into His heavenly realm.

Dear Jesus, I thank You that You continue to teach us Your Truth in Your Word and Your Holy Spirit guides us into all Truth. Teach us, oh Lord, Your Way and what it means to be resurrected into new life in You. You are our resurrection and You are our Life. Thank You, Lord. Amen.

January 13th

The Grain of Wheat

"Most assuredly, I say to you, unless a grain of wheat falls into the ground and dies, it remains alone; but if it dies, it produces much grain. He who loves his life will lose it, and he who hates his life in this world will keep it for eternal life."
(John 12:24-25, NKJV)

When Jesus calls us to deny ourselves, take up our cross, and follow Him, He calls us to die,[1] as Bonhoeffer attests. The willful heart will not allow this to happen out of fear or selfishness. But Jesus clearly calls us to give up the life that we know that we have and exchange it for the life that He wants to give us. It is in the dying to self. He has our purpose, the purpose for our specific existence, in His life.

When we move beyond the door of grace into the life of His Kingdom, we become regenerated, a new creation. The love we have for ourselves cannot be stronger than the love we have for Him. Our sight on His Light will keep us forever, but we have to give up all that we are, to be born into Him. We do this once and for all as we turn our eyes upon Him and we then continue to walk in His Light as He is in the Light. Then, we have fellowship one with another.

It is to His holy love that He draws us unto Himself. In all that He has done for us and in all that He is doing in us, we celebrate our willingness to fall into the ground and die as the grain of wheat; knowing that in our death and burial, He brings us into true life in Him. This is the abundant life that He speaks of and so willingly gives to those who seek Him.

The Kingdom of God is the treasure of life and all who dwell there dwell in Him. *"And I, if I am lifted up from the earth, will draw all peoples to Myself."*
(John 12:32, NKJV)

January 14th

Believe in the Light

"While you have the light, believe in the light, that you may become sons of light." (John 12:36, NKJV)

Today is the day to walk in His light. Jesus is the light of the world. His light is pervasive and penetrating. His light is all-encompassing. His light is the life of men and in Him there is no darkness at all. His light shines upon our paths so that we know the way that we should go and we are determined not to veer off His path of light.

His Word is a lamp to our feet and a light to our paths. His light pierces the darkness and the darkness flees as His light prevails. He who follows him shall not walk in darkness but have the light and life dwelling in him. (John 8:12)

His Word is hidden in our hearts so that we will not sin against Him. We meditate on His Word through the night watches and we are strengthened as we contemplate upon Him. (Psalm 119)

His light causes us to become the light of the world as He is the light of the world. The fullness of His light shines forth, in and through our lives, that others will see good works for His glory. (Matthew 5:14)

Today is the day to walk in the light as He is in the light, let your light so shine before men and glorify Him today! Praise the Lord!

January 15th

Willing to Submit

"So when He had washed their feet, taken His garments, and sat down again, He said to them, 'Do you know what I have done to you? You call Me Teacher and Lord, and you say well, for so I am. If then, your Lord and Teacher, have washed your feet, you also ought to wash one another's feet.'" (John 13:12-14, NKJV)

Our willingness to submit the totality of our wills to Him is going to be tested. What will our wills do when the time comes to serve another disciple in Christ? What will our wills attest to when we are confronted with the challenge to love our enemies and not curse them? What will our wills permit when others say all manner of things against us, even falsely? Will our wills continue to submit to Him through all things?

When it comes to something easy in that we could help or serve our brother, do we serve in love and unrestrained willingness? Do we place ourselves under compulsion to serve and resent it all the while? Or, if we think we have graduated to the pulpit, do we think we no longer have to serve as He served?

Jesus has given us the standard first. Although He is our Lord, our Master, and Teacher, He first served rather than being served. It is to His glory that we serve as He served and knowing that He is in us for every good work, it is Him serving all the while we submit to Him presenting our bodies in worship as a sacrifice.

He is then able to use the vessel that bears your name for His glory and His service. If you call Him Lord and Master, for it is well and true that He is, then He is alive in you to love through you the ones that need love today. Allow His love to pervade the darkness through your tender voice, your tender touch, and your tender hug. Serve the Lord with gladness of heart and as Jesus said, "If you know these things, blessed are you if you do them." (John 13:17, NKJV)

January 16th

Loving One Another

"By this all will know that you are My disciples, if you have love for one another."
(John 13:35, NKJV)

The Holy love of God is the love that Jesus speaks of here. Because He first loved us, we have the opportunity to receive His love. This is not the love of the world that loves because it is loved, or a romantic love that we might see in some movie, nor is it the sentimental love that causes us to emotionally feel and do things that we would not ordinarily do.

Holy love is Holy. It is the love of God poured out on us in grace, unmerited, and freely given because He is love. Holy love is unlike anything in this world. Holy love is not of this world. An unregenerate man cannot love with the love of God. Someone who is not born again does not have the love of God in him. Many Christian churches are filled with unregenerate people who do not know God, nor do they have the love of God in them.

Do not measure your love, or the lack thereof, by other people's version of love. Other people can be quite unloving and judgmental. Measure what is inside of you by the love of God. Do you know Him? Has He remade you unto Himself? Are you born again as Jesus spoke to Nicodemus about in John chapter 3?

If you are set apart by Him, have been made new in Him and consider yourself a disciple of His, you have no excuse not to love. His love bears witness of itself. God loves through you to love others. If you are His disciple, you will love one another. If you find yourself constantly in a state of being unloving, then question yourself as to whether you are truly a disciple of Jesus or maybe you just think you are. Get real with Him and allow Him to tell you the truth.

Holy love is the love of God being poured into your heart and then being poured out of your heart to others. Allow His love to grow inside of you and to be constantly moving, not stagnant. Always forgive. Always forgiving. Let love abound and you will see that you can love with the Holy love of God for His purpose and His glory.

January 17th

Keep My Commandments

"If you love Me, keep My commandments." (John 14:15, NKJV)

You have heard it said by many believers that they love the Lord. They are happy that Jesus loves them and that God loved the world so much that He gave His Son to die on the cross for them. However, when it comes to knowing His word and keeping His word, then it becomes something entirely different for the person who is not seriously involved in a relationship with Jesus Christ.

Jesus admonished His disciples to keep His commandments. His commandments are many and are not suggestions. The words that He spoke are His commandments. We are not exonerated from His word because we are ignorant of it. He clearly states that if we truly love Him, we will keep His commandments, it's not an option.

As we said earlier, an unregenerate man, one who does not know God, cannot love with the love of God, but a born again, new creation man can. As well, an unregenerate man cannot obey the word of God. But, a born again believer who has been made new in Christ is given the power of the Holy Spirit to love and obey. The power of the Holy Spirit comes to the new creation man and it is the power of God that reveals the word in truth and gives the ability to obey. If there is no obedience to His word, then the disciple simply is acting unbecoming himself and is in a state of not submitting to his Lord. If there never has been any obedience to the word of God, most likely there has never been a commitment to Jesus as Lord.

The Holy Spirit gives the power to the disciple of Jesus Christ to obey, to forgive, to love, to submit, to turn the other cheek, to give, as well as, many other attributes of godly and loving behavior. It is the will of man to choose to submit, or not, in the moment by moment opportunities that present themselves every day. Choose to submit to Him in the morning and in the each and every moment of the each and every day. Watch and pray and see what the Lord does in your life. He is amazing! You will find yourself loving when you could not love and obeying Him when you knew it was only His power and grace that did it in you.

January 18th

The Gift of the Holy Spirit

"And I will pray the Father, and He will give you another Helper, that He may abide with you forever-the Spirit of truth, whom the world cannot receive, because it neither sees him nor knows Him; but you know Him, for He dwells with you and will be in you."   (John 14:16-17, NKJV)

The promise of the Holy Spirit is real and true from Jesus Christ. The Holy Spirit of God is the gift of God Himself to dwell in us who are disciples of Jesus Christ. The Holy Spirit's work is to convict the world of sin, and of righteousness, and of judgment. (John 16:8) The Holy Spirit's work is also to guide us into all truth and to speak the word of the Lord and to show us of things to come. (John 16:13) The Holy Spirit will not speak on His own authority, but will speak what He hears. He will glorify Jesus Christ. (John 16:14).

The Holy Spirit is the promise of God to His believers who proceeds from the Father and testifies of the Son. (John 15:26) He will teach you all things, and bring to remembrance all things that Jesus has said. (John 14:26) The mystery of the gospel of the Kingdom of God is Christ in you, the hope of glory. (Colossians 1:27)

Allow the work of the Holy Spirit in your life. He is the gift of God Himself to dwell in you to teach you all things according to the word of the Lord.

Father, I pray that Your Holy Spirit quicken me to Your word. Your word is truth. Incline my heart to hear and understand Your mystery and believe in the work that You have done. Your promise of peace is certain. The gift of your Spirit is sure. Thank You, Father, for guiding me into all truth. Amen.

January 19th

How Little We Know

"Every branch in Me that does not bear fruit He takes away; and every branch that bears fruit He prunes, that it may bear more fruit." *(John 15:2, NKJV)*

The fruit of the Spirit of God is love, joy, peace, patience, kindness, goodness, self-control, gentleness and faithfulness. (Galatians 5:22) Jesus clearly states that His fruit comes from Him. He is the vine, we are the branches. Apart from Him, we can bear nothing. Apart from Him, we can bear no good thing in the Spirit.

If we call on the name of Jesus Christ, which is to desire after Him, we are to deny ourselves, take up our cross, and follow Him. His redemptive work is complete. He is the One who saves us. We cannot save ourselves, nor can we save anyone else. In the submissive process to Him, His Holy Spirit does the work in our lives of a new birth. His Holy Spirit continues to work in and through our lives and that is who other people will see and hear when they come into contact with you. They hear and see the fruit of the One Who dwells in you.

If we are honest with ourselves, we know when we have set ourselves on the throne and taken up residency where the Holy Spirit should reign. That is the part that gets pruned. What is not like Him needs to go and He does the work of pruning with shears of love. He will not share His throne with any man. He is the cleanser and the pruner and He will use whatever means necessary to remove what is not like Him. Our disposition reveals what is in our heart. He will remove what does not abide in Him and throw it in the fire.

Abide in Him and you will be fruitful…full of the Spirit of the Holy One.

Stop treating Him like you're making a phone call and then hanging up on Him because you have something better to do. Allow His Spirit to work His work in your countenance and disposition so that there is nothing between Him and you. Be glad in Him for He is keeping you in His grace and the depth of His love knows no bounds.

January 20th

Abide in Me

"Abide in Me, and I in you. As the branch cannot bear fruit of itself, unless it abides in the vine, neither can you, unless you abide in Me."
(John 15:4, NKJV)

Abiding in Jesus Christ is the only place to be. The abiding place is the person of Jesus Christ. This is not a noble suggestion; it is just as much a command as any command of the Lord.

Fascinatingly enough though, if we have realized Who He is, and what He has done for us in the saving grace of redemption, we will want to be with Him. He is God of the entire universe, our Creator; who wouldn't desire to be with Him? He is wonderful, counselor, mighty God, the Prince of Peace. He is in all things and through all things and He is more than we could ever imagine.

And yet, He knows there are those who will choose not to abide in Him. To abide in Him is to live in Him, stay with Him, dwell in Him and stay there. He Is and always Is. He doesn't leave us, although we do seem to leave Him by neglect or selfishness.

Stay in the secret place with Him. It is an each and every moment choice to be with Him. It is not because He is needy; it is because we need Him. Acknowledge Him in the morning and do not lean upon your own understanding, but seek Him and dwell with Him where He is.

He has promised that as we abide in Him, He abides in us. Believe that! The mystery of the all-encapsulating Presence of the Holy One abides in us.

Jesus said, "If you abide in Me, and My words abide in you, you will ask what you desire, and it shall be done for you." (John 15:7). He is our desire and it is not a trick. When you desire Him with all your heart, soul, and spirit, He has promised to abide in that place. His promises are real and true and He is forever faithful to His word. Bless the Name of Jesus!

January 21st

Be With the Overcomer

"These things I have spoken to you, that in Me you may have peace. In the world you will have tribulation; but be of good cheer. I have overcome the world."
(John 16:33, NKJV)

Two things Jesus speaks of here that are very plain to see, and yet many of us too often forget. First of all, we have to believe Jesus when He says anything because it is the Truth. He says that 'in Me' you may have peace. The abiding place and person is Jesus Christ. Abiding in Jesus Christ is going through the Door of the Kingdom into His Life. The Kingdom of God is the dwelling place of peace, real peace, not peace that the world gives, but true spiritual peace. This peace, that passes all understanding, will guard our hearts 'in' Christ Jesus our Lord.

Secondly, Jesus states that we will have tribulation in this world. Tribulation is trouble, distress, or turmoil because of oppression or persecution. Trouble is going to come, that is, if you're not already in distress, it may be coming your way shortly. This is as a result of being oppressed for naming the name of Jesus, doing good, or displaying the Holy Spirit. In this, you will be persecuted. Our task is not to become bogged down because of persecution or tribulation. We cannot allow the ways of the world to win over our minds and hearts.

Jesus has emphatically declared that He has already overcome the world. Anything that the world has to throw at us has been conquered. Jesus Christ is victorious over sin, death, hell, and the grave. What can man do to me? Whom then shall I fear?

Jesus says abide in Me. Stay with Jesus. Stay with the King. Stay inside of Him, dwelling in His Kingdom where the peace of God passes all understanding. Be of great cheer, He has overcome and you're with Him! Bless His Holy Name!

January 22nd

The Author of Eternal Life

"Jesus spoke these words, lifted up His eyes to heaven and said, 'Father, the hour has come. Glorify Your Son, that Your Son also may glorify You, as You have given him authority over all flesh, that He should give eternal life to as many as You have given Him. And this is eternal life, that they may know You, the only true God, and Jesus Christ whom You have sent.'"
(John 17:1-3, NKJV)

It is wonderful to know the author of my salvation…it is the Lord, strong and mighty. It is stupendous to be in the knowledge of the author of eternal life…it is the Holy Lord, Most High!

He is the author and the finisher of our faith, His Name is Jesus. He continues to declare our abiding in Him that as we give our lives to Him, we know that He has all authority over all flesh.

He that was in the beginning will be with us through the end and forevermore.

The atmosphere of heaven is glory. It is there that the glory resides in splendor. Glory comes from heaven on high. Glory surrounds His throne and Jesus sits at the right hand of the Father.

Eternal life is knowing Him. Jesus Christ declared, 'And this is eternal life, that they may know You, the only true God, and Jesus Christ whom You have sent." Eternal life is knowing our Lord in Jesus Christ. You can know the Lord today. Eternal life is not about time and space; it is not about a point in time in the future when you die and go to heaven. No! Eternal life is for now! Eternal life is the Presence of God, it is a state of being, not a state of time. Eternal life is being in Him now and forevermore.

Get through the Door of Jesus, that wonderful blood stained door and do a walk-about in His Kingdom. Dwell in Him today and dwell in Him forevermore. Amen!

January 23rd

Being One in Christ

"I in them, and You in Me; that they may be perfect in one, and that the world may know that You have sent Me, and have loved them as You have loved Me."
(John 17:23, NKJV)

There is so much to the Kingdom of God it is not too difficult to just go on and on about the treasure of knowing Him. When we get through and out of ourselves in our submission to Him, we find our true self that He created us to be dwelling in Him. What could a man give in exchange for his soul…even the whole world… never! To find myself knowing Him in his Kingdom is knowing Him forever.

The Father sent the Son, named Him Jesus, the Christ, and as the Father and the Son are one, so Jesus prays to the Father to make us one in them. How rich is that?

The Father Creator of the entire universe, being in Jesus Christ, and being one together now desires that the disciples the Father has given Jesus (verses 20-22) be one in them. The Father is in Jesus and Jesus is in the Father. I am in Jesus and Jesus is in me. The Father and Jesus are one and Jesus and the Father come and make their home in me. (John 14:23). Isn't that fantastic?

Can we understand the mystery of the Christ in you, the hope of glory? (Colossians 1:27b) Jesus said that the Kingdom of God does not come with observation, but the Kingdom of God is within you. (Luke 17:21b) And Paul said that "the mystery which was hidden from ages and generations, but now has been revealed to His saints…" (v. 26) His Holy Spirit is the revealer.

You don't have to wait till you die your fleshly death to be one in Him. Be one in Him today, love the Lord with all of your heart, keep His word, and the Father will love you and the Lord of all, in Jesus Christ, will come and make their home in you…today! (John 14:23)

January 24th

Hearing the Voice of Truth

"Pilate therefore said to Him, 'Are You a king then?' Jesus answered, 'You say rightly that I am a king. For this cause I was born, and for this cause I have come into the world, that I should bear witness to the truth. Everyone who is of the truth hears My voice.'"   (John 18:37, NKJV)

Throughout life, I have found that we want to be critical of others who do not believe what we believe. I have discovered that most religious and political beliefs are exactly that, beliefs. Although beliefs require us to think about what we believe, when it comes to religious or political philosophy, it isn't so much about the intellectual as it really is about what a person believes. This is why, at times, we feel like we could talk till 'we're blue in the face' to others and they still do not understand what we're talking about, let alone agree with us.

As far as spiritual matters are concerned, it is not that people do not have the intellectual capacity to believe what we believe, or simply hear what we have to say, they just do not have the ears to hear, or the faith to believe. We cannot create faith in other people, nor can we make people hear Jesus when it is not their time to hear. Jesus said that everyone who is of the truth will hear His voice. It is the Lord

God that decides who hears and who does not hear. Even when a heart is pricked by the Holy Spirit, a person's ability to receive becomes a matter of their personal will. Narrow is the way and few there are who follow in it.

If you have found yourself with the ability to hear His voice, then hear Him and walk in His truth. Be obedient to the calling that is inside of you and be thankful that your name is written in the Lamb's book of life. Continue to be faithful and obedient to the call to go and make disciples.

But in all of this, be careful not to allow a judgmental spirit within yourself to be critical and condemning of others who have not been given the ability to hear Truth. Trust the Lord that those who are of the truth will hear Him when He calls. It is the Holy Spirit's work to convict the world of sin, not yours, and it is the right of our Holy Lord to judge and not ours. (Matt. 7:1-6)

January 25th

Continue in Praise

"I will bless the Lord at all times; His praise shall continually be in my mouth. My soul shall make its boast in the Lord; the humble shall hear of it and be glad. Oh, magnify the Lord with me, and let us exalt His name together."
(Psalm 34:1-3, NKJV)

As we go to the secret place to pray often with our Lord, we learn as we grow that He hears the prayers of the heart whispered in secret to Him. He hears our heart's cry. And, there are times that should be more often, that we can declare with great fervor and with a loud voice His praises.

He alone is worthy of all praise. This is not the time for reserved meditative worship, but the time to open our mouths and let the praise sing to His glory. Do not wait for a Sunday service to praise Him for what He has done; praise Him with a loud voice now! Do not wait for the next week to roll by and for time and space to be spent on the frivolous; praise Him now with a glad and thankful heart! The Psalmist declared that His praise would continually be in his mouth. Continually is ongoing, never ceasing. Imagine that!

Would it be that my mind and heart be so joined to Him in continual abiding grace that my thoughts stay ever abiding in Him. Would it be that my heart be filled with such an overflow of His Spirit that the effervescence of His glory could not be contained, but be shouted from the rooftop that He is Almighty! He has done so many things for us…speak of those things.

The Lord is good. He alone is worthy of our praise. Praise Him where you are. Praise Him where you're going and praise Him when you get there. The Lord is great and greatly to be praised. Shout Hallelujah!

January 26th

Being in Him

"Trust in the Lord, and do good; dwell in the land, and feed on His faithfulness. Delight yourself also in the Lord, and He shall give you the desires of your heart." (Psalm 37:3-4, NKJV)

Trust in the Lord – place all that you are in Him. Know that He is good. Know that He is able to deliver you. Know that He is Lord of all and there is none like Him. Trust Him with your heart, soul, mind, and spirit. Give your all to Him and be filled with His Holy Spirit.

Dwell in Him and feed on His faithfulness – As we abide in Him, He has promised to abide in us. He is faithful to His word. He is faithful to Himself and will do what He has said He will do. Do not count His faithfulness as the world counts it. When we examine ourselves, we see that we are unfaithful in so many things that it's difficult to believe that true faithfulness can even exist. But, He Is faithful. Trust in His faithfulness and rely on Him. Seek Him, know Him, be with Him and incline your heart to rest in Him.

Delight yourself in Him – Be ever joyful in His Presence. Be glad in Him. He is true joy and peace. In Him we find true contentedness. When all the world seems to go astray, take joy in knowing Him and being with Him.

He will give you the desires of your heart. As we trust in Him, dwell in Him, and delight in Him, He gives us His desires. We find ourselves becoming unified and one in Him. Our desires become His desires and His desires flow into our hearts with such joy that we begin to understand His holiness and purpose for our lives.

The joy of the Lord is our strength. Being in Him brings Him joy and brings us strength in our inner man. Be strong in the Lord. Delight yourself in Him and He will fulfill His purpose in you today!

January 27th

Submitting Now

"Preserve me, O God, for in You I put my trust. O my soul, you have said to the Lord, 'You are my Lord, my goodness is nothing apart from You.'"
(Psalm 16:1-2, NKJV)

What will will I will today, His, or mine? Most Christians seem to think that they don't have to submit today, for after all, 'I did that the day I was saved…' This is perhaps the reason why so many so called Christians have no idea what the will of God is. They believe that they did something some time ago and their past experience is supposed to last for an eternity.

God is eternal. Salvation is eternal. But were you really converted on your day of discovery, or did you, as some of our preachers preach, simply gain some knowledge of the Lord, and pray an eight second prayer and then you were done with it all? Jesus said, 'You must be born again.'

If you have been born again into Christ and He lives inside of you, then daily submission is the order of the day, in pleasant surroundings. A true disciple of the Lord willingly lays down his will and submits to the Lord for the Lord is the Lord, isn't He? If He is not your Lord, then He is not your Lord, and you do not know Him and He doesn't know you.

But if you say, 'Lord, Lord', and He is real and true in you today, then every day is the day to say, *"Preserve me, O God, for in You I put my trust. O my soul, you have said to the Lord, 'You are my Lord, my goodness is nothing apart from You."*

Submission to Him is now, in the each and every moment. I know that I need Him. I know that I am desperate for Him. I know that I know that I know that He and I know each other and His joy is my strength. Sing to the Lord, He is my Light and my salvation, sing His praise, glorify His name, and in daily submission to Him, you'll not have to wonder what His will is, you'll be in it.

January 28th

A New Creation

"Therefore, if anyone is in Christ, he is a new creation; old things have passed away; behold, all things become new." (2 Corinthians 5:17, NKJV)

'Dearly beloved, we are gathered here today to say good-by to an old friend, a fiend of sorts, sometimes a good guy, sometimes a bad guy, you never knew which day would be which with our old fiend, I mean friend...'

If you have truly given your life to Jesus Christ, having been born again, then you have become a new creation. If you know in your heart that you really never became a new creation, then today is the day to drive yourself back to the Lord and submit to Him in truth and in Spirit. Get things right, and see new things emanate from your inner man. This is between you and God right now, not me, and certainly not some preacher man. Wholly lay your life down to Him, and recognize that because He paid the price for our sin by His death on the cross, we can go to Him and ask to be a part of Him in His Kingdom.

He willingly laid His life down for you and for me, and we must willingly lay our lives down before Him, denying our very selves, and in a very miraculous way… in this process of submitting to Him and us recognizing Him as Lord, He makes us a totally new creation. My wants are no longer my wants. I don't have to sin. I am not perfect, but He dwells in me towards my perfection in Him. I am not holy, but He is holy in me, and because He is holy, I am made righteous and holy in Him. I am not complete on my own, but my completion is found in Him. You and I do not have to sin because His power is in us and He has conquered sin, death, hell, and the grave. He is Almighty.

Be the new creation today and smile the smile of glad heart, a grateful heart that you are His and He dwells in you as He said He would. Don't pick up the old things any more. You have a choice and a strength now that strengthens your inner man not to sin and not to go back to the old fiend that you might have been some time ago.

January 29th

A Prayer of Faith

"For He made Him who knew no sin to be sin for us, that we might become the righteousness of God in Him." (2 Corinthians 6:5, NKJV)

Dear Father, You sent Your Son, Jesus Christ here to this earth to be born of the virgin Mary. He lived the life You chose for Him to live on this earth. He obeyed You. He performed many signs, wonders, healings, deliverances, and miracles in Your power and for Your glory. He glorified You. He taught us to pray, really pray. He taught us what it is like to obey, to suffer, and give up His life for us all. He laid down His life willingly for the sin of the whole world. It was for this reason that He bled, suffered, and died. In this, He bore the sin of the whole world, including my sin. He paid the price for my sin once and for all on the cross. Because He did this, I know I do not have to sin.

Father, as He laid His life down for you, I lay my life down for Him. I submit my life to You. I deny my self and any claim to my self and place it at Your cross. You have promised to make me a new creation, a new man, a born again man/woman. I trust in You that You will do as You have said. I receive You into my life as my Lord, my Master, my King. I submit to You.

I walk by faith and not by sight. My dwelling place is with You in Your Kingdom. Lead me through the door of the cross into Your life giving Presence. I choose this day to abide in You and I know that You will abide in me. Forever I will abide in Your Presence in the life of Your Kingdom. I am forever Yours and forever is today and forevermore.

Thank You, Lord, for making me and continuing to make me into You. Eternally grateful, Your son and Your daughter. Forever is today and forever is forevermore, bless You Jesus!

January 30th

Be Still

"Be still, and know that I am God..."   *(Psalm 46:10a, NKJV)*

The word of the Lord admonishes us oftentimes to cry out to Him, to shout praises to His name, to praise Him with a loud voice, to enter His courts with praise and thanksgiving, to rejoice with a loud voice, and in the quiet times we are admonished to be still.

Being still implies just that, being still. Stop the movement both physically as well as the mental churning of thoughts that we get so preoccupied with. It doesn't say not to think, it says to be still. Being still is most assuredly being quiet before Him for the purpose of listening. Be quiet before Him to meditate on Him and His goodness. Reflect on His grace that He has bestowed on you. Know Him in quietness before still waters.

Being still requires us to stop talking and begin listening. If you're talking, you're not listening, and if you're not listening, you're not learning. Learn from Him and learn to lean upon Him for He is good and His mercies are new each morning.
Being still implies rest. Rest from worry and rest from anxiety, be free for whom the Son sets free is free indeed. Relax in the breath of God. Take your self out of time and into Him and breathe…just breathe.

Our Father, Who knows no time or space, is waiting in the secret place for you. Go to Him there and be still in His Kingdom. Rest on Him, relax on His bosom, allow Him to hold you and comfort you. Quiet your spirit in His Presence and in humbling trust, know that He knows and cares for you.

January 31st

Where Is He?

"The kingdom of God does not come with observation; nor will they say, 'See here! Or 'See there!' For indeed, the kingdom of God is within you."
(Luke 17:20b-21, NKJV)

If you believe you are a disciple of Jesus Christ, then answer this question…where is God? We have been taught in the word that He is on His throne in heaven. We have been taught that He is omnipresent, that is, He is present everywhere; He is the all-knowing, all-sufficient, all-wise King. He is indeed everywhere at all times; He is that big of a God.

So, how big is your God? Is He big enough to be everywhere at all times? Is He big enough to be on His throne in heaven and big enough to send His Holy Spirit to this earth to dwell inside of you…all at the same time. You see, if He is on His throne in heaven, in the kingdom of heaven and He dwells in you richly, and the kingdom of God, as Jesus declared, is within you, then where is He? He is on His throne in you!

If that is the case, and it is, why do you cry out in lonely need imploring the Lord to come to you? He is already there. If it is the case that the kingdom of God is within you, and it is, why do you keep asking God to tell you His will? He is His will, and if He is in you to will and to work His good pleasure, then His will is already at work inside of us.

I have seen many cry out to God as if He is in a far off land and is so far off that they seem to need to scream for Him to hear them. He is near. The word says to acknowledge Him, draw near to Him, seek Him, know Him, and we act like we have never heard that before because our level of understanding relies on the plain of the flesh. We think we need to feel Him. He is not a feeling. He is Spirit and those who worship Him, must worship Him in spirit and truth.

Jesus said that if we would abide in Him, He would abide in us. He said that He is the vine and we are the branches. If we are His, we dwell in Him. Past teaching has taught us that He is in a far off place. He is and He isn't for He is risen in you! Bear the fruit of knowing where He is. "At that day you will know that I am in My Father, and you in Me, and I in you." (John 14:20, NKJV)

Trust *'in'* Him, for Jesus also said, "I in them, and You in me; that they may be made perfect in one, and that the world may know that You have sent Me, and have loved them as You have loved Me." (John 17:23, NKJV)

February 1st

Search Me, O God

"Search me, O God, and know my heart; try me, and know my anxieties; and see if there is any wicked way in me, and lead me in the way everlasting."
(Psalm 139:23-24, NKJV)

As we continue to discover more of Him, we are quickened by His Spirit to know more about ourselves. Coming into contact with holiness and purity enables us to see ourselves for who we really are. If we have been born again of Christ's Spirit, then we are justified through faith, and are made clean in Him.

We can praise the Lord for His goodness that allows us into His Presence of holiness; we can live long and prosper in that alone. However, we are still on this earth walking around in an earthly suit that He fashioned for us. Flesh is still flesh and it wars against the Spirit of God.

I found myself one night becoming so angry watching the evening news that as I was preparing a potato for the evening meal and stabbing it with a knife, I stabbed my thumb in the process. My anxiety had taken over the focus of what I was doing. As ridiculous as that may sound, it is actually funny to me now, but my thumb was terribly sore from the wound. Anxiety and anger are not funny though and there is something in me that I allowed to frustrate me to the point where I could blame the television, or my lack of focus, or whatever there is about me to blame, other than what is truly on the inside.

That's why we need a holy God to check us in the deep recesses of the heart. He goes where no man is able to go. As I continue to learn to submit to Him, He makes my way clearer and all the while He is making my way cleaner and more holy as well. I am changed because He is changing me. Bless God for His Holy Spirit!

February 2nd

The Power in Him

"And He got up rebuked the wind and said to the sea, 'Hush, be still.' And the wind died down and it became perfectly calm."   *(Mark 4:39)*

"Who stills the roaring of the seas, The roaring of their waves, And the tumult of the peoples."   *(Psalm 65:7)*

"You rule the swelling of the sea; When its waves rise, You still them"
(Psalm 89:5 NASB)

Are there greater powers in the earth than the power of wind and the power of the waters of the seas? Who stands against the tides of winds in a storm, in a hurricane no less, and is stronger than the strength of the gales, the gusts, and the storms and the squalls?

Who stands in the midst of wind and rain that pounds with overwhelming ferocity;

of wind with such force and speed that moves even the mightiest of structures? Who stands in the midst of the waters that rage against the ship and shore with such dynamic torrent that nothing stands in its path, nor is untouched by its bursts? Who stands against the tidal pull of waters that cause the waters to recede and spring forth at its command? Can one or a thousand so stand against the tide that pulls the powerless to their death? Is there a power in the earth greater than death?

No man can stand against God's creation and yet of all the powers of wind and sea, gust and storm, tide and death, there is a power known to man that is as great as the storm of the sea and that is the power of man's will. For it is the will of man that a man chooses to believe or to act in his will alone. It is the will to live, the will to die, the will to work, the will to rest, the will to believe or not believe. It is man's will that he embraces in his own world to believe what he believes and so chooses to abandon all against his belief.

There is one, though, who has stood in the midst of all of the powers of the earth and said, 'Peace, be still.' There is one who was slain in the midst of death and rose above even that. There is one who did not submit to his will, but submitted to the will of His Father. The powers of the earth had no power over Him as the Son of God and the power of will of man had no power in Him as the Son of man. It was in this He taught us, "If any man desire to come after Me, let him deny himself, take up his cross and follow Me."

It is only in the laying down of the power of our will to the far greater power of the will of God that we see that the power of God is far greater than any power in the earth. He demonstrated to us in that when any power comes against us, the power of God is greater in us than any power on the earth. In our surrender to Him we find that we can say, 'Peace, be still,' to whatever power that we think has power over us. In this, He stills the storm because He can and will. These words are Spirit and they are true.

February 3rd

My Redeemer Lives

"For I know that My Redeemer lives, and He shall stand at last on the earth; and after my skin is destroyed, this I know, that in my flesh I shall see God, whom I shall see for myself, and my eyes shall behold, and not another."
(Jeremiah 19:25-27, NKJV)

As the sun rises in the east, bright and beaming, the dark clouds are forming in the west; blowing and fiercely moving eastward towards the sun to estrange the sun's rays and warmth from my face. As a sense of darkness covers my portion of the heavens, will I believe that the sun no longer is? Will I believe that the sun no longer shines? Will I believe that if I do not see the sun, that no one else does as well?

For when I do not see the sun, the sun still is…still shines…still shines on whom the sun is shining regardless of my circumstance.

The sun still is. The clouds are temporal.

In all things I know that my Redeemer lives! Not only does my Redeemer live in the above and beyond, but my Redeemer lives in me. The Son that I know pierces through the darkness and shines such a light that only light can know. He witnesses to Himself, and as the Son rises, His glory rises within me; and there is no darkness at all.

February 4th

Worship

"The hour is coming, and now is, when the true worshippers will worship the Father in spirit and truth; for the Father is seeking such to worship Him. God is Spirit, and those who worship Him must worship in spirit and truth."
(John 4:23-24, NKJV)

Be careful of your presumption of the authority you believe you have in your field of expertise or in your own mind. It is one thing to know a thing and quite another to come off as all-knowing of all things and you lose your audience, your customers, your job or your spouse.
How do you tell the truth of God to someone who believes in a concept that isn't true without destroying the person in the process?

What is right theology and who has obtained it?

Jesus said, regarding the work of the Holy Spirit in the believer, "However, when He, the Spirit of truth, has come, He will guide you into all truth; for He will not speak on His own authority, but whatever He hears He will speak; and He will tell you things to come." (John 16:13)

It is the Holy Spirit of God who is right and who judges rightly.

Oh, that I may know Him in the power of His resurrection so that I may be found in Him in Holy Love. Only the Holy Spirit truly knows and it is only the Holy Spirit who truly loves. Worship is not singing a song, although one can worship while singing. Worship is not putting on fancy clothes and going to a building although one can worship Him while there.

Worship is…hmmm. My heart breathes sighs and longs for Him.

Is a life worth living, a life worth giving to a Life worth receiving all glory, honor and praise? I will worship that Life, the One True Living God in Christ Jesus this day; this day in Him. Breathe in His Holy Spirit and breathe out the living waters of God.

February 5th

A Moment of Decision

I would have missed moments in time with Him to be out of time in Him if I had left Him and remained with my thoughts; for my thoughts were driving me to do as they desired. I almost obeyed my thoughts. Instead, I remained in Him. It became a clear delineation of a choice in time. I chose Him. I'm sorry to say that that doesn't happen every time.

Who or what is driving you?

Is the sound coming from above or behind? Is the thought coming from without or within? Again, I ask, "Who or what is driving you?"

"Finally, brethren, whatever things are true, whatever things are noble, whatever things are just, whatever things are pure, whatever things are lovely, whatever things are of a good report, if there is any virtue and if there is anything praiseworthy – meditate on these things." (Philippians 4:8, NKJV)

It is a clear choice that we have in moments in time to choose to honor Him and be in Him and recognize that if we are in Him, He is in us. Abide in Him all the day in the each and every moment, wherever you are and in whatever He has placed your hands to do. Allow Him His rightful place in you; the honor of a King. Give Him praise!

February 6th

Judging Others

"And do not judge and you will not be judged; and do not condemn; pardon, and you will be pardoned." (Luke 6:37, NKJV)

If you judge, you will be judged. If you do not, you may not. If you condemn others, you will be condemned in like measure. What has the church taught us in judging others and what condemnation has the church brought upon itself through the condemnation of other folk? People judging and condemning another, it should not be.

In this passage, the person who judges or condemns another is likened to a blind man leading the blind into a ditch. There is a difference between the ability to discern something as being true, or not, and taking the discernment into a completely different realm of condemnation.

"And He also spoke a parable to them: 'A blind man cannot guide a blind man, can he? Will they both not fall into a pit? A pupil is not above his teacher; but everyone after he has been fully trained, will be like his teacher.'" (Luke 6:39-40, NKJV) Judgment is for the One True Judge…God Himself.

If you have a problem with judging others, how do you come out of it? That is, the problem of looking at others and judging or condemning them? Some may say, 'I've done it for so long, that's just what I do…I'm good at it…" Are you really good at something that was never intended for you to do and you have no authority to do?

You see, in the judgment of others, you take the authority of the One True God for yourself. You do not see, nor do you really know. Judgment is not ours to make or take. You either believe that or you don't. Jesus warns us not to take the judgment of others upon ourselves for ever how we judge others is how we will be judged. And, we will reveal just how blind we really are. Another thing, stop judging yourself!

We heap coals upon ourselves and bring trouble to ourselves unnecessarily. Perceived knowledge in the mind of a student puffs the pride. There is always something we do not know. Allow Him to be Lord in you and through you for His sake and for the sake of others that have been brought into your life. Allow His holy love to flow and you will see others with His eyes…eyes of compassion, mercy and grace.

February 7th

Renew Your Mind

"And do not be conformed to this world, but be transformed by the renewing of your mind, that you may prove what the will of God is, that which is good and acceptable and perfect." (Romans 12:2, NASB)

Renew your mind by presenting your body to the Lord. How do you do that, but in humility? Renew your mind in true worship, submitted to Him in love. Renew your mind in right believing, in right thinking, in right thoughts.

Renew your mind with His Spirit renewing you in the each and every moment.

Drop off the old, oftentimes you don't see it coming. Still, at other times, the old is around like an old coat…comfortable…comfortable thinking like you used to think. Stillness sets in and the regrets and hurts of yesterday rise to the heart seeking solace and relief in talk and vengeance. Drop off the old. Renew your mind. Put on the mind of Christ and walk in the Light as He is in the Light.

Renew your mind with right beliefs, right thoughts, right thinking on right thoughts. Think on these things…whatsoever is holy, just, pure, loving, holy love, think on these things.

Allow the Christ in you to love through you and hug through you today!

February 8th

Live From the Secret Place

"How lovely are Thy dwelling places, O Lord of Hosts! My soul longed and even yearned for the courts of the Lord; my heart and my flesh sing for joy to the living God." (Psalm 84:1-2, NASB)

The Lord reigns in majesty high above all that we know or could ever imagine. He is above all in the heavenly places. According to the word of God, if we are true worshippers of Him, we have been seated in heavenly places with Him in Christ Jesus. (Ephesians 2:6)

Jesus Christ told His disciples that when they pray they should "go into their inner room, and when you have shut your door, pray to your Father who is in secret, and your Father who sees in secret will repay you." (Matthew 6:6, NASB)

The dwelling place of the Lord is that secret place in you. The 'courts of the Lord' is the heart of the penitent believer. Go to Him, abide with Him, He has promised that if we would abide with Him and keep His commandments, that He and His Father would abide in us. (John 14:23-24, NKJV)

The heart of the believer is the dwelling place of the Lord Most High. Stay in Him, rest in Him, trust in Him in the heavenly places, for in Him abides His grace and love today and forevermore.

February 9th

The Counsel of the Lord

"Many are the plans in a man's heart, but the counsel of the Lord, it will stand. What is desirable in a man is his kindness, and it is better to be a poor man than a liar."   (Proverbs 19:21-22, NKJV)

When the Spirit of the Lord speaks to us, hopefully, we hear His voice because we recognize His voice. His counsel is to be coveted more than any weight of gold. The Lord is good and His loving kindness is forevermore. His mercy endures to all generations. Who can know the depth of His love or the depth of His wisdom?

Many are the plans of man indeed through ideas and dreams, visions and thoughts. Man can get what he thinks to be the greatest idea of all time and come to find out, it was thought out and failed years ago without his knowledge, and so he goes about with his idea only to find the same demise. I see that in restaurants in just about every city, there is always a couple of locations that 'seem' to be the perfect location, right on the corner of a busy street; and year after year, one by one, the restaurant owners come and invest their time, energy and many thousands of dollars, only to see it vanish because there never was any support in the community for a restaurant in that location.

What stands in the end and who decides what stands or falls? I am not merely speaking of business ideas and man's best laid plans. Here, we see if we believe the word of the Lord, it is His counsel that stands amidst the plans in the minds of men. The word of the Lord speaks peace in counsel, not turmoil. His counsel is not burdensome. That is not to say that all will be rosy for we still live on this earth in earthen vessels. But that is the point. His counsel is not of flesh, but in the Spirit.

When His Spirit speaks, we need to listen and heed His word. He knows all things. His word is Truth. He speaks in kindness and so should we. God does not lie and neither should we. Truth is in His counsel, as well as, kindness and wisdom. Seek the Lord and you will hear Him in the quiet, 'Walk this way'. You'll not regret it.

February 10th

Listen to Counsel

"Listen to counsel and accept discipline, that you may be wise the rest of your days" *(Proverbs 19:20, NKJV)*

In my younger days, I would read and read the Proverbs because they spoke often of getting wisdom and obtaining knowledge and I knew that that was the right road for me. As I grew older out of my teen years, I would read more and more of His Word to be with Him, but mostly for enlightenment and wisdom. I wanted to know His will for my life, so I would pick out some scripture and let that expound on my heart for a few moments and if it suited the situation, I would go in that direction. Needless to say, I've made quite a few errant decisions in my life by allowing the wind to prognosticate the pages and then my finger magically land on a verse that was supposed to define my destiny. I laugh now at my ignorance of God and the poor use of His Word. I have made many mistakes along the way.

So, how is it that we are to 'listen to counsel' from the Lord? In my getting of understanding, I have been able to surmise this: spend large amounts of time getting to know the Lord by abiding in Him. Do not rely on your own interpretation of scripture…get help. Get to know what other men have said in commentaries. Listen to pastors and teachers as they preach. Examine their fruit. Again, do not rely on your sole interpretation, that's dangerous. There's a good fifty per cent chance that you could be wrong in relying on your own designs. Get godly counsel from godly men and women who have been seasoned by time in the knowledge of the Word and have the Spirit of the Lord guiding them, the fruit of their character will reveal much.

Pray, pray, pray in the Spirit, but again, do not rely on your sole interpretation of things. If you're married, speak often with your spouse. Learn to respect and love in your spouse's conversations. If you're not married, get Godly counsel. Too many advisors cloud issues, so be wise in the counsel you receive.

In all things, trust in the Lord; do not lean upon your own understanding. Learn to know the difference between your own internal voice and the voice of the Lord.

The more time you spend with Him, the more you will get to know His voice. Then, when the word of the Lord does come, you will be rested and refreshed by His Spirit that says, 'Walk this way' and His Spirit will provide the faith to hear and believe.

February 11th

In the Name

"The name of Jesus has healed this man – and you know how lame he was before. Faith in Jesus' name has caused this healing before your eyes."
(Acts 3:16, NLT)

It is in the name of Jesus Christ that we as Christians live today. In Matthew 10, Jesus spoke of doing and receiving in the name of prophet, a righteous man, or a disciple. He spoke earlier of being willing to confess Him before men that He would confess us to His Father in heaven. What is it about this confession and the belief in Him that His prophets, righteous men and disciples have in common?

The common denominator is His nature, His Spirit. He who confesses Jesus Christ as Lord and receives Him as Savior is accepting Him into his/her life. They are receiving the message of the Kingdom of God of grace in grace. The follower of Jesus Christ is accepting the Spirit of God into their lives and along with the Spirit of God is His nature. The name of the disciple should be consistent with the name of his Lord. The same is true of his nature. The nature of the disciple, prophet, righteous man or woman is to be the same nature of the Christ. So, when we pray in Jesus' name, we pray in His nature with all of the authority and power that rests in Him.

Jesus speaks in actual terms to explain the spiritual. Everything He talked about was spiritual, but manifested in the natural. Everything to the spiritual man is 'in'. 'In' is where we deny, where we leave the old and become new. In is where we construct upon the new birth. In is where He Is and abides. In Him, I live, and move, and have my being.

Will I deny the outer husk of myself and submit to His life and order? Have I given others a taste of Him, or do I continue to exemplify myself in my expressions? Confession, nature, message, receiving is all done in Him. I have to ask myself, where do I dwell? Do I dwell in Him? As He flows His love and life through me, He touches others in the same love and life whether it be in the voice, the touch of the hand, or a solid embrace.

So we find that praying or moving in His Name is not a three word formula, "in Jesus' Name," to get what we want, No! In His Name is in His Nature, so we pray and move within Him, moving as He moves. Be in Him today and He will be in you what others need and He will get the glory.

February 12th

The Name of Jesus

"Some Jews who went around driving out evil spirits tried to invoke the name of the Lord Jesus over those who were demon-possessed. They would say, 'In the name of Jesus whom Paul preaches, I command you to come out.'"
(Acts 19:13, NIV)

The seven sons of Sceva, a leading priest, learned an invaluable lesson here. When they approached the demon possessed men, the demons responded, 'I know Jesus, and I know Paul, but who are you?' Then, the demonic spirits, through the actions and power of the demon-possessed men, beat with violence and tore the clothes from the sons of Sceva and sent them running. There was no power in the sons of Sceva for they did not know the Christ, they were using and abusing His Name.

When, we as a born-again believer pray, we pray in His Name, in His nature. He dwells in me and I dwell in Him and His will should be expressed as He would express it. Therefore, when I pray in Jesus' name, I'm praying as He would pray. I pray humbly as the Son going to His father. I pray as a loving, obedient, and humble son; that is Jesus' nature: humble, obedient and loving, always abounding in unquestionable faith. The Father knows the Name of Jesus for He sits at the right hand of the Father.

We need to be careful here that we are not simply attaching Jesus' name to our own prerogatives and selfish ambitions. We have been taught by many religious leaders to attach the three words, 'in Jesus' name' to the end of our prayers, no matter what has been prayed and no matter what our motives. It is as though we have been taught a magical three word phrase as a formula to get whatever we want, 'in His name'.

The idea of commanding Almighty God to our beckon call by using the authority of His name is placing the authority of God into the mouth of a fool who chews up His grace and declares it as some type of spell to get what he wants. The event of the sons of Sceva is recorded in the book of Acts for a reason. Let us all learn to say the Name of Jesus as He would declare His obedience in humble submission to His and our Father.

Thy will be done, that we would be humble and reverent in speaking your Name to the heavens. We can go boldly to Your throne knowing that You are our Father and we are mere mortals bearing Your Name and Your Spirit. Teach us, O Lord, how to pray that Your will be done today.

February 13th

Who Is This Jesus?

"The book of the genealogy of Jesus Christ, the son of David, the son of Abraham." (Matthew 1:1, NASB)

The question is asked, 'Who is this Jesus?' because the question is not, 'Who was He?' or 'Who is He to be?' for He Is. The genealogy is written to establish the line of nationality and ethnic origin. This was important to Jews and should be equally important to us today, although, I've not heard many sermons, or messages on Matthew 1:1. This is, after all, the Word of the Lord, and why the Lord would have inspired the writer to include the genealogy is the Lord's purpose and not man's.

It is kindly reasoning, but insufficient to include man's justification for this genealogy for it serves God's purposes most of all. God deemed it necessary to exemplify the lineage all the way back to Abraham to show that Jesus Christ was a Hebrew, a Jew, and a generational son of Abraham, the father of the faith of the Jews. Jesus responded to the Pharisees questions one day with this, "Later, as Jesus was teaching the people in the temple, he asked 'Why do the teachers of the religious law claim that the Messiah will be the son of David? For David himself, speaking under the inspiration of the Holy Spirit, said, 'The Lord said to my Lord, "Sit in honor at My right hand, until I humble your enemies beneath your feet." (Ps. 110:1). Since David himself called him Lord, how can he be his son at the same time? And the crowd listened to him with great interest.'" (Mark 12:35-37, NLT)

I will ask this question to you, "Who is this Jesus? Who is He, and who is He to you?" For He is not only the son of Abraham and the son of David, He is also the Lord of Abraham and the Lord of David. Have you chosen as of this day who you will serve? In the beginning, the Word already existed, He was with God, and He was God." (John 1:1, NLT) Jesus has always been, not in the flesh, but in Spirit, for not only was He the Son of God, he became the Son of Man, for our sake. Jesus Christ is Lord. Is He your Lord? If so, walk in Him, abide in Him and the Father will give you the Holy Spirit to walk in obedience to Him and He shall be Lord to you indeed.

February 14th

The Beginning of the Consummation

"To Abraham was born Isaac...and to Jesse was born David the king."
(Matthew 1:2a, 6)

So it had begun, the first of three sets of fourteen generations which begins with Abraham and continues with King David. A careful perusal of the verse of Matthew 1:2-6, gives a history of the lineage of Jesus Christ, but also confirms the early portions of the Old Testament story. Each person listed regards someone of specific significance and their story of how they progressed through life is equally significant. We can never underestimate the significance of others, nor of our own significance.

What we continually need to realize is how important personal significance and specificity of the Lord God truly is. How is it that things are as they are and how is it that things have come to be as they are? Family leaders and fathers are significant; never underestimate that as a fact. Jesus Christ was a son of Abraham and a son of David and in the lineage, the prophecies of the Lord concerning the Messiah, the Expected One are fulfilled. The Lord speaking to David through the prophet Nathan said, "And your house and your kingdom shall endure before Me forever; your throne shall be established forever." (2 Samuel 7:17)

It was Moses who prophesied in Deuteronomy 30 about 'choosing life in order that you may live, you and your descendants, by loving the Lord your God, by obeying His voice, and by holding fast to Him for this is your life and the length of your days, that you may live in the land which the Lord swore to your fathers, to Abraham, Isaac, and Jacob, to give them.' (v. 19b-20) How is it that inheritance comes about if there is no proof of lineage? What is the land and what is the kingdom? In both instances, the Lord God referred to a specific land that still exists today. But in the spiritual word of the Lord, He not only promises an actual land, but a real land, a spiritual reality of the Kingdom of God, that is not made with human hands. If you name the Name of Jesus Christ, His Kingdom dwells within you and that Kingdom is forever in Him.

February 15th

Following the Faith of Kings

"…and to David was born Solomon by her who had been the wife of Uriah."
(Matthew 1:6b)

As the kings and leaders are listed here in verses six through twelve, we are reminded of the faith that men have towards their God. When the prophet Samuel spoke to the King Saul about his end of being a king, he said, "But now your kingdom shall not endure. The Lord has sought for Himself a man after His own heart, and the Lord has appointed him as ruler over His people…" (I Samuel 15:14)

It was the shepherd David who was to be king, a man after God's heart, a man chosen to do the will of the Lord, a man who worshipped and had the faith of a true king. We need to see that it is the Lord who chooses and appoints the rulers over His people. In the beginning of the line of kings, these were men full of faith and courage. However, their sons did not always follow as their fathers. David's prayer over his son, Solomon, was a prayer of faith that men should always pray for their children. "…and give to my son Solomon a perfect heart to keep Thy commandments, Thy testimonies, and Thy statutes, and to do them all, and to build the temple for which I have made provision." (I Chronicles 29:19) Solomon is known for his prayer of faith to receive the wisdom of the Lord and the Lord had favor on him.

It was said of Uzziah in 2 Chr. 26:4, "And he did right in the sight of the Lord according to all that his father Amaziah had done." Hezekiah was a man of prayerful faith, "…Hezekiah did throughout all Judah; he did what was good, right, and true before the Lord his God. And every work which he began in the service of the house of God in law and in commandment, seeking his God, he did with all his heart and prospered." (2 Chronicles 31:20-21)

Oh, that it would be said of us what was said of the lineage of Jesus, that these were men who sought after God's own heart, that what we do is right and just and true before the Lord. What magnificent men of faith that we have to follow whose testimonies stand before the Lord as a witness that following the Lord is done in faith and obedience. God's grace gives us today the power to continue in that faith. Following the Lord is exciting. The road may be long and full of trials as it was for each of these kings, but it is the road appointed for us to walk in Him and He will direct our paths.

February 16th

The Lineage Continues

"And after the deportation to Babylon…and to Jacob was born Joseph the husband of Mary, by whom was born Jesus, who is called the Christ."
(Matthew 1:12a, 16)

The deportation to Babylon came as a result of hundreds of years of disobedience to the Lord God. Jeremiah, the prophet, lamented, "Her, *(Israel)* adversaries have become her masters, Her enemies prosper; for the Lord has caused her grief because of the multitude of her transgressions; her little ones have gone away as captives before the adversary." (Lamentations 1:5). As was stated earlier, not all of the sons of kings followed the way of the Lord, but did what was right in their own eyes. Although the Lord may be slow to anger, He is just in all of His ways.

We are reminded here that even though His people rebelled, even for hundreds of years, there was always a remnant of the faithful. It was the remnant of the faithful ones while in captivity in Babylon that the lineage was able to continue. God knows all things and He knows all things from the end, not just from the beginning. The prophecies of the Lord will come to pass no matter how many of His people disobey and no matter how strong the adversary may seem to be. God is faithful all of the time. God can be depended upon always, that is an absolute. One of the prophecy's concerning the birth of the Christ is from Micah 5:2, "But you, Bethlehem Ephrathah, though you are little among the thousands of Judah, yet out of you shall come forth to Me the One to be Ruler in Israel, whose goings forth are from old, from everlasting." So, not only does the lineage continue from the generations, but the prophecies concerning the Christ also unfold. "And He shall stand and feed His flock in the strength of the Lord, in the majesty of the name of the Lord His God…" (v. 4a)

The Lord has been and always will be faithful to His word and faithful to Himself. He will do what He says He will do. He is the ultimate in dependability and faithfulness. We, as humans, are faithful in our unfaithfulness. We are unreliable; we fear when we do not have to fear. We run when we should stand in the power of His might. What we have to come to know and understand is that His wonderful faithfulness can abide in us, if we submit and give up the claim to the rights to ourselves, and abide in Him. He will come to us and abide in us in the Holy Spirit. He gives us the strength to do all these things…submit, give up, abide, remain and the most pleasant of all, rest in Him.

His faithfulness in grace is that powerful. He doesn't make us follow Him, but He empowers us from within to love and obey. Faith is from Him and in Him.

Holy love is Him and from Him and in Him we have life…that, my friend, is the Kingdom of God.

February 17th

The Establishment of a Nation

"Therefore all the generations from Abraham to David are fourteen generations; and from David to the deportation to Babylon are fourteen generations; and from the deportation to Babylon to the time of Christ fourteen generations."
(Matthew 1:17, NASB)

The lineage continues indeed in truth by the testimony of the generations. It was prophesied that the Messiah would come from the lineage of Abraham and David. In Genesis 12:3, the Lord declares to Abraham, "And I will bless those who bless you, and the one who curses you I will curse. And in you all the families of the earth shall be blessed."

In Psalm 89:3, David records the promise from the Lord, "I have made a covenant with My chosen; I have sworn to David My servant, I will establish your seed forever, and build up your throne to all generations." This he was told by the prophet Nathan in 2 Samuel 7:16. The coming Messiah of the Jews would be a son of Abraham and a son of David.

I've often wondered at the times and the seasons and why God chose that particular time period to give birth to His Son in the earth. The fulfillment of three sets of fourteen generations had been completed with the birth of the Christ child. God never does anything without reason, so there must be His reasoning and wisdom to place the birth at this time. It is not my case to question God as to why, but what it does allow me to do is watch how God plans all things. He knows all things from the end to the beginning. All of His prophecies from His chosen prophets come to pass. In the book of the Revelation, He tells us how all of time is going to end.

Jesus Christ was born in a time of God's choosing. The time had come for Him to be in the earth. As Solomon wrote in Ecclesiastes, 'to everything there is a season,' and for us, it is as well. We live in times of constant uncertainty and the time that He has chosen you and me to live is the time set for us. God does not make mistakes. What is it then that He has purposed for you? Why did He birth you from out of time into time in this season? The answer lies in Him.

February 18ᵗʰ

The Son of God

"Now the birth of Jesus Christ was as follows. When His mother Mary had been betrothed to Joseph, before they came together she was found to be with child by the Holy Spirit." (Matthew 1:18)

The time of the Kingdom of God had come. The Son of God was to be born of a virgin, untouched by the world. The Holy Spirit is the Father of the Son of God. It was the Holy Spirit who gave the seed for the Redeemer of the world to be born. This is just one of the mysteries regarding the Kingdom of God.

The angel Gabriel, as recorded in Luke 1:35, said to Mary, "The Holy Spirit will come upon you, and the power of the Highest will overshadow you; therefore, also, that Holy One who is to be born will be called the Son of God…for with God nothing will be impossible." (v. 37)

Another mystery is the mystery of the Trinity, the Father, Son and the Holy Spirit. When Jesus was speaking to Nicodemus at night, He told him, "Most assuredly I say to you, We speak what We know and testify what We have seen, and you do not receive Our witness…no one has ascended to heaven but He Who came down from heaven, that is the Son of Man who is in heaven." (John 3:11, 13). We have to realize in truth and reality that the consummation of the Christ child was performed by the Holy Spirit. Jesus was from the beginning…in the beginning was the Word and the word was God. (John 1)

So much has been made from our religious traditions regarding the Christmas season that not very much is said about the conception of the child; we just want to celebrate His birth and open our presents. The presents, I would suppose might represent the true gift of Christmas, but the True gift is originally given by God Himself through the power of the Holy Spirit in the conception of the child.

We are convicted of our sin by the power of the Holy Spirit. We are born again into the Kingdom by the power of the Holy Spirit. It is the work of the Holy Spirit that draws men unto Himself. It is the power of the Holy Spirit that convicts that world of righteousness for Jesus' sake. (John 16:5-11)

If you haven't already, take the time now to be filled with the Holy Spirit in your life. Jesus said, "If you, then, being evil, know how to give good gifts to your children, how much more will your heavenly Father give the Holy Spirit to those who ask Him!" (Luke 11:13) This is how we are born into the Kingdom of God by the power of the Holy Spirit because of the completed work of Jesus Christ on the cross at Calvary. Being born again is nothing we can do on our own; it is the work of God. Give your life to Him and allow the Son of God to be born in you today.

I pray that you will seek Him while He may be found. Worship while you have breath to breathe. Abide in Him and the Kingdom of God will be open to you in such a way that any question you may have of your purpose, you will find it in Him. His grace is all-sufficient. He is forevermore and the life that He gives to us not only lasts forever, it is for your breath even now.

February 19th

The Possibility of Betrayal

"And Joseph her husband, being a righteous man, and not wanting to disgrace her, desired to put her away secretly." (Matthew 1:19)

Mary, the mother of Jesus, had received a visit from the angel Gabriel before she had conceived of the Holy Spirit. The announcement was a celebratory time after a time of reflection of what was really happening to her. This has been recorded in Luke 1, along with Mary's visit to her relative Elisabeth, the soon to be mother of John the Baptist.

Joseph and Mary were betrothed; they were engaged. They had had no sexual relations for Mary was indeed a virgin. When Joseph hears of Mary's pregnancy, even though we may be certain he had heard the story of the angel, he desires to put Mary away secretly, that is, to allow her the dignity of not having public humiliation from canceling the engagement and being pregnant out of wedlock. This was the natural human response to the possibility of him being betrayed by Mary. He still loved her and did not want her disgraced.

A key point here is that Joseph was a righteous man and in our season of time, it may be that we really do not know what that means. If the word of God calls a man righteous, that means that he was a man in right standing before God. It means that he knew the law of God and kept it in obedience. It means that he knew how to worship and follow the Lord in his ways. He knew how to live right before the Lord. It is this righteousness of his that made him what he was before God, His Father. He was an honorable man. It is to these characteristics that we have to ponder the disappointment he must have felt at the news of Mary's pregnancy. Joseph was not in the meeting with the angel Gabriel and Mary. He was hurt and disappointed, but he did not intend to disgrace Mary out of love and honor. Could we be that right before God today? How shallow is our disappointment before it reaches the lowest depths of anger?

Shortly thereafter, an angel meets with Joseph in a dream to inform him of all that is happening, but it was that brief amount of time that elapsed that we are discussing here where Joseph didn't really know what to do. He was in the ultimate challenge of his life. Have you been there when you felt abandoned by all and you had no way out but on your knees? It is times like these we can thank God that we know Him and that He desires His best for us. Always trust in Him.

February 20th

They Shall Call His Name Immanuel

"...Joseph, son of David, do not be afraid to take Mary as your wife; for that which has been conceived in her is of the Holy Spirit." (Matthew 1:20b)

A welcomed dream came by night to Joseph for him to take Mary as his wife as the angel expressed the occurrence of the conception of the Christ child. Joseph did all that the angel told him to do and that was to accept Mary in her condition as his wife, kept her as a virgin until she gave birth to a Son and they called His name Jesus.

The prophet Isaiah spoke the word of the Lord, "Therefore the Lord Himself will give you a sign: Behold, a virgin will be with child and bear a son and she will call His name, Immanuel." (Isaiah 7:14) This birth fulfilled the prophecy of the expected One, God with us.

During all of these events, the dreams, the visions, the conception and the plans, both Joseph and Mary fully cooperated and obeyed the Lord in all they were told.

What has happened to us since then? We don't have to wait on a dream or vision, we have the very Word in front of us and we still have a difficult time with obedience. We have all of the necessary means of understanding and knowledge of the word through commentaries, the internet websites, a plethora of Bible versions, preachers preaching on the television or internet twenty-four hours a day and we still can't seem to find just the right time to be with the Lord in prayer and study. Is it because of all these things that we do not take time to pray? Has our culture determined our relationship with our Lord in self-determined self-gratification 'I want it now' mentalities? A preacher's presence is no substitute for His Presence.

Joseph and Mary were the standard at the time in the denying of the self for the purposes of God to come to pass. They had to give up all that they were and ever hoped to be in order to bring the Christ child into the earth. They obeyed in all things required of them. And, because they obeyed in all, the Immanuel child, God with us, was protected, nurtured and grew in the admonition of the Lord. Oh, that we would be that attentive to the Lord and His desires for us. Obey the Lord in all that He has you to do and you will see His Holy Spirit at work in you and through you. Then, when He's done all through you…rest and remain in Him.

February 21st

Born in Bethlehem

"Now after Jesus was born in Bethlehem…"   *(Matthew 2:1a)*

The Son of God was born of the virgin Mary in a stable in a town called Bethlehem. Although Bethlehem is a place and still is, its significance is something far greater than we can imagine. Bethlehem was known as 'little' by the prophet Micah. Bethlehem means 'house of David' and had historical significance as David himself took care of Saul's sheep in and out of Bethlehem.

The real significance, however, lies in God's plan. This was to be the place of the Messiah's birth. Oswald Chambers had the spiritual idea that we become the spiritual Bethlehem as we allow the Christ to be born in us. Through regeneration, also referred to as the new birth, we become born again and then are able to enter into the Kingdom of God. When He is born in us, we become the new creation that Paul talked about. Again, Immanuel means 'God with us'. Have you been born again? Jesus told Nicodemus specifically that unless we are born again, we cannot enter the Kingdom of God. (John 3). When the Holy Spirit speaks to us in the conviction of who we really are, we can choose to deny Him or choose to deny ourselves and allow Him to make us new. It is His life that makes us new; there is nothing we can do to become born again, except believe. And even the faith that it takes to believe in a Holy God doing something so miraculous in us as to make us a new creation comes from Him. It takes a God-kind of faith to believe in what He can do in us.

Jesus said that it takes a child-like faith, trusting without fear; otherwise, we cannot see the Kingdom of God. With all that is in the Bible about what Jesus Christ did for us on the cross of Calvary, how His blood was shed for our sins…for the sin of the whole world, it takes a God kind of faith to believe that the One man could save the whole world from its penalty of sin. So, do you see the significance of Bethlehem? It is the birthplace of the King.

Again, I ask, is your life the birthplace of the King, the Bethlehem, the little city that birthed the Son of God who was the Son of Man who is the King of kings and the Lord of lords? Have you been born again?

February 22nd

Wise Men Seek the Lord

"…Behold, magi from the east arrived in Jerusalem, saying, 'Where is He who has been born King of the Jews? For we saw His star in the east and have come to worship Him.'"   *(Matthew 2:1b-2)*

The magi, presumably oriental scientists or commonly known as wise men, sought the child who, according to their astrological estimations, predicted the birth of a ruler. They were astrologers among their many characteristics and were able to follow the star of Bethlehem. This star wasn't just any star and they knew that the time had come for this birth of the King of the Jews. They traveled to Jerusalem in search of the child who would be King.

These magi could also have been kings from other lands as they had a very real understanding of what a king was, as well as a kingdom, because every true king possesses a kingdom, otherwise, he is not a king. This is what so gravely disturbed Herod the king for he was extremely jealous of the news; he was not going to share any of his kingdom in Judea with anyone; that is not what kings do.

These were wise men bearing wealth. They had come to worship this new king. It is quite astounding today the folk who believe they possess sufficient intelligence and wealth and think that they do not need a God to submit to for they already possess all that they think they need. What is it that drives wealthy wise men to their knees to worship a king that they do not know, but through their wisdom have sought that which they know is greater than themselves? We worship what we bow down to and spend our time and money on. It is the course of life and in the natural, our tendencies are to bend towards that which gratifies and satisfies our selfishness.

Perhaps, that is the major difference here, the willingness to give up time, energy and wealth to a higher calling, a higher purpose and a higher God than ourselves. In wisdom, learn to submit to the One who is greater than all, the True King of kings and the True Lord of lords. In time and at the end of time, every knee will bow and every tongue will confess that Jesus Christ is Lord. Be willing to submit to Him in worship in love, adoration and truth. He came to love you and He still does.

February 23rd

The Underlying Reason

"...For out of you shall come forth a Ruler, who shall shepherd My people Israel." (Matthew 2:6b)

When Herod the king heard the prophecy concerning the Christ child, he commanded the wise men to go and search for Him and to come back and tell him where He was so that Herod could go and worship Him as well. It is very clear here that not everyone who seeks the Lord is doing so with pure intentions. If we are truly led to worship the Lord, we will have been led to the place of worship by the Holy Spirit. It is the Holy Spirit that guides us into all truth. (John 16:13)

There are so many reasons why people tinker with the Lord as they do. For Herod, it was to find Him and kill Him. Still others have sought the Lord for a sign of peace, a sign of wealth, a sign of things to come in order that they might know the future. Some seek the Lord for mercy from the guilt of their sin and after believing they have received their due forgiveness, go back to their home of addiction to wallow all the more. (Matthew 12:44) Others seek the Lord for personal gain and riches in the business world while others seek the Lord for a simple morsel of bread.

It has been the usual and customary for the many to seek the Lord for very personal reasons, not the very least being the religious traditions brought on by family and culture. Oftentimes, children grow into adults doing the same religious exercises that their parents and grandparents did, but not really knowing the reasons why. They go to church. They give a tithe or an offering, whichever suits them for the day. They may usher or serve in some simple capacity to soothe their conscious, or the conscious of their spouse or parents. Yet they simply do not understand the why, but they've been told that there is a reward up in heaven someplace waiting for them when they get there...wherever there is.

The wise men sought a king, the long-expected One, the King of the Jews. This King, named Jesus came preaching the Kingdom of God. That is His Kingdom where He rules and reigns. If you seek Jesus for real, you are seeking a Ruler, a King, the Author and finisher of your faith, the Deliverer and the divine grace. If you seek Jesus, the only response to Him when you find Him is to bow down at His feet and worship Him and give your life completely to Him. That is, if you are seeking Jesus Christ.

February 24th

What Do You Give a King?

"And they came into the house and saw the Child with Mary His mother; and they fell down and worshipped Him..." (Matthew 2:11a)

Much of what is taught in religious traditions today do not have as much to do with scripture as much as they do with the observances of men from days gone by. Always listen to the leader's words along the way by examining the fruit of their words and the conduct of their character. Jesus said that you will know them by their fruit for every good tree bears good fruit and every bad tree bears bad fruit. (Matthew 7:15-20)

The heart of any real Christian leader will always lead God's people to the Word of God, the worship of God and the ways of God. This is not Christian perfection par excellence, but the fruit of a heart towards God. The followers within any traditional church setting will eventually exemplify the standards of their leaders, the good and the bad. Not everyone is a leader and not every leader is a man or woman of God. There are always underlying reasons why people choose their professions as well as their church body. Remember, Herod sought the Child to kill Him.

Jesus exemplified true worship by always giving glory to His Father. He did not speak on His own accord, but only spoke what the Father had Him speak and do. (John 8:49-55). He honored and revered His Father in heaven in Truth and in Spirit. We worship Him by the giving of our lives in honor to Him.

Worship has been taught throughout the ages as a song, a hymn, a gift or an offering. Worship has been taught as a lifting of the hand or an attendance to a meeting. True worshippers worship in Spirit and Truth. (John 4:24) True worship is a humble heart falling down at His feet in submission. The humble heart gives the very best that it can give and that is its life.

One cannot presume to know the heart of another as to the nature of Truth in another. God knows and that is sufficient enough to worship Him as the True God and King that He is. True Spiritual worship is the gift we give to our King.

February 25th

The Gifts Prophesy

"…and opening their treasures they presented to Him gifts of gold and frankincense and myrrh." (Matthew 2:11b)

The gifts that the wise men gave to Jesus were gold, frankincense and myrrh. The scripture here says that they opened their treasures, that is, they came prepared to honor the future King of the Jews with gifts befitting a king. The gift of gold, first of all, has always been the finest and wealthiest gift to give anyone, especially a king. This gift of gold was given to a baby of the poor. God always supplies the needs of His own. God is and has always been faithful to care for the needs of His children. The gift of gold prophesied of His greatness, of His Kingship, and the honor that they gave Him being kings themselves.

Isaiah 60:3-6, prophesies of the Gentiles bringing gifts of gold and incense in honor, blessing and glory. The gifts were in prophecy and the gifts continued to prophesy. The frankincense was given as an aromatic fragrance denoting His Divinity. The gifts themselves told who they believed He was. What do your gifts foretell?

Myrrh denoted bitterness and was chiefly used in the care of the dead. Could the wise men have known in those days of His purpose in suffering? Jesus was known as the suffering servant. He came to die for the sin of the world. Again, the gifts given prophesy of the King's domain and the King's purpose.

It is to these gifts given that we look at the gifts we've given over time to our Lord and King. It has been said that the register in a man's checkbook reveals what kind of man he is, where has he spent his money will reveal where his priorities lie. Jesus said, "For where your treasure is, there your heart will be also." (Matthew 6:21). But in worship, we are not just talking about money, oh, no! In worship, we are talking about a life completely given over to Jesus Christ in reverential submission and honor.

Men may give some money to the church or to the poor, but that is not the point of worship. Treasure in the Kingdom of God is not about money. Your treasure is what you treasure and that could be anything. What you treasure prophesies about your life and the truth about what is in your heart. Even the gifts of the wise men prophesied more than just money and so does your life. Your treasure tells the truth about you. It's time for you to tell the truth about your treasure because your treasure tells the truth on you.

February 26th

Divine Providence

"Now when they had departed, behold, an angel of the Lord appeared to Joseph in a dream, saying, "Arise and take the Child and His mother, and flee to Egypt, and remain there until I tell you…"   (Matthew 2:13a)

How marvelous it is to be in tune with God. Oftentimes, many have to look back through the years to see God's hand of providence in their lives and some never see His hand of direction at all. Although, the Lord communicated via an angel in a dream to Joseph, at least a couple of times, the Lord did communicate and Joseph was attentive to the word of the Lord through the angel. The Holy Spirit is ever present and because of that, I believe that He is always communicating.

To be in tune is to be on the right frequency, the right pitch. The sound will sound the same albeit, at times, of direct attack and at other times of simple harmony.

When God speaks, do we have ears to hear? Even the ability to hear the Lord's voice comes from the Lord. That is why Jesus spoke in parables to that generation, '…Hearing you would hear and not understand, and seeing you will see and not perceive…" (Matthew 13:14b, NKJV)

Not all hear the Lord and not all understand when they hear the Word of the Lord. The power in hearing the scripture comes from the illumination of the Holy Spirit. Do all see? Do all hear? Do all understand the words they read in the scripture? The Lord spoke to Joseph in dreams and he obeyed all. The Lord knows who hear His voice.

"To him the doorkeeper opens, and the sheep hear his voice; and he calls his own sheep by name and leads them out. And when he brings out his own sheep, he goes before them; and the sheep follow him, for they know his voice."   (John 10:3-4, NKJV)

It is to our own ignorance and dismay through laziness, complacency and busyness that when the Lord does speak to us through the Holy Spirit, that we are either too busy to listen or too tired from the voices of the world to hear the still, small voice of the Lord, saying, 'Come, follow Me." He has promised to protect those who trust in His name, Psalm 91:14, but it is our responsibility to listen in our trusting. That is a good word for us today; that those who say they trust the Lord, also know and listen to His voice, and are kept from many a danger and many a foolish decision.

February 27th

Into Egypt

"And he arose and took the Child and his mother by night, and departed for Egypt." (Matthew 2:15b)

God knows the end from the beginning. An angel of the Lord warned Joseph in the dream and Joseph obeys and goes to Egypt. Subsequently, Herod, in his determination to kill the Child King sends a contingency of soldiers to Bethlehem and its surrounding region and murders all of the male children two years of age and younger. The Lord, in His Divine providence, had protected the Christ Child from the hands of Herod and had given them supply for their journey from the hands of the wise men.

It is gravely disturbing to hear of the slaughter of babies. Jeremiah, the prophet, prophesied of the time, "A voice was heard in Ramah, weeping and great mourning, Rachel weeping for her children; and she refused to be comforted, because they were no more." (Matthew 2:18; Jeremiah 31:15) The depravity of man knows no end. There are no boundaries that men of a depraved mind can be limited to when it comes to protecting themselves from their perceived enemies. It is the evil depravity of man guided by the dark forces of satanic structures that murder babies, whether it be in the form of a soldier with a sword or a doctor performing an abortion. Murder is murder.

It behooves us to listen to the Lord intently with ears set to hear His voice so that when He speaks, we hear Him and obey. The opportunity for the Lord to speak to us is usually not just for us alone, but for those around us as well. The Lord speaks His direction for leadership, for comfort, for healing and for protection. Hear the word of the Lord!

It is for those whom you know that the Lord speaks to you, saying, "Walk this way!" Other people are watching you and following your guidance. We are not alone on this earth and it is up to us to remain in Him, in tune with His voice, ever listening for Him to say, "Come here," and we obey and are saved.

February 28th

Following the Dream

"But when Herod was dead, behold, an angel of the Lord appeared in a dream to Joseph in Egypt, saying, 'Arise and take the Child and His mother, and go into the land of Israel…" (Matthew 2:19-20)

This is the third time in the book of Matthew that it is recorded that an angel of the Lord appears in a dream to Joseph and tells him what is going on and what he is to do. In various times, the Lord has spoken to His children in the particular as with Adam and Eve; in the still, small voice with Elijah, in prayers with the prophets and through the voices of the prophets, in the dreams and visions of Daniel and Ezekiel, in the light on the Damascus road with Paul, as well as, the revelation of the Holy Spirit in the Word. God has been speaking for thousands of years and He is still speaking today.

When the angel of the Lord spoke to Joseph in those dreams, the angel of the Lord was speaking what the Lord desired. When Jesus spoke on the earth, He spoke only what the Father had told Him to speak. (John 8:28). When the Holy Spirit speaks truth, "He will not speak on His own authority, but whatever He hears He will speak; and He will tell you things to come. He will glorify Me, for He will take care of what is Mine and declare it to you." (John 16:13b-14, NKJV)

When we say we have a dream, we are saying that we have a strong desire to do something particular. When Joseph had a dream and he followed his dream, he was following the Lord in what the Lord said in the dream. There is considerable difference here in what we sometimes choose to follow. Oftentimes, we are following a whim, an impulse, a lust labeled as a desire, our imagination or some other outer influence that has gotten hold of our minds and we think that it is divine, but is far from it.

How do you know the difference? Again, Jesus said that His sheep hear and know His voice. (John 10) The best way to know His voice is to be in His word, reading what He has said and knowing His nature. He will not speak against His own nature. Abide in Him and He will abide in you. The fruit of the Spirit is love, joy, peace, patience, kindness, goodness, faithfulness, gentleness, and self-control. (Galatians 5:22) His nature is His fruit. His nature is Light, not darkness. Practice being in His Presence. Walk in the Light as He is in the Light and you will have fellowship with Him and know Him in the Kingdom of His love.

February 29th

The Guidance of a Father

"...and being warned by God in a dream, he departed for the regions of Galilee, and came and resided in a city called Nazareth, that what was spoken through the prophets might be fulfilled, 'He shall be called a Nazarene.'"
(Matthew 3:22b-23)

This is the fourth dream of Joseph recorded in the book of Matthew. On this occasion, he is warned in a dream not to go to Judea, so instead, he is led to the region of Galilee. This is where they set up their home to raise a family.

Joseph has been in tune spiritually and completely obeys the Spirit. God, our Father has promised to protect and to guide and Joseph acknowledges the Father in listening obedience resulting in safety, health and prosperity.

We cannot underestimate the will of man in the equation of speaking and listening. When God is speaking we are not always listening. At times, God is completely silent, yet directing through our circumstances. We hear Him in the Spirit, not in clamor. We hear with ears in tune with Him, not in the busyness of our self-inclinations.

We hear with our ears, literally, and oftentimes, we miss His voice in a friend, a spouse, a co-worker, or a child. Too often, we're waiting for God to drop a rock on our heads for a sign, yet He comes in the unexpected. Too often, again, He has told us repeatedly what to do and because we were insistent on hearing Him the way we want to hear Him, we completely miss the boat.

Too often, I've seen opportunities for His healing hand, His soothing Spirit or His prospering us and we simply let Him slip away by our impertinence or neglect. The Holy Spirit is a gentleman and we need to be abiding in Him in a heightened spiritual awareness in order to see and hear and receive all that He has for us.

"Trust in the Lord with all your heart, and lean not on your own understanding; In all your ways acknowledge Him, and He shall direct your paths. Do not be wise in your own eyes; fear the Lord and depart from evil, it will be health to your flesh and strength to your bones." (Proverbs 3:5-7, NKJV)

March 1st

Repent

"Now in those days John the Baptist came, preaching in the wilderness of Judea, saying, 'Repent, for the kingdom of heaven is at hand.'" (Matthew 3:1-2)

Repent – change your course of direction and go in the opposite direction. Repent – change your mind and take on a new way of thinking. Repent – consider your ways and change your mind. Repent – think rightly with a new disposition. Even the ability to spiritually repent comes from the Lord.

All of these are right and even more so is the theological expectation of the word repent. To repent here is to see the direction that your life is taking with an understanding that you are not going in the right direction which is the way of God. In order for us to go in God's direction and be under His direction is to change our minds, our way of thinking, our ways of acting.

We cannot continue to think impure thoughts or dwell in darkness. This is far more than the idea of positive thinking over negative thinking. Just because someone thinks positively about themselves and their worldview doesn't mean that they have repented. Here, the repentance comes as repenting of your sins. Stop sinning; stop going away from God and turn to Him! Once you have been born again in His Spirit, His Spirit empowers you so you do not have to sin. It then becomes a choice, rather than a nature.

The change has to take place in the mind and in the heart first, before it can take hold in the actions. If you consider yourself a Christian, a believer in Jesus Christ, your actions will reveal the transaction in your heart. If there is no change in the behavior, there hasn't been a change in the heart. John the Baptist said, 'Bring forth fruits of repentance…' That is, confess your sins, stop your ways, and prove it by the way you live your new life.

Again, this isn't making a good man better. The introduction of Jesus Christ and the Kingdom of God doesn't make us better. He makes us a new creation, with a new heart, and a new mind. Paul implored his disciples to 'put on the mind of Christ'. We are to love the Lord our God, with all our hearts, all our minds and all our strength. We cannot do this if we choose to love ourselves more than Him. Change your mind towards Him and the fruit of repentance will be that we will no longer depend on ourselves, religion or anything else but Him.

March 2nd

The Way of the Lord

"For this is the one referred to by Isaiah the prophet, saying 'The voice of one crying in the wilderness, make ready the way of the Lord, make His paths straight!'" (Matthew 3:3)

It is the way of the Lord to have one man appointed to usher in the Day of the Lord. It is the way of the Lord to have one man announce the Lord's arrival. The message that John preached had been spoken of in the times of the prophet Isaiah. It is the way of the Lord that Isaiah referred to when the Lord spoke through him, saying, "'Comfort, O comfort My people,' says your God. 'Speak kindly to Jerusalem; and call out to her that her warfare is ended, that her iniquity has been removed, that she has received of the Lord's hand double for all her sins…Let every valley be lifted up, and every mountain be made low; and let the rough ground become a plain, and the rugged terrain a broad valley." (Isaiah 40:1-2, 4)

As John the Baptist literally came preaching in the wilderness of Judea, "Repent, for the kingdom of heaven is at hand," (v.2), he was literally ushering in the way, the Kingdom of God way, into the earth. The Kingdom of God was the message of John the Baptist and Jesus Christ. To make ready the way of the Lord is to, again, change your mind…get your mind ready for a change of thinking, of living, of behaving. Get ready to change!

The way of the Lord and His paths lead to the heart of God and it is His way to lead the heart of man on a straight path; where every mountain has been made low and every valley has been lifted up. What mountains are there in your life that He cannot make a plain? What valley in your life can be so deep that He cannot raise you up out of it?

This is the way of the Lord in His Kingdom, that when He is lifted up, He draws men unto Himself. He is higher than any valley and greater than any mountain. Make the way straight in your own mind. Get up out of the stinking thinking of your current circumstance and by the power of the Lord, be lifted into heavenly places. In the heavenly places, there are no mountains to climb and no valleys to get lost in. There is no fear in the Kingdom of God; there is no fear in perfect love.

If you name the Name of Jesus Christ, your warfare has ended and your iniquity has been removed. He has already won the war over sin, death, hell and the grave. Now give God praise!

March 3rd

Provisions for the Prophet

"Now John himself had a garment of camel's hair, and a leather belt about his waist; and his food was locust and wild honey." (Matthew 3:4)

It is God Himself who calls the prophet a prophet. No man can take the name of a prophet lest God Himself call him by that name. It is God Himself who supplies the needs of His prophets. John had come eating locust and wild honey. His clothing was a garment of camel hair and leather. He was not arrayed in the finest of clothing, raiment, robes and suits of clothing. He was fed by the Lord and he was dressed by the Lord.

This prophet's message was the message that the Lord had given him. He didn't make it up and he didn't expound on his own opinions. He kept everything close to the heart of God and whatever he was told to preach, he preached.

In the gospel according to Luke, they spoke of John, "And all who heard them kept them in mind saying, 'What then will this child turn out to be?' For the hand of the Lord was certainly with him. And his father Zacharias was filled with the Holy Spirit, and prophesied, saying, 'Blessed be the Lord God of Israel, for He has visited us and accomplished redemption for His people…and you child will be called the prophet of the Most High; for you will go on before the Lord to prepare His ways; to give His people the knowledge of salvation by the forgiveness of their sins…and he lived in the deserts until the day of his public appearance to Israel". (Luke 1:66-68, 76-77, 80)

It is by the testimony of the Lord in His word that John was the prophet that was foretold in the earlier days of Isaiah, and was acknowledged by the Holy Spirit speaking through his own earthly father, Zacharias. This is a testimony to the life and calling of a prophet with God as his mission and message.

Beware of men and women who name themselves the title of prophets and priests, apostles and bishops. It is God Who calls men and women to do His work. It is God Who supplies His faithful servants with their needs, not their fancy houses and vehicles. It is God Himself Who supplies the message of the faithful servant, not the opinions of those who are led by their desire for power, money and fame.

Make ready the way of the Lord, make His paths straight. The way of the Lord is the Kingdom of God and all who enter into it only enter in through Jesus Christ by the grace of the Father. No present day prophet, apostle, priest or bishop can supply your need or your way into the Kingdom, but if they follow in the way of

John, they will deny themselves, take up their cross and preach the message of repentance and confession of sin. It is the Lord's message. Follow the way of the Lord Jesus Christ. His path is plain and His ways are filled with grace.

March 4th

The Prophet and the People

"Then Jerusalem was going out to him, and all Judea, and all the district around the Jordan; and they were being baptized by him in the Jordan River, as they confessed their sins." (Matthew 3:5-6)

There had been no known prophet in Israel since the days of Malachi. The word spread quickly about John and the people came from all around to hear his message, confess their sins and be baptized in the Jordan River. The people left their comfortable surroundings and went out to the desert wilderness to hear the prophet of the Lord.

John's message was clear, 'Repent, for the Kingdom of heaven is near." He baptized them 'as' they confessed their sins. To enter into the Kingdom of God, it is not optional that we repent or confess our sins. The way has been made plain. The message is clear, repent of your ways and confess your sins. Be baptized, symbolizing the death and denial of your present ways, be washed clean in a river of death and be raised into new life in Him. The Jordan River was dirty; in no way would a repenting sinner be made to think that this 'washing' was ceremonial, or literal. This was a spiritual washing away for the remission of sins.

It is this message that the people took to heart then and it is the message that we have to take to heart today. We live on the other side of the cross of Jesus Christ. We have been given so great an opportunity to hear the message of grace that not even John was able to see. But even with the greatness of the grace of our Father through Jesus Christ, John's message still rings true. We still have to repent of our sins. We still have to change our ways and our ways of thinking.

Jesus Christ's conquering of sin means that even though we may find ourselves committing a sin, His power in us in His Kingdom means that we do not have to sin. It is our choice. No one makes us sin. In the grace and power of Jesus Christ, we do not have to sin. The devil was defeated that day on the cross and we do not have to live defeated lives, but live victoriously in the Spirit. We do not have to live a drudgery life filled with anguish and defeat from the darts of the evil one.

Repent of your sins, dive into the grace of Jesus Christ and having been washed clean live out the washed clean life in Him. He gives you the grace to overcome and to abound in Him. Commit your ways to Him and this day, walk out of the Jordan into His blessing!

March 5th

Fruit in Keeping with Repentance

"...every tree therefore that does not bear good fruit is cut down and thrown into the fire." (Matthew 3:10b)

Have you ever wondered at what it is that annoys you with people who do not tell the truth? What about when you think you've told the truth and another person just looks at you with a disgruntled grin and you realize that they know differently?

If we say we have repented of our sins and have been born again of the Spirit of God, then do we act like it? John the Baptist was talking to the Pharisees and Sadducees of the Jewish Sanhedrin, the religious lawmakers and scribes, and asked them, 'Who told you to come down here and get baptized?' He called them a 'brood of vipers' for they had no intention of living out their impulsive response to John's message of repentance, confession of sins and baptism.

Here, the word hypocrite comes to mind when we look at today's church and see people saying one thing and doing another. We are somewhat led to question if anything is real anymore by how so-called Christians tend to live a different life than what is prescribed in the scriptures. Does anyone know how to live a Christian life? Does anyone realize that you really cannot mimic Jesus Christ, or 'do what Jesus did'? Only Jesus can do what Jesus did.

It is, perhaps, the fault of the church itself and its wrong teachings that have led the outside world to look at the church in judgment and say, 'you don't quite live up to what you preach!' The truth is…we can't. We cannot live up to the teachings of the church or the traditional ways of looking at the scripture. That was what the Law was all about. The Jews could not live up to the Law and we cannot live up to Jesus Christ. It has been a false teaching to say that we could.

That was the purpose of the coming of Jesus Christ. He came to do something and everything that we could not do for ourselves. We cannot save ourselves from our sin and we cannot keep ourselves from living unbecoming lives before God. But, praise God, Jesus' gospel of the Kingdom of God says that He lives His life through us. He died on the cross for us, we don't have to. His death on the cross conquered sin, death, hell and the grave. We cannot do any of that, but allow Him, through the power of the Holy Spirit, to live His life in us and through us.

That is the fruit of repentance. Living out what He has done in us. He lives His life through us, so that when a witness is needed, He testifies through us in fountains of living water. It's up to us to give our lives to Him, completely and totally. That way, the fruit of the Spirit of love, joy, peace, patience, goodness, kindness, gentleness and self-control are His fruits exhibiting that He is working through a life given completely to Him.

March 6th

Have You Been Baptized?

"I indeed baptize you with water unto repentance, but He who is coming after me is mightier than I, whose sandals I am not worthy to carry. He will baptize you with the Holy Spirit and fire."   *(Matthew 3:11)*

Throughout the centuries of Christendom, baptism has taken on meaning after meaning with the form of baptism being left to the various denominational practices and interpretations. Some interpret the baptism as a sprinkling of water at specific ages of youth and others interpret it as John the Baptist was referring to here as a complete immersion into and out of water. Most, if not all, interpret that the baptism is necessary after some type of decision, or commitment to Christ has been made by the person willing to be baptized.

But is that what this passage of scripture is referring to?

John the Baptist came baptizing people in the Jordan River. He baptized people who had had repented of their sins, that is, turned away from their sin to live a better life for God. He said that Jesus, the One who was mightier than he, would baptize with the Holy Spirit and with fire.

Jesus Christ came to die. He was beaten, crucified on a cruel cross, died, was buried, and then He was resurrected. No other god can make that claim. We serve a risen Lord.

Baptism, then, is likened unto this…we die to ourselves, are buried…as the grain of wheat falls into the ground, and then, we are resurrected, born again, made into a new creation, a new life, born of His Holy Spirit. Are you born again with a new life? Have you been baptized into His death, burial, and resurrection? Has the Holy Spirit been God-breathed inside of you so that you know His new life lives inside of you?

It is Jesus Christ that baptizes with the Holy Spirit that cleanses and makes all things clean and all things new. It is Jesus Christ that baptizes with fire to burn up anything and everything that is not like Him. (v. 12) No outward appearance, ordinance, church function or church dignitary can save anyone.

I'll ask you again…have you been baptized? Have you been baptized with the Holy Spirit and with fire?

Father, teach us the truth by your Holy Spirit on what it means to be baptized with the Holy Spirit and with fire. Examine our hearts and lead us into all of Your truth.

March 7th

Being Baptized into Him

"As for me, I baptize you with water for repentance, but He who is coming after me is mightier than I, and I am not fit to remove His sandals; He will baptize you with the Holy Spirit and fire." *(Matthew 3:11)*

John came baptizing a baptism of repentance. His message was for all people to repent of their sins, confess their sins and get baptized into the river, into water. John was the forerunner. His message was the forerunner's message. Jesus said of John, 'I say to you, among those born of women, there is none greater than John; yet he who is least in the kingdom of God is greater than he." (Luke 7:28)

John said that the One to come would baptize with the Holy Spirit and fire. The Greek word for 'with' could also mean 'in' or 'by'…that you would be baptized in the Holy Spirit. When we come to Christ, we are invited into His Kingdom of peace and rest. We come to the door of the cross and because He paid the debt we could not pay with His own blood, He is the door into His Kingdom. He is His Kingdom. Everything about being with Him is being in Him.

When we give up ourselves, He not only comes into our lives and makes us a new creation (2 Cor. 5:17), we go into Him (2 Cor. 6:16); we are baptized into Him (Rom. 6:3-4) and we are to remain in Him (John 15:11-16). He is the way, the truth and the life. His Holy Spirit gets into us and we get into Him. That is how we are baptized in the Holy Spirit. It is the fire that burns up anything that is not like Him. (Hebrews 12:26-29). If you are born into Him, you are in Christ with a heavenly Father; outside of Christ, our God is a consuming fire.

The baptism of water is symbolic of the remission of sins, the washing away. It is also symbolic of being lowered into death, His death, and then being raised into life, His life. (Romans 6). When we are baptized into Him, His Holy Spirit is the One covering us completely, inside and out. It is as though we are covered in a pool of water, inside and out; we are completely enveloped in Him.

Remain in Him. Rest in His goodness. Reside in His Spirit. Reveal the peace of God that only the Holy Spirit can reveal. He does all of the work; this is His story. It's not about you or me. It's about Jesus and the work that He did in saving grace two thousand years ago. He is still about it today. Rest in Him and He will work all things together for your good, to those that are the called according to His purposes in the earth.

March 8th

The Coming Judgment

"And He will gather His wheat into the barn, but He will burn up the chaff with unquenchable fire." (Matthew 3:12b)

Too often we want to hear only the good, peaceful words that tickle our fancy. We want to feel good and we have been led to believe that positive goodness leads to positive words and affirmation which leads to prosperity and all the good things that some preachers promise, but never can deliver. Empowered ignorance is dangerous.

We've been told to think good thoughts; that the power of positive thinking will see us through. These sentiments may make us feel good in a moment, but are only temporary; they are not the joy that Jesus spoke of in John 15:11, "These things I have spoken to you, that My joy may remain in you, and that your joy may be full." Jesus was speaking to His disciples about remaining in Him, abiding in Him, obeying His commandments and abiding in His love.

Those that remain in Him, abide in His love and that keep His commandments are the ones who will bear the fruit of the Holy Spirit. (John 15) Not everyone is going to believe in the saving grace of Jesus Christ and even fewer folk are going to abide and remain in Him for narrow is the way and few there are that find it. (Matthew 7:13) Not everyone is going to heaven.

We are not to judge as to who gets to go to heaven or not. We are not to judge as to who is saved, or not. We don't have the capacity to judge rightly and we have been admonished by the Lord not to judge. So stop judging others.

The word says here that, 'HE will gather HIS wheat into the barn, but HE will burn up the chaff with unquenchable fire." (Emphasis mine) The Holy Spirit is the One Who convicts of sin, who judges with righteousness and who illuminates the truth into the hearts of men and women. (John 16:8-13). He is the One who does the work. We are to be the mouthpiece, just like John the Baptist. We are to allow the overflow of the Spirit of God emit from us so that a world that needs Him will come to know Him through the vessels that bear our names.

If you name the Name of Jesus Christ, rejoice that your name is written in heaven, but take no credit for anything that He does through you. Glorify Him in all things and remain in Him and His joy will be full in you.

March 9th

Jesus is Baptized

"Then Jesus arrived from Galilee at the Jordan coming to John, to be baptized by him." (Matthew 3:13)

Humility is a strong character trait and is often looked upon with great admiration. But is humility truly humble when the person is conscious of their own humility? A deliberate act of kindness to a lesser qualified person is kindness, but does it come with a motive? Conscious humility is viewed as pride and eventually seeks a reward. Have you ever known someone who wanted to be viewed as humble, but you seemed to think they were after something because of their ulterior motives. We don't really know why people do what they do, but eventually we will see it in their fruit. A good tree will produce good fruit and a bad tree will produce bad fruit. A truly humble person will perform humble acts because it is in them to do so. They do not seek credit or glory for having done something good for their fellow man.

The trait of humble obedience is in many a person; it was certainly in Jesus Christ. Jesus Christ was the Son of God, yet He humbled Himself to do all that He did in the earth, including being baptized by John the Baptist. The baptism of John was to exemplify the remission of sins, but Jesus, being the Messiah, the long-expected One, the Son of God had no sin to be remitted of or confessed. No one knew that at the time. We know that now because we believe what was written of Him. So, why did Jesus come to be baptized of John?

Of the many wondrous things we could say about Jesus Christ, we can never forget that He was God in the flesh. He was fully God and fully man. He, in the form of human flesh as the Son of God, was in humble obedience to His heavenly Father in purity and in Spirit. John recognized this and tried to prevent Him from this act. John believed that he, John, should be baptized by Jesus, for John believed he was not worthy to even loose the sandals on Jesus' feet.

Humble obedience is Jesus Christ. He had the power to lay His life down for us all and when we give our lives to Him, His power of humble obedience is at work in us. All that Jesus did was to glorify the Father. It is our pleasure to glorify the Lord in our bodies and in all that we do, to glorify Him. Humble yourself in the sight of the Lord and in due time, He will lift you up; not to glorify you, but to bring you unto Himself in His eternal Kingdom.

March 10th

The Confirmation

"After being baptized, Jesus went up immediately from the water; and behold, the heavens were opened, and he saw the Spirit of God descending as a dove, and coming upon Him, and behold, a voice out of the heavens, saying, 'This is My beloved Son, in whom I am well pleased.'"   *(Matthew 3:16-17)*

If there was ever a time in Jesus' ministry in the earth that God smiled in heaven, this had to be the time. God, the Father, was well-pleased with His Son and said so. A smile is an extravagant expression that has lost its way among the busyness of life. The reflection of the joy of the Lord is a smile, born in heaven and filled with peace. The smile is the tender heart woven by His Spirit and flows in grace to another's eyes.

Smile a smile away and smile once more. It is a gift from God that never ceases to give its pleasure to the giver and the receiver.

Jesus' humble obedience to His Father made the heart of the Father glad. In our humble obedience to Him, we follow in our Lord's path of peace, even though we may think the path be rocky, the internal joy that He gives sees us through. What John saw that day as the Spirit of God descending upon Jesus as a dove was the reflection of God's heart. The Spirit of God touched Jesus in approving love and affirmation.

The Father said, 'This is My Son! I am well-pleased in Him." This was a pronouncement; it was a confirmation; it was a loving Father sincerely glad of heart smiling down from heaven at the sight and sound of loving, humble obedience.

Why do we do what we do for our Lord? Why, indeed. For the Lord, it is He Who does His work and it is our opportunity to gladly and humbly submit to our Father in Christ, saying, "What would you have me do, Lord? Your will be done, oh, God, and not my own." It is in our humble obedience to Him that the smile of God falls upon us. It is not that we do anything for His favor for we cannot do anything to deserve Him. But, we humbly obey out of love and sincere desire to be with Him, not just for eternity, but for this very moment that we breathe our breath in Him.

Smile a smile away and smile once more. His smile is gladness of heart, peace and joy in the Holy Spirit. Be glad in Him! The Kingdom of God is here, be blessed in Him today.

March 11th

Led By the Spirit

"Then Jesus was led up by the Spirit into the wilderness to be tempted by the devil." (Matthew 4:1, NKJV)

After Jesus is baptized and declared to be the Son of God, He proceeds to be led of the Spirit of God into the wilderness to be tempted to along the lines of this – Whose will will you follow? Whose way will you walk? Whose life will you live? Who do you ultimately submit to when you are totally depleted of all resources? In whom will you find your sustenance?

It says that He was led of the Spirit into the wilderness, the place of being alone. The wilderness is the place of trying and doubt. It is the place that we are watched to see what we will do. What is it that you do when you think are alone? In quiet times of total separation from other people, what do you really do with the time you have been given?

In the times you think you are alone, do you do what you want to do because no one sees, or you think that no one hears? Whom do you serve with the time allotted? Be honest with your past and your present. We are never totally alone, are we?

In our opportunities of testing, we are influenced to do things in particular ways that are completely incongruent with the Spirit of God. In these opportunities, we may be asked to simply look the other way. We may be implored to ignore the obvious for a lower road. It is in the self that we are tested. What is it about yourself that you would be willing to give into for some temporary gain? What would a man get in exchange for his soul…the whole world?

Jesus was led by the Spirit and He chose the Spirit's path and way. He denied the flesh, the self, the human will. Jesus was led by the Spirit. Are you?

March 12th

Who Commands the Body?

"And after He had fasted forty days and forty nights, He then became hungry." (Matthew 4:2, NKJV)

Is it even imaginable to fast and go without food for forty days and forty nights? Simply because I have found myself unable to do something that Jesus did, it doesn't mean that He didn't do it. I believe the word of God is the Word of God and when it says that Jesus fasted for this length of time, I believe it. What seems to me to be unimaginable is all the more reason to look at Jesus Christ with awe.

The Spirit led Jesus into the wilderness. His food became the word of God. His time was spent with God, not in contemplation of His next meal. The changes that must have taken place in His body during this time must have cried out to be satisfied and yet He remained faithful to His task. In all of our getting, get understanding. The things we think we need to get us through our day are not the things we need to get us through our day.

Our preoccupation with our personal needs and desires keep us dwelling on those things. If we think we're hungry, we satisfy our craving for food, whether we're hungry or not. We seek pleasure in entertainment and words intended to gossip rather than Words that edify the spirit. We do more to satisfy our self-esteem than we do to satisfy the Lord.

Paul said, "…but I buffet my body and make it my slave, lest possibly, after I have preached to others, I myself should be disqualified." (1 Cor. 9:27). He also said, "I urge you therefore, brethren, by the mercies of God, to present your bodies a living and holy sacrifice, acceptable to God, which is your spiritual service of worship." (Romans 12:1)

We have to get our bodies under control, rather than our bodies making unjust demands on our minds, saying, 'I need to eat NOW!' or 'Feed my eyes with lust!' or 'Satisfy my cravings for…whatever!' We choose to satisfy our senses, our carnal selves. The things that we see, taste, touch, hear, and smell are the temporary things of life. They come and go, but some folk treat these temporary things of life as little gods to be satisfied at every whim.

You command your body. Take charge over your life by submitting it to Him in the each and every moment of each and every day. Commit your ways to the Lord and He will direct your steps.

March 13th

The Spiritual Conversation

"And the tempter came and said to Him, 'If You are the Son of God, command that these stones become bread.'" **(Matthew 4:3)**

The tempter has always come to deceive with slight of hand and doubting truth. The deceiver came to the garden and said to Eve, 'Has God indeed said...?' (Gen.3:1). He questions the Word of God. 'You will not surely die.' (Gen 3:4). He lies about the Word of God. 'For God knows that in the day you eat of it your eyes will be opened, and you will be like God, knowing good and evil.' (Gen 3:5). He speaks that which is not true in order to deceive and manipulate the mind. He came to Jesus with the same tactic. 'Give up what is rightfully yours and I will give you what is rightfully God's.' Needless to say, the tempter has nothing to give but trouble.

The tempter comes with a doubt, 'If'. He desired that Jesus prove Himself before him so that he could manipulate Jesus' denial of the self. The tempter was saying, 'Prove yourself to be the Son of God. Prove yourself to be satisfied when you have the power to do it for yourself. Take matters into your own hands and take care of yourself, but do it my way, no, do it your way, but just do it.'

Not much has changed since those days, we get tempted in the same manner, maybe different tactics under different situations, but it always revolves around taking matters into our own hands and taking the rights to ourselves and doing things our way. Oswald Chambers says that it is denying the rights to ourselves. Jesus said, "If any man desire to come after Me, let him deny himself, take up his cross daily and follow Me." (Luke 9:23, NKJV) When we are tempted, it is on the line of our perception of our rights to ourselves. The Christ follower has no rights. He gives up his rights to himself at the cross.

Jesus Christ is the Door to the Kingdom of God and when we walk through that Door into Him, we give up our self and walk into new life in Him. No flesh gets to go into the Kingdom. Learn to daily deny the self. Learn to daily deny the flesh. Learn to daily take up your cross and follow Him. It is not once and for all, but in the each and every moment. We are not speaking of salvation here, so please do not misunderstand. This daily following is getting into Jesus and Him getting into you. The Word of God is certain and when the tempter comes, be certain of God, trusting in Him for His grace is sufficient for your every need.

March 14th

How Do You Live?

"But He answered and said, 'It is written, "Man shall not live by bread alone, but by every word that proceeds from the mouth of God"'. (Matthew 4:4, NKJV)

If we have been born anew in Him and recognize that His Holy Spirit is what lives inside of us, then how do we live? How can we live if not by His grace and His grace alone? His Kingdom does not come with observation, but is within you. We live, truly live, the abundant kind of living kind of life, by the very breath and word of God.

Man does not live by bread alone, the outward fleshly manifestation of your outer man. But we who are alive in Christ live by the very word of God. He is His word. We live in Him and He lives in us. (John 14, 15) We live and move and have our very being in Him.

He is our daily bread. He is the bread of Life, the true life, the abundant kind of living kind of life. Do you get it? He is the living water, and out of you shall flow fountains of living water…

So, how do you live? You live by His Spirit living inside of you. His Kingdom is real. His Kingdom is for today. He is His Kingdom and He is the treasure that all men seek.

Thank the Lord for new life in Him. Thank the Lord for His daily bread, the daily word of Life. Paul said, 'I die daily…' We give up our rights to ourselves in order to die with Him in His death, and then live in Him in new Life!

Bless the Lord for His mercies are new each morning. Abide in Him, learn and obey His word, and the promise of the Father is to live in you and make His home in you. Bless the Lord for new life. Bless the Lord and all that is within me, bless His Holy Name!

March 15th

The Testing Continues

"...and said to Him, 'If you are the Son of God, throw yourself down...'"
(Matthew 4:6a, NKJV)

Have you ever done something in faith, just knowing that what you're doing, you're doing for the Lord and you are proving it by walking out in faith? Then, after some time, you find out that it was all a big mistake and you felt quite foolish about the whole thing. Well, if you haven't, I can tell you that I have and it's quite embarrassing when you claim to be doing something in faith and all you're doing is proving that you don't know the difference between faith and foolishness.

The word of God says to test the spirits, not to test God. Jesus responded to the tempter's tale with the Word, "On the other hand it is written, 'You shall not put the Lord your God to the test.'" (v. 7) It is not a wise choice to test God with what you think is His need for you to do something, when it is really your secret desire to move on, quit something, say something you shouldn't say, or do something really stupid…you just don't know it's stupid, so you do it anyway because you think you are all spiritual.

The true case is that if we were all that spiritual, we wouldn't have the need to put God to the test, or ourselves, because we would already be led of the Spirit and not of doubting questions.

Jesus Christ had just been told by His Father that He was His Son. He had the Holy Spirit in Him and on Him, so He knew very well Who He Was and Is. The tempter is the foolish one here and he is still the foolish leading the foolish today. Jesus knew He was the Son of God and although He had the need of hunger from fasting, He commanded His body, His mind and His Spirit. He knew the Word of God, He knows Himself. The devil wants to question that! And so, the deceiver comes to question and debilitate us with impertinence, foolishness and stupidity, and stupidly, we give in way too often. I speak from personal experience.

In Him, I have learned and am learning to acknowledge Him in all of my ways, to commit every way to Him and to deny that which I believe to be the self in order that His grace covers in all and through all. His grace is sufficient for my every need so I need not tempt my Lord with a selfish desire. Now, if I throw myself at anything, I am throwing myself at His feet, and that's a very good thing.

March 16th

The Attempted Takeover

"Again, the devil took Him to a very high mountain, and showed Him all the kingdoms of the world, and their glory; and he said to Him, 'All these things will I give You, if You fall down and worship me.'" *(Matthew 4:8-9, NKJV)*

As Jesus Christ clearly knew Who He was, He also knew who the tempter was and what power he had on the earth. It is spoken of the devil in the Word of God that he, "prowls around like a roaring lion looking for someone to devour," (1Peter 5:8); he will lay a snare or a trap in order to take them captive to do his will, (2 Timothy 2:26); a murderer and a liar, (John 8:34); the prince of this world, (John 12:31); the god of this age, (2 Corinthians 4:4); the prince of the power of the air, (Ephesians 2:2), as well as , many other names and devices.

The devil has authority in his realm and only in his realm. He had no authority over the kingdoms of this world as he put it; nor does he have full authority over all things in anything. But that doesn't give him an excuse to speak the truth for he is the father of lies. It is his deceptive influence that simulates authority and is what deceives most people.

Know who you are in Christ. Know that you are wonderfully made in Him. You are a new creation dwelling in His Kingdom. Perfect love casts out all fear; God is perfect and holy love and in Him we move and have our being. Your trust is in Jesus Christ and the work that He did on Calvary was His all-sufficient grace for the salvation of the world. Know who you are in Christ for we battle not against flesh and blood, but against principalities in high places.

If you are in Christ, you have been made alive in Him, and He has raised us up together to sit in heavenly places in Him. (Ephesians 2:6). In Him, we are being built together for a dwelling place of God in the Spirit. (Eph. 2:22). In Him, you have put on the new man who was created according to God, in true righteousness and holiness. (Eph. 4:24). In Him, we are being filled with fruits of righteousness which are by Jesus Christ, to the glory and praise of God. (Philippians 1:11). For us to live is Christ, and to die is gain. (Phil 1:21). In Christ, He has delivered us from the power of darkness and conveyed us into the kingdom of the Son of His love, in whom we have redemption through His blood, the forgiveness of sins. (Colossians 1:13-14)

Know who you are in Christ, for whom the Son sets free, is free indeed. Do not have conversations with the devil. Submit to the Lord in all things. Resist the devil and he will flee. (James 4:7). The power is in the Holy Spirit and you have been baptized with the Holy Spirit and with fire. Walk in the knowledge of Who He Is, for He dwells in you. Always remember that the battle is the Lord's and we do not battle according to the flesh for the weapons of our warfare are not carnal but are in the Spirit. Abide in His Holy Spirit and His Spirit will show you the way!

March 17th

The Response of the Spirit

"Then Jesus said to him, 'Begone, Satan! For it is written, "You shall worship the Lord your God, and serve him only."' (Matthew 4:10, NKJV)

"You shall have no other gods before Me." (Deut. 5:7, NKJV)
"You shall not make for yourself an idol, or any likeness of what is in heaven above or on earth beneath or in the water under the earth. You shall not worship them or serve them; for I, the Lord your God am a jealous God…" (Deut. 5:8-9a, NKJV)
"You shall not take the name of the Lord your God in vain, for the Lord will not leave him unpunished who takes His name in vain." (Deut. 5:11, NKJV)
"If anyone wishes to come after Me, let him deny himself and take up his cross daily, and follow Me. For whoever wishes to save his life shall lose it, but whoever loses his life for My sake, he is the one who will save it. For what is a man profited if he gains the whole world, and loses, and forfeits himself?" (Luke 9:23-25, NKJV)

The response of the Spirit of God spoke through the mouth of Jesus of Nazareth. He spoke the Word of God to only worship the Lord God. Jesus did not argue with the devil, why would you?

Oftentimes people make themselves out to be the god of their self and say it is the Lord God leading them to do such and such. Be wary of the person who says, 'The Lord wills it!' when, in fact, it is their secret desire to do a thing. Confusion abounds in the matter of will against will in the conditions of life. When a person has to do battle and labor to get their way, it is a sure sign that the Lord is not in it. If the Lord can sway the hearts of kings, what is it that is in you that makes you think you have to viciously argue someone down just to get your way and then you call that, 'God's will'?

It is life in the Kingdom of God that is the unknown quantity here. Life in the Kingdom of God is peace. If you are disturbing the peace with your selfish desires, where exactly do you dwell? It is the Lord's work to fight the battles for we do not wrestle against flesh and blood; it is the Spirit of God that fights the fight of faith, we merely stand in His Presence knowing Who is in us and Who we are joined to. Constant bickering for your way is not of the Holy Spirit, but is of the evil one who has set its way to worship its way and damn the others that get run over in that way.

That way is not the way of the Kingdom of God, but of the wide and foolish way of the world that chooses another god to serve called the will of man in the power of the self. Check your demeanor and disposition the next time you want to do a specific thing and you run up against disagreement. The Lord God is all powerful and all mighty, be certain of Him and only certain of Him.

March 18th

The Reward of the Spirit

"Then the devil left Him; and behold, angels came and began to minister to Him."   (Matthew 4:11, NKJV)

After Jesus' severe trial of fasting in the wilderness for forty days and forty nights, He becomes hungry. I do not know that we can comprehend the hunger that He felt at the time. I do not believe that we can comprehend what His body was going through at the time, particularly His mind. He would have been, perceivably, completely exhausted…starving for food to replenish His body. His mind would have been weak as His body was weak.

At the end of the fasting, the devil comes, in Jesus' greatest perceived weakest state. The devil tempts Him to do the devil's wishes, to the point of worshipping him, but Jesus will have none of it and dispenses the devil with the Word of God and the confidence of the Son of God.

When the devil left Him, angels came and ministered to Him. It is the comfort of God, the Father, to minister to His Son in the time of trial to replenish His Spirit. We do not know what the angels did at that time, nor do we know how long it took. Be very careful here of what men may say about angels, for the Word of God is very specific with what it says and what it doesn't say. All we know is what it says, the angels ministered to Jesus, we do not know what they did.

The point here is that when we go through trials of testing and temptation and, in the Sprit, overcome, we are ministered to by the Holy Spirit. The Holy Spirit comforts us in our times of need. The Holy Spirit knows our needs and our weaknesses. He knows our times and our days. He provides us with the Word to encourage us; He speaks Truth to us in times of sorrow, threat, fear and loss. He guides us into all Truth. He is our great deliverer.

The Holy Spirit prays in us and for us, "And in the same way the Spirit also helps our weakness; for we do not know how to pray as we should, but the Spirit Himself intercedes for us with groanings too deep for words; and He who searches the hearts knows what the mind of the Spirit is, because He intercedes for the saints according to the will of God." (Romans 8:26-27)

Just as Jesus Christ was ministered to by the angels, so are we ministered to by the Holy Spirit. He sees us through. "And He has said to me, 'My grace is sufficient for you, for power is perfected in weakness.' Most gladly, therefore, I will rather boast about my weaknesses, that the power of Christ may dwell in me." (2 Corinthians 12:9, NKJV) Let Him Who knew no sin, but dwelt among us as we are, minister to you in the power of the Holy Spirit. He knows our needs before we even ask. Abide in Him in the each and every moment. Trust Him with your life through the good and the bad. He loves you so!

March 19th

Prophecy Fulfilled

"This was to fulfill what was spoken through the prophet Isaiah…"
(Matthew 4:14, NKJV)

After the time of the fasting and temptation in the wilderness, Jesus withdraws into the region of Galilee and settles in Capernaum, which is by the sea. This fulfills the prophecy of Isaiah 9:1-2:
"But there will be no more gloom for her who was in anguish; in earlier times He treated the land of Zebulun and the land of Naphtali with contempt, but later on He shall make it glorious, by the way of the sea, on the other side of the Jordan, Galilee of the Gentiles. 'The people who walk in darkness will see a great light; those who live in a dark land the light will shine on them.'" (NKJV)

The gospel of Jesus Christ was and is the gospel of the Kingdom of God. He proclaimed that He was the Light of the world and in Him, there is no darkness at all. He came to set the captives free, to set at liberty those who were bound; to open the eyes of the blind. His Spiritual Light opens the eyes of the spiritually blind that they may see the Light of the Lord. The Light of the Lord shows us the Way into His Ways, His Kingdom.

In His Kingdom, He is the Prince of Peace, the Wonderful Counselor, The Mighty God and the Everlasting Father. In Him, there is shown a great light to light the way of nations that the love of the Father is so great and His mercies endure forever.

His grace had come in the form of a Man, known as the Son of Man and the Son of God. Jesus Christ was and Is prophecy fulfilled. We can believe all that has been written of Him since before the foundations of the earth. (Isaiah 40:21, Matt. 13:35, Matt. 25:34, Revelation 13:8)

God knows all and sees all. "In the beginning was the Word, and the Word was with God, and the Word was God…in Him was life, and the life was the light of men. And the light shines in the darkness, and the darkness did not comprehend it." (John 1:1, 4-5, NKJV)

Jesus declared we, too, are the light of the world and that while we have the light, we are to believe in the light so that we become the children of light. Apostle Paul said to walk in the light as He is in the light and there we have our fellowship with one another. Continue to abide in Him for His light abides in you for the purpose of the True Light shining in the darkness for the people that you meet and the places that you go. We are His handiwork and if we are abiding in Him, His Light will shine through us to a lost and lonely world. Allow His Light to shine through you today!

March 20th

The Gospel of Jesus Christ is the Kingdom of God

"From that time, Jesus began to preach and say, 'Repent, for the kingdom of heaven is at hand." (Matthew 4:17, NKJV)

Throughout the last two thousand years, many different people and cultures have had their thoughts and sermons on what they believed to be the Gospel of Jesus Christ. Some have said the gospel is salvation. Some have said that the gospel is Jesus Christ and Him crucified. Still others have said that it is the Good News, but have varied in their definitions of what they thought the Good News was.

Some men have said that the gospel is grace or the way to get saved, the way to heaven, or the way to new life, or the way to be born again, or the way to…and the list goes on and on. The same is likened unto it when you ask a minister what is the Kingdom of God and it all depends on who and when you're asking the question as to what the answer of the day will be. There are many variations of answers when it comes to the questions, 'What is the Gospel of Jesus Christ?' and 'What is the Kingdom of God?'

Always go to the Word of God for the answer to any question regarding the Word of God. Man's opinions are just that, they're opinions, and men have a strong tendency to be awfully wrong at times. If you want to know what Jesus said about a matter, ask Jesus in the Word.

Jesus began to preach and say, 'Repent, for the kingdom of heaven is at hand'. That is the Good News. That is the Gospel of Jesus Christ. But, that is just the beginning of what He had to say because in all that He did, He was teaching and preaching the Kingdom of heaven; the Kingdom of God. He healed the blind so they could see. That's what spiritual healing is all about. He alone gives the ability to see so that 'seeing you can see'. He alone gives you the ability to hear 'so that hearing you can hear'. He heals us of all our dis-ease. He is the ultimate healer. He alone gives life, eternal life that is for now and eternity. Eternal life is a way of life, not just a season of life. Jesus said that the Kingdom of God does not come with observation, but is in you!

Besides all the definitions of what the Kingdom is, who is Jesus Christ to you? Is He the deliverer and savior of the world to you? Is He the King of kings and Lord of lords to you? He is a King with a Kingdom. He ushered in the Kingdom of God and sealed it with the gift of the Holy Spirit. He desires a relationship with you this moment! He is Life forevermore and He is His Kingdom. "If any man desire to come after Me, let him deny himself, take up his cross daily and come, follow Me." (Luke 9:23). Abiding in Him IS dwelling in His Kingdom, abide in Him today!

March 21st

Being in a Safe Place

"From that time Jesus began to preach and to say, 'Repent, for the kingdom of heaven is at hand.'" (Matthew 4:17, NKJV)

Everyone in their right mind wants to be in a safe place. Few of us who consider ourselves normal go out and look for trouble, or do things to others that make them want to hurt us in some way. Many of us make mistakes, by accident, or by deliberation, but we certainly do not want to dwell in an unsafe environment.

The promise of God is that if we will repent of our sin and self, and give our lives over to Him, He will make us a new creation. He gives us that new life in Him so that we can be in His kingdom, the dwelling place of God. He has provided a way for us to be in His kingdom abiding in Him through the saving grace of Jesus Christ. Believe God, through Jesus Christ, that He provided the atonement for our sin so that we would have the entry way opened to us into His kingdom. His Kingdom is the safest place I know because this spiritual kingdom is Jesus Christ, Himself.

Jesus said that in this world we would have tribulation, but He has overcome the world. This means a couple of things. First, we will have trials, temptations, pains, hurts, and sorrows in this world. We are not exonerated from being human. Secondly, because He has overcome the world and if we dwell in Him in his kingdom, we can live content in Him. We may be hard-pressed on every side, but in Him, we have peace. We may be confronted with terror on the outside, but in Him, we can have life forevermore. We may be struck down in the flesh, but we will never be abandoned by Him in His kingdom. He is in your mind and heart to change your thinking from the inside.

Although the world is sometimes a dangerous place, we can know that the safe room is in the safe place, the trusting place of His Spirit. His Spirit is life and joy and peace. Dwell with Him there and be safe forevermore.

March 22nd

The Calling of Disciples

"And He said to them, 'Follow Me, and I will make you fishers of men.' And they immediately left the nets and followed Him."   (Matthew 4:19-20, NKJV)

When Jesus calls a person to Himself, He calls out specifically to those Whom He calls. This is not to say who that there are those who He calls and those who He does not call for He said Himself that "God did not send the Son into the world to judge the world, but that the world should be saved through Him." (John 3:17). Jesus calls men and women to Himself, but not all hear, nor do all answer the call. Nevertheless, Jesus is specific in calling His disciples.

It is up to us to answer His call. We now have the Holy Spirit to call and convict the world of sin and that call comes through the avenues of the written Word and the preached Word. Someone might come to know Jesus Christ through these writings because it contains the written Word. I know people who have read the Bible without someone helping them along and they come to know Jesus Christ. People are called in church services, or evangelistic services through the voice of a preacher. Others are called when they've heard the voice of a parent who has ministered the Word to them as a child. Still others, it was a friend or co-worker that led them to Christ by the Word through the marvelous work of the Holy Spirit.

If you are reading this, I would suspect you have answered to the call of Jesus Christ, through the work of the Holy Spirit in your life. It doesn't matter the manner of vehicle that you came to know Him as much as it does with what have you done with Jesus Christ since hearing Him call your name. Simon, who was called Peter, and Andrew his brother, left their nets and followed Him. The representation here is not that you leave your work and become a preacher, but that you hear Him and respond to His call with the denying of the self. When He calls and you answer that call, you are entering an entirely different domain, the Kingdom of God.

Again, we repeat the words of Jesus when He said that if someone desires to come after Jesus, let him deny himself, take up his cross daily and follow Him. When we choose Jesus, He makes us what He has wanted us to be all along and only He can answer that specifically for your soul. He is interested in you so much so that He was willing to die for the salvation of the world of all time. And, as you are reading this, the call has come to you, even now…follow Him!

March 23rd

The Call Continues

"And going on from there He saw two other brothers, James the son of Zebedee, and John his brother, in the boat with Zebedee his father, mending their nets; and He called them." (Matthew 4:21, NKJV)

The call of Jesus Christ to a disciple, that is, one who follows under a teacher and assists in spreading those teachings to others, is specific. He calls Simon and Andrew and then goes over to Zebedee's boat and calls James and John. They were all fishermen and knew what it took to catch fish. He says to Simon and Andrew, 'I'll make you fishers of men.'

Each of the four men left their nets and followed Jesus. Have you ever wondered at that interaction? One might suppose that since Jesus had just moved to Capernaum, they probably had never heard of Jesus of Nazareth, a carpenter by trade. But once Jesus appears, He talks to them and they leave their life's work to go and follow (disciple after) Him. What was it that they sensed that day on the seashore? Were they moved by the Spirit of God? What was Jesus' voice like? It was said that Jesus spoke as one having authority, did He speak to them with the voice of authority?

Was Jesus that much of a motivational leader, or was it the supernatural work of the calling of the Spirit of God on Jesus? Do you actually believe that Jesus was a motivational power of positive thinking type leader or was He simply led by the Holy Spirit? The power of positive thinking has its place, but not in the pulpit. That kind of preaching diminishes the power of the Holy Spirit into, 'I think I can, I think I can, etc.' The positive thinking preacher preaches positivity over the Spirit.

There have been many writers and speakers to make much of the leadership of Jesus Christ as if we could lead others as He led others. Let's always remember that He was the Son of God. Perhaps what was leading the men to follow Jesus was the specific call on their lives by the supernatural work of the Holy Spirit. The nature of God in the Bible is as such. All of the leaders in the scriptures were specifically called-out ones with a very specific task during a very specific season. Always take the individual verses of scripture in context of the paragraph, the chapter, the book, the testament, and most of all, the nature of God in the totality of the whole. Don't pick and choose individual verses to try and make them mean something that our Lord was really not saying. Even today men try to create books and conferences on leadership in the church and they make it rather worldly and completely leave out the work of the Holy Spirit.

It is the power of God to call men and women to Him. We are not called to men, but to God. No man deserves the honor and worship of God because they call themselves an apostle, bishop or other type of church leader. Jesus said, 'Follow Me!" It is our duty to make sure of our calling in the following of Jesus Christ. Follow Him and He will make you what He has called you to be.

March 24th

Proclaiming and Healing

"And Jesus was going about in all Galilee, teaching in their synagogues, and proclaiming the gospel of the kingdom, and healing every kind of disease and every kind of sickness among the people." (Matthew 4:23, NKJV)

The gospel of the Kingdom of God according to Jesus was what He preached, taught, talked about, and illustrated through healings, miracles and wonders that no man had ever done. All that Jesus talked about and performed led to the way of the Kingdom of God. John the Baptist came preaching the Kingdom of God and so did Jesus Christ.

Jesus taught as one having authority, as His authority came from God alone, not as the other scribes and people were amazed at His teaching. (Mark 1:22). Jesus would say, 'The time is fulfilled, and the kingdom of God is at hand; repent and believe in the gospel." (Mark 1:15) The time fulfilled is the arrival of the kingdom of God. The time fulfilled is the arrival of the Day of our Lord. Jesus came preaching, but His healing was what drew the crowds.

He could heal every disease and every sickness; there was no disease too difficult for Him. There was no sickness that could not be healed by His touch. He was revealing the power of God among the people. He had called ordinary men to be His disciples and he was healing the ordinary people of their ailments and lifelong issues of life…exciting times indeed!

The marvelous work of Jesus Christ was powerful and it still stands as a testament to His power today. We may not see exactly what Jesus did in those times, but the wisdom of God can work its work in medicine today unlike we have not seen before. God's miraculous power can work through the eyes and hands of a skilled doctor or medical practitioner.

But what of us today, are we left to the medical community alone for our healing? I don't think so. I have seen the answer to prayer in the healing of saints in need and I have seen the answer to prayer as He brings a person home to Him. We are to believe in the power of God today just as they saw the power of God then. Simply because you have not experienced a healing in your life, or in your closest friend, does not mean that the power of God is not available to you today. Pray, pray, pray in the Spirit and believe in faith, not doubting. Stand in Him in your time of need and He will direct your paths. He does not always answer our prayers the way we want, but He does hear us and answers according to His perfect will. Always remember that the healings of Jesus were as a sign to the age that the Kingdom had arrived in power and the greatest power on earth, death, was conquered by Him. Spiritual power conquered spiritual death. Jesus' words are Spirit.

March 25th

Coming to Jesus

"…and they brought to Him all who were ill, taken with various diseases and pains, demoniacs, epileptics, paralytics; and He healed them."
(Matthew 4:24b, NKJV)

Everything in the Word of God is there for a reason. Jesus was preaching the gospel of the kingdom and in His kingdom Jesus has all authority. He had all authority over every disease at hand. It did not matter what they brought to Jesus, He exhibited all authority over people's physical, mental, and spiritual health. This is power and grace in the Kingdom of God.

If you really have a need, bring it to Jesus. That was what was being spread throughout the region and even beyond the Jordan. As Jesus preached, He healed. He was that close to people. His preaching wasn't from some far away pulpit being guarded by security, He was among the people. He could touch the direst of need to remove evil spirits from people so they would no longer be controlled by another force. He could touch the most severe and excruciating pain and make it go away. He could touch the minds of the lunatic (Greek term) and bring them back from suffering to reality. He could touch the malformed, the couldn't walk, the broken body and everyone could see them move about with normalcy.

Excitement was being declared throughout Syria, Galilee, and beyond. Huge crowds were gathering wherever He went because of the magnificence of the healings. The power of God was among the people...wouldn't you have been excited? Overwhelmed, we would be declaring to our friends and neighbors, come and see the One Who healed me of all my diseases!

Jesus came healing people initially because He came to heal and to preach the Good News. (Luke 4:18-19). The healings exhibited the power of God over all disease. They represented authority over any authority in humanity. The healings also depicted a freedom from bondage to a diseased body. These healed people were allowed to be free to worship and be with other people as well, for they would no longer be considered 'unclean' by the religious hierarchy and the teachings of the day. The freedom from bondage is particularly clear here. They were freed to gather and listen to Jesus' teachings. There is nothing like being free from pain, physical discomfort, sores, disease, and the unknown. The healings represented the inner healing of a soul set free from any and all sin, regret, bondage, stress or fear. Jesus was expressing the power to forgive sins in all of His healings. (Mark 2:5-11)

Be free in Jesus and when you find yourself diseased in your body, seek Him where He may be found and rest in His Words of life. The Holy Spirit is here for you. Call out to Jesus now in faith knowing that He hears your heart and the confessions on your lips.

March 26th

The Gathering of the Multitudes

"And when He saw the multitudes, He went up on the mountain; and after He sat down, His disciples came to Him. And opening His mouth, He began to teach them..."   (Matthew 5:1-2, NKJV)

The multitudes had gathered. They had come from far and wide, from Galilee, Syria, and beyond the Jordan. Jesus had healed many of them of their diseases and freed them from demonic oppression. He had given them health and wholeness in their minds and bodies and now, He has gone up to a mountain to speak to them the gospel of the kingdom.

The words that Jesus is about to speak are words of life in the kingdom of God. They have been referred to as the Sermon on the Mount or the Be-Attitudes. These teachings of Jesus are some of the oft quoted words of our Lord throughout time. The foundation of entire Christian denominations have been built on the interpretations and perceived philosophy of His teachings throughout the scriptures.

When Jesus came preaching, He was preaching repentance and teaching the Kingdom of God. The words of the Sermon on the Mount are just that…teaching the multitudes about the Kingdom of God and what it was like. He was teaching them that if they enjoined to repent of their sins and follow the way of the Kingdom, they would be able to see His teaching manifest in their lives.

Jesus spoke words of edification and of blessing. He spoke on the differences between what the current scribes and teachers have taught and what the Kingdom was really like. He spoke, having authority because He did not speak from the teachings of the scribes, which was their earthly authority, no, He spoke from heaven down. He came with His own authority. As we read and meditate on the words of Jesus Christ, we have to realize that He was teaching about life in the Kingdom of God. No man can live out His words literally for His words are lived out only by Him. He was the only One who could perform His teachings.

So often, we find ourselves thinking we can 'do' His Word, when essentially, He did not come that we would 'do' His Word, but 'become' His Word. His teachings were His teachings in that if we give our lives over to Him completely, then He is able to re-create us into Himself where He abides and that is in His spiritual kingdom. In the Kingdom, He is the One doing the work and we are the ones being in Him while He is being in us. He fulfills the teaching, not us, so stop trying so hard to act like Jesus because you can't.

Only Jesus could do what Jesus did. Be in Him and He will birth in you a life that is the abundant life, the eternal life that is here and now and forevermore. Be in Him, remain in Him, rest in Him and the treasure that you find is above and beyond anything you could ask or think.

March 27th

The BE-Attitude

"Blessed are the poor in spirit, for theirs is the kingdom of heaven."
(Matthew 5:3, NKJV)

If we call ourselves His disciples, then we have come to the knowledge of His saving grace through the power of the Holy Spirit. It is the Holy Spirit that convicts the world of sin and it is His power that draws us to Him. We cannot do this work without God, we must be born again.

Because of Him we have been made new in Him, dwelling in Him and He in us. It is His power to become poor in spirit. This has everything to do with humility of heart and lowness of spirit, not material poverty. This saying of Jesus has nothing to do with money, but has everything to do with attitude and motive. Happy are they who are humble in spirit, for their spirits are as the Spirit of the kingdom of heaven. For Jesus, who is our Savior and leader, first humbled Himself and became obedient to the point of death, even the death of the cross.

"Blessed are they that mourn, for they shall be comforted." (Matthew 5:4). It is the power of God for us to behold when we humble ourselves, repent of our sins, and continually seek after Him in a renewed dependence daily. It is only by His grace that we have the opportunity of eternal life, and we get there by the loosing of our rights to ourselves, all the while being comforted by the Holy Comforter Himself.

When we lose our lives for His sake, we find the true life He meant for us to have in Him. There is no room in the kingdom of heaven for the pride of man. In mourning, we give up that life to demand our own way. Dead men have no desires. In joy, we find that He gives us the desires of our hearts. Happy is he who can find life in his right purpose and destiny and can live that life to the fullest today!

March 28th

Blessed are the Meek

"Blessed are the meek, for they shall inherit the earth."
(Matthew 5:5, NKJV)

Happy are the meek, not the weak. The world looks at Christians with the expectation that they can simply run rough-shod over them because they are supposed to be like Jesus, and Jesus was thought to be weak for the way He denied Himself. He voluntarily laid His life down so that the world, through Him, would be saved from the power of sin. The internal strength of purpose within Jesus Christ puts us all to shame when we catch a glimpse of what He went through to die on a cross for the atonement of the sin of the world.

Meekness is a gentle contentedness of knowing who you are and your purpose in this earth. Meekness is quiet submission to God; knowing when to speak, when to give a soft answer, and when to remain silent. Jesus was the purity of meekness speaking the right words at the right time and remaining silent even in the midst of rage. It is humbled self-control. Jesus was never weak. We find ourselves to be weak when we forget whose we are and that He has promised to always be with us. At times, we refuse to be meek because we don't want to be deemed as weak. So, we pick ourselves back up and give other people what we think they deserve, when we should be remaining silent, or should be offering a merciful response to an angry situation. A soft answer turns away wrath.

It is the power of the Holy Spirit dwelling in us to afford the response of meekness and humility when confronted with rage. It is the power of the Holy Spirit that endures through us to offer up non-violence to a violent situation. Standing in surrender with your back against a wall with no place to go for safety, and you have to rely on the power of the Holy Spirit for your next breath; that is the revelation of meekness flowing through your body into an atmosphere of terror. Peace is greater than fear and meekness is a far greater strength than any strike of the hand. Happy are the meek, for they shall inherit the earth. This is part of the mystery of the kingdom of God, the Christ in you, the hope of glory, doing in you what you could not possibly do yourself.

March 29th

Hungry and Thirsty for Righteousness

"Blessed are those who hunger and thirst for righteousness, for they shall be filled."   (Matthew 5:6, NKJV)

Our minds are places of critical thought, meditations, right and wrong thinking, pure and impure thoughts, and a plethora of many ideas and concepts too many to mention. We usually decide what we will think about and what we will not, albeit there are so many outer influences desiring to constrain us one way or the other we sometimes do not know what to think about some situations or complexities we find ourselves in. Wrong, or impure thinking takes us down roads that we simply do not need to go down and we have to work at not having stinking thinking.

The word of God admonishes us to think on things that are pure, noble, just, higher than what we would normally think about. Think about things that are right and positive, rather than things that are wrong and negative.

But what Jesus is talking about here…hungering and thirsting after righteousness is far more than just positive thinking. Righteousness is being right with God but because of our sin nature, we are unable to be right with God. Being right with God is being in alignment, in oneness with Him. Only His righteousness is totally and completely right. Only God is holy.

Hungering and thirsting implies being empty; therefore craving, desiring, and going after that which we know that we need is the response necessary to being filled.

When we submit to Him, repent of our sin, and are born again of His Holy Spirit, we are then made righteous before God because of Jesus Christ. It is the righteousness of Jesus Christ that makes all things new. He makes all things right within us. Jesus Christ becomes our righteousness. When we abide in Him, He abides in us and only then do we who hunger and thirst after righteousness receive the infilling of that which we hunger for. Go after God.

Again, this is far more than just positive thinking…this is life in the Kingdom of God!

"For if by the one man's offense death reigned through the one, much more those who receive abundance of grace and of the gift of righteousness will reign in life through the One, Jesus Christ." (Romans 5:17, NKJV)

March 30th

Obtaining Mercy

"Blessed are the merciful, for they shall obtain mercy."
(Matthew 5:7, NKJV)

If we had to be merciful of our own choosing, most of us would simply pass others by and go about our own business. A compassionate heart goes a long way towards helping others in need, but a compassionate heart is not likely to forgive when it is wronged over and over again.

We need a Savior and His name is Jesus Christ. We need God's mercy and grace because we do…we need His mercy, His overwhelming compassionate grace. We need His forgiveness, kindness, and benevolence. God is merciful to sinners. God is holy love.

When we dwell with Him in His kingdom abiding in Him, we are filled with His Holy Spirit. When mercy is needed in any given situation, His mercy rules our hearts and is an overflow through us to those who need compassion. When we live submitted lives to Him, He is able to be Himself in us and because He is full of mercy, His mercy fills our hearts to the full and beyond. Because we have been forgiven, it is our blessing to forgive, for it is in forgiving that we obtain forgiveness. Jesus asked the Father to forgive us our debts as we forgive our debtors. The power to forgive and to be merciful to others in their time of need is found in the indwelling power of the Holy Spirit.

If you find yourself being mean-spirited and lacking compassion in varying situations with others, you need to go back to Jesus Christ and ask Him to search your heart and see if there is anything in you that is not like Him. Also, ask Him if there is anything in you that is exactly like Him, He will show you Himself and your lack. An unforgiving spirit has no part in the Kingdom of God.

If any man desires to go after Jesus, let Him deny himself, take up his cross, and follow Him. Happy are you who do this and His merciful loving kindness will follow you and will be in you all the days of your life.

March 31st

Pure in Heart

"Blessed are the pure in heart, for they shall see God."
(Matthew 5:8, NKJV)

Jesus said in Luke 18:17, "Assuredly, I say to you, whoever does not receive the kingdom of God as a little child will by no means enter it." (NKJV) It is the purity in the nature of a child's heart that longs for and desires to be with his Daddy, to sit on his lap and have the Dad hold him. The purity and innocence of a little child desires love and wants to give love.

Purity is spotless, blameless, having no censure. Jesus Christ was the spotless Lamb of God that took away the sin of the world. (John 1:29) It is the absolute purity of Christ alone that was worthy to be the ultimate sacrifice for our atonement. Oswald Chambers calls it the "at-one-ment".[1] We, being at one with Him, by His grace, are made unto Him righteous and pure in heart. We are not pure and certainly not innocent so it takes His pure nature in us to cleanse us of ourselves and our thoughts.

It is His righteousness and purity, alone, that cleanses us and makes us a new creation. The purity of heart is His; the purity of conduct is ours. The life giving breath of God in His Kingdom cleanses our hearts and purifies our minds as we dwell with Him, putting on the mind of Christ…thinking on those things that are true, noble, just, pure, lovely, and of a good report. (Phil. 4:8). It is the thought conceived in His holiness that breeds purity in the heart.

Begin today to lose yourself of yourself and stop trying to be holy, you cannot do it. He alone is holy. But, Jesus told us to take His yoke upon us, for His burden is easy and His yoke is light. In submitting to Him in the each and every moment, we will see Him in His purity and know Him as He truly is. He is holy, He is pure and He dwells in you to make you as He is. Happy are you who have Christ dwelling in you for you know Him and He knows you and now you see clearer than you did before. His purity cleanses our eyes to see Him in the glory of His Kingdom.

April 1st

Blessed are the Peacemakers

"Blessed are the peacemakers, for they shall be called sons of God."
(Matthew 5:9, NKJV)

Jesus Christ, Who is our peace, dwells with you in the kingdom of God for He is His kingdom. We have been made to sit in the heavenly places in Him. (Ephesians 2:6). It is because of what He has done for us out of His great love that we can even know His mercy and grace. He is our peace. Peace, not of this world, but peace that passes all understanding and guards our hearts in Him. "Therefore, having been justified by faith, we have peace with God through our Lord Jesus Christ…" (Rom. 5:1, NKJV)

In the old west of the United States, a peacemaker was a pistol, a gun that would take care of any unruly person. This is not the peace that Jesus speaks of. His peace is the inner peace of knowing Him and being in Him. Contentedness in Christ is peace. Peacemakers make the peace because the Creator of peace dwells in them.

Peacefulness is a settled spirit. It is a spirit that does not lack and has learned to be content in whatever state of condition it has found itself to be in. A peaceful spirit knows who is in control even though circumstances may throw, seemingly, everything into a tale-spin. God is in control. He engineers our circumstances. A man of peace doesn't look for trouble, although trouble may knock on his door. Peacemakers learn of His Spirit in their responses to trouble, violence, and hate.

Peacemakers do not have to respond to violence with violence, nor do they have to respond to hate with hate. The holy love of Jesus Christ is the holy love of the peacemaker and when violence and hate come knocking, it is the power of God that settles the score for the peacemaker on the inside. Though some may cower in fear, not so for the peacemaker, for he is able to trust in His Savior through all things. As Jesus laid down His life for us all, so we, as His sons and daughters, have learned in the earth shattering dwelling place of peace to lay down our lives in holy trust of Him. It is the peace of Christ that others will see and not my own. As we dwell in the glory of His grace, others will see Him and He will be glorified in His peace.

April 2nd

Under Persecution

"Blessed are those who are persecuted for righteousness sake, for theirs is the kingdom of heaven." (Matthew 5:10, NKJV)

To be persecuted is to be oppressed, subjugated, driven away, or exterminated because of religious or origin reasons. (Webster's) Throughout the centuries and particularly just after Jesus' time on earth, the early Christians were hunted down as animals, imprisoned, tortured, beaten, mocked, and murdered. Many peoples throughout time have been oppressed for their religion, race, creed, or national origin.

Jesus is very specific here, though, and He is not talking about all people everywhere throughout all time if they are oppressed or otherwise seemingly denied their rights as human beings. No! This is not what He is saying.

The word of God says that "there is none righteous, no, not one; there is none who understands, there is none who seeks after God". (Romans 3:10-11, NKJV) And since we have no righteousness of our own, when Christ paid the price for our sin on the cross and subsequently rose from the grave, He became our righteousness. All who believe and confess the name that is above all names bows before that name in submission to Him. "…and be found in Him, not having my own righteousness, which is from the law, but that which is through faith in Christ, the righteousness which is from God by faith." (Philippians 3:9, NKJV)

Christ, who has become our righteousness in Him, is the one who is persecuted here. If you call on the name of Jesus Christ, the righteous One, and He dwells within you, then for certain, persecution is coming your way in some form or fashion.

"But even if you should suffer for righteousness sake, you are blessed. 'And do not be afraid of their threats, or be troubled.' But sanctify the Lord God in your hearts, and always be ready to give a defense to everyone who asks you a reason that is in you, with meekness and fear; having a good conscience, that when they defame you as evildoers, those who revile your good conduct in Christ may be ashamed. For it is better, if it is the will of God, to suffer for doing good than for doing evil."
(1 Peter 3:14-17, NKJV)

April 3rd

Persecuted Because of Jesus

"Blessed are those who have been persecuted for the sake of righteousness, for theirs is the kingdom of heaven. Blessed are you when men cast insults at you, and say all kinds of evil against you falsely, on account of Me."
(Matthew 5:10-11, NKJV)

For the one who has given their life to Christ Jesus and has forsaken all for Him, the road is narrow and few there are who walk in it. There are no other allegiances or loyalties to this one save Christ Jesus. And because of the faithfulness of these followers of Jesus Christ who endure and persevere until the end, there will be suffering for His sake.

No matter where you go in life, people want you to agree with them, share with them, be loyal to them; do what they do or go where they go. To the follower of Christ, when the decision is made to remain faithful to Him, the world looks at that type of faithfulness as being unfaithful to them. Here is where the mettle meets the soul…will I press on toward the mark of the high calling of Christ, or will I give in to a lesser road? When you give in to the way of the world, the world applauds and is gratified. When you go the way of the cross, the world despises that way and all who walk in it. Leaders who demand loyalty to themselves have no part in the Kingdom of God for they are idols unto themselves.

The world looks at the true disciple of faith and says all manner of things falsely, demeaning, accusatory with the angst of evil by its side, most of the time they don't even know what they do. Jesus says that these who are faithful are blessed, that they are the happy ones. Jesus says that when they say these things about you or to you, they are talking about Him, not you, for it is Him that they are seeing and hearing in their minds when you speak.

For the disciple dwelling in Him, in the Kingdom, all the riches are there in His fullness of glory. The world looks at this follower and does not see the riches of His glory, but sees a person whom they believe to be beneath them. They see someone who isn't quite strong enough, so they decide to push and persecute with toil. To this follower, Jesus says, "Rejoice, and be glad, for your reward in heaven is great, for so they persecuted the prophets who were before you." (Matt. 5:12)

Be faithful unto death. Continue in the calling that He has for you. Never give up, never give in. The reward is in heaven and only the faithful will see it in the fullness of time. He is faithful in you and you will know Him in the power of His resurrection, be thou faithful in Him unto death.

April 4th

You Are the Salt of the Earth

"You are the salt of the earth; but if the salt has become tasteless, how will it be made salty again?"   (Matthew 5:13a, NKJV)

The gospel of grace stands alone. It cannot be joined to works or the law. When Jesus came into His ministry, He came preaching repentance and the Kingdom of God. The only way to enter the Kingdom of God is by the grace of God. There is no other way. You cannot work your way into God's grace nor can you try to obey all of the law of God, you simply cannot do it. That's why the gospel of the kingdom is so necessary.

It was the needed custom to obtain pure salt for flavoring, seasoning and whatever they had need of it to do. But if the salt obtained was tainted, or blended with other minerals, it was simply not fit for use. The tainted salt would be thrown out to the roadway to be walked upon. If the salt becomes tasteless, it is of no use. "It is good for nothing anymore, except to be thrown out and trampled underfoot by men." (Matt. 5:13b). Here Jesus speaks of the necessary purity of the salt mineral to remain untainted by any other substance. What good is salt if it doesn't salt the food or provide the necessary ingredient for medicinal purposes? It is good for nothing.

This is why the person who thinks he is a Christian, but he isn't born again; he is a most miserable person. He thinks he's had some experience at church or he's trying to read the Bible and follow all the rules, but he just can't do it and fails miserably at trying to be what only Jesus can make him to be. This is the person who keeps running to an altar because they can't quit their personal sin because there's no power in them to overcome and, again, they are miserable.

Stop all of this and be made clean in Him. Jesus said to be made perfect and only He is perfect. Only He can make this possible through the life changing opportunity of being born into His Kingdom. He calls it the new birth. Unless one is born of water and of the Spirit, he cannot see the kingdom of God. (John 3:3-8). This is the real deal. This born again of the Spirit of God opportunity is the true salt, the true light where there is no mixture of works or law involved. Only by the grace of God are we brought into His marvelous light and it is only by His grace that we remain. Be the salt of the earth; be the true righteous flavoring in the earth and His grace will flow through you as a fountain of living water to those who need His grace.

April 5th

You are the Light of the World

"You are the light of the world. A city set on a hill cannot be hidden."
(Matthew 5:14, NKJV)

We take light for granted. We see the sun rise every day and every day we enjoy the light being given to us. We take light for granted for in our time, we can turn on a light with the flick of a switch and the area we are in immediately has light. And, it doesn't matter the size of the area or room, there's always enough light to go around.

We take the Word of God for granted as well. Some of us have read and heard so much scripture that we are numb to its power. We take the Word of God for granted because we're ok most of the time and when we aren't, we can pray our simple prayers and read a verse, or two and somehow we get an inkling of feeling better and we're on our way.

But you, when you truly need the Light of Christ in your mind from emotional turmoil, from mental anxiety and stress, from the compaction of work and duty, you cry out to God, 'Please save me from this mess!' You, then, go to the Word of God, or church and pray with fervor, knowing the last time you got yourself into a mess, He delivered you and now you need Him again. You need the Light of the world and you're not ashamed to let a few people know it.

Again, you take the Light for granted because you know He's there, for He's always there. He's there when you sleep, He's there when you awake. He's there with you and your family and He's there when you're alone. He is always there for you and maybe next time you will have the strength to be the light in someone else's life when all of your mess seems to be under control.

Jesus said, "You are the light of the world...no one lights a lamp and puts it under a basket, but that it lights the whole house...let your light so shine before men, that they may see your good works and glorify your Father in heaven." (Matt. 5:14a-16, NKJV)

If you name the Name of Jesus Christ, stop taking the light for granted and glorify God, He created it for you! Stop taking the Light of the world for granted, He's given His life for you! Stop taking the Light in you for granted for it was given to you for others to have the Light in them...stop taking and start giving Him away. Be the light of the world!

April 6th

The Power to Fulfill

"Do not think I came to abolish the Law or the Prophets; I did not come to abolish, but to fulfill." (Matthew 5:17, NKJV)

Jesus, being filled with the Holy Spirit, speaks of the plan of God in the fulfillment of all things. Jesus was and is the fulfillment. He went down into Egypt and 'came out of Egypt' as a baby, just as the people of Israel had done years before. He is a picture of Israel fulfilled in obedience. And what they could not do by obedience to the Law of God, He became obedience in the flesh. What the people of Israel refused to listen to in the Prophets, He became the fulfillment of in the Spirit. Of all that is written in the Law and the Prophets, what we now know as the Old Testament; and of all that had been preached to the people of Israel to obey throughout their history, there was none of it that was continually obeyed for they would not and could not fulfill it by themselves.

It is now being preached that since we live in the time of grace that the Law and the Prophets don't matter, but those who preach such do not read all the Words of the Christ. He says, 'until heaven and earth pass away, not the smallest letter or stroke shall pass away from the Law, until all is accomplished." (Matt. 5:18b, NKJV) But why would there be an expectation of God on us in this dispensation of time that if the people of Israel could not keep all of the Law, why are we who are the called out ones expected to do something that they could not do?

People could get stuck here because now they are thinking about their pocketbooks, their finances, the things that they have accumulated, their rights to their stuff and what is it that we have obeyed or not obeyed. When Jesus Christ said He came to fulfill, He did just what He said. Paul stated, "But before faith came, we were kept under guard by the law, kept for the faith which would afterward be revealed.

Therefore the law was our tutor to bring us to Christ, that we might be justified by faith. But after faith has come, we are no longer under a tutor." (Gal. 3:23-25, NKJV) "…He condemned sin in the flesh, that the righteous requirement of the law might be fulfilled in us who do not walk according to the flesh but according to the Spirit." (Rom. 8:4). Jesus Christ fulfilled all things in that the righteousness of God became our righteousness in Him. We do not have any righteousness of our own, but in Christ, He is all that we need. When we abide in Him, we live in the fulfillment of the Law and the Prophets. He is the fulfillment.

As Oswald Chambers puts it, 'give up the rights to the right to yourself.'[1] It is the Christ in you, the hope of glory that is your way into the Kingdom of God…He is your King. In Him dwells all of the power to fulfill all things in you. Allow the power of the Spirit to work in you. And all that He is will flow from you in glorified obedience. Then, you won't be concerned about the cares of this world that choke the Spirit of faith. You will have overcome and know that it was Jesus living in you to fulfill His Kingdom life through you to His glory forever.

April 7th

The Power to Complete

"For I say unto you, that unless your righteousness surpasses that of the scribes and Pharisees, you shall not enter the kingdom of heaven."
(Matthew 5:20, NKJV)

Oh, to be on the side of the mountain when Jesus said these words. They must have struck fear in the hearts of his followers and those who sat to listen. It was the glory of the scribes, the lawyers and writers of the law, and the Pharisees, the purveyors of control over the religious lives of the community, that unless your righteousness…your right doing and living was beyond that of them…you would not be allowed in the kingdom of heaven. One can almost hear the deep shudder of breath of 'what am I to do, I cannot keep the law as those men do?'

But Jesus didn't say, 'Do as those men do.' No, He said that your righteousness would have to surpass, exceed, that of your religious leaders. And the question still gets asked today, 'Does my righteousness, my right doing, working, helping, serving, or giving add up to my entrance into heaven?' For what Jesus was teaching here was that no one could help, serve, give, obey, work or do right in order to obtain a heavenly pass. No, it takes the blood of a blameless one, a perfect sacrifice laid out on an altar of death and who can be that blameless one, certainly not you or me? Who can bear our infirmities, our weaknesses, our sin, even the sin of the world and give in return the righteousness of a holy life given unto God? There is no other than Jesus Christ.

What hope does the world have in that it really doesn't care in the acknowledgement of a Holy God? That's just it, the world wants to act like it doesn't care, but if you ask a single person, "Do you want to go to heaven when you die?" in their quiet reflection, they'll admit that no one wants to go to the alternative which is hell… even if they don't admit that there is a heaven or hell.

Jesus Christ came to fulfill, to complete, the Law and the Prophets and He did, yet, all things have not yet come to be accomplished. The world, as we know it, has not ended, but it will. A new heaven and a new earth will come to pass. Jesus Christ is the True and Faithful One who will bring all things to their fulfillment. It is only in Him that we have entrance into the kingdom of heaven by His blood over the Door of which He is. He is the way and all of the righteousness of the Holy Spirit is in Him. Be found in Him. Give your life to Him, abide in Him and He will fulfill all in you to His glory and the glory of the Father. Then, the cares of this world will not choke or even matter to you for the glory of His Kingdom will be in you and the righteous Light will shine in the darkness to bring others to Him in His glorious Light. Give Him praise!

April 8th

Matters of the Heart

"But I say to you that everyone who is angry with his brother shall be guilty before the court…" (Matthew 5:22a, NKJV)

It is what is in our hearts that condemn us before a Holy God, not just the actions before men. People fear getting caught for doing something terrible, particularly murder. But murder doesn't begin with the hand; it begins in the heart with anger towards another. Anger is an emotion born from a thought, a reflection, a response to a wrong, or an indictment of someone who simply lives in anger and doesn't remember the reason why. The matters of the heart are deep wells and those who keep their wells in order keep their hearts and minds stayed on pure things, noble things, things that are higher. God said, 'My thoughts are not your thoughts, My ways are not your ways…' (Isaiah 55:8a, NKJV) "Above all else, guard your heart, for everything you do flows from it." (Proverbs 4:23, NIV)

But who can keep their own hearts pure? Does anyone fear God in the midst of anger towards another? People fear God when they've done wrong. They fear the court when they've gotten caught doing wrong. But do you fear God in the midst of your walled up separation from your fellow man when anger has gotten hold of you and you choose not to let it go?

It is what is in our hearts that condemn us or free us unto a righteous and Holy God. Who or what is in your heart? "If our hearts condemn us, we know that God is greater than our hearts, and He knows everything. Dear friends, if our hearts do not condemn us, we have confidence before God and receive from Him anything we ask, because we keep His commands and do what pleases Him." (1 John 3:20-22, NIV).

The power of God in Jesus Christ enables us to have Him fulfill and complete the law of love in us. Christ died for us and if we name His Name, He lives His life in us. In this, our heart and mind, soul and body belong to Him. He is the One who knows our hearts and it is He who guards our hearts and minds even when we do not have the strength to do it ourselves. Submit to Him and you will find yourself not submitting to anger given to resentment, bitterness, or worse. In your submission to Him, His love and peace will guard your heart in Christ Jesus. In Him, you will find the all-sufficient One to be all-sufficient in you. Be free from anger! Release and forgive.

April 9th

The Depth of Anger

"...and whoever shall say to his brother, 'Raca,' shall be guilty before the supreme court; and whoever shall say, 'You fool,' shall be guilty enough to go into the fiery hell." (Matt. 5:22b, NKJV)

There are depths to our emotions that we may or may not be aware of. The thoughts we entertain are not all good and wholesome thoughts. It is where our heart resides as to where our conscious finds itself in the Lord or in something else entirely. We have constant unabated thoughts firing on all cylinders and, at times, we are not sure where they emanate from.

If we abide in anger towards another person, surely the anger will remain and fester as a cancer. The cost of anger dwelling is incalculable. It causes internal and external stress, resentment, burden bearing, fault finding, joy stealing, a combative nature and unholy alliances. If we allow a minute opportunity to fester into something larger, we allow the resentment to turn into bitterness which turns into consternation which could lead to rage. All of this derives from the anger pit.

Jesus is emphatic that if we allow anger to stew within us, it is in our hearts going to differing levels that, externally, will turn into separation from the offending party; that leads to more frustration leading to confrontation and, depending on the variable responses of humans, could lead to physical alternation to violence to murder. Some of this may be intentional, but usually in the confines of a civilized society, most people say 'they never intended it to go that far'.

What most people forget, however, is the severe consequence of the results of unguarded anger. There are internal stressors at work that debilitate the body and mind when preoccupied with being angry towards another person. The stress leads to poor health and debilitating effects in the body, internally as well as externally. Stress kills. So, the consequences begin in the heart and flow through the body to be exhaled.

Our lot is to listen to Jesus and acknowledge the depth of the possibility of anger and acknowledge the depth of the consequences. The Word says to "be angry, but do not sin, do not let the sun go down on your anger." (Ephesians 4:26, ESV). Get rid of the anger before it gets hold of you. Anger will take you down a spiritual road that you do not want to be on and will ultimately lead to death by rejecting the very power that has tried to save you. Believe in the Lord Jesus Christ that not only can He save your soul from hell, but He can also save your life from being a miserable angry creature while on this earth.

This is the sum of the Kingdom of God. He gives us life eternal for today and forevermore…life eternal is a way of life in the Kingdom. Jesus said, 'If anyone loves Me, he will keep My word; and My Father will love him, and We will come to him and make our abode with him." (John 14:23, NKJV)
The internal dwelling of the Holy Spirit in us keeps us in Him and in Him, there is no darkness at all. Remain in Him and even the darkest darkness that attempts to come your way must flee in the light of His glory and grace.

April 10th

The Acts of the Heart

"You have heard that it was said, 'You shall not commit adultery'; but I say to you, that everyone who looks on a woman to lust for her has committed adultery with her already in his heart."   (Matthew 5:27-28, NKJV)

When Jesus says, 'You have heard it said, but I say…' He is communicating the transition from one mindset to another; one dispensation of time to another. The mindset of the Law of God began with the Ten Commandments. This particular commandment, "You shall not commit adultery." (Exodus 20:14), is very specific as are all of our Lord's commands. This command is action specific. It is when a married person has physical sexual relations outside of the marriage bond. Earlier Jesus had said that He did not come to abolish the law, but to fulfill it. The transition is leading to the gospel of grace.

In the fulfillment of the law, the law is no longer relegated to being written on paper or stone, it then becomes a law written on the hearts of men and women. The time of the Kingdom is the time of the heart and all that matters is what is in and on the heart of man. If a married person desires in their heart to view with their eyes another person other than their spouse in the spirit of lust, then, in the matter of the heart, that person is already committing adultery.

It has been said by some men that 'they may be a Christian, but they're not dead.' That is to say, 'I'm still a man and a man's gonna look at women lustfully and that's just life!' Well, Jesus our Lord has already spoken to that and it would be true, that when a man says, 'I'm not dead', is correct in that he has not denied himself or died to himself. Paul understood the life of a true disciple when he said, 'I die daily'. This is no joking matter. Viewing internet pornography would be a most egregious adulterous act that a married man or woman could perform when it comes to the matters of the heart. Jesus equates the lustful viewing the same as the act.

This may be a difficult subject for some people. However, the power of the Holy Spirit is more powerful than any proposition or influence of the evil one. Remember, Jesus was tried to be tempted and succeeded in not succumbing to the devil's attempts, not just because He is the Son of God, but that He knew who He was and applied the power of the Spirit and the Word to the onslaught of the evil one. We, too, need to rely on the Holy Spirit and just say, 'NO!' when the urge or thought arises to view a person who is not your spouse in a lustful manner.

Dwell in the Spirit of God by dwelling in the Word and bathing in prayer. The 'NO!' will be easy when the Holy Spirit is in charge. Submit to the Lord, resist the devil and the devil will flee. (James 4:7)

April 11th

Seeing the Matter

"And if your right eye makes you stumble, tear it out and throw it from you; for it is better for you that one of the parts of your body perish, than for your whole body to be thrown into hell." (Matthew 5:29, NKJV)

Jesus continues His message of the person that looks at another with lust in their heart with a very specific line of thought concerning what the eye is viewing and the need to make corrections if need be. This is also a great example that Jesus' teachings on the Kingdom of God were not to be taken literally, but spiritually. The Kingdom of God, then and now, is not a physical kingdom on earth, not yet. Jesus said Himself that "My kingdom is not an earthly kingdom. If it were, my followers would fight to keep me from being handed over to the Jewish leaders. But my kingdom is not of this world." (John 18:36, NLT). The Kingdom of God is a spiritual kingdom and Jesus' words are spiritual words, so do not consider plucking your eye out literally, be focused spiritually on Jesus Christ in the power of the Holy Spirit.

It is a far better thing to guard our hearts by guarding our eyes first. At times, our eyes see someone that could lead us down the road of desire or lust. It is a conscious decision of the heart in a faithful continuance to pursue the person with the eyes to the point where your imagination takes over into something unnatural. It is not natural for a man to pursue a woman with a heart of lust. If it were, all men would be looking at all women all of the time with lust in their hearts for sexual gratification. A person learns this type of behavior and then decides whether or not to control themselves when a woman passes by or they are in their presence. It is animalistic to believe that all men lust for all women at all times, that just isn't the case. A man makes the decision to lust or not. It is a matter of the heart and here, Jesus is explicitly attacking the decision to control what your eyes are set upon and what you are thinking as you are looking. The best road is if an opportunity presents itself in the world to look with lust in the heart, then just like saying, 'No!' to any sin, turn your head and look away. It's called self-control.

If you cannot control yourself, and many choose not to, then the Spirit of God is here. This is the offering of the Kingdom of God. When a person is led to follow after Jesus Christ, the Holy Spirit breathes new life into the person and the person becomes born again. With this new birth, the person then has an enabler in the Spirit of God to follow after God totally and completely. If you find your eye is set upon another in an ungodly way, it is a matter of the person having taken themselves back up again and doing what they want to do. According to Jesus, it would be better to pluck your eye out than to follow down a road of spiritual rebellion. One of the fruits of the Spirit of God is self-control.

Submit to the Lord. Resist the devil and he will flee. Opportunities to look with lust are only temptations. In the power of the Holy Spirit, you do not have to sin. Remember that!

April 12th

The Work of the Hand

"And if your right hand makes you stumble, cut it off and throw it from you; for it is better for you that one of the parts of your body perish, than for your whole body to go into hell." (Matthew 5:30, NKJV)

The work of your hands comes from the desires of the heart. Jesus speaks of committing adultery in the heart, that is, it is concentrated in the mind. It is your eyes that lust first after another woman or man that is not your spouse, and it is your hands that you choose to use to take something that is not yours to take. We take with our hearts first and then take with our hands what our heart's desire. Jesus is saying, 'Do not steal, do not covet; do not take that which is not yours to take.' Still, it is the desires of the heart that lead us astray and nobody makes us sin, it is always a decision of the heart.

If we think through what we use our hands for, we can be thankful to God that He has provided such a wonderful body to be on this earth. The use of the hands represents our work, our pleasure, our fun, our skills…there are so many usages for our hands. We can give and we can take away; we can greet another with a wave or a handshake; we can give directions and signs with our hands. There are so many natural, positive things we can do with our hands.

With our hands, we can hit or slap, jab or choke another person. With our hands, we can kill, steal, or destroy another, just with the stroke of a hand. How important are our hands? Our hands can be used for godly purposes or ungodly means.

We can clasp our hands in love and gratitude to another or we can form a fist and attack. It is all a matter of what is in our heart that makes us who and what we are and how we use our hands. It's not just our mouths that are extensions of our hearts, but our hands are as well. With our minds, we choose to work or not. We can choose to work with our minds or our hands, but whether we use our minds and/or our hands to work, we have chosen to do the better thing to work rather than being idle.

Jesus has shown us that it is in the seeing and the doing that shows what we desire. Desire the Holy Spirit and your hands will never be idle, nor will they be used for violence. Desire the Holy Spirit and your hands will be clasped in love and prayer, lifted in adoration and praise, giving to those in need and not taking. What are you doing with your hands?

Father, I pray that our hearts are focused on You and You alone. Thank You for being so wonderful to us that You gave and You keep on giving by being with us and in us as You are. Be in our hearts. Be in our eyes. Be in the beauty of our hands and the work that You have given us to do, may it be to Your glory and Your glory alone. I love You!

April 13th

The Matter of Divorce

"And it was said, 'Whoever sends his wife away, let him give her a certificate of divorce'; but I say to you that everyone who divorces his wife, except for the cause of unchastity, makes her commit adultery; and whoever marries a divorced woman commits adultery." (Matt. 5:31-32, NKJV)

In Jesus' Sermon on the Mount, He begins with the 'Blessed are...' that is, happy are those who 'are' in the state of being that He specifically speaks about. The state of being emanates from the heart. If the heart is pure, then what flows from the heart leading to the mouth and the hands will have pure motives and peaceful offerings to give to others. Likewise, if the heart is bad and filled with anger or lust, then the outcome of the eye and the work of the body will be as a result of what lies in the matters of the heart. Each of the messages within the sermon go together for He is beginning His teaching ministry on the Kingdom of God.

The heart is the seat of these matters and as Jesus later teaches, the Kingdom of God does not come with observation, as the clouds and seasons of weather, but is within the heart of those who are born of the Spirit of God.

Just as an impure heart of anger leads to murder in the heart and an impure eye leads to adultery in the heart, so does the impure relationship of a married man and woman lead to divorce when the heart of the two are not one. Jesus goes back to the Law and refers to the ability of a man to 'put away his wife', that is, to put her on the shelf for any reason that the man chooses. The disposition of a man who would do such a thing would reveal that the man and woman do not get along and the heart of their marriage is in error so much so that the differences in their marriage are irreconcilable and they choose divorce as the only way out of their differences. Jesus basically says, 'This is not to be so!' The pride of a man certainly leads to a fall.

Marriage is built on a faithful continuance of love, forgiveness, respect, communication and a willingness to prosper even in the midst of any and all of the issues of life. Anger must not lead to resentment and bitterness in marriage. Neither should there be a lustful eye leading to adultery. This is not to be so in life and especially not in marriage.

The holy love of God must be realized within the heart of the ones given to marriage. There is no fear in love and there isn't any such thing as irreconcilable differences in marriage in the Kingdom of God. All of this is a choice and our choices occur every moment of every day in the recesses of our minds. Keep your hearts stayed on Him, in Him. Make the commitment to Jesus Christ as Lord of your life and Lord of your marriage. He loves you both, not just you. Do not let the sun go down on your wrath and keep your eyes focused in Him and not the world around you. Marriage requires it of you for the two are to be one and what God has joined together, let no man divide. "For I hate divorce!" says the Lord, God of Israel. 'To divorce your wife is to overwhelm her with cruelty,' says the Lord of Heaven's Armies. 'So guard your heart, do not be unfaithful to your wife.'" (Malachi 2:16, NLT)

April 14th

To Swear an Oath

"Again, you have heard that the ancients were told, 'You shall not make false vows, but shall fulfill your vows to the Lord.' But I say to you, make no oath at all, either by heaven, for it is the throne of God, or by the earth, for it is the footstool of His feet...'"   *(Matthew 5:33-34a, NKJV)*

Jesus is saying here, 'Let your yes be yes and let your no be no.' (v. 37). This is to say, tell the truth in all that you say. An oath is beyond the common word of man where a verbal or written contract is needed in order to obligate both parties towards each other. If we take these spiritual words literally, then we wouldn't be signing any contract ever, making any vows of marriage, wouldn't be allowed to borrow money and the list goes on and on of how our world works in everyday life. Again, these are spiritual words for which truth is to be the prominent domain of our relationships in the world. If we say we are going to do something, do it. If we say we are not going to do something, then don't do it. Do not encumber yourself by making false claims, or by making vows that you cannot, or will not keep. Then, you become a liar. Tell the truth; always tell the truth for you do not abide in this world alone, it is He who abides in you and when you speak, you are speaking the overflow of God...or, are you?

If the Christ be born in us, it is the Spirit of God who is guiding, blessing, prospering and speaking. We are His hands in this world. What we join ourselves to is vitally important. Beware of what you join yourself to. Do not join yourself to a harlot nor join yourself to the world that is constantly badgering and taking. Since Jesus is the 'way, the truth, and the life', then the truth of the way in you is to be the way of truth in your heart and in your mouths. You have joined your heart to the Spirit of God and your commitment is to Him.

To swear an oath in this context is to add to your words and, in Christ, your words are sufficient. Be honest and truthful. The art of many words add to pretense and may possibly cause doubt in the hearer. Let your yes be yes and your no, be no. The Lord says, "I will not allow deceivers to serve in my house, and liars to stay in my presence." (Psalm 101:7, NLT).

"Those that speak for themselves want glory only for themselves, but a person who seeks to honor the one who sent him speaks truth, not lies." (John 7:18, NLT)

April 15th

A Response to Violence

"You have heard that it was said, 'An eye for an eye and a tooth for a tooth.' But I say to you, do not resist him who is evil; but whoever slaps you on your right cheek, turn to him the other also."   (Matthew 5:38-39, NKJV)

The Russian writer, Leo Tolstoy, took the literal road of Jesus' words in the Gospels and eventually developed "the doctrine of non-resistance to evil by force"[1] having his writings and ideas influence people such as Mahatma Gandhi and Martin Luther King. Since Jesus' day, this verse has been taken literally whereas other verses are taken spiritually. It would seem that if one is to 'turn the other cheek' in the midst of violence, then one seemingly has taken the upper hand by taking the upper road. But, if you take this verse literally, then it would stand to reason that you must take all of Jesus' words literally resulting in most of Jesus loving Christians walking around eyeless from looking at others with lust, and handless, from having walked in offense towards their fellow man.

What are we to do with Jesus' words, then, for He certainly meant to have them lived out? He wasn't just spending time frivolously talking like many of us do these days philosophizing and dreaming of better days. If we take these words to be spiritual words, then what of it? Does it mean that I can hit someone back if they hit me? It is the cowardly who attack the non-violent. When we abide in Christ, who is our Lord and standard, we abide in the power of the Holy Spirit. It is He who has overcome the evil one, death, hell, and the grave. It is He who lives in you. So, when the world says all manner of things falsely against you, or when the world decides to slap you on the cheek, they are doing so in order to slap the Jesus out of you and you know they cannot do that. "But you belong to God my dear children. You have already won a victory over those people, because the Spirit who lives in you is greater than the spirit who lives in the world." (1 John 4:4, NLT)

Was all of this a forewarning of the horrific persecution that came to the Christians of the day and for all of us who choose to follow Him? Certainly yes, but it has also been just as certain that persecution by violence has been used throughout the last two thousand years and is still used today, and not just in certain countries, but here in our communities. I have witnessed it myself.

Remember this transition from living under the Law to living in the law of grace. If Jesus came to fulfill the Law, and not to abolish it, then how does He do that in this instance of not taking an eye for an eye, or by taking instinctive retribution for a harm done? He is saying here that the law of love and grace in the power of the Holy Spirit is far greater than any harm done by the evil one. "For we know him who said, 'Vengeance is mine, I will repay. And again, 'The Lord will judge his people.'" (Hebrews 10:30, ESV) Do you trust God in that He will do what He said He will do, or do you, in your unbelief desire to take matters into your own hands in order to judge others to the point of your own sense of retribution? Do you have the right to defend yourself? In the Kingdom of God, do you have any rights?

Make the commitment to live, abiding in Him. Will you be offended, most certainly! Will you be harmed physically? Possibly, I do not know, but what I do know is that He will give us the words to say when we are brought before wrong judgment and it is my heart's desire for Him to speak in that time of duress rather than my own selfish sense of personal vengeance and wrongful desire to defend my body in the midst of spiritual warfare and persecution. The man who takes to violence as his way of dealing with life has no part in Him.

April 16th

Management versus Ownership

"And if anyone wants to sue you, and take your shirt, let him have your coat also." (Matthew 5:40, NKJV)

In the Kingdom of God, we do not own anything. The Kingdom of God is not about material things. We dwell in a Kingdom with a King who is the Creator. All things were made by Him and without Him, nothing was made. (John 1:2b). "Every good and perfect gift is from above coming down from the Father of the heavenly lights, who does not change like shifting shadows." (James 1:17, NIV)

"Then He said to them, 'Watch out! Be on your guard against all kinds of greed; life does not consist of an abundance of possessions.'" (Luke 12:14, NIV)
"The Lord answered, 'Who then is the faithful and wise manger whom the master puts in charge of his servants to give them their food allowance at the proper time? It will be good for the servant whom the master finds doing so when he returns. Truly I tell you, he will put him in charge of all his possessions.'" (Luke 12:42-44, NIV)

We have been given a certain amount of time on this earth in the earthen vessels that bear our name. We came into the world with nothing, owning nothing and we will depart from this world taking nothing with us. In the matters of the heart, the ability to give away that which has been given to you to manage is particularly a Spiritual matter. It is the gift of God to give for you have been freely given, so freely give. You see, in light of this spirit, the one who decides to take you to court desiring the items you manage, let them have it, for they are taking from God, not from you. The preponderance of these sentiments is not so much on the literal undertaking of Jesus' words here, but it is the spirit that enables you to not be attached to anything in this world. Be carefully careless of things in this world. You will know by how much you care for something by how deeply you are attached to it.

Are you tight fisted with the things the Lord has given you to manage, or are you open handed?

Is it poor management to give away the Lord's possessions? No, that isn't management, but the work of a hireling. Know the Lord and inquire of Him, He will tell you when it is time to part with what He has given you to manage. That is the point here, seeking Him and His desires.

We cannot do these things by ourselves in the flesh; it is only by His grace in the Spirit that He works His work within us. It is our flesh that wants to fight to keep things to protect our rights and to dwell on our perceived personal possessions. If you know that you have been bought with a price and that He owns all and has allowed you to manage His possessions, then it is a far greater blessing to give rather than to fight with someone over something that is not yours to begin with. It is the person who has not given up themselves to Christ who believes that they own the rights to themselves. In Christ, we are a new creation, new in Him and only in Him.

April 17th

Go On with God

"And whoever shall force you to go one mile, go with him two. Give to him who asks of you, and do not turn away from him who wants to borrow from you."
(Matthew 5:41-42, NKJV)

It was as a custom that the Romans in their ruling military could command someone to carry their belongings a certain distance. Jesus, being aware of this egregious custom, made note of it in His message. He did not denigrate the custom, but made it a point of illustration for the Kingdom believer to go the 'second mile' if commanded to go the first mile. This is to sum up the nature of the Christ moving ever forward in God as He was delivered all the way unto death.

We bicker and complain at having to do practically anything that requires effort out of our comfort zone. If we want to do something for someone, then it's usually ok with us to do it, if we have the time, but once someone commands us to do something, whether we want to or not, then, that's a difficult, if not impossible arrangement. Most people simply do not want to be told what to do, let alone, be made to do something for someone when there's absolutely no benefit to us. How unseemly that is to us, thusly we complain.

Jesus says, 'Have none of that complaining and murmuring about yourself!' In the giving up of our rights to ourselves to God, we move forward in Him as Jesus Christ did. To my knowledge, no one is going to command you to be crucified on a cross for Him, as He did for us. He did all that He did in the power of the Holy Spirit with the purpose and glory of the Father in Him. We are no less. He indwells us with His Spirit, and it is His Spirit that gives us the power to do all things, that includes walking a second mile, if need be, for someone else's baggage or giving to someone who is in need. In Him is the power to give way beyond what we believe is reasonable. In Him, is the power to love other people above and beyond how we could ever love others ourselves. He loves through us. He lives through us and He gives through us. He is our supply, our never-ending supply of living water and life giving bread.

No person can literally do all of these teachings of Jesus, that's why He desires to accomplish these things in us and through us. Jesus gives the admonition, "Give, and it will be given to you. A good measure, pressed down and shaken together and running over will be poured into your lap. For with the measure you use, it will be measured to you." (Luke 6:38, NIV). Give to Him all of you. That is the best measure one can measure. If you complain about the jot and the tittle, that will be as much as you'll see. Give it all to Him and you will be able to find the rest for your soul that you've always needed. He has already taught us how to give by the giving of Himself first and loving us through it all. You'll not marvel then at how you can give, but how much you love in the giving.

April 18th

Loving Those Who do not Love You

"You have heard that it was said, 'You shall love your neighbor, and hate your enemy.' But I say to you, love your enemies and pray for those who persecute you..."   *(Matthew 5:43-44, NKJV)*

Being with God in the earth is not being God Himself, but allowing Him to be Himself in us. He leads us by His Holy Spirit in teaching us the Father's desires. It is He who does all of the work of the Holy and the Righteous in us for we cannot or dare not do it ourselves.

How far does our love go before we are exhausted and become tedious with others in our own lack of forgiveness, patience, goodness, kindness, and so on? We are not who we think we are. We are not loving and forgiving and we need the Holy Love poured into our hearts and minds so that He pours it out of us. If our enemies and persecutors crush us under the weight of meanness, is it enough that we can have the love of God squeezed out of us as trampled grapes?

We cannot love our enemies on our own. It is oftentimes troublesome just to love our spouses as we should, or our mothers and fathers, sisters and brothers. Who can love as God has loved, save God Himself? No man can love as God has loved. He gave Himself from heaven down; down to the death on a horrendous cross and the grave; to conquer hell and all that is against us He did conquer. Who can love as He has loved?

It is too easy for us to hate the enemy and despise those who despise us. It is the impossible at work in the love of God to do the impossible work that only He can do. He is the God of all possibilities for He is the God of all love. It is this same God, through Jesus Christ and His power delivered in us through the Holy Spirit birth that we catch a glimpse of Holy Love. When we see and hear and touch Holy Love, Holy Love reaches back to God through our hearts, our hands, our embrace in the love of another, even when it is our enemy or our persecutor. In the moments of touching Holy Love, we see His Kingdom at work in our lives.

But this Kingdom work is not for ours to keep. It is His work in us to share. He shares His Holy Love through us. Embrace Him now in the power of the Holy Spirit and be made new in Him. He still loves the world so much that He continues to give through us "in order that we may be sons of our Father who is in heaven; for He causes His sun to rise on the evil and the good, and sends rain on the righteous and the unrighteous." (v. 45, NKJV) In the beginning in being with Him, you cannot love with His holy love, but as He loves with His love through you, you learn what that is like. Submit to Him and the more love your receive from Him, the more He abounds in you.

April 19th

Be Perfect as Your Heavenly Father

"Therefore you are to be perfect, as your heavenly Father is perfect."
(Matthew 5:48, NKJV)

Be perfect…come to completeness in all things! No need for anything else!

Holiness is of the Father…complete, sacred, divine character, holy, pure…be as He is.

The Father is Holy Love…the same Love which is in Christ Jesus is the same Love He sends to us in the Holy Spirit. God is Love. Be perfect as your heavenly Father is perfect. Be of the same Spirit. Be of the same Holy Love. Be in Him and Him in you. Perfect love casts out all fear. "For this is the message we heard from the beginning: We should love one another." (1 John 3:11, NIV)

"And this is his command: to believe in the name of His Son, Jesus Christ, and to love one another as He commanded us." (1 John 3:23, NIV). "Dear Friends, since God so loved us, we also ought to love one another." (1 John 4:11, NIV)

"I have loved you even as the Father has loved Me. Remain in my love. When you obey my commandments, you remain in my love, just as I obey my Father's commandments and remain in His love. I have told you these things so that you will be filled with my joy. Yes, your joy will overflow! This is my commandment: love each other in the same way I have loved you. There is no greater love than to lay down one's life for one's friends." (John 15:9-13, NLT)

To be perfect as our heavenly Father in heaven is perfect is to die to ourselves in Him so that He can live His life in us. We go to the cross; He has shown us the way. These are spiritual words…spiritual words indeed. We go to our cross and as the seed is sown in the ground, we are sown into death, so that in dying we can live again in Him. This is the new birth. These are spiritual words. We are born again of His Holy Spirit and without this born again life; we will not enter the Kingdom of Heaven. You must be born again! We must be born of water and the Spirit. Otherwise, this thing that many call Christianity has not happened for you. Submit to Him now and pray the Holy Spirit come and raise you to new life in Him! Then, be perfect as your heavenly Father is perfect.

April 20th

On Practicing Righteousness

"Beware of practicing your righteousness before men to be noticed by them; otherwise you have no reward with your Father who is in heaven."
(Matthew 6:1, NKJV)

The lesser-than motive lingers about when we do anything seemingly spiritual in public. The lesser motive is doing something to be seen by men. No one knows the heart of a man except that man and God, therefore God knows why we do what we do for Him and for other people. Jesus says to beware of your motives that you would not be found a hypocrite, acting spiritual in public for the express purpose of being seen by men thereby fulfilling your selfish pride rather than fulfilling the desire of the Lord in Him and for Him only.

The spiritual work of the Holy Spirit within a person is just that…within. The Holy Spirit delivers life out of a vessel born of the Spirit to others that are drawn by the Spirit. If we are led by the Spirit, we will also walk in the Spirit and not fulfill the desires of the flesh. The desire of the flesh is constant, the flesh wars against the Spirit until there is no more battle, and one or the other will win out with the decision being made by the vessel in submission to the one or the other. Do not fulfill the desire of the flesh; just say 'No!' The Holy Spirit is in you and gives you the power over all flesh and all darkness that may come by way of influence and supposition.

The standard of being led by the Spirit is Jesus Christ. We do not do what He did. We cannot do what Jesus did, so do not fall into that trap. If we are born of the Holy Spirit, then the Holy Spirit is our guide into all spiritual things. The same Spirit that led Jesus Christ while on earth is the same Sprit that leads us today. Submit to the Holy Spirit's work and leading in your life and you will do as He guides you. The more you pray, the more the Holy Spirit grows in you to where you hear His voice and know it. The more you pray, the more you realize your need for Him to be in Him and it is only by Him that we can be or do anything in the Spirit.

How can we who are led by the Spirit of God take any credit for anything that He is doing in us and through us? To take credit for giving, praying, helping, serving, preaching, teaching, or leading in the Spirit is to take the glory of God for ourselves. Brethren, that ought never to be. We have seen those who take the Lord's glory for themselves, but you, you shall have none of that! The reward of the Father is His Presence in our living, in our giving, in our doing. He is the Giver. He is the Healer.

He is the Lover of our souls. How can we take credit for being holy and righteous when we have no righteousness of our own? Give God the glory in all things, for all things and through all things. Do what the Spirit desires to do and be joyful in Him.

April 21st

The Secret Giver

"But when you give alms, do not let your left hand know what your right hand is doing that your alms may be done in secret; and your Father who sees in secret will repay you." (Matthew 6:3, NKJV)

According to Jesus Christ there is only one type of real giver and that is the one who does his/her giving in secret. There is to be no trumpet playing when we give, no public spectacle, no public applause or even a careful nodding of the head of another who approves of us giving to Him or to someone else in His Name. People who need the approval of others while they perform their spiritual acts, according to Jesus, have their immediate reward given to them in their pride and that is all the reward that they will receive. This may sound harsh, but Jesus is the one who is saying it, and why would we be giving to the church, the Lord, or the whatever, if it is not us giving it to Him? If He is the receiver of the gift, the alms, or the offering, then shouldn't He be the one who decides how it should be given?

Again, these are spiritual words and those who are given to understanding receive them spiritually. There is the spiritual kinship we have in loving and serving our Father in heaven, but our kinship is born of His Spirit alone and only what He desires to do in us is what satisfies Him. This is the testimony that He receives; the testimony of agreement in Him and with Him. Our minds and hands fulfill the desires of the Spirit's leading in our lives. If He desires to give, then we give. If He desires to witness through us, He does so with our open hearts and mouths. The agreement is the secret. He is the one doing the work. We cannot please Him with any righteous act because we do not have any righteousness of our own. The secret is done in Him and not for the witness of man. The flesh agreement between the right hand and the left hand leads to applause.

Our dilemma in doing things publicly comes because of the religious traditions that have been taught over the last two millenniums. Religious teachers of Jesus' day gave publicly so that others could see what they were giving and they gave out of their plenty rather than giving out of their leading of the Holy Spirit.

Beware of your motives in giving. This is not only what you give, but how you give, how much you give, and to whom you are giving. It is the power of the Holy Spirit who will lead you into the ways of the Lord in all these matters. Follow Him rather than following a man who tells you what to give and how to give it. Follow the Holy Spirit's leading and you will receive your reward from your Father in heaven and His reward is all-sufficient now and forever.

April 22nd

The Motive of Prayer

"And when you pray, you are not to be as the hypocrites; for they love to stand and pray in the synagogues and on the street corners, in order to be seen by men." (Matthew 6:5, NKJV)

The hypocrite is the one who does something publicly for ulterior motives and is trying to present a persona that he really doesn't quite live up to. The hypocrite is the one who is seemingly doing something spiritual, but performing it in the flesh with fleshly motives. Stop right there and stop judging others right now. You think about you. Have you performed for others a spiritual act only for the performance? Jesus directs our attention specifically to doing anything to exude righteous behavior…giving and praying in public…even if it's only one person watching you; ask yourself, "Why am I doing this? Is it just to put on a show to prove to others that I can be spiritual, too? After all, I'm a spiritual person and deeply spiritual people do deeply spiritual things because they think I think deeply spiritual thoughts…" Are you serious?!

Has that ever been your motive for giving or praying? Have you ever seriously pondered how to pray and give secretly? Jesus tells us in His message how to give and pray secretly, but religious traditions tell us to do otherwise. Which is right, Jesus' words or religious tradition?

Haven't you ever been curious about the majority of religious traditions performed in church services because most of them don't quite seem to be consistent with the Word of God?

But you, you take care of you and your motives and why you do what you do at home, at a church service, or anywhere else you find yourself in public doing something outwardly spiritual. Again, these are all matters of the heart. Secret giving waits for no applause. Secret prayer is prayed in the secret place and only the Spirit of God knows your heart. Read Jesus' words and compare them to what you've heard from others in church services. Trust in Jesus and trust Him in His word. This is life in the Kingdom of God. You've been given opportunity to know Him completely, that is your motive in prayer. It is the Spirit of God leading to give and trusting Him fully in what He desires you to do. Wait on the Lord, He will surely show you the way.

Jesus did all that He did on the earth to glorify His Father in heaven. He was led of the Holy Spirit. If we have been born of His Spirit into His kingdom of light and love and grace, then the overflow of the Spirit will flow out of you in light and love and grace. You don't have to perform unnecessarily in the flesh, our Father abhors hypocrisy. Allow the Spirit to move through you and be obedient when He does, that is a tremendous key here. Know His voice and obey Him.

April 23rd

When You Pray

"But you, when you pray, go into your room, and when you have shut your door, pray to your Father who is in the secret place; and your Father who sees in secret will reward you openly."   (Matthew 6:6, NKJV)

Just before Jesus made these statements, He had talked about the hypocrites, who love to stand in public to pray to have their voices heard for the purpose of having people believe that they are very spiritual people, or that they have a direct line to God that others do not have.

No matter the rationale for the folk who Jesus referred to as hypocrites, what makes them a hypocrite is their motive in praying, not the prayers themselves. Motive is what is on the inside of a person, and only that person and God truly knows the motives of men. God knows the hearts of men, their thoughts, their personal pride, and their rationale for doing what they do.

Because Jesus knew their hearts, He was not only teaching us about the fruit of those who do spiritual things in public for personal glory, He was teaching us the reasons for prayer as well as the mode of prayer.

By Jesus' own words here, He is teaching us that prayer is having a personal private relationship with the Father, first and foremost. Prayer is honoring our Father with relationship time, speaking with Him in reverence, getting to know Him more completely and us listening to Him more intently. Prayer is loving Him and loving to be with Him privately and personally. Prayer is breathing His Spirit in and breathing His Spirit out.

Honoring our Father in secret where no one knows is only between Him and you. In that, He is able to grow in you and you grow in Him. When you walk outside and others see you again, they see and hear the Spirit of the One who is your Father. There is reward in humility and obedience. That was Jesus' example that He set for us to walk in. Take the time to pray as He has taught us to pray…be in Him and be thankful that your name is recorded in heaven.

April 24th

What to Pray

"And when you pray, do not use vain repetitions as the heathen do. For they think that they will be heard for their many words. Therefore do not be like them. For your Father knows the things you have need of before you ask Him." (Matthew 6:7-8, NKJV)

Many of us have been to a church service and have seen what Jesus is talking about here. We have heard public pray-ers pray in vain repetition. Did Jesus pray much in public? The word of God does not offer many illustrations to that idea, does it? But praying in public is not what He is talking about here. What He is prescribing in prayer here is knowing our Father in a complete, loving relationship and in that relationship of prayerful communication, not repeating over and over again what you say. You don't do that in a conversation with other people, do you? Why would you say something over and over again to a perfect Creator God who hears you and already knows your needs before you ask Him? The reasons are endless when we hear public prayers in church services and in other venues that are repetitive and ranting about personal need. Jesus refers to this as 'heathen'.

Personal prayer is just that, personal. Jesus informs us that our Father knows our needs; He is the only very personal all-knowing God who loves us. He wants us to go to Him in love; to desire Him above all else. He wants us to seek Him and His righteousness and all the things that we need will be added to us.

Trust Him that He knows you and knows your needs and go to Him, honor Him with a life submitted to Him. You know it is an honor for someone to come to your dinner table when you invite them. They honor you with their presence and you honor each other with respect with the invitation to dine and the courtesy of a positive response.

How much more so is your Father in heaven when He, through Jesus Christ, invites us to dine with Him at His table of love, rest, and peace. Pray with your Father often and pray with Him more, He is waiting.

April 25th

In This Manner, Pray

"In this manner, therefore, pray: Our Father in heaven, hallowed be Your name." (Matthew 6:9, NKJV)

"Holy, holy, holy, is the Lord of hosts; the whole earth is full of His glory!" (Isaiah 6:3b)

"Speak to all the congregation of the children of Israel, and say to them: 'You shall be holy for I the Lord your God am holy.'"
(Leviticus 19:2)

"For the Lord Most High is awesome; He is a great King over all the earth…God reigns over the nations; God sits on His holy throne. The princes of the people have gathered together, the people of the God of Abraham. For the shields of the earth belong to God; He is greatly exalted." (Psalm 47:2, 8-9)

Our Father is holy. He is the One True God. He is set apart above all that is or will ever be. He is spirit and those who worship Him, worship Him in spirit and truth. Worship and honor and glory belong to Him and Him alone. He will not share His throne with any man. He is our creator, our beginning and our end. In Him is life, real life. Trust in the Lord as Lord of all and acknowledge Him in all your ways.

We can do nothing but submit to our Father who is holy and holy love. In this manner, reverence Him, honor Him and glorify Him. Love Him with all your heart, all your soul and all of your might. In this manner pray…submitted in holiness and holy love. Jesus is the standard. Begin every prayer with honor to our Father who is holy. "Blessed are the pure in heart, for they shall see God."

April 26th

Your Kingdom Come

"Your kingdom come, Your will be done on earth as it is in heaven."
(Matthew 6:10, NKJV)

The Kingdom of God is the abiding place of the Most High God. It is the place where He sits on His throne in glory. The Kingdom of God is the place where He reigns supremely in holiness, mercy, and grace. His will is performed in His Kingdom. Jesus prayed to our Father that His kingdom come and His will to be done on this earth as it is in heaven.

Jesus told His disciples, 'And as you go, preach, saying, 'The kingdom of heaven is at hand.' (Matthew 10:7). In Matthew 11:12, He said, "And from the days of John the Baptist until now the kingdom of heaven suffers violence and the violent take it by force." All through the book of Matthew, Jesus introduced His parables with the phrase, "the kingdom of heaven is like…"

In Luke 17:20, Jesus answered the Pharisees with, "The kingdom of God does not come with observation; nor will they say, 'See Here!' or 'See there!' For indeed, the kingdom of God is within you." Where the Holy Spirit of God resides on His throne is where the kingdom of God resides. God is sovereign in His Kingdom.

Jesus Christ came preaching the gospel of the Kingdom of God. (Luke 4:43). It was and is the will of God that He continues to desire that His will be done in the earth. Is Jesus Lord, Master, and King in your life? Is His will being done in your life? Paul said of the mystery that had been hidden from earlier generations, but was revealed now that being, the Christ in you, the hope of glory. He 'conveyed us into the kingdom of the Son of His love.' (Col. 1:13). Abide in Him today throughout the day and He will abide in you and the kingdom of God and His will will be made known in the earthen vessel that bears your name. Hallelujah!

April 27th

Our Daily Bread

"Give us this day our daily bread." (Matthew 6:11, NKJV)

As Jesus was teaching His disciples how to pray, He touched on every need known to man. He said to pray first giving honor to our Father and asking for His will to be done on earth as it is in heaven. That alone covers our needs as humans, but as long as we are here in this fleshly body, we need to eat and have our basic necessities met in some way. Food, clothing, and shelter are the basic needs of life and asking for our daily bread is just that…relying on God for those needs.

But as I continue to study this exemplary prayer, I realize that I personally do not pray enough. Not only do I not pray enough, I don't pray about the things that He told us specifically to pray for. I guess I do thank Him for my food as I prepare to eat it, or even after I've eaten it, I know that it comes from Him. But, I'm not so sure that is what He's talking about here.

He is telling us that whatever basic necessity in life that we need, we can have the freedom to go to our Father and ask Him for it, without being redundant and without fear of being too simple. He knows our needs before we ask Him, but it is in the asking that what we are really doing is recognizing that it truly is coming from Him and not our own hands. This way, we recognize what He is continually doing for us in this realm and we honor Him by recognizing His gifts of love. He is love and He is generous.

Always be reminded that He is the giver of every good and perfect gift; that includes our basic necessities of life. It doesn't mean that we don't have to work, but what it does mean is that we honor Him in our work and know that everything that we see, touch, taste, hear, and smell comes down from the Father of Light. This includes our work, our home, our clothing, and the simplest of things…our daily bread.

April 28th

On Forgiveness

"And forgive us our debts, as we forgive our debtors."
(Matthew 6:12, NKJV)

Let's take a look at this scripture inverted, 'As we forgive our debtors, and forgive us our debts.' Jesus is clearly telling us to pray in such a way that in this particular, it is conditional. Forgiveness is conditional. Ever how we decide to forgive others, if we do forgive, is how we will be forgiven. How else can a holy God be just in His forgiveness? He is holy, completely set apart in righteousness and sacred; in the atmosphere of glory. Can He impart something to us, that is, after we have been made a disciple, that we take upon ourselves to use it for our own benefit, but not in right representation to Him?

You see, all of us who are made righteous in Him are forgiven our sin. We receive the justification of our sin, just as if we had never sinned. He has paid the price for the wages of sin is death. However, do you really believe that you can walk in unforgiveness and walk in Him at the same time? Those are two distinct and entirely different spiritual realms. Unforgiveness towards another person is harboring a sin unto myself that I believe someone else has offended me with. If I choose not to forgive another of their sin, He has stated that He will not forgive ours. The problem is that we want to blame God for being unjust here, but it is not God who is unjust, it is the person who chooses not to forgive who does not understand what justice and forgiveness is all about.

As He has loved us, we are to love, and allow His love to flow through us. As we realize His power to forgive us, we are able to dwell in that same Spirit and power to forgive, and allow His forgiveness power to flow through us to forgive others. If you are finding yourself living in unforgiveness, make things right by submitting to the Lord first. His abundant grace covers you. Then, He makes the way plain for you to be able to forgive. He forgives through you. He is holy. He is righteous and just. He is love and forgiveness. When we realize we are powerless to forgive, we can allow His forgiveness to flow through us. This is the wonder of grace. Submit to Him and you will see His will being done in the earthen vessel that bears your name. *"For if you forgive men their trespasses, your heavenly Father will also forgive you. But if you do not forgive men their trespasses, neither will your Father forgive your trespasses." (Matthew 6:14-15, NKJV)*

April 29th

Deliver Us from the Evil One

"And do not lead us into temptation, but deliver us from the evil one. For Yours is the kingdom and the power and the glory forever. Amen."
(Matthew 6:13, NKJV)

Always look within the context for the true meaning of any passage of scripture. Look within the context of the verse, the chapter, and the book. When we look for deliverance from temptation, in this context, we look for deliverance from an unforgiving spirit. For it is in unforgiveness that a human harbors the spirit of resentment, being offended, withholding love, withholding peace, withholding the grace of God. God has given us memory to remember where not to go again and to remember where we've been. Our memories are not to be harbors for unforgiveness, but for gratefulness in grace.

A spiritual place that is without love, forgiveness, and grace is a place that is ripe for the evil one to take possession of. Do not fool yourself that you think you can be a disciple of Jesus Christ and be full of hate, bitterness, and unforgiveness. That is not a bearer of the Holy Spirit of God. Do not be deceived, God is not mocked, whatever a man sows is that which he shall reap.

"Yours…" is the Your children, Your people, Your disciples. "Yours is the kingdom…" that which dwells in Him is His and is as He is, not as the evil one is. Jesus says to pray to the Father in such a way that we would always walk in His kingdom in love, mercy, forgiveness, and grace for such is the Kingdom of God.

Be delivered from the evil one by abiding in Him. Live in Christ and He has promised to live in you. Be born again of His Spirit and be made new, a totally new creation. Then, you will see His kingdom reigning in you and forgiveness, love and grace will flow through you as He flows through you today!

April 30th

Be Moved with Compassion, Release and Forgiveness

"For if you forgive men their trespasses, your heavenly Father will also forgive you. But if you do not forgive men their trespasses, neither will your Father forgive your trespasses." (Matthew 6:14-15, NKJV)

Do you know the recesses of your heart? The inner places where you haven't been and you refuse to allow anyone else to go there because of what you may be harboring there. How can a man know the depths of his heart without a counselor? The Psalmist pleaded with the Lord for the Lord to search his heart and see if there was any wicked way in him.

Have you been offended, or taken offense? Have you been harmed by another? Betrayed, or rejected? For it is in these moments of terror, fear, harm, and debt that we keep ourselves safe from further harm by subduing the emotion and memories and storing them deep inside our hearts. It is possible to believe that you have forgiven others of the harm they intended for you, when in truth the bitterness and harmful effects reside in dark places.

The Holy Spirit is our conviction, our Comforter, and our guide. Be moved with compassion and open yourself up to His loving searchlight, knowing that He loves you. Be released from the ties that have you bound. Repent of any agreement that you have had with darkness and reject its bondage over you. Ask for forgiveness from the One who is the great forgiver and walk in His forgiveness as you forgive others their trespasses against you as He makes you aware of the consequences of their sins in your life. Do not allow others to have a stronghold over you by harboring unforgiveness. Let it go and be free. Do not relive the episode by talking about it with others, bless, and do not curse. His power and grace is in you, you are more than a conqueror…you are a forgiver!

"Then the master of that servant was moved with compassion, released him, and forgave him the debt." (Matthew 18:27).

May 1st

The Pride of the Religious

"Moreover, when you fast, do not be like the hypocrites, with a sad countenance. For they disfigure their faces that they may appear to men to be fasting. Assuredly, I say to you, they have their reward." (Matthew 6:16, NKJV)

There are quite a few obstacles for the world to get through to the understanding of the heart of Jesus and the majority of them have to do with the religious and how they act in public. Here, Jesus tells His disciples to wash their face and anoint their head and not to act out in public that they are fasting so as not to draw attention to themselves. The pervasive pride of men in religion prevents the true Spirit of the Christ being seen because men want to be seen for their works so that they may glory in themselves for their piety.

Jesus tells us to go to the secret place where our Father resides in times of fasting, praying, and abiding in Him. This is a condition with a promise that the experience of being with Him in the secret place brings with it an open reward. However, Jesus' words are Spirit and be certain that the open reward will be spiritual as well. We are not to obey our Lord for personal, selfish gain. Many religious people desire wealth and riches and teach others to obey God for monetary gain. I do not believe that is Jesus' heart in anything that He said.

Jesus was all about the Holy Spirit having His way in our lives and the secret place is the place of beginning the day in Him…in prayer, in fasting, in love, in abiding in Him. This is a very personal relationship with a very personal Lord and Master. When we walk out of the secret place into the public places of men, they will see and hear the Christ who dwells in us and that is reward enough. If our Father decides to reward you openly with anything in addition to His abiding grace, it will be His permissive will that allows it, so give Him glory that is due to Him and to Him alone.

May 2nd

The Treasure That You Seek

"For where your treasure is, there your heart will be also."
(Matthew 6:21, NKJV)

What is it about the work of men and women that causes us to desire more and more? If we get paid a salary, we want more. If are able to obtain an object, then we work to obtain another. If we work to obtain credit, we work further to obtain more credit. Our natural human tendency is always about the more. More is the insatiable desire for what we do not have, but want the more just the same.

Jesus tells us not to store up treasures that will decay. The temporal things of the world are here today and gone in some tomorrow that always comes. The things we see, taste, touch, hear, and smell are definitely the temporal things of our existence that we look to make our lives more comfortable, more manageable, and more, more, more that will soon be gone.

When we go to the secret place of prayer and abiding grace, the place of seeking His Kingdom and righteousness, it is there that He gives us our daily bread, as well as, meets our daily needs. The treasure of the heart can be His Spirit, His wisdom, His Presence, the dwelling place of the Almighty. Or, the treasure of the heart can be the dwelling place of greed, corruption, and the seeking after whatever the world has to sell you that day.

We cannot serve God and mammon, which is, basically our selfish desires. We have to believe Him when He said, "But seek first the kingdom of God and His righteousness, and all these things shall be added to you." (Matthew 6:33, NKJV)

Trust Him with all your heart, your life, your soul, and your strength and the greatest treasure will be found in Him…His Presence!

May 3rd

How Do You See?

"The lamp of the body is the eye. If therefore your eye is good, your whole body will be full of light. But if your eye is bad, your whole body will be full of darkness, how great is that darkness!"   (Matthew 6:22-23, NKJV)

In the quest for knowledge men see many things, but not all men see the same thing when they view the same object. Some see more, some see less, and some see some things entirely differently. It is the individual's personal perspective that is arrived at, but how does each individual arrive at different conclusions when each person has been given the same information. It is, after all, how we as individuals see things. We see things from our own perspective, whether how we see it to be the truth, or not, we seemingly believe our own perspectives.

If the lamp of the body is the eye, then what the eye sees is what it sees and becomes the filter through which the body is illuminated with what the eye sees. It is 'how' the eye sees a particular thing that will determine its value, its rightness, its wrongness, or what it sees is indifferent, thereby becoming a sense of neutrality regarding the subject matter. Do you see with your eyes, or your 'mind's eye'? Remember, these are spiritual words.

If the eye is bad, that is, the perspective is altered to a bad state, then, whatever that eye sees will be altered according to the condition of the eye, or perspective. What is it that you see with, your physical eye, or your mind's eye? It is what is in your mind that you see with; you see with your mind's eye, and if your mind is in a 'bad' state, that is how you will see things.

Conversely, if your 'eye' is good, that is, your mind's eye, your personal perspective about things, if it is deft, then what your eye sees will be good. The eye will be clear to see what is real and true without being altered by a "bad' spiritual or emotional influence.

If you have been born of the Holy Spirit, then the Holy Spirit will illuminate from the truth of the holy. We have a choice, to see life from the Spirit of Truth, or, to see life from an altered state of personal perspective. How do you see son of man?

May 4th

Determine Your Loyalty

"No man can serve two masters; for either he will hate the one and love the other, or else he will be loyal to the one and despise the other. You cannot serve God and mammon." (Matthew 6:24, NKJV)

We make choices everyday with the abundant and ever coming opportunities that begin the moment we wake up. We decide to do, or not to do, whatever it is that we are engaged in and the circumstances that God engineers around us will either play havoc with our course of decisions, or our decisions will play havoc with our circumstances and then the fun, or the stress begins with each and every daily decision.

If we have been baptized with the Holy Spirit, then the Holy Spirit enables us to move about in His kingdom with ease because His Spirit will be guiding us according to His will. The moment we decide to pick ourselves back up again, is the moment we decide to serve our self rather than the One Who is our Lord. Advertisements, influences, friends, as well as, enemies, work schedules, work, free time, money, credit, and the list is endless, are all on the road of decision. How do you decide what to do with your time, money, resources, family, and friends?

Do you permit others and outer influences such as advertisements, television or radio to make your decisions for you? If you don't make a decision when you need to, that in itself is a decision, and someone, or something will make the decision for you. It comes down to - what do you believe and who do you love?

Do you truly love the Lord, your God and Master, or do you love yourself, or some other personality? You will ultimately do what you will to do. You will love and serve yourself, or you will deny the self, take up your cross daily, and abide in Him. Abiding in Him is not an option for the true disciple. If you do abide in Him, His Spirit guides you into all truth.

You will serve who or what you love. The question remains, 'Who or what do you love?'

May 5th

Worry or Obsessing

"Therefore I say to you, do not worry about your life, what you will eat or what you will drink; nor about your body, what you will put on. Is not life more than food and the body more than clothing?"   (Matthew 6:25, NKJV)

As Jesus takes us further into Himself, we see that He wants us to see life from His truth, rather than our personal perspectives. As Paul stated, He has seated us in heavenly places. Life in His Kingdom is the ever-abundant life giving kind of life. The eternal life that has no end, but eternal life is also a state of being in the present. Eternal, kingdom life is for now.

He wants us to see with Holy Spirit eyes that His kind of life is far more than food and clothing. Your heavenly Father knows you need these things, but these things are not the things that we wake up to in the morning. These things are not limited to just these things either, but He is making the point that even the minutest of things we deem absolutely necessary still do not match to our life in Him. The food that we eat is gone in a matter of minutes and the clothing we buy that we think we need to wear will eventually wear out. All things are here today and gone in some tomorrow. These are the temporal things in life. The things we hear, see, taste, touch, and smell are the sensual things of the life we believe are normal. But His Life is anything but normal. His Life is extraordinary. His Life is in Him. In speaking with folk, oftentimes they will say, 'I'm not worried about it." But what they have done is spent an inordinate amount of time in thought about something that ultimately will not be here in the very near future. Or, they will spend money that they don't have and buy items on credit that, again, ultimately will not be here in the very near future. People may not think they worry, but they sure do get quite obsessive with their thoughts and cantankerous with their money.

Complete submission to Him, beginning in the morning, and throughout the day in the each and every moment, takes the hard work of worrying and renders it unnecessary, because by dwelling in Him, those things that were once important to us, we trust will be worked out in Him. "And we know that all things work together for good to those who love God and are the called according to His purpose." (Romans 8:28, NKJV) Submit to Him and enjoy His rest today!

May 6th

Get Outside

"Look at the birds of the air, for they neither sow nor reap nor gather into barns; yet your heavenly Father feeds them. Are you not of more value than they?"
(Matthew 6:26, NKJV)

In the process of letting loose of the self, the things we thought that mattered to us become less burdensome in thought and deed. It's not that the things of this life are not important; they're just not the most important. We need to heighten our sight and see our lives and needs from His truth, rather than our own personal perspectives. See with the eyes of the Holy Spirit and breathe with the breath of God.

When was the last time you got outside and seriously observed the birds of the air? The next free moment, go and see the birds that He created. When was the last time you went outside and observed the grass of the field or the flowers that are around you? The next free moment, go outside and see, really see the beauty of the earth as He has created it, the colors of the spectrum are for us to enjoy in the great outdoors.

Seeing life that He created, whether it is the life of an animal, or the life of a plant helps us to get out of ourselves and into what He deemed as 'good'. His creation is beautiful and is wonderfully made. And in all of that, man is created to be a little lower than the angels. He is mindful of you and knows your every need. He knows your thoughts and He has plans for your future. He wonderfully made you and cares for you more than you could ever imagine. He so loves you. He loves you so.

Smile a glad smile in Him today. Look to the earth and sky and see His creation, that what He made is good to Him and good to you. Then, the things you thought were important won't seem as important as they did moments ago.

May 7th

Consider the Lilies

"So why do you worry about clothing? Consider the lilies of the field; how they grow: they neither toil nor spin;"   (Matthew 6:28, NKJV)

We have so much to do, so much to think about, so many places to go and people to see that we keep ourselves so busy that we do not notice much around us anymore. Have you stopped to breathe? Do you notice your breath? Be still and know the Lord.

If you are into devotions and being devoted to the Lord, are you so tied up into your devotional that you forget to pray? When was the last time you prayed nonstop for twenty minutes? Have you ever done that…prayed nonstop for twenty minutes, thirty minutes, an hour, or hours? When was the last time you took a walk outside and observed the Lord's creation in quiet communion with Him?

We are so careful at times to be full of care for so many things that we make grave attempts at obeying the Lord and do not obey in the very simplest of things. Jesus said, 'consider the lilies…' Lily bulbs are placed in the ground and lie dormant until their right season to push up through the earth to make the earth green and full of flower. Lilies do not have a choice in what variety of lily they will be. Whatever kind of lily they are, that is the flower that they will display in the blooming season. Consider the lilies…lilies are.

Your mind's eye can see your favorite lily, or your favorite bulb plant, a tulip, a daffodil, or other. The Lord God is their provider, yet how much more so are we to Him. He provides for you with His Presence, His Son; He feeds you and cares for you. He strengthens you. He gives us the strength to push through the earthen mess around us to reach up towards the Son and with our arms and hands lifted high, wave before Him and allow Him to receive the beauty that He has created in us. He has created the beauty of glory inside of you. He has clothed you with beauty in the innermost parts. Reach to the Son and give Him His glory!

May 8th

Do Not be Anxious

"Do not be anxious then, saying, 'What shall we eat' or 'What shall we drink?' or 'With what shall we clothe ourselves?'…for your heavenly Father knows you need all these things." (Matthew 6:31, 32b, NKJV)

Jesus continues in His discourse of 'do not's' with specifically saying, 'do not be anxious' five times during Matthew 6:25-34. If Jesus Christ says something five times in the matter of moments in His sermon on the mount, then it must be something extremely important that hits everyone at their basic needs. Do not be anxious…that is, don't have anxiety about your basic necessities. Do not worry; obsess, or constantly think and dwell on your needs. Your heavenly Father knows you have to eat and drink and wear clothing. Seek Him first and His Kingdom.

It is the cry of unbelief that yearns to worry over basic necessities. What you are actually doing is telling God that you do not trust Him for these needs. You may say you trust Him, but your heart-filled words tell the truth on you. Crying in unbelief, murmuring, and complaining about your lack is proof positive that your heart is not with Him. Your heart, then, is on things and you're choking yourself in desperation from their absence. Check your needs and see if what you're complaining about is a real need. God is not a liar like men. God is faithful in all that He does and He is faithful in all that He knows and He knows what you truly need.

Nervous anxiety is stressful and stress kills the body. Nervous debilitating stress is antichrist thinking. It is distrustful of the Lord in that it portrays a misrepresentation of who God really is. The importunate beggar acts like he's not a child of God because he really doesn't rely on God, so how can he trust Him? The child of God waits in earnest expectation for the fruition to come to pass. Earnest expectation is not worry, but is a persistent trusting and knowing that God will provide; it just hasn't appeared on the seen yet. Do you understand the difference?

Do not be anxious for anything, but trust in the Lord with all of your heart and do not lean upon your own understanding. That is a major key…when you lean on your own understanding, nothing ever quite measure's up. You seem to always have too much need. But God, in His holy Love knows that you have need of these things and He will provide His provisions for you. You may need food or a home, wait on Him. You may need a job or a new business, trust in Him. You may need a husband or a wife. Wait on Him. He is faithful and He will provide His provisions.

You may need relief from trouble. Dwell in Him and allow His wisdom to shine. We do not always get what we ask for, but in Christ, He is all that we need. Walk in the light of His love and rest and not in agitated worry. Know the difference between the two. He loves to give to His children. Breathe in peace and breathe out rest. This is the place of grace, the dwelling place of the Most High.

May 9th

Seek First the Kingdom of God

"But seek first the kingdom of God and His righteousness, and all these things shall be added to you." (Matthew 6:33, NKJV)

It is a new day dawning. You are not who you were ten years ago, five years ago, one year ago, or even yesterday. Today is a new day. Start the day in Him. Jesus tells us to seek first the kingdom of God and His righteousness. How do you do that?

First, recognize that the abiding place is in Him. If the abiding place is in Him, it is Him. The Kingdom of God is Jesus Christ. He wants you to seek Him first each new day and each new moment. Seek the Lord Jesus Christ with all of your heart, soul, and mind. Be with Him. Speak with Him. Listen to Him by reading His word. Allow His word to wash over you as the rain falls.

Secondly, seek His righteousness. He is His righteousness. He is our righteousness because we have no righteousness, no right thinking, no right doing, and no right being on our own. If we are to have any righteousness in us, it will be His righteousness dwelling in us.

Seek the Lord and know that He is good. Know that He is right here with you now, right now in the right now place, the dwelling place of the Most High. Jesus said that the kingdom of God does not come with observation, but dwells within you. Abiding in Him comes with a promise…He will abide in you.

It is a new day! Shout "Hallelujah!"

May 10th

Tomorrow Worries

"Therefore do not worry about tomorrow, for tomorrow will worry about its own things. Sufficient for the day is its own trouble." (Matthew 6:34, NKJV)

All through Matthew chapter 6, Jesus admonishes us to not worry about tomorrow. He tells us to consider the lilies of the field and how they grow, they neither toil, nor spin, nor do they worry. The lily of the field is. It does what it was purposed to do, and that is to lie beneath the surface of the earth and in its season, it is to push through the earth and set its site on the sun. In its flowering season, it produces a flower that stretches towards the sun in glory. It gets its nourishment from the sun and the earth and the rain.

Jesus tells us to seek Him first and His righteousness. So, every new day we have a decision to make and the choices that we have are between focusing on the life and love of Jesus Christ or focusing on our lives and on our stuff.

How easy it is for us to ponder, think through, meditate, worry, quarrel, and exasperate ourselves with the 'next thing'. The 'next thing' has our minds and hearts in contemplation all the way to stressful worry. Jesus told us not to worry about our lives.

If our dwelling place becomes tomorrow, then our dwelling place is worry for tomorrow worries. Worried thinking is debilitating thinking, filled with anticipation and the road to stress.

Set your mind on things above, things that are pure…Jesus; things that are right… His word; things that are holy…His Holiness; things that are righteous…Jesus Christ. Deliberately choose to seek Him and relax in Him. Breathe Him in and breathe Him out.

Choose Him today and the Holy Spirit will light the path and illumine the way.

May 11th

Judge Not

"Judge not, that you be not judged. For with what judgment you judge, you will be judged; and with the measure you use, it will be measured back to you."
(Matthew 7:1-2, NKJV)

A part of the treasure of the Kingdom of God is knowing that we serve and worship a Holy God. He is righteous and just in all His ways. He is the one true judge and life giver. He is just because He knows all things. He knows our hearts, our thoughts, our motives, and our ways. He knows when we fail and when others fail against us.

Oswald Chambers refers to this passage as a law of God and that of retribution.[1] Jesus implores us not to judge and if we do, ever how we have judged, it will be measured exactly back to us as we have judged others. Our Father is holy and just, there is no other like Him. We certainly aren't. We cannot take what is His alone and use it as we please in order to fulfill revenge, a payment, or a trespass against us. We will reap what we sow, so if we sow judgment that is certainly what we will reap.

We can discern what others have done and know for certain right from wrong, sin from righteousness, and light from dark. We do not have to follow others down a wayward path. Sin and wickedness abounds in high and low places. We can know the truth and speak the truth in wisdom and love. We can teach our children well. However, if we go beyond the acknowledgement of sin into the spirit of condemnation and give ourselves the right to judge another to hell, we will reap what we have sown.

Look into your own life and see what is inside of you that warrants the searchlight of holy grace and only speak what God is speaking. When all the world is giving way to its own selfish desires, keep on keeping on desiring Him, and He will rebuke in due season. If you trust Him as Savior, then trust Him as Lord and you will see to trust Him as judge over all for He is in control.

May 12th

Work it Out

"And why do you look at the speck in your brother's eye, but do not consider the plank in your own eye?" *(Matthew 7:3, NKJV)*

"Therefore, my beloved, as you have always obeyed, not as in my presence only, but now much more in my absence, work out your own salvation with fear and trembling; for it is God who works in you both to will and to do for His good pleasure. Do all things without complaining and disputing, that you may become blameless and harmless, children of God without fault in the midst of a crooked and perverse generation..." (Phil. 2:12-15a, NKJV)

Oswald Chambers has also said to work out what God has worked in.[1] God has worked in you as a disciple of His, His good will, His good pleasure. Work that out in your life by not complaining and badgering others for their faults. Stop the attacks and the fault finding…even secretly. No one knows what you're thinking but God and that is enough.

Stop and consider all the mighty works that God has done for you and in you. Consider that there is none righteous, no, not one; that includes me and you. Before you go on the internal, by secret thoughts, or by the external, opening your mouth to criticize…consider! Do all things without complaining and do all things to His glory.

It is enough what Christ did for us on the cross, but to be allowed to walk into His Kingdom and believe that you had anything to do with it, is again, taking holy judgment that is rightfully God's and placing yourself on His throne.

Allow His love and grace through your life right now and humble yourself in His sight. In the secret place, He sees and knows you. Abide there wherever you go and you will see you for who you really are, a child of God saved by grace. Stop and consider that for your friends and your enemies. Bless and do not curse. Let His love abound through you.

May 13th

Righteous Judgment

"Do not give what is holy to the dogs, nor cast your pearl before swine, lest they trample them under their feet, and turn and tear you in pieces."
(Matthew 7:6, NKJV)

We have established that there is one true God that has the authority and holiness to act as a righteous judge. He is holy and all that He does is holy. Judgment is for Him alone. When we take upon ourselves what is only His, we take what is holy and give it to the lesser than. Anything other than God Himself is lesser than God.

As wild dogs fight over territory, food, or presence, so it is when we take judgment upon ourselves to the demise of another. We tear one another with our words, attacks, the gnashing of teeth, seething anger, and unrelenting rage. You may say, "Not me, I've never done such a thing." But, if you have ever taken God's throne for yourself and performed even a silent judgment against your brother, your spouse, your parent, your friend, or your enemy; you, my friend, are guilty.

Whatever judgment you judge, you will be judged. Jesus talked about murder and hate as they are synonymous. It is not 'like' they're synonymous. They are indeed synonymous. When you judge another in condemnation, you will be judged in condemnation. You will reap what you have sown.

It is taking a holy thing and giving it to feed the hogs. They will fight for it and tear it to shreds along with you if you decide that's where you want to go. If you go to a fighting arena, you will find yourself in a fight. This is what it is like if you take what is rightfully God's, you do so at your own peril.

Speak the word of God in Spirit and truth. Speak it into your life and into your children's lives. Allow the Holy Spirit to do His work. The Holy Spirit will convict the world of sin when we have the word written in our hearts and spoken in our mouths. He will bring to remembrance what needs to be said to a lost and dying world. God loves the world through you. It is not your right to condemn the world to hell. But, we are to go to the world and in His Spirit, make disciples, washing the world by the word of truth. You'll be so busy in His work that you won't have time to judge it.

May 14th

The Secret Place

"But you, when you pray, go into your room, and when you have shut your door, pray to your Father who is in the secret place; and your Father who sees in secret will reward you openly." (Matthew 6:6, NKJV)

Go now, meet Him now, meet Him in the secret place. You, yes, you…go now. There are words and Word and seeds to sow. Seeds of healing and relief. Will you go now? Do not be choked by the cares of this world.

Pray and submit in prayer and learn to submit and pray in His will.

"Ask, and it will be given to you; seek, and you will find; knock, and it will be opened to you. For everyone who asks receives, and he who seeks finds, and he who knocks it will be opened."

Did you know? Did you forget? I Am here…

Spend the time you have now in prayer with Him. Today is a day of prayer.

May 15th

Trust in Him

"Or what man is there among you who, if his son asks for bread, will give him a stone? Or if he asks for a fish, will he give him a serpent? If you then, being evil, know how to give good gifts to your children, how much more will your Father who is in heaven give good things to those who ask him."
(Matthew 7:9-11, NKJV)

How far will a man go to get what he wants? How far have you gone to get what you want? What did you give up in order to obtain that which you sought? Did you make a purchase, a deal? What did you trade? Did you trade more than what you received? Did you bargain your soul in the process?

In the Kingdom of God, Jesus tells us what the Father has to give us if only we would ask. It is a hard thing for a man to lay his life down, isn't it? And yet, no one is fooled here in truth that in order to get to the place of the Kingdom of God and resting in the secret place of the Almighty sitting at His feet and be willing to ask, something first must take place.
No flesh shall see God. The giving up of oneself for the self that He gives is that new creation born again life that is found in Him, but only after…asking. The pride of life is a pervasive spirit that prevents truth from reaching the need of true life. Being willing to submit to Him is being able and willing to trust in Him.

He is to be First. He is not first and foremost, as if to say He is first among many, no! He is First and Only.

The man pleaded with Jesus, 'Lord I believe; help my unbelief." (Mark 8:24b). He gives us the faith to believe. It is His faith that we believe with. It is faith in Him and in Him alone. Trusting is faith active. How much the Father has been willing to give, to help, to heal, to give of Himself to us…if only we would trust Him and ask. Go to Him now!

May 16th

Focus Your Faith

"Therefore, whatever you want men to do to you, do also to them for this is the Law and the Prophets." *(Matthew 7:12, NKJV)*

The beginning of Matthew chapter 7 starts out with Jesus saying, "Judge not..." He goes on to talk about the consequences of human judgment and the severity of those consequences. Then, He speaks about asking the Father for whatever it is that you need. What exactly is He saying in the context, then, that whatever you want men to do to you, do also to them?

He is leading us to right faith. Faith in believing and doing what He says...building upon the rock, a sure foundation. In order to do that, you must first take your eyes off of men and focus in Him. You cannot focus your faith in Him when you are preoccupied with what another person has done to you, or said about you. Focus your faith. Do not set your hands to the plough in the Kingdom and look back at your brother or your enemy and judge them for anything...stay focused in Him.

Focusing your faith in Him will keep you abiding in truth in Him and will also allow Him to abide in you for Him to do His will in and through your life. In all of this, your faith will lead you to the treasure of Him and you will automatically leave the judgment of the world and your brother to the One True Judge who is holy.

Jesus said, "Do not think that I came to destroy the Law or the Prophets. I did not come to destroy, but to fulfill." (Matthew 5:17). He has fulfilled the Law and the Prophets in love. He has done it. He performs this truth in love in and through you. Faith in Him, trusting in Him is love active. Judge not, but love. Do unto others as you would have them do to you; Holy love is the fulfillment. Holy love is God above. Dwell in His Holy love and no matter what the world does to you; His love will be fulfilled through you. This is life in the Kingdom of God.

May 17th

The Narrow Way

"Enter by the narrow gate; for wide is the gate and broad is the way that leads to destruction, and there are many who go in by it. Because narrow is the gate and difficult is the way which leads to life, and there are few who find it."
(Matthew 7:13-14, NKJV)

Always be careful to be examining yourself first when it comes to the word of the Lord. Oftentimes I have heard this scripture explained away in regards to the 'other people' who are in the broad way and it is used in judgmental ways as to say, 'I know the way, all those others do not, they're going to hell, and I'm not...' Be certain of the road that you are on. Look within to see what spirit is leading and has been leading, do not deceive yourself; for it is too easy to do.

Jesus said that He is the way, the truth, and the life, and that no man comes to the Father but by Him. This way is Him. He is the gate, the door, the entrance into the Kingdom of God. He is the only way. There are not two doors and He is not just one of many. To enter in by Him is to be changed by Him into His new creation, abiding in, living in, led by His Spirit, constantly renewed by Him in His kingdom. To make a decision for Him in a one-time experience and then walk away is to be as Jesus said, "…No one, having put his hand to the plow, and looking back, is fit for the kingdom of God." (Luke 9:62). How do you know that your one-time experience was real? Are you willing to bet your eternity on your one-time experience if you have decided to will your own will and walk your own walk? It is a far better thing to believe that my first-time experience led me to a life-time walk with Him.

The broad way is the way where many follow their own will, not having given up themselves, or their ways of living. The way of the many is the way that all are invited to come as they are, to stay as they are, and lead others to be whatever they want to be. It is a difficult thing to 'unbecome' another's belief that they can live as they choose and be what they want to be. That way is broad and as Jesus said, leads to destruction.

Jesus was quite fascinating in this regard: He set the course of truth, declared the way, allowed and continues to allow others to make their own decisions without hateful judgment. He was telling the truth in all things, but in this area, His followers have had a hard time following. Walk in His way…tell yourself, your family, your friends, and your enemies the truth about Jesus Christ and allow them to make their decisions about the way in which they will walk out their lives. Narrow is the way and difficult is the path in truth. I pray that you and I walk in truth in His way, the way that He has chosen. Be comforted.

May 18th

Bearing Good Fruit

"Even so, every good tree bears good fruit, but a bad tree bears bad fruit. A good tree cannot bear bad fruit, nor can a bad tree bear good fruit."
(Mathew 7:17-18, NKJV)

Again I say to you, look within. Let's continually be honest with ourselves about our lives in what we say and do according to the scriptures and not as we may possibly have deceived ourselves by not living out what we say we believe. Are we honorable to God with our confessions and actions because it is what is in the hearts of men that will proceed from their mouths? We speak and act on the outside what is really on the inside.

In this passage of scripture, Jesus is imploring us to look at our leaders' fruit. If the fruit is bad, the heart is not good. This is such a hard saying, but Jesus has forewarned us that the way is narrow and few there are who find it. We must be discerning of ourselves and of our leaders. Does what they say they believe match how they walk in the home, the church, the community, and the nation? Blessing and cursing do not come from the same fountain. If it does, how do you know which one is real? The source of its stream is either one, or the other. Bad does not come from good. If you find yourself debating with that, you are debating with Jesus Christ.

We cannot always know when someone is telling us the truth. We cannot always rely on our feelings and emotions, because we can become easily deceived when someone is speaking to us about what we really want. At times, we deceive ourselves with another's deception because our need is greater than truth itself. That is why it is so imperative to live a submitted life before Christ, following Him and Him alone.

We have to know the truth in Christ so as not to be deceived by the world or the spiritual forces in dark places. It is right for a man or woman of God to discern the spirit of the one's they follow. Again, we have to be careful not to walk around in unlawful judgment, but to rely on the Holy Spirit to guide us into all truth according to the word of God. Jesus makes it plain, bad comes from bad and good comes from good. Our job is to know what good is and Jesus said, "No one is good but One, that is, God. But if you want to enter into life, keep the commandments." (Matthew 19:17b)

The walk must match the talk, for me, for you, and for all who name the Name of Christ.

May 19th

The Will of My Father

"Not everyone who says to Me, 'Lord, Lord,' shall enter the kingdom of heaven, but he who does the will of My Father in heaven." (Matthew 7:21, NKJV)

Just as the walk must match the talk in our leaders, the walk must match the talk in our lives in every personal way. Jesus goes to the depths of the core of our existence; if we call Him Lord, He has to be Lord, not us. Bad fruit comes from bad trees and selfish willfulness does not exist in the kingdom of heaven.

Many people get angrily intimidated by the sense of a narrow mindset from judgmental believers. Again, we have to judge ourselves so that we are not out unlawfully judging others. Jesus makes it plain, if someone names the Name of Jesus Christ as Lord, that person will be doing the will of our Father, and not their own will.

Workers, teachers, pastors, preachers, prophets, apostles, and evangelists will be judged by Christ in the matter of His will versus their own. Doing the work of a Christian does not guarantee entrance into the kingdom of heaven, but being in the will of our Father as He desires for you to be does. How do you know the difference?

You can know the difference if you know who is doing the work. If you're doing the work according to your own willfulness, which is one of the mightiest powers in the earth, you will have your immediate temporal reward. If you have submitted to Him in His will and His will is Him and He is doing the work through you, you will know and that is all that matters. He does His work in you as you submit to His will and through you as you freely give. In this, He is glorified and His glory is forever.

Who writes this write, and who works this work? What is the source of this work and of yours? Does the work of the Holy Spirit work His will in me…in you? I do not want Him to say to me in my time with Him, "…I never knew you, depart from Me, you who practice lawlessness." (Matthew 7:23b). It is, then, 'Oh, that I may know Him in the power of His love and grace'.

Trust in Him, do His will and He will receive the glory. He calls that good. Be thankful that your name is written in the Lamb's book of life. Bless His Name today and bless His Name forevermore!

May 20th

Hear and Obey

"Therefore whoever hears these sayings of Mine, and does them, I will liken him to a wise man who built his house on the rock: and the rains descended, the floods came, and the winds blew and beat on that house; and it did not fall, for it was founded on the rock." (Matthew 7:24-25, NKJV)

One of Jesus' sayings was, 'He who has ears to hear, let him hear." (Matthew 11:15, Matthew 13:43b, Mark 4:9, Mark 4:23, Mark 7:16, Luke 8:8, Luke 14:35, etc.). The point that Jesus continued to make was the idea of being able to hear what He had to say. Not everyone is going to 'hear' and understand Jesus Christ. He said that Himself. (Matthew 13:13-16)

So, in order to do the will and sayings of Jesus Christ, one would have to be able to 'hear', that is, understand with spiritual ears what He was actually saying and then do what He said in the spirit. Those who worship Him, worship Him in spirit and truth.

We hear with spiritual ears to as a result of knowing Him in an abiding relationship. He is the foundation of that which He speaks. When we receive the God kind of faith to believe with a God kind of belief, we are then able to work out what He has worked in, that is our faith. We believe 'in faith'. We do not believe in faith, we believe in Jesus Christ in faith. We are saved by faith; we walk by faith.

It is going to rain on the just and the unjust. Bad things are going to happen to all; death will come to each of us, but the life that is built on Jesus Christ is the life that has a sure foundation for abundant living today and life forevermore forever.

Hear Jesus, read and know His word, but do not stop there. The Holy Spirit is the One who gives us the power to obey. So then, we can obey Him in all that He had to say. We can obey Him when He speaks and obey His spirit when He convicts. Trust in Him and do not let go.

The reward is that He will not let go of you. Build on a sure foundation in Jesus Christ. God is faithful, especially in the midst of a storm that you think is tearing the foundation out from under you because that is what He is doing…until only He is left as your rock from which you stand.

May 21st

The House of the Foolish

"But everyone who hears these sayings of Mine, and does not do them, will be like a foolish man who built his house on the sand: and the rain descended, the floods came, and the winds blew and beat on that house; and it fell. And great was its fall."   (Matthew 7:26-27, NKJV)

Just to make sure we understand here, Jesus is talking about the foundation a person builds his life in, and not about a literal house. Although this is definitely true if He were talking about a literal house, but Jesus said that His words are spirit, and they have to be heard with spiritual ears. To those who have ears, let them hear.

The reward of obedience to Christ is eternal. The reward to disobedience to Christ is also eternal. Jesus Christ came that people might have life, and that more abundantly. The abundant God kind of life is found in Jesus Christ alone. This life is true and real and lasts forever, and begins at the moment of transformation in Him. We pray with Him, talk with Him, get to know Him and His word, and His word continues to transform our lives into His good pleasure.

To every action, there is an equal and opposite reaction. The moment you deny yourself before Him and repent of your sin, His action is to make you a new creation, a new creature, giving you a new birth. He gives you the power to hear what He has said and the power to obey every word.

If a person hears the gospel of Jesus Christ, which is the Kingdom of God and His sayings, and does not do them, then that person has no foundation in Jesus Christ and has no part with Him. The foundation of that man's life is as a vapor because he will have no foundation. Do not be fooled by the riches of this world. Jesus' words are spirit and are sure. He speaks here of life and life eternal…eternal life in Him or eternal destruction in everlasting fire. What will will a man will to do…to hear and obey? I choose to serve the Lord.

May 22nd

A House for the Lord

"Thus says the Lord: 'Heaven is My throne and earth is My footstool. Where is the house that you will build Me? And where is the place of My rest? For all these things My hand has made, and all these things exist,' says the Lord. But on this one will I look: on him who is poor and of a contrite spirit, and who trembles at My word.'"   (Isaiah 66:1-2, NKJV)

What do you give the person who has everything? What do you give the person who knows everything? What is it about self-adulation that is so disturbing to the humble?

It is in quiet moments that we can be still, and know the Lord. The Lord is good. He is great in mercy and loving kindness. The Lord God is our creator; He fashioned our days from before the foundations of the earth. He is Master and Lord of all. He is the King of all kings. He is holy, set apart, blameless, righteous, just. God is holy love.

There is none of us righteous, no, not one. The pride of man drives him to a fall. We are like sheep, led astray, in need of a good shepherd, a savior to save us from our sin and from our selves. In all that we are, He asks, 'Where is the place of my rest?' And, in the still, small voice, He tenderly calls and says, 'But on this one will I look: on him who is poor and of a contrite spirit.' He who humbles himself in the sight of the Lord, he shall find rest in Him and the Lord will find rest in him.

To be poor and contrite in spirit is to be known in humility and repentance; surrender and submission; turning the other cheek; meek, hungering and thirsting for righteousness. To be poor and contrite in spirit is to be merciful, peacemakers, pure in heart, forgiving as He is forgiving. 'On this one will I look...'   Is He looking at you?

May 23rd

Recognized Authority

"And so it was, when Jesus had ended these sayings, that the people were astonished at his teaching, for He taught them as one having authority, and not as the scribes."   (Matthew 7:28-29, NKJV)

In our lives and work, we all answer to somebody. We are not alone, even in our perceived alone times, we really are not alone. Husbands and wives answer to each other, children answer to parents, employees answer to employers, CEO's answer to board members, the self-employed answer to their customers, and on and on in every area of our lives, we generally answer to somebody. Political leaders are supposed to be servants of the people and should listen to the people, but most do not.

When we see authority in operation, we usually respond in two ways, we agree and follow, or we disagree and go another way. Oftentimes, we do have a choice to follow our teachers and leaders, or not. Sometimes we simply wait and think about what we are told, or led to do, but obedience or refusal are the usual choices, unless there is an opportunity for more options. People like options because they like to satisfy themselves.

Leadership comes in a variety of means and just because someone is in a position of leadership doesn't mean that they are a real leader, they just hold the position of such. Real leaders are recognized in the authority they display. Not all leaders have real authority. The leaders may hold positions of authority, but choices are made in the follow-ship as to whether the authority will be recognized as real and true. People will follow a leader if they perceive realness and truthfulness, and that usually coincides with the connection of the walk matching the talk. Does the leader substantiate his leadership by his life and his work, or is he a hypocrite? Does the leader have the nature of the position of authority?

"As one having authority…" is to say that the people were astonished at the truthfulness and reality that Jesus displayed in His speaking. There was the drawing and wooing of the Holy Spirit in Jesus' breath that led the people to believe that 'this man has authority!' When they compared His life teaching to that of the scribes who knew the scriptures but were unable to live out the love of God in what they taught; the comparison was too easy to make. Real authority exudes from the heart and if the leader has no heart in the matter, he has no real authority. Jesus was all heart and Spirit and His authority was recognized by the people as real and true. He was filled with the Holy Spirit and the power of the Holy Spirit was always speaking through Him. His authority exuded from heaven down.

Do we display true authority as He did when we speak in His Name? Or, are we viewed as a scribe who knew the letter of the law, but not the author of it?

May 24th

Following Authority

"When He had come down from the mountain, great multitudes followed Him."
(Matthew 8:1, NKJV)

The authority that Jesus displayed in His teaching on the mount was a kind of authority that had not been seen before by the people. They had had their scribes, teachers, and leaders, but nothing like Jesus. What Jesus had to say was true and real, and He spoke from the seat of an indescribable authority that could only be followed for they wanted more of what He had to say. If real authority exudes from the heart and spirit of a man, what is it about ourselves that either turns people on to Christ, or turns them away?

You see, if we name the Name of Jesus Christ, we are the ones who represent Him in the earth. Today's church has found itself in a quagmire of hypocrisy, false humility, and propagating hate while preaching the word of God. People followed the Spirit of Jesus to hear truth and He didn't hate the people in the process.

The religious did not like what He had to say for it was to their discredit that they were the ones who didn't get the love of God in their knowledge, teaching and writing out the law. And, it is to the religious today, that the world looks at the church and doesn't want to hear what it has to say because of how the Life and the Word has been displayed.

First of all, the world doesn't really want to hear the word of God, because if they really heard it, it would require a change on their part and ultimate follow-ship of all that Jesus was saying. But, so many of the world's children now refuse to enter into an arena of listening ears because of the church's hypocrisy and the lack of validation of true authority.

It is not so to be with us, so I say, "No more to the hypocrisy!" If it takes days and weeks and years of lives to get ourselves right in the Kingdom of God, let's start by doing so today. Abide in Him, and He will abide in you. Remain faithful to Him, He is always faithful. Know His word; His Holy Spirit will bring to remembrance at the right time when His word is to be rightly spoken. Be real and true in Him and the authority of the Holy Spirit will be heard through you and me to a lost and dying world that so desperately needs a Savior. Submit to the Lord and commit your every way to Him today and allow His Holy Spirit to do the work through you in holy love. Let them follow Him.

May 25th

You Can Make Me Clean

"And behold, a leper came and worshipped Him, saying, 'Lord, if You are willing, you can make me clean.' Then Jesus put out His hand and touched him, saying, "I am willing; be cleansed." Immediately his leprosy was cleansed."
(Matthew 8:2-3, NKJV)

The people recognized the authority of Jesus as one who had authority that had not been given by any man. The people recognized the divine in Him and they were willing to follow Him, not just to hear more, but to get at what He had inside of Himself.

The people followed Him from the mountain, but it was the leper who approached Him personally that day. It was the leper that had the greatest apparent need and he was willing to go all out in his belief that Jesus was real and true and divine. The leper needed a healing that no man was able to give him.

This is what it is like in the life of the Kingdom of God. A great many people may recognize the authority of Jesus Christ and many are willing to follow His authority, but far fewer people are willing to lay their lives down in their pitiful need of saving, of healing, and overwhelming tremendous need. Recognizing Him as Lord and following Him to worship Him is a choice opportunity that many have been afforded, only to wink at Him and say, 'Maybe next time,' but not so with the leper, the man of tremendous need. The leper knew his plight and knew that his death was imminent.

It is to be so with us. I am the man with the tremendous need of a Savior. I am the man who needs cleansing. I am the man who needs saving from myself and the sin that abounds around me. Jesus Christ stands at the door of my heart and says, 'I am willing; be cleansed.' And in my moments of submission and worship, I know that He has changed me and has cleansed me for all eternity. This is the power and the life in the Kingdom of God.

May 26th

Faith in His Authority

"Now when Jesus had entered Capernaum, a centurion came to Him, pleading with Him, saying, "Lord, my servant is lying at home paralyzed, dreadfully tormented."   (Matthew 8:5-6, NKJV)

This story is told early in Jesus' ministry, the story of a man who understood rule, order, and authority. This centurion was a Roman military man over 100 men, plus servants and detail. He understood military rule and authority and believed in it because he was ruled by the same authority over him.

This man recognized Jesus' authority as divine authority as it was real and true. This man was a real leader. He followed leadership and he exhibited leadership with the expectation of his men obeying his words. He knew real authority when he saw it. However, he didn't stop at simply recognizing Jesus' authority; he decided to follow Jesus' authority in faith.

This man realized the expectation of divine power and authority as great and believed that Jesus' divine power and authority was more powerful than any disease or demon. Jesus volunteered to go to his house, but this man knew that true power and authority in the spirit is all-encompassing. He was able to surmise in faith that Jesus' power and authority was not limited to space. He implored, 'Speak, and it will be done.' Jesus declared his faith to be great, even greater than all Israel.

We, too, must realize the power and authority of Jesus Christ. We, too, must have the faith to say to Jesus, 'Speak, and I will be healed. Speak, and my child, my parent, my servant, my friend, my enemy, will be healed.' The faith, the God kind of faith that believes in the power and authority of the Christ must be realized in us. Jesus is waiting for you to believe. He's waiting for you and me to believe in His power and authority as our Creator, our King, our Lord, and as our Healer:

"Bless the Lord, O my soul, and all that is within me, bless His holy name! Bless the Lord, O my soul, and forget not His benefits: Who forgives all your iniquities, who heals all your diseases, who redeems your life from destruction, who crowns you with lovingkindness and tender mercies, who satisfies your mouth with good things, so that your youth is renewed like the eagle's."   (Psalm 103:1-5, NKJV)

May 27th

Are You Getting It?

"Now when He was asked by the Pharisees when the kingdom of God would come, He answered them and said, 'The kingdom of God does not come with observation; nor will they say, 'See here!' or 'See there!' For indeed the kingdom of God is within you."   *(Luke 17:20-21, NKJV)*

The totality of the word of God, what most would call the Holy Bible, is a finely woven tapestry of time and space, both historical and revelatory of the future. It is the inspired word of our Holy Lord from times past and times to come. It speaks of real experiences that were and real experiences that are yet to come. The old was a foreshadowing of the new and the new is a preview of things that are and are to be. The word of God is carefully spoken, holy inspired, and wholly true.

When Jesus came and preached in the countryside and the cities, He said, "I must preach the kingdom of God to the other cities also, because for this purpose I have been sent." (Luke 4:43). Jesus went about preaching the kingdom of God and what He preached, we have written in the four gospels. What He preached was the life of the living in the kingdom of God that required repentance to obtain. "Repent, for the kingdom of heaven is at hand." (Matthew 4:17b). The Kingdom of God is not seen because of a building, a steeple, a place to meet, or a place to greet. He said, 'The kingdom of God is within you.' All of His life was poured into that message of life for now and life forevermore.

Repent – turn from the old, about face, no more to move in the old ways and old thinking. Be made clean and new in Him, for the kingdom of heaven is at hand. The power of the Holy Spirit comes to convict, to cleanse, and to give new birth to the life in Christ.

When He made you a new creation and you became born again of His Spirit, He led you into life forevermore which begins today. Abundant life is a state of being in Him. He is His kingdom and as we abide in Him, He has promised to abide in us. Get to know Him by His word and obey every saying of His. He is faithful to His word, His words are spirit and they are true. Continue with Him, in His Kingdom, for His Kingdom has come and in His kingdom, His will is done. The still, small voice is speaking, "Follow Me."

May 28th

As You Have Believed

"Then Jesus said to the centurion, 'Go your way; and as you have believed, so let it be done for you.' And his servant was healed that same hour."
(Matthew 8:13, NKJV)

In another passage, when Jesus asked his disciples, "Who do people say the son of man is?' (Matthew 16:13, NASB), He wanted the disciples to know what other people said and believed about him. When Jesus asked them who do they, the disciples, say that He is, Peter exclaims, "You are the Christ, the Son of the living God!" (v.16). Jesus told His disciples that day that flesh and blood had not revealed this to Peter, but that His Father in heaven had revealed it to him.

It really does matter what you believe about Jesus Christ. The centurion saw Him face to face and believed that His divine authority superseded any disease or any other spirit. The centurion understood authority and believed in faith that Jesus had authority over all. He was close enough to have this private conversation with Jesus and trusting enough that divine healing could be accomplished with only a word from Jesus.

Again, it really does matter what you believe about Jesus. Are you going to believe what other men and women say He is, or is not? Are you going to believe a good teaching about Jesus Christ and believe in someone else's belief that may, or may not be complete, or entirely correct? Jesus wanted to know the obvious; that many people will have their opinions and beliefs, but you, you have to know what you believe about Jesus Christ. Who is He to you? What do you believe? Just as sure as you are reading this writing, it is certain that it will be done for you as you have believed. Do you know Him personally and do you know that He knows your name? (Luke 10:20)

If you name the Name of Jesus Christ you know that He is Lord over all things, His Holy Spirit will have revealed this to you. Believe that and as a new creation, walk in the power of His Name and teach others to do the same.

May 29th

He Comes into Your House

"Now when Jesus had come into Peter's house, he saw his wife's mother lying sick with a fever. So He touched her hand, and the fever left her. And she arose and served them." (Matthew 8:14-15, NKJV)

Having a true relationship with Jesus Christ is for all times and all places. So many times we see people who try to act right by going to a church service only to come back home and act any way they please. It is easy to judge other people's hypocrisy by not living up to Christian standards in the home or in their places of business because hypocrisy is so easy to see and so very rampant in our religious societies. For years, people have tended to believe that God is 'at church', or up in heaven somewhere and so they leave Him there when they walk out of the doors of the church facility or the place of meeting. This is the belief of the religious.

If we have truly given our lives to Christ, we know that this is not the truth. The Holy Spirit has come to reside in us and us in Him.
God is above all and in all. Abiding in the life of Christ is to cheerfully know that He comes to our house and lives in us. We are the temple of the Holy Spirit. This is the new birth that Jesus spoke of. Although this may sound redundant, too many folk still do not realize the truth of the life of the kingdom of God that He dwells within you. So, no matter where you go, the Holy Spirit is there abiding in you. (John 16). It is wonderful to know that no matter where you are, the Holy Spirit is there to be with you, to touch, to heal, and to spiritually guide you into all wisdom and truth.

Jesus is showing us that just as He went into Peter's home, He desires to come into your home and He sees and knows all your needs even before you ask. "And all things you ask in prayer, believing, you will receive." (Matthew 21:22, NASB). The relationship of our Lord with His disciple is as we see here with Peter. Allow Him to be Lord in your life and all that He is, He will be in you…in your house today.

May 30th

Getting Deeper into Him

"When evening had come, they brought to Him many who were demon-possessed. And He cast out the spirits with a word, and healed all who were sick, that it might be fulfilled that which was spoken by Isaiah, the prophet, saying: 'He Himself took our infirmities and bore our sicknesses.'"
(Matthew 8:16-17, NKJV)

Jesus shows us the power of faith in Him. It is as we believe, He says. He teaches and He heals and He does all in His life that His Father had anointed Him to do. (Luke 4:18-19). As we continue to go deeper into His word and deeper into the life of the Kingdom, we see that all He was then, He is in us today. He did not abandon us. The Father sent us the Holy Spirit.

The Holy Spirit teaches us that the war is in the spirit. (Ephesians 6:12) Just as Jesus came and warred in the spirit through healings and the freeing of the demon-possessed, He revealed that the war is in the spirit realm. He displayed all authority over all realms. What we see in the flesh with our own eyes, is a symptom of what is going on in the spirit.

When we pray, we pray in the spirit. When we worship, we worship in spirit and truth. When we seek Jesus' healing in our lives to be free from whatever bondage that may have us or attacked us, we pray in the spirit that the power of the Holy Spirit will set us free. This is to be free from any spiritual bondage, no matter how it is seen in the flesh.

"For though we walk in the flesh, we do not war according to the flesh, for the weapons of our warfare are not of the flesh, but are divinely powerful for the destruction of fortresses." (2 Corinthians 10:3-4)

It is the power of the Holy One to heal, to set free, and to deliver. That power has not changed, nor has He diminished. Any and all needs are to be brought to Him. He came that we might have life, abundant life, and that includes not only being set free from the wages of sin, but being set free from any power that hell has to offer us.

May 31st

Understand That We Don't Understand

"Now when Jesus saw a crowd around Him, He gave orders to depart to the other side. And a certain scribe came and said to Him, 'Teacher, I will follow you wherever you go." (Matthew 8:18-19, NASB)

Too often we think we completely understand things in the scripture and as certain as our understanding seems to be, we realize we were wrong all along. How many times have we found ourselves thinking, 'Now, I've got it!', but only to realize, no, I only got half of it. Or, I really do not understand Jesus. I really do not understand the Holy Spirit. I really cannot do this thing called Christianity; it just doesn't seem to work for me.

It is a very good thing to come to a level of understanding that we do not fully understand, or believe, and we can go to Jesus and say, 'Help my unbelief; I need You in Your wisdom.'

It is in the state of humility and being 'poor in spirit' that we truly can submit the self to the refiner's fire and be baptized into truth, rather than prolonging our self-life into thinking we have it all together, because, eventually we will find that we do not understand all things.

John the Baptist said, 'And the axe is already laid at the root of the trees; every tree therefore that does not bear good fruit is cut down and thrown into the fire." (Matt. 3:10) It is the self that has to go first, because the self has to be denied in order for the fruit of the Holy Spirit to be exhibited. There is so much to the Kingdom of God and His word that we do not understand and still we jump at the opportunity to 'follow Jesus' just like the scribe desired to do. And, just like us, the scribe had no idea what he was getting himself into because Jesus responded to him, "The foxes have holes, and the birds of the air have nests; but the Son of Man has nowhere to lay His head." (Matt. 8:20)

Be careful of making promises that you know you will not keep. That is the inherent danger of making spontaneous decisions at an altar. The decisions made at an altar in a church service usually get forgotten within a very short time span. The point here is this: get to know Jesus in a full-time loving relationship instead of making empty promises that make you feel good for the moment, but make you a fool by speaking vows that you cannot, or will not, keep. (Ecclesiastes 5:1-7, Matthew 5:33-37)

June 1st

Getting Into Your Boat

"And when He got into the boat, His disciples followed Him."
(Matthew 8:23, NASB)

Jesus told His disciples that if any man desired to come after Him, that he would have to deny himself, take up his cross daily, and then follow Him. (Luke 9:23) All through the gospels Jesus was teaching in everything He said and did. It is easy to see and hear His teaching, the words written in red, so to speak. But, oftentimes we fail to see that everything Jesus did, every action, every miracle, and every healing, He was teaching the disciples and us what the kingdom of God was truly like.

In all that Jesus did, He glorified His Father. He did not do, or say anything, that His Father had not ordained. Being that all of this is true, then what was He teaching by getting into the disciples boat? This passage is also in Mark 4:35-41 and Luke 8:22-25. It follows the passage about people desiring to follow Him, but not really knowing the depth of the following and where Jesus would ultimately lead them.

In this passage, Jesus desires to cross over to the other side, but a storm arises and the disciples believe they are going to die as a result. In the Luke sequence, Jesus asks the disciples, 'Where is your faith?' This was after He had calmed the storm. There are many aspects of this short trip across the lake for the disciples and I want us to see something here that you may not have gotten earlier.

If you desire to follow Jesus, you have to deny yourself. He wants to get into your boat; you, yes, you, your boat. When He gets inside of you, He will spiritually take you places that you would not go on your own. He will take you to depths that you cannot get to on your own. Are you going to continue with Him? Will you take up your cross daily and follow Him? Will you trust Him that He is with you and will you continue to trust Him with your soul?

You see, we do not understand all things, but we can have faith in Him that He will guide us through any storm at any depth. Do you still desire to follow Him? Then go out with Him into the depths where the storms and the big fish are and don't be afraid.

June 2nd

Where is Your Faith?

"And they came to Him and woke Him up, saying, 'Master, Master, we are perishing!' And being aroused, He rebuked the wind and the surging waves, and they stopped and it became calm. And He said to them, 'Where is your faith?' and they were fearful and amazed, saying to one another, 'Who then is this, that He commands even the winds and the water, and they obey Him?'"
(Luke 8:24-25, NASB)

When Jesus led His disciples out into the open sea and the storm came and rocked the boat to the point to where they thought they were going to die, the Almighty power of God spoke to the wind and the water and said, 'Peace, be still.' The Creator has power over all. After this, Jesus turns to them and asks, 'Where is your faith?'

These were disciples, like us, in that they had not fully understood the following after the Almighty. He knows and understands our every need in the midst of every storm and He keeps asking, 'Where is your faith?' Have we responding yet with the full affirmation that 'You, Jesus, You are my faith! Your Holy Spirit dwells within me to comfort and to guide, to strengthen me and to glorify the Father!'

We are born of the Spirit and of fire into Him. His Holy Spirit resides in us. Jesus has admonished us to abide in Him and He will abide in us. We are to obey His sayings, His commands, and He and the Father will come and make their home inside of us. (John 14:16-24). If we choose to take up our cross daily and follow Him, we are at His command, being led of His Holy Spirit. This is life in the Kingdom of God.

So He asks again, 'Where is your faith?' If you know with great certainty, then you know that your faith is in you. He is in your boat, the vessel that bears your name. Give voice to the One who abides in you and speak to the storms of life and say, 'Peace, be still!' And watch the power of God move through you as fountains of living water to a lost and dying world that needs so desperately to hear the voice of God speaking once again, 'Peace, be still!' Have courage enough to realize that the Holy Spirit is at work in you and speak the word of God so that the work of the Holy Spirit gets out of you into the lives of people who need to hear His Good News. Be fruitful and multiply, He has ordained it.

June 3rd

The Other Side of Following

"And when He had come to the other side into the country of the Gadarenes, two men who were demon-possessed met Him as they were coming out of the tombs; they were so exceedingly violent that no one could pass by that road."
(Matthew 8:28, NASB)

Earlier in the day, Jesus had given orders to the disciples to cross over to the other side. He leads them through the raging storm of wind and waves, the forces of nature that frighten even the best of us to succumb to fear. His power is so great that it quiets the storm to calmness. Now that they are on the other side of the sea, a different kind of storm is revealed. This time it is the storm of raging demons. He is not afraid.

As the story is told, the two men frighten the villagers with violence and no one desired to even go on the road they possessed. But Jesus, they recognize, even though they had never seen His person, the demons knew His Spirit. They cry out in fear for they know who is confronting them. With words of power, Jesus dis-possesses the two men of the demonic spirits and casts the spirits into the neighboring herd of swine.

Jesus' power to rule and reign over the forces of nature and the forces of the spirit realm are being revealed. It is His power that rules and we dare not be afraid in the midst of any storm or in the midst of any force. "Be still, and know that I am God. I will be exalted among the nations, I will be exalted in the earth!" (Psalm 46:10, ESV)

It is to the follower of Jesus Christ that we leave all behind and trust Him for our present and our future. He is all-powerful over all things. For us to cry in fear, or fear in life is to tell Almighty God that He is not Almighty to us. That is the cry of unbelief. These events in the life of Jesus Christ are here to teach us truths about His life, His power, and the Kingdom of God. Know for a fact that no matter the storm or force that sets itself against you, 'greater is He that is in you, than he that is in the world.' (1 John 4:4) Be of good cheer, He has overcome the world. Be courageous for He is courageous. Allow His courage inside of you to quiet you and quiet the forces that surround you in His power and in His might.

June 4th

Whole-Hearted Rejection

"And, behold, the whole city came out to meet Jesus; and when they saw Him, they entreated Him to depart from their region." (Matthew 8:34, NASB)

It is remarkable and quite astonishing how the world takes offense at Jesus Christ. In the witnessing of Christ, we get offended at times, when people reject us, but they are actually rejecting the Holy Spirit that inhabits us. We shouldn't get offended, nor should we glory in rejection through prideful self-pity. It is to the dismay of our Lord that an individual rejects the call of Christ, let alone an entire city.

This passage is here to teach us, though, that the rejection of Jesus Christ is imminent. It is baffling at how different people view God and how they simply cannot understand why anyone would give up any rights to themselves to something that they cannot see, or believe in. The world likes itself as it is and is blinded to its demise and chains of selfishness, greed, and perceived freedom from religion. Jesus Christ is not religion.

Even though Jesus displayed a power to them that they could never achieve on their own, they rejected Him nonetheless. It is to this day that people still reject Him and as we continue on our journey with Him, we discover the depth of rejection and the pain it brings.

It is actually very painful to be rejected. Jesus Christ was the ultimate Man of Sorrows; His own people rejected Him, His teachings, His miracles, His power, and all that He had to offer. Be careful here with your feelings and emotions when you are rejected, for self-pity is distasteful to our Lord. It means that we care more for our self than we care about Him. Find your sustenance in Him. Be strengthened in Him. It is He who has given you life, be thankful for Him, for He loves you so. Do not wallow in anything but His grace, for His grace is sufficient for all your needs.

"Blessed are you when men hate you, and ostracize you, and cast insults at you, and spurn your name as evil, for the sake of the Son of Man. Be glad in that day, and leap for joy, for behold, great is your reward in heaven; for in the same way their fathers used to treat the prophets." (Luke 6:23-24, NASB)

June 5th

Faith in Action

"And, behold, they were bringing to Him a paralytic, lying on a bed; and Jesus seeing their faith said to the paralytic, "Take courage, My son, your sins are forgiven." (Matthew 9:2, NASB)

Over the years, I've met hundreds, if not thousands of people. In talking with them about their faith, individually, and in small and large group settings, people of faith usually place themselves in one or two categories: those that are willing to share their faith somehow, some way and the other group who says, 'My faith is private, it's my personal business.' The latter group is typically someone who does not understand the concept of denying the self, but one would not want to automatically presume that of the sharing group. It requires, however, a denial of the self in order to allow the Holy Spirit to speak as He speaks to witness of the Lord.

Not everyone is comfortable 'sharing' their faith in street witnessing or even talking to their neighbor about a relationship with the Lord. This is extremely common, however, and really should not be. Too often people of faith excuse themselves from sharing their faith by saying they are uncomfortable, it's not my personality, the timing isn't right, I'm too busy, isn't that the evangelist's, or the pastor's job, and on and on the excuses flow. One of the reasons people do not share their faith is that they think they have to, for all practical purposes here, 'street witness', and so most Christians will shut down in talking about their faith.

Let's look at the opportunity the way this particular scripture talks about it: the people know a man in need, they knew a man who could help him, they took the sick man to the helper, and the helper made him well. Jesus looked at this event as – Jesus seeing their faith! The faith they had turned into action to help another man by taking the time and energy to go to his house, pick him up, along with his bed, and then take him to Jesus. The faith was in what Jesus could do, not in what they could do.

The fascinating thing about our lives today is that if you really are a born again believer in Jesus Christ, then the Holy Spirit abides in you. So, wherever you go, you're taking the Spirit of God with you. It is the power of the Holy Spirit to convict the world of sin and the power to draw men to the Father. (John 16). Jesus said, 'as you go, make disciples...' So, the next time you have the opportunity to share your faith, allow the Holy Spirit to have His way in you. It doesn't have to be like going to the dentist. Just relax, stop the quivering, and open your mouth.

And, you will be amazed at how He witnesses to Himself through you to a lost and needy world. (Acts 1:8; Matthew 10:20) Be pleasantly obedient to let Him use your voice, your hands, and your feet and be amazed at what God does through you!

June 6th

Your Sins Are Forgiven

"…Take courage My son, your sins are forgiven."
(Matthew 9:2b, NASB)

All power, in heaven and earth, has been given to Jesus Christ. Jesus said, "For which is easier, 'To say, your sins are forgiven,' or to say, 'Rise and walk'? But in order that you may know that the Son of Man has authority on earth to forgive sins" – then He said to the paralytic- 'Rise, take up your bed, and go home." (Matthew 9:5-6, NASB)

Jesus Christ came to save people from their sin. Jesus made an outer showing of an inner working. He healed the man of his paralysis. The man became strong enough to not only get up and walk; he carried his bed as Jesus told him to. The people marveled and glorified God that God had given such 'healing' power to a man.

We have to believe Jesus' words. Jesus showed us that He could heal. He stated emphatically that He had power to forgive sins. We have to believe all of Jesus' words and walk in Him as truth. That means that your sins and my sins are forgiven. You and I do not have to carry our past around with us as though we still have need of a suitcase load of sin needing to be taken care of. Many a person is weighted down with their past sin unnecessarily. Sometimes our memories have more power over us than the words of Jesus Christ. When anything has more power over you than Jesus Christ, it is unbelief.

Unleash the power of the past from your mind. Let it go by going to Him and giving all to Him. Do not hang on to anything. Too many folk still say, "But what about this; but what about that?" Or, "What I did doesn't deserve forgiveness, it was too awful…" Stop the maddening guilt and let God have His way in you making you fully clean. Believe Him. Don't believe me, believe Him! He said that He could make you 'whiter than snow', believe Him and let Him do His work in you. Then, just as He said to the paralytic, take up your new life in Him and walk, giving Him glory for the power to heal you and forgive you of all your sin. Shout 'Hallelujah!'

June 7th

Spiritual Determination

"...But in order that you may know that the Son of Man has authority on earth to forgive sins,' then He said to the paralytic, 'Rise, take up your bed and go home.'"   (Matthew 9:6, NASB)

Jesus Christ's words are spirit and are true. He displayed the power to forgive while exhibiting the power to heal. The healing represented the forgiving. The healing is in the spirit just like the new life is in the spirit. When you became a born-again new creation in Him, you did not get a new body, did you?

Have we determined what is spiritually real and what is temporal? The things that you see, taste, touch, hear, and smell are the sensual things, the temporal things of the earth.[1] These things do not last, but the spiritual reality of the Holy Spirit is what is now and forevermore. While Jesus was here on earth, He healed that we might be healed. He died that we would be forgiven.

The power of God to heal through and in the Name of Jesus Christ is alive today. I have prayed for it, witnessed it, and seen others receive healing in His Name. I have also prayed and seen many others pray and not receive healing. I have seen saints of God die from their diseases, but is it because they did not pray? Is it because they did not have enough faith? NO! But we who pray, pray in earnest believing that the power of healing from God rest upon the soul who is in need. It is a matter of the will of the Father to heal, or not to heal. If I speak in error as some may believe because they think I do not have enough faith, or the right kind of faith, as they quote scripture out of context that 'He heals all my diseases', then why do all people die? Why is it that it is appointed for all men to die? If the healings of Jesus Christ imply that we are to be healed of all our diseases, then why is it that the prayers for the sick seemingly go unanswered?

Perhaps the answer lies in that these prayers do get answered, albeit not as they desire. We have to be praying 'Thy will be done on earth as it is in heaven", and when we pray that prayer we first have to be submitted to our Lord as Lord and not us as Lord. It is the heart of the prideful that believes he can command the Lord God Almighty. Jesus tells us to go to Him praying and believing, but we must understand that prayer is a mechanism of getting us in line with His will.

Get to know your heavenly Father in such a way that you know, beyond any shadow of a doubt, what His will is in each and every case of need. Pray the prayer of faith for yourself and your friends and believe that your heavenly Father knows your need, even before you ask. Pray, and do not doubt. Ask, and you shall receive.

Believe, but think about this before you pray…Jesus would go to the mountains and pray all night, that is where He learned and became the will of the Father. How about you?

June 8th

The Call of Levi

"And as Jesus passed on from there, He saw a man, called Matthew, sitting in the tax office; and He said to him, 'Follow Me!' And he rose, and followed Him." (Matthew 9:9, NKJV)

The call of Jesus upon Matthew was very specific. The life and work of Matthew was also very specific, he was among the worst of the servants of Israel for he was a tax collector. These were men who would sit in their office, or alongside of the road and take a tax from the merchants and folk who passed by. The usual and customary way of a tax collector was to exact enough money from the villager so as to give to the Roman governor his due and to make enough money on top of that as the tax collector's payment of collections. Their dealings were ruthless and self-satisfying and as some would attest, the tax collectors were viewed as legal thieves among the population albeit Jews themselves who knew their villagers personally. These 'thieves' from among the people were hated by their fellow brothers of Jews and yet protected by the Roman government of whom they served.

It is the specific calling of this man, Levi, son of Alphaeus, whom Jesus called Matthew that made notice to all that Jesus had come to save sinners; this included the most despised. Matthew was in his calling, his vocation, when Jesus called him to Himself to leave what he was doing to come and follow Him. Matthew obeyed.

The representation we are to see here is not that when Jesus calls men to leave their vocation and sit at Jesus' feet and subsequently become pastors and preachers. Although tradition has taught that this is so, that is not the teaching here. I've been around enough ministers and so-called Christians, for that matter, that left what they did to follow Jesus, but they did not leave who they were…their mean, ornery selves. The essence of the call of Jesus is that He has called you and me to leave who we are and what we are and go and follow Him.

There is a vast difference here in stating that we are to leave what we are and who we are, as opposed to leaving what we do. Matthew did both, he left his line of work, but he also left behind what he was, that of being a despised thief among his people, a sinner, to follow the teacher of righteousness that had the power to save him from himself. The power in Jesus' authority to save sinners from themselves was recognized from the beginning of His ministry and He is the only way that we can be delivered from the penalty of sin, the power of sin and the only means of departing from an old life and receiving a new life in Him and that new life is forevermore. Leave who you are and go…follow Him! In Truth, you will bear the fruit of the Holy Spirit and then you will know that you are His.

June 9th

Bringing Others to Jesus

"And it happened as He was reclining at the table in the house, behold many tax-gatherers and sinners came and were dining with Jesus and His disciples." (Matthew 9:10, NKJV)

If we believe the Word of God to be True, then every person mentioned and every event detailed is there for a reason. When Matthew, the sinning tax-collector was called and subsequently followed Jesus, he did what was normal and natural, that is, he fulfilled his need to eat. It's that simple.

He had a dinner at his house and invited the friends that he knew along with Jesus and His disciples. His current collective of friends involved other tax-collectors and 'sinners', by what nature we do not exactly know, but let it suffice that these people were not honorable men. We can presume that they were the wretched parts of society by trade and by means of who they were. In this passage, nothing is spoken on what they talked about or what they ate. The passage is clear and simple…Matthew is bringing others to meet Jesus and he is bringing Jesus to meet them and they all needed to eat.

Matthew is a vessel and he uses what he has at his disposal to give a lot of people an opportunity to eat at his table, the same table that had been supplied by means of perceived theft and extortion through the avenues of tax collecting. The food that was served was certainly a part of Matthew's profits from his 'sinning' ways. No righteous man would be found in Matthew's house, let alone partaking of his profits. And yet, there they were, all together, the tax-collectors, the sinners, the newly called disciples, and the Man of God, Jesus.

If you name the Name of Jesus Christ, then keep it simple. Allow Jesus to be Himself in you and make the invitation to others who need Him at your dinner table. Invite who you know and who you are comfortable with; start there. In Truth and in Spirit, allow the Holy Spirit of God to join you and your friends at the table. Enjoy a meal with Jesus and watch Him work His work and all that He touches will be blessed.

June 10th

The Call of the Self-Righteous

"And when the Pharisees saw this, they said to His disciples, 'Why is your Teacher eating with the tax-gatherers and sinners?' But when He heard this, He said, "It is not those who are healthy who need a physician, but those who are sick."'   (Matthew 9:11-12, NKJV)

By means of a call, Jesus goes out and calls His own disciples unto Himself. By the means of a different call, the Pharisees, who are the self-righteous ones, make a call of their own. They stand outside the house of Matthew putting the disciples to the test and inquire, 'Why is your teacher eating with the tax-gatherers, the worst of the lot of sinners that we know?' The Pharisees didn't even want to talk to the tax-collectors; they brought their grievance to Jesus' disciples. They thought they held the proprietary rights to righteousness.

We have to take note, first of all, that the self-righteous folk have no righteousness of their own. Their righteousness is only a personal perception. Paul said that "there is none righteous, no, not one." (Romans 3:10). Isaiah prophesied, "For all of us have become like one who is unclean, and all our righteous deeds are like a filthy garment; and all of us wither like a leaf, and our iniquities, like the wind, take us away." (Isaiah 64:6). We all need the deliverance from who we are, what we are and what we have done. None of us are exempt.

You see, anytime we take judgment upon ourselves and judge the heart of another; we take that which is not ours to take. Even if we name the Name of Jesus Christ and truly believe that we are His, we are only His because of His righteousness and not our own. There is no such thing as self-righteousness, but there is self-deception…thinking we are something that we are not. Be willing to follow Jesus Christ to the fullest. That means having a full understanding that we did not do anything to deserve His grace and neither can anyone else. None of us has any righteousness of our own. His grace alone saves us from the penalty, the power and the consequences of sin. His power alone gives the power to be born again, a new creation.

This helps us to understand that your friends and co-workers are in need of a Savior just like you and me. Do not condemn, but love. Do not judge, but persevere. And when the self-righteous, who think they have the right to criticize, wag their tongue at you and judge you falsely, remain in Him. He will speak in time, but you, you go in peace.

June 11th

The Sick Have Need

"But when he heard this, He said, 'It is not those who are healthy who need a physician, but those who are sick. But go and learn what this means, 'I desire compassion, and not sacrifice, for I did not come to call the righteous, but sinners." (Matthew 9:12-13, NASB)

Although Jesus came to save all who are lost and all who have sinned and fallen short of the glory of God, not everyone is going to believe Him, and not everyone is going to see their need of Him. This is more than unfortunate, it is disturbing to know that there have been and will always be people who do not recognize the power of God or their need of Him. There are many reasons why people think that they do not need God.

Take a look at your own life and you will discover the inner workings of rebellion and unbelief in your past that thwarted the power of God from your heart. We all have taken too much pleasure in our sin and too much pleasure in ourselves. We all have refused to see the need to change. We all do not comprehend the power of darkness in the world and the eventual end of it. At times, there are those who think they are good enough and just simply do not have the need of a 'god way up there telling them what to do'. The justifications for living without God are endless.

But the point Jesus is making here is that even the religious who think they have it all together…don't, not really. It is the humbled sickened soul that knows he needs a Savior that Jesus has come to heal. If a person thinks his religion or religious works will save then surely he will have his reward, but it won't be in Jesus Christ.

There are none too bad and none too good that do not need a Savior. We all need Jesus and we all need His saving grace to carry us into His Kingdom. No man's religious works save. Jesus said that we must be born again. We must be completely undone and not everyone is going to believe that. Some will mock the idea of being born again, but it was Jesus who first said that and not some writer long ago.

He desires love, compassion, and life…not sacrifice. We cannot work our way into His life. It has to be done His way, the way of grace. Go and learn what it means that He desires compassion and not sacrifice. Love Him more than yourself and dive into Him today.

June 12th

New Wine in New Skin

"Nor do men put new wine into old wineskins; otherwise the wineskins burst, and the wine pours out, and the wineskins are ruined; but they put new wine into fresh wineskins, and both are preserved."   *(Matthew 9:17, NASB)*

Jesus went about preaching, saying, 'Repent, for the kingdom of heaven is at hand.' (Matthew 4:17). He kept telling one story after another, in parables, giving illustrations in various ways, in healings, travels, miracles, and teachings on what the Kingdom of God is all about. Jesus came preaching the gospel of the kingdom.

Jesus told Nicodemus, 'You must be born again.' (John 3:3). Here in Matthew, He tells John the Baptist's disciples these illustrations of putting a new patch on new clothing and new wine in new wineskin. It is all a part of the revealing that we have to give up the old in order to receive the new. You cannot stay the person you are and say, 'I "invite" Jesus into my heart,' as some men have taught us to say, no, Jesus is the One who says, 'Come unto Me.' You have to become an entirely new creation, born again, as Jesus would say. The Holy Spirit knows when a man just wants a piece of His power, but is not willing to submit to Him as Lord. It is the power of Christ that comes into the surrendered life and is born inside of him. He makes you new. You cannot do that yourself. It is the power of Christ to forgive sin, to heal, to make new, and to cause a person to become born again in His Spirit. If a man will lose his life for His sake, He will find the new life in Christ that He has promised. This is life in the Kingdom of God!

We have to leave our traditional mindsets of self, religion, and of conventional thought and get into Jesus' gospel of the kingdom of God. Jesus said to 'repent', that is to completely turn from one direction and do a 180 degree 'about face' into Him. When we give up ourselves to Him, He miraculously makes us new in Him. He is birthed into our lives and the Holy Spirit comes in and lives within us. The new wine will not go into an old wineskin. He is the new wine and the surrendered life is the new wineskin. The Holy Spirit cannot and will not come to a person who refuses to be made new in Him. The Holy Spirit is the change agent, not you, and this occurs as you believe in Him, giving your life over to Him. You cannot 'patch up' an old life, it just doesn't work anymore than religion works over a man who thinks he can work his way into heaven. Let Him have His way today!

June 13th

Speak What You Believe

*"...for she was saying to herself, 'If I only touch His garment, I shall get well."
(Matthew 9:21, NASB)*

Jesus responded to the woman who had the need of healing from her bleeding hemorrhage of twelve years with, "Daughter, take courage, your faith has made you well." (v.22) My heart has to smile with the fact that Jesus healed this woman through her faith in Him. She had spoken in her heart what she believed and that was to get close enough to Jesus to touch the hem of His garment. She acted on her belief.

The faith driven life is the life driven after Him. If I can only get to Jesus, well, if you are born again of His Spirit, He is right where you are. Know His word, obey His commands, abide in Him, and He will abide in you. Believe! Place the faith that He has given you back into Him, and let Him lead you to where you need to be.

Trust in Him. Be healed in Him, and speak that out loud. Speak out what He has put in. The faith that you have in Him is a 'walk about' in His Kingdom. In Him there is life, and that, more abundantly. There is nothing mundane or boring about the life of Jesus Christ.

Walk in healing in your spirit, your mind, and your body. I still have to wear eyewear for my nearsightedness. He has not healed me of my nearsightedness, but I can wear glasses that correct my sight to near perfection. Does that mean I do not have faith, no, I don't believe that. What I do believe is that His will is for me to see how He wants me to see. Am I healed of all my physical ailments immediately? No, but I can go to a doctor and ask for help and guidance. I do believe that He heals me with help from the medical field with knowledge and medicine.

Many of our ailments come from the abundance of stress. Stress is toxic and leads people down the road to unending physical derailment when left unchecked. In Christ, I believe that I am healed; I have to speak that out loud. My healing comes in my soul from Him. As I am made new in Him, He has healed me of all my diseases, the diseases of my mind, my heart, my soul, and my body. I have trusted Him with my life and I have spoken that aloud. I am not ashamed to call Him my Lord. It is as I believe because He is my belief. My trust is in Him and not in my beliefs. Keep your eyes on Him and know that He is closer than your garment. He abides in you. Believe in Him for your peace and rest in Him.

June 14th

They Began Laughing at Him

"He began to say, 'Depart for the girl has not died, but is asleep.' And they began laughing at Him. But when the crowd had been put out, He entered and took her by the hand; and the girl arose."   (Matthew 9:24-25, NASB)

In this setting of a synagogue official's home, his daughter has died and the official has implored Jesus in humility to come to his house to heal his daughter. His daughter had been dead long enough for the family and friends to know and for them to be making preparations in a funeral. The man believed that if Jesus would come and lay His hands on her, that she would be healed and brought back to life. Jesus agreed.

When Jesus arrived at the man's house, the instrumentalists, and the purveyors who worked the work of a funeral had already arrived on the scene preparing the family in their sorrow. What met Jesus there, though, is what we have seen today… mocking laughter. Have you ever been in a church service, or other venue, and seen people laugh, or smile their smiles when someone who truly wants to believe in God to do the miraculous? It's as if the few people who truly believe with the God kind of faith to believe God will move to heal are surrounded by derision, mockers, and unbelief.

Which group have you been a part of, the faith, believing faith, or the scorning mockers?

Jesus removed the faithless from the house and He was able to do His work. This is a faith fact. You cannot laugh at God in unbelief and expect Him to move on your behalf. Nor can you surround yourself with scorning unbelief and expect God to move, not because God is not able, but because the unbelief gets into the person of need and you do not have agreement with the very person who needs the healing. When Jesus asks you, 'Do you believe?' He wants to know if you agree with Him. He knows He can heal you or whoever of all their diseases, but do you agree with that same belief? He continually asks the people, 'do you believe?' He wants them to voice their agreement out loud because He already knows what's in their hearts. He wants you to voice agreement with Him out loud. Do you believe? If the answer is a faithful resounding, yes, then speak with your voice and say in faith what you believe He can do. Allow the Holy Spirit to do His marvelous work through you in believing, audible faith.

June 15th

Do You Believe?

"And after He had come into the house, the blind men came up to Him, and Jesus said to them, 'Do you believe that I am able to do this?' They said to Him, 'Yes, Lord.' Then He touched their eyes saying, 'Be it done according to your faith.' And their eyes were opened." (Matthew 9:28-30a, NASB)

In my opportunities of prayer and life walk with my Lord, I have seen people healed from the Lord, almost immediately, and I have seen people healed over time. I have seen it when people were prayed over by many saints and elders and I've watched them die. I have seen saints prayed over and be healed and I've seen, for the most part, people walk away truly wanting to be healed and yet depart believing their prayers went unanswered.

What is it about us that we continue to search for the holy grail of healing in our bodies and leave the truly spiritual life to hucksters? There are those in the church and in the world who simply are into what they can do for others so they can make a dollar off of it and then they want you to move on so that you don't give them away in their false lives. There are still ravenous wolves raping the church of its life and you have to be aware that the word of God is true in this. The hypocrite does not recognize his own hypocrisy.

One reason why we do not see the kind of healings taking place today that we see in the 'Jesus days' is this – we have not experienced this kind of faith and these kinds of miracles and because we have not personally experienced it, we tend to believe that it doesn't exist for us today. Another reason, just mentioned, is the fact that there are so many false teachers in the church today that as we watch these false prophets at work, we then find ourselves either mocking the whole experience in unbelief, or completely turning away in disgust. False prophets and teachers do much wrong to the body of faith.

Because I have seen people healed from all types of diseases and ailments, I have experienced healing faith in Jesus' Name and Presence. Because of false teachers, my faith is debilitated and weakened. What are you and I to do as a result?

Do this with all of your heart: Never cease to pray, it is the easiest thing to do and yet the hardest thing to get going, but never cease to pray. Secondly, never cease to believe in the power of God to anything that you have prayed for in faith. Keep believing, do not stop believing. Jesus told His disciples to watch and pray; so watch and pray believing with all of your heart and leave the results to God. Leave the results to the Almighty who is more than anything we could ask or think. Trust in Him, not in your faith, or the lack thereof. Wait on the Lord and watch in faith for His good work to come to pass. "Do you believe I am able to do this?" Jesus continues to ask. I know that He Is and you do, too!

June 16th

A Spiritual Revelation

"And as they were going out, behold, a dumb man, demon-possessed, was brought to Him. And after the demon was cast out, the dumb man spoke..."
(Matthew 9:32, NASB)

How many times have we observed people and wondered at what drives them to do what they do? Do we wonder at ourselves at some of the things we've done only to say to ourselves, 'Now why did I just do that?'

When we look to the word of God for knowledge, wisdom, truth, or just a word to get us through a moment, we look with eyes of our own education, experience, former teachings, and oftentimes curiosity at what really happened and what does it really mean for us today. We have been taught with traditional teaching and conventional thought often with such repetition that it seems all of the teachers, past and present, are saying the same thing. What drives our minds and hearts to think what we think about the scripture?

If we look at this passage within its context, it goes along with a line of healings that Jesus had performed. All the healings that Jesus performed not only provided healing power to the person in need but also demonstrated the power of God to heal in all instances, because nothing is impossible with God.

This is true and it is also true that Jesus was teaching us about the kingdom of God in everything He did while on the earth because everywhere He went He preached the gospel of the kingdom of God. He was His preaching and everything He did exhibited true life. In this healing, the man is healed from his inability to speak caused from a demonic force that possessed his natural ability to communicate.

There is physical healing of all types of diseases and ailments and there is spiritual healing of all types of diseases and ailments. In this instance, the inability to speak, the dumbness of the man, was healed by the casting out of a demon. This is a faith fact. It is true whether you believe it or not. Again, I ask the question, 'What is it that drives people to do the things that they do?' What causes these extremely debilitating diseases that seem to exist only to drive the person to such ill health that, at times, death seems to be the only recourse? We need to know who our real enemy is...

"We do not wrestle against flesh and blood, but against principalities, against powers, against the rulers of the darkness of this age, against spiritual hosts of wickedness in the heavenly places. Therefore take up the whole armor of God that you may be able to withstand in the evil day, and having done all, to stand."
(Ephesians 6:12-13)

June 17th

The Gospel of the Kingdom

"And Jesus was going about all the cities and the villages, teaching in their synagogues, and proclaiming the gospel of the kingdom, and healing every kind of disease and every kind of sickness." (Matthew 9:35, NASB)

Jesus went to all the cities and villages, teaching in the synagogues and in the streets, proclaiming the gospel of the kingdom. We know what men have said they believe was the gospel of Jesus Christ, but hardly anywhere you hear preachers preaching the 'gospel of Jesus Christ'…the gospel of the kingdom. Many apostles, prophets, evangelists, pastors, and teachers teach and preach well, but not many preach what Jesus proclaimed and that is the gospel of the kingdom of God. Christ Jesus is the Kingdom of God, the Kingdom of Grace.

The word of God is explicit, John the Baptist and Jesus Christ preached, 'Repent, for the kingdom of God is at hand.' (Matthew 3:2, 4:17) Jesus' entire ministry was His life teaching and that teaching was the kingdom of God. (Mark 1:15, 2:2, 4:11, 4:30, 10:15; Luke 7:22, 8:10, 18:17). These are just a few of the scriptures that speak of Jesus' preaching the kingdom of God.

All of His parables were teachings on what the kingdom of God was like. He exhibited the true life in the kingdom. He was and is His kingdom.

Everything He professed about the kingdom He illustrated with healings, miracles, teachings, proofs, and the ultimate proof was the giving up of His life for the sin of the world so that we could have that same life in His kingdom. We do not have to die a physical death on a cross. He's already paid that price that only He was worthy to pay.

Everything He did while on this earth was a detailed illustration of how we enter into that life and what that life is all about. We have to give up ourselves (Matthew 16:24-27) to enter into this life of the kingdom of God. We must be born again (John 3:3) What Jesus preached is not what men and women preach today; the preaching of the truth of the gospel of the kingdom of God got lost somewhere in time and space because of religion. But just because the preaching got lost, the truth of the gospel of the kingdom did not. Learn from Jesus what His gospel was and is. And, I pray that your eyes and ears will be opened that seeing, you will see; and hearing, you will hear. Bless Jesus Christ on your journey in this gospel of the kingdom of God!

June 18th

He Sees You, Do You See Others?

"And seeing the multitudes, He felt compassion for them, because they were distressed and downcast like sheep without a shepherd."
(Matthew 9:36, NASB)

How is it that we could care as He has cared for us? Some may say that they care and love as He loved us, but I seriously doubt it. He left His throne in heaven to come to this earth as a baby, defenseless and full of every need. Although He was God incarnate, He lived on this earth and grew up as a child into an adult for the sole purpose of pleasing His Father. It was His Father's purpose for Him to preach the kingdom of God, as well as, to die on a cruel cross for the sin of the world.

He was punished for our transgressions; He was bruised for our iniquity. The sin of the whole world was placed upon Him so that we could have life with Him in His kingdom. The atonement had to be made and He was that blood atonement.

He has seen the multitudes and had compassion, but can we understand and know the depth of His compassion? He has seen us as individuals over time and space and had compassion and has even known the number of hairs on our head, He knows us that well. Still, in His holy compassion and love, He died for us. You see, we may say we care, but how much we care is seen in the height and depth of our actions. We may say we love, but the breadth and width of our love is observed in our actions.

Do we really see the world as He sees the world? A thought with past weight not reconciled droops the face.

He sees our hearts and knows us intimately in the power of His love and compassion. In truth, I cannot love you as He loves us. But the proof of His love being in us is a renewed life birthed of Him in us. They will know us by our love, the holy love of Christ Himself flowing through us to a lost and needy world.

"I was hungry, and you gave Me something to eat; I was thirsty, and you gave Me drink; I was a stranger, and you invited Me in; naked, and you clothed Me; I was sick, and you visited Me; I was in prison, and you came to Me...Truly I say to you, to the extent that you did it to one of these brothers of Mine, even the least of them, you did it to Me." (Matthew 25:35-36, 40b, NASB)

June 19th

The Harvest is His

"Then He said to His disciples, 'The harvest is plentiful, but the workers are few. Therefore beseech the Lord of the harvest to send out workers into His harvest.'" (Matthew 9:37-38, NASB)

It is the prayer of the faithful to the Lord of the harvest that Jesus speaks of here. The harvest, all of the lost souls throughout time, is His to bring in. He is the One who calls and commissions the preacher, the pastor, the evangelist, the missionary, the minister, the witness, the priests of the faith. The Holy Spirit is the one who convicts of sin, of judgment, and of comfort. He alone delivers and saves the lost from their sin.

But how can they hear without a preacher? How can they hear without a faithful servant of the Most High God who has been called to a very specific time and place and people?

If you have been covered in the blood of Jesus Christ and have entered into His Kingdom through the power of the cross, then abiding in Him has been your due course. Open your heart to the madness in the world and allow the Holy Spirit to speak through you to the times, the seasons and the peoples that He has placed you in. Pray to the Lord of the harvest, He is Lord of all. And always remember that His harvest is His body is His church, so be nice when His witness is flowing through you.

The saying attributed to Edmund Burke that, 'all that is necessary for evil to triumph is when good men do nothing' is certainly appropriate here. We are to pray that the Lord of the harvest will send laborers into the fields of the world to gather the harvest. But in our earnest prayer, let us be honest in all sincerity that the possibility of the laborer in your field of life's work is you.

June 20th

The Calling of the Apostles

"And having summoned His twelve disciples, He gave them authority over unclean spirits, to cast them out, and to heal every kind of disease and every kind of sickness. Now the names of the twelve apostles are these..."
(Matthew 10:1-2a, NASB)

The twelve disciples that Jesus called are named in Matthew 10:2-4. These very specific men were given a very specific authority to deliver a very specific message of the kingdom to a very specific people. The authority to heal every kind of disease came from Jesus Christ and subsequently the apostles came back with excited news of success.

There is no spiritual sickness that the power of the Christ cannot cure. The question remains to each individual, however, and that is this: do you believe that the power of Jesus Christ exists in the earth today to physically heal every kind of disease, every kind of sickness and does He still deliver people from unclean spirits?

As He asked the blind men in Matthew 9:28, "...do you believe that I am able to do this?", so He continually asks us today. Do you believe He is able? Do you believe that He will?

We have seen so much confusion, error and false teaching that it is extremely difficult to believe because of the pride of errant men and women of the cloth. It has been said that some do not experience the healing of the Christ because they do not believe. It has also been said of the reverse that some cannot believe because they have not experienced the physical healing of the Lord.

There has been conjecture of the many who would debate that healing was for then and not for now and the other side says that healing was then and is for now and always. I have seen both sides. I have seen people prayed for and die and I have seen people prayed for and live in healthful healing. There is no specific formula in any of my personal experiences other than this...it is the Lord God who heals whom He will heal and I will never let it be said of me that I lacked the faith to believe that He can heal anyone and that He will heal anyone that He chooses to heal. He has been given all authority over all things and that includes my mind to believe in His power to heal in any given circumstance. Walk in the faith that He has given you.

June 21st

The Kingdom of Heaven is at Hand

"…but rather go to the lost sheep of the house of Israel. And as you go, preach, saying, 'The kingdom of heaven is at hand.'"   *(Matthew 10:6-7)*

In the beginning of the ministry of the apostles, Jesus gave them directives on what to do and who to do it with. The gospel of the kingdom of heaven was first preached to the house of Israel. The kingdom message implied the domain of a king with a kingdom, the king being God in His indescribable domain of heaven. Specific declaration of these words was not suggested, but demanded by Jesus the Christ. The apostles were to go and say specifically, "The kingdom of heaven is at hand."

This message taught the hearers that heaven had come upon them in such a way as it was not only imminent, that is forthcoming, but that the kingdom of heaven was here. All authority had been given by Jesus Christ and He gave His apostles authority to proclaim His message that He, being the son of God, had arrived on the scene. He gave them authority to heal and to work miracles which was to signify the power of the kingdom of heaven which was in Him and on them.

We don't have to wait to get to heaven to see the power and authority of God in the earth. All we have to do is to look to Christ Jesus Himself and know that it was the grace of God coming down to earth to redeem the world of its powerlessness to save itself from itself. We have to believe in faith of His wonderful grace that was exemplified then in the hands of His apostles and know that that same gift of grace is for us today. It was freely given and it is freely received.

We can smile a smile today knowing that the power of the Christ arrived over two thousand years ago and that same power still exists for us today. Believe in the power of the kingdom of God, it is as close as your hand and as dear as your heart. His grace that has delivered the millions over the years is still delivering today. Receive His grace and speak what the apostles were given to speak, 'The kingdom of heaven is at hand!' This message was given to initiate a new covenant, not made with the hands and work of men, but freely given by God, through grace. It is believed in faith and lived out in faith and no man can do any work to deserve the life-changing, healing bringing power of the Almighty God into the souls of men.

June 22nd

The Representation of the Kingdom

"...the kingdom of heaven is at hand. Heal the sick, raise the dead, cleanse the lepers, cast out demons; freely you have received, freely give."
(Matthew 10:7b-8, NASB)

The kingdom of heaven has arrived in the earth. Jesus later told the Pharisees in Luke 17:20b-21, "The kingdom of God does not come with signs to be observed; nor will they say, 'Look, here it is!' or 'There it is!' For behold, the kingdom of God is within your midst." (NASB) The New King James version says, '...the kingdom of God is within you.' The Greek word here *'entos'* means inside or within.[1]

At the onset of Jesus' ministry in Nazareth, Jesus proclaimed His anointing to preach the gospel to the poor, to proclaim release to the captives, recovery of sight to the blind, to set free those who are oppressed and to proclaim the year of the Lord's favor. (Luke 4:18-19). He then set out and physically performed many healings and miracles to display that the power of God had come upon the Hebrew people.

He did not heal everybody physically. The healings were a foretaste of the spiritual healing that was to come from His death on Calvary and His ensuing resurrection and that is for everyone who will be given the faith to believe.

In this passage in Matthew, He gives His authority to preach, to heal and deliver to His chosen messengers, the apostles. This authority represented the power of the kingdom of God that Jesus continued to preach throughout His earthly ministry. The physical manifestation of all of those healings and deliverances represented the spiritual deliverance that comes from the receiving of the kingdom of God into a person's life.

It is by His stripes that we are raised from the death of sin into new life in Him. It is by His death, burial and resurrection that we are released from the power of sin, death, hell and the grave. It is by His freely giving His life for us on Calvary that we can freely receive new life. We can be born again with the ability to abide in Him in His kingdom being healed from all our diseases, all our infirmities and delivered from the oppression of evil in our spiritual lives. We can have all of this in Him for Christ, Who is our peace, is peace to those who receive Him. The kingdom of heaven is at hand. Will you walk in His light as He is in the light receiving all that He is and all that He offers to you today? Abiding in Him in His kingdom delivers us from spiritual destruction and keeps us forevermore in His wonderful life giving grace.

June 23rd

How He Provides

"Do not acquire gold, or silver, or copper for your money belts, or a bag for your journey, or even two tunics or sandals, or a staff; for the worker is worthy of his support."   (Matthew 10:9-10)

When Jesus sent his disciples out to deliver people from unclean spirits and to heal them of their sicknesses, He told them not to take any additional clothing or any money of any kind to provide for themselves. Although this is not an extended journey covering a long period of time, it is a journey that would require shelter and food for a period of days, if not weeks.

Scripture should always be viewed within the context…the context of the verse within the chapter, the chapter within the book, the book within the old or the new covenant and the context of the nature of God Himself. Jesus is speaking to His disciples to do something specific in a specific way. Jesus expects them to obey His directives in the way that He has told them. Why are we so very different now than what He originally told His disciples? What has taken over the church that the simplicity of Jesus' directives in the beginning with just twelve men having been freely given authority over unclean spirits and every kind of disease and sickness and that they were to freely give freedom away. They were not to accept any payment for God's service other than the shelter in people's homes and the food that the hosts would provide.

Many men of the cloth throughout time have taken the 'additional' and have proven in false pretense that they deserve it somehow in that God takes care of them just like anybody else in the corporate world and as some preach, better than anybody else. But, that is not what Jesus said. Men, over time, have taken the words of our Lord out of their context and made it to mean what they want it to mean and have profited handsomely as any corporate thief.

Jesus taught His disciples to trust Him for their provision. He has taught that to us all and He has been faithful to His promises. The Word has been given freely. New Life has been given freely. Healing and wholeness, deliverance and peace, they are all free. Trust in Him and freely receive His goodness.

Beware of the wolves in sheep's clothing for they are hirelings, salesmen and marketers who try to sell the Lord's word and work as if it was their own. You will know them by their fruit. We have to continually pray before God in His Spirit that He leads us to a right teaching regarding the provision of spiritual leaders. Church leaders are not CEO's of the corporate world, but some think and act as though they are. Any church leader that presents himself as a CEO is exactly that and should leave the pulpit alone and go and start up his own company. That way he would be telling the truth. The real church of our Lord is His body, not some corrupt group of people who are led by hirelings making the most of every tithe and offering that passes through the offering plate.

Paul stated that the worker is worthy of his hire. It is the 'in between' interpretations that we have seen in the system of the church where some ungodly men have taken advantage of the church for their own gain in order to make a profit off of God and the backs of the people in the ministry.

And then there are other men of God who have lived in lack from the egregious selfishness of the people that they were given to oversee in the spirit. The Holy Spirit is never wrong and the people of God have to submit to the work and power of the Holy Spirit in all things, including their own personal provision and the provision of the spiritual leaders in leadership.

June 24th

A Greeting of Peace

"And into whatever city or village you enter, inquire who is worthy in it; and abide there until you go away. As you enter the house, give it your greeting. And if the house is worthy, let your greeting of peace come upon it; but if it is not worthy, let your greeting of peace return to you." (Matthew 10:12-13)

The disciple's life is not to be a solitary life. He is to be out and about proclaiming and doing the Lord's will. The disciples then were to inquire as they entered the city or village as to who might there be that would be kind to receiving them. They were to ask this before going further into the city so that they would not be going from house to house finding rejection and discord rather peace. Jesus laid out a pretty good plan, didn't He?

It is our responsibility to seek the Lord and acknowledge Him before we do anything, not after we have already failed or have been met with rejection. Too often, we, as believers fail to see the simplicity of His directives to His disciples thinking that we are above and beyond that of those days…but we are not. These directives were given as a plan for us all. Even good business men and women perform a market analysis before they move into a city with their business.

The plan is this: In every city there are worthy receptors of His grace and peace.

We are to inquire who they are before we enter a city or village. If we would obey this first directive, it would save us from so much failure, rejection and discord that our lives would prove to be more fruitful in Him simply because we understood the concept of honoring Him by listening to Him.

How many doors do we have to knock on in disquieted rejection before we seek the Lord of peace and ask Him where the peace dwells in the city? How many hornets' nests do we have to fight off because we didn't get clearance from the gospel of wisdom?

When peace is freely given to you, return it with a smile. God knows our hearts for sure. Peace usually comes with a smile and a handshake or a hug. Let your greeting be one of peace and may your greeting be returned in peace. In this manner, the Lord's Spirit will prevail in your destination and He will be glorified in all that is accomplished there in His name. Bless the Lord!

June 25th

Knowing When to Walk Away

"And whoever does not receive you, nor heed your words, as you go out of that house or that city, shake off the dust of your feet…"   *(Matthew 10:14)*

There is nothing like the feeling of being received, loved and honored. People who honor others well display gifts from God. To honor and receive someone into your home is to respect and offer a peace that passes understanding. Not everyone knows how to do this. Not everyone has the gift of hospitality, but they receive the Lord's work nonetheless. Some folks' hospitality is further along than others, and so is their cooking.

Jesus implored His disciples to seek after peace in the duration of their work. Here, He also implies that there would be instances where the disciples would not be received and neither would their message of the Kingdom of God.

Jesus did not tell them to despise and hate the rejecters. He did not tell them to perform any malice or to display any malcontent upon the homes or cities that refused them and their message. Simply put, if their peace was refused; if their message was rejected; if their persons were not received, then simply shake the dust off of their feet and move on. Jesus exclaimed that the rejecters would be admonished by the Lord. Judgment is solely His. And, as the disciples were deliverers of God's grace, so are we are to be purveyors of His goodness to those whom He sends us to.

When we are met with rejection, we are not to stick around and complain about it or to fight to gain some foothold for ourselves and call our judgmental disposition holy love. We are to leave and leave the resulting judgment to God. He is just and He will perform His judgment and His grace. We are not the deciders of the future of His children or His enemies.

Be obedient to the call of God in your life. Be the holy priest that He has called you to be. Allow the Holy Spirit to do His work and if His work is rejected, then move on in peace.

June 26th

Sheep, Serpents and Doves

"Behold, I send you out as sheep in the midst of wolves; therefore be shrewd as serpents, and innocent as doves." (Matthew 10:16)

Before sending His disciples out to deliver the message of the gospel of the Kingdom of God, Jesus describes how He wants them to be as they go about Jesus' business of delivering, healing and preaching. He tells them to be as sheep, Luke 10:3, depicts their manner to be as lambs. The mild mannered disposition of a lamb who intends to do no harm to anyone is the manner of spirit here. The warning is explicit, you will be among wolves who will be pleased in persecuting and attempting to devour you, so in your manner of being and doing as you deliver the gospel, it is inherent that the gospel of peace be delivered in peace.

Show yourselves to be shrewd, that is, wise, having the knowledge that even in the midst of speaking grace to the hearers, there will be those who are determined to undermine that which is spoken in love. Persecution comes from within and without; from twisted minds who intend to do harm to the speaker as well as to the message.

If they persecuted and ridiculed the Son, they will certainly persecute His disciples. To be as innocent as a dove is to go about with the internal confidence that what is inside of you, you did not create, but is there abiding in you to be a fountain of living water to a thirsty generation. Do no harm. The gospel of peace and grace comes with power to deliver from wicked forces, power to heal diseases and sicknesses and the power to set people free from the penalty and power of sin. The power is in the Spirit of God and emanates from Him. It is His gospel, not yours. We are to be vessels of grace and peace, moving about as a harmless dove.

Be ever thankful that your names are recorded in heaven, Luke 10:20. Cast all your care upon the Lord. Allow Him to His work through you as you have been freely given, freely give. As you go about, know that you may be treated as a snake, but be wise in your expectations. As you go about, know that you will be confronted from the least likely of souls to the most demonstrative. Do not fear, but be of good courage, He has overcome the world!

June 27th

The Coming Persecution

"But beware of men; for they will deliver you up to the courts, and scourge you in their synagogues; and you shall even be brought before governors and kings for My sake, as a testimony to them and to the Gentiles." (Matthew 10:17-18)

Jesus tells His disciples just how far the persecution will go for them. He foretells all of this that it is most definitely in their future. The persecutors will take their cause to the government so as to quiet the message and eliminate it if they could through court cases, imprisonment and constant aggravation.

All of these things happened to the disciples in time. Each of them were eventually mistreated, persecuted, imprisoned, or killed in some fashion. There is little comfort in receiving such warnings because they trusted Jesus at His word. He was telling them the truth.

In warning them, he wanted them to count the cost of their discipleship. Although His message was freely given, it would be delivered with a very high cost and that would mean their lives.

I thank God for obedient men, servants of the Most High God who were willing to suffer persecution, pain and rejection for the sake of the gospel. I thank God, through Jesus Christ, for His leadership in all these things that He, most of all, suffered for my sake, and for the world, that He destroyed the yoke of the bondage of sin. He destroyed the curse of sin, death, hell and the grave.

Jesus told them in advance what the cost would entail. And, in like manner, He continues to tell us that persecution exists even until today. Be faithful to Him in the Spirit of the Lord. He is faithful, so you be faithful. He alone is good, so allow

His goodness to shine as a Light among men who so desperately need to hear the gospel of the Kingdom of God. He is near. Tell that to all He leads you to tell. The Holy Spirit will convict and comfort Whom He will, so you can rest in Him.

June 28th

Who Does the Speaking?

"But when they deliver you up, do not become anxious about how or what you will speak. For it is not you who speak, but it is the Spirit of your Father who speaks in you." (Matthew 10:19-20)

It is a wonderful thing that when we trust our lives to Jesus Christ, we know that in the laying down of our lives to Him, we are raised in Him. In the gospel of John, Jesus told His disciples to 'abide in Him' with the promise that if we abide in Him, He will abide in us.
We are responsible to do the abiding in Him; that is our part. He will fulfill His promise because He is faithful to His word.

He also told them in John 16:13, that when the Holy Spirit comes, "He, the Spirit of truth, comes, He will guide you into all truth; for He will not speak on His own initiative, but whatever He hears, He will speak; and He will disclose to you what is to come." Jesus not only promised provision of food and shelter, protection and deliverance, He also promised that even the words that they speak will be provided. The Holy Spirit will speak through them what the Father has for them to speak. Amazing! Isn't it?

Do you believe that this was just for then or can it be that our Lord meant this for all of His disciples throughout all of time?

This message was for then and still is. When we dwell in Him and honor Him, He will determine when and what to speak through us. We don't have to make it up nor do we have to be compelled to speak for Him. He is the One who does the speaking which means I don't have to worry about what I'm to say or be afraid of saying the wrong thing. He is that amazing!

Trust in Him as you flow in Him. He has promised to flow through you as fountains of living water. Let your light so shine among men that His Light is expressed to the world that you come in contact with. Trust Him in all things and He will heal, deliver and speak.

June 29th

The Hard Road before You

"And brother will deliver up brother to death, and a father his child; and children will rise up against parents, and cause them to be put to death. And you will be hated by all on account of My name, but it is the one who has endured to the end who will be saved."   (Matthew 10:21-22)

What manner of cause can be ever made from the likes of personal persecution from your own family? How heated does the disdain of the gospel have to be in order to separate the bond of blood to capitulate disagreement? How far have the enemies of Christ gone in order not to hear holy words from a Holy God?

We need to remember that Jesus Christ told His disciples to be as sheep, harmless as doves, but wise as a serpent. There will be persecution, but under this admonition, do not go out and cause your own pain by being hateful and spiteful as you communicate the gospel of peace. I have seen it when Christians cause their own destruction by how they handle, or mishandle other people. Then, when the persecution comes, it comes from vengeful retribution towards the person just for being hateful. This is not to be! We are not to be harmful to people when communicating the gospel of grace. Let the words we speak be the words of the Spirit.

Trouble will come soon enough for the person who delivers the kindness of the Lord. There are those who truly disdain that which is holy. They do not believe in God and do not intend on ever believing. Nor do they want anyone within their listening range to hear the gospel either. Trust Jesus Christ, there will be trials and tribulations. But also trust Him that He is guiding you into all truth. That is, if you have completely submitted to Him.

The promise that He gives is for all of time. The encouraging promise is that the one who has endured to the end will be saved! Be faithful unto death, neither fear nor tremble, the Lord God is with you forevermore. Bless the Lord God Almighty!

June 30th

Follow the Lord

"But whenever they persecute you in this city, flee to the next; for truly I say to you, you shall not finish going through the cities of Israel, until the Son of Man comes." (Matthew 10:23)

There are a couple of things here that our Lord had told His disciples. Whenever they are persecuted, do not stand around and fight against the persecution. Many folk have interpreted standing as standing their ground. It is not your ground. He told us to flee, not get into a battle over turf or words or for any reason. Let the persecutors have their domain for it is not the domain of the Lord. As He said He will do, He will punish those who refuse His testimony.

God used the persecution of the messengers to the Jews to fulfill the taking of the message first to the House of Israel, then to the Gentiles. They were to go into all of the cities of Israel and speak the Good News. The disciples had to be obedient to the call. He empowered them to do so and gifted them with the power to perfume many spiritual miracles in His Name. Their obedience in all these things was a necessity even in the face of severe persecution, trial, and danger. They had to speak healing, speak the Kingdom message and move on.

Let's stop here and take note of our own commission. If you name the Name of Jesus Christ, you are not exempt from spreading the Good News of the gospel of the Kingdom of God. You are not exempt from persecution or trial or tribulation. We have all been warned about it in His Word for it has come and will continue to come no matter how sweet we think we may have been to someone, the persecution comes because of an antichrist spirit. We do not have to take persecution personally and have ourselves wallow in defeat. Do not look for your own success or for people to love you because you are expressing the Spirit of God. If they attack you for His Name's sake, they are attacking Him.

As Jesus Christ bore suffering through rejection, sorrow, mocking, beatings and death by crucifixion, we who are called to follow Him are to follow Him all the way on whatever road He has placed us on. Be thankful you are called to be His.

July 1st

He Knows

"A disciple is not above his teacher, nor a slave above his master. It is enough for the disciple that he become as his teacher, and the slave as his master. If they have called the head of the house Beelzebul, how much more the members of his household! Therefore do not fear them, for there is nothing covered that will not be revealed, and hidden that will not be known." (Matthew 10:24-26)

As we have stated earlier, all of the miracles, healings and deliverances that Jesus performed were very specific with very specific people. All that He did, He did for a reason and all that He did, He did for the glory of God. The Kingdom of God was preached in every event and in every story. The same is true for His suffering.

Jesus foretold of the disciples suffering because it was going to happen, and it did. Here, Jesus refers to the event when the Pharisees said that Jesus cast out demons by the power of Beelzebul and in like manner, the disciples will fall under the same accusation. They were to deliver people from evil spirits, what do you think the naysayers were thinking when they saw demonic spirits come out of people? You see, Jesus delivered people from evil and the evil was seen in the convulsing. What the eyes see that do not see is the evil being revealed rather the deliverance taking place. Resentful accusations were always around Jesus and so it would be for His disciples.

Jesus was explaining here that whatever He encountered, His disciples would encounter the same. We are not exempt from his suffering.

Christians think that Jesus has already done all of the suffering so they don't have to, but that is misguided and misleading. Christ died once for all for the penalty of sin, to save the world from its sin. When we, as disciples, deliver the message of Truth, we will encounter whatever Jesus encountered. We are not above our Master. As Jesus said, He already knows all things for there is nothing covered that will not be revealed.

What desperate men do to His disciples, no matter how secret they think they may be in their transgressions and their depravity; whatever is done in the dark will eventually be shown in the light. "'Vengeance is Mine', says the Lord," trust Him in that. Have faith and do not fear for He has overcome the world.

July 2nd

Fearless Obedience

"What I tell you in the darkness, speak in the light; and what you hear whispered in your ear, proclaim upon the housetops. And do not fear those who kill the body, but are unable to kill the soul; but rather fear Him who is able to destroy both soul and body in hell."   (Matthew 10:27-28)

The hearing disciple is the disciple whose ear is able to hear, quick to listen and slow to speak, but speak when he/she must. The listening disciple is the disciple whose ear is bent to the Lord and Master and is ready to obey. The obedient disciple is the one whom He knows has been with Him and hears His voice for His sheep know His voice and are in tune with Him. The readied disciple is the disciple who is filled with the Holy Spirit and as Isaiah 30:21 says, "And your ears will hear a word behind you, 'This is the way, walk in it,' whenever you turn to the right or to the left."

When we have spent time with the Lord, we recognize His voice, speaking to us and giving the words for us to say. When we abide in Him and Him in us, rivers of living water will flow through us to ears that need to hear of His grace and mercy, the Good News that the Kingdom of God is at hand. This is His nature, that we become vessels of Truth, not just for ourselves in ourselves, but vessels of Truth for the world to hear His gospel.

Be obedient to what He says. Not every person is the same and not every situation will call for the same words. There is no formula to being a witness save the nature of the Christ and His Holy Spirit working through you to someone who needs healing, deliverance or faith.

Do all that you do for the glory of God without fear for He goes before you in all things and through all things. I have to admit that I have been afraid at times and at other times I've simply been too lazy or reluctant to be obedient to the Lord's call in saying something to someone who needs to hear from the Lord. I have become unsure or just downright disobedient to His call and I am the one who has missed the blessing of faith and the reward of obedience. Say, 'No more!'

We all can be the effervescent breath of God through abiding in Him, recognizing His voice, hearing Him and releasing Him into the lives that so desperately need Him. Be faithful even as He is faithful. Be willing, even as He wills Himself to care for you and not only that, but to care for others through you!

July 3rd

He Knows You

"But the very hairs of your head are all numbered. Therefore do not fear; you are of more value than many sparrows."   (Matthew 10:30-31)

The word of the Lord came to Jeremiah, saying, "Before I formed you in the womb I knew you, and before you were born I consecrated you…" (Jeremiah 4-5a) God knows us before we know ourselves. There is a great deal of blessing in the level of intimate love that God has for us. He knows our hearts, our minds, and our prayers before we pray them and yet, we still pray our prayers.

He so cares for you that He gave Himself for you to die on a cross for the sin of the world. His love is beyond anything we can ask or think. Paul exclaimed, "…so that you Christ may dwell in your hearts through faith; and that you, being rooted and grounded in love, may be able to comprehend with all the saints what is the breadth and length and height and depth, and to know the love of Christ which surpasses knowledge, that you may be filled up to all the fullness of God." (Ephesians 3:17-19

"For you formed my inward parts; You covered me in my mother's womb. I will praise You, for I am fearfully and wonderfully made; marvelous are Your works, and that my soul knows very well. My frame was not hidden from You, when I was made in secret, and skillfully wrought in the lowest parts of the earth. Your eyes saw my substance, being yet unformed. And in Your book they were all written, the days fashioned for me, when as yet there were none of them. How precious also are Your thoughts to me, O God! How great is the sum of them! If I should count them, they would be more in number than the sand; when I awake, I am still with You."   (Psalm 139:13-18, NKJV)

Oh, how He knows you and oh, how He loves you. How great is His love for you! Bless the Lord!

July 4th

The Choice to Come

"Everyone therefore who shall confess Me before men, I will also confess him before My Father who is in heaven. But whoever shall deny Me before men, I will also deny him before My Father who is in heaven."   (Matthew 10:32-33)

As we have to know our Lord through abiding in Him, we come to understand His love, mercy and grace. John 1:17 says, "For the Law was given through Moses; grace and truth were realized through Jesus Christ." Although we live under grace and not under the Law, it does not mean that all things are permissible and we can simply sin so that grace can abound all the more. No!

Jesus Christ, knowing that He had called His disciples to Himself, He also knew that they knew they had a choice to follow, or not. Here, He makes it very clear for those who choose to follow Jesus Christ, confession before men is eminent, that is, noteworthy, as well as, imminent, forthcoming…about to happen. We all have a choice in or very near future. Will we confess Jesus Christ before men?

Although we live under grace, do not overestimate your interpretation of grace to mean that Jesus Christ will not do as He said He will do. Jesus Christ is faithful to His word, all of it. The choice will be the test. The test will be for the ones who have said they follow Jesus Christ and in the simplicity or the grandeur of the situation, the answer will be spoken. The test will be simple and may come without notice or warning.

If you name the Name of Jesus Christ as your Lord, then by all means be faithful as He is faithful. Remain in Him and what He has revealed to you in the dark, speak in the light. Tell of His excellent mercy and grace. Speak often of His goodness. Allow Him to be Himself in you as you follow in His will. Allow His will to be done in your life and when the time comes to confess Him before anyone, He will flow from you as a living stream and the joy of the Lord will be your strength now and forevermore.

July 5th

The Grace of Loving God

"Do not think that I came to bring peace on the earth; I did not come to bring peace, but a sword."   (Matthew 10:34)

Jesus tells His disciples the truth. The cost of following Him will cost them everything. Many people believe that if they stand strong in faith concerning their belief in God or country, they might be willing to lay their life down for the cause. But, Jesus Christ makes it very personal in that He warns them that their own family members, their wives and children, will be divided against each other in their love and follow-ship of Jesus Christ.

In the ensuing verses 35-39, Jesus makes it plain that anyone who loves anyone else more than Him is not worthy of Him. Jesus wants all of you; all of your love, your mind, your strength, your body, your soul, your desires, your will. All of that is presented to Him and given over to Him and in return, He will give you eternal life.

The sword that He speaks of is the sword of division. It is His life against the flesh, even flesh and blood. Otherwise, we will be found unworthy, untrustworthy and unreliable. Jesus stated in Mark 12:30, "The foremost is, 'Hear, O Israel! The Lord our God is one Lord; and you shall love the Lord your God with all your heart, and with all your soul, and with all your mind, and with all your strength." This is also in Deuteronomy 6:4.

If all of this sounds too difficult, it may very well be. However, when we have given all to live in Him, we find that He lives His life through us and in that His life, love and grace fills us to overflowing. In fact, if we do not give our all to Him in submission, it is impossible to please Him in anything. But with God, all things are possible. The peace that Jesus Christ brings is spiritual. Spiritual peace is a settled rest in Him. He is our peace. Love Him with all of your heart and allow that love to flow through you to your spouse, your children, your in-laws and all that you meet. Trust Him and let His faithfulness be faithful in you.

July 6th

Be Willing to Lose Your Life

"And he who does not take up his cross and follow after Me is not worthy of Me. He who has found his life shall lose it, and he who has lost his life for My sake shall find it."   (Matthew 10:38-39)

A vicissitude is an unwanted change from the norm. If a person expects that the 'unbecoming' of the self, that is, the life that they know as themselves, is unnecessary or unwanted, then it would stand to reason that the person would not desire to anything to lose the 'self'. However, it is in the 'unbecoming' of ourselves that we see ourselves for who we really are and what we truly are before a holy God.

The person who lives in the realm of the protected state from being released from themselves is actually protecting themselves from the truth of who they truly are and the reality of what truly is. The unbecoming of the self is the exchange of 'what would a man give in exchange for his soul' (Mark 8:37). In Jesus Christ, he obtains eternal life if he does so. Otherwise, he clings to that which will lead to his eternal death, that being his present self. Thus, the seeming vicissitudes of the unbecoming of the self, prevent reality and truth from being sought.

Psalm 139:15-16 (NIV), tells it well when the Psalmist said, 'My frame was not hidden from You when I was made in the secret place, when I was woven together in the depths of the earth, Your eyes saw my unformed body. All the days ordained for me were written in your book before one of them came to be." Our Lord knows who the real you is. The real you is the new creation, born again you and you have to lose what you think you know to be real for what He knows to be real.

Be willing to lose yourself, to take up your cross and follow after Him. Ever-present eternal life is the exchange for your current life. Your self is not destroyed; you simply give up your claim to your rights to it. That's what the cross bought for you; to remove the penalty of sin away from you so that you can have this life evermore. The choice is yours. Choose life, but you have to give up yours in the exchange.

July 7th

The Grace of Receiving

"He who receives you receives Me, and he who receives Me, receives Him who sent Me. He who receives a prophet in the name of a prophet shall receive a prophet's reward; and he who receives a righteous man in the name of a righteous man shall receive a righteous man's reward." (Matthew 10:40-41)

Just to be plain here, if we receive the messenger (ie., the testifier, preacher, pastor, witness, etc.) of Jesus Christ, we are receiving the message of Jesus Christ and His Father who sent Him to deliver the message. If we receive a prophet or a righteous man in the Name of Jesus Christ, we receive the message of Jesus Christ and the reward of it.

But, what is this reward? What is the reward of a prophet or a righteous man?

The reward is this – the gift of eternal life!

It's that simple.

Pray for the laborers in the field, whether they be pastors, teachers, evangelists, witnesses, testifiers of His grace, pray-ers, priests, parents, friends who are made righteous in Him…in the Kingdom of God, we all are ministers of the gospel of grace. There is no hierarchy nor is there any disciple excluded. If you name the Name of Jesus Christ, we are all in this together to give our lives as such that He witnesses to a lost and dying world through us.

If you have given your life to Him, He has received you unto Himself and you have received Him into yourself. The grace of receiving is abundant and overwhelming to the point that the overflow is the result. Pour out what He has poured in and the flow will be constant forevermore.

July 8th

The Gift of Cold Water

"And whoever in the name of a disciple gives to one of these little ones even a cup of cold water to drink, truly I say to you he shall not lose his reward."
(Matthew 10:42)

Sometimes the simplest of things makes all the difference in the world to the loving care of another human being. Taking care of loved ones is what family members should do, but to take care of others in simple tasks, even that does not go unnoticed by our Lord.

Sharing a cup of cold water on a hot day is the very least we can do for someone; to do it in the name of Jesus is being propelled by the Spirit to offer that which is a basic need, albeit voluntarily to another. It is the art of loving kindness shown to one who cannot take care of themselves. We all have our opportunities to help someone, sometimes daily, oftentimes when no one is looking. What we do with our opportunities to aid someone else in the name of our Lord is viewed in heaven and recorded.

"For I was hungry, and you fed me. I was thirsty, and you gave me a drink. I was a stranger, and you invited me into your home. I was naked, and you gave me clothing. I was sick, and you cared for me. I was in prison, and you visited me." (Matthew 25:35-36, NLT)

How these things are recorded, I do not know. But, Jesus makes it clear, the opportunities that we have every day of our lives are more than just opportunities, they are tests of our belonging to and following the Spirit of our Lord. I do not believe that all opportunities are meant to be tests, for they are in the natural course of life, providing the basic of needs. But, they become tests in our hearts when we hesitate to help. When we hesitate, we take a second thought about the opportunity and in those moments of hesitation, we miss the blessing of the Lord upon someone else. In the second thought, the proud will say to themselves, 'I'll be rewarded for this' and that is true, but most likely, the reward will only be in their minds. Do not let your right hand know what the left is doing. Be careful that your motivation to help is not simply to earn a reward.

Jesus' words are profound and yet very simple…to be able to give a basic necessity to a person that is completely unable to return the favor is to be in His nature because He died for the sin of the world and that is something that none of us could do for ourselves.

July 9th

Jesus Preached the Kingdom

"When Jesus finished giving these instructions to his twelve disciples, he went off teaching and preaching in towns throughout the country."
(Matthew 11:1, NLT)

Have you ever wondered what it was that Jesus taught and preached as He went about the countryside? If you've been a Christian for any length of time, then you've heard a few people preach, teach and pray. Is what we hear today what He preached then because, as you well know, the Bible, as we know it in the New Testament, didn't literally exist at the time. It was being performed so that it could be recorded and written down for us to know.

Matthew 4:17, says, "From then on, Jesus began to preach, 'Turn from your sins and turn to God, because the Kingdom of Heaven is near." In verse 23, it says, "Jesus went about Galilee, teaching in the synagogues, preaching everywhere the Good News about the Kingdom." (NLT).

All of the words of Jesus Christ were what He was preaching. He was consistent with His message. It was the same message that the Lord God had given John the Baptist, 'Repent, for the Kingdom of God is at hand.' All of the healings, miracles and corollary events were illustrations to His teachings. He came to heal the sick spiritually, so He healed the sick in the natural. He came to open the eyes of the spiritually blind, so He healed the physically blind to sight. He came to set the captives free, to set at liberty those who were in bondage, so He freed people from their demonic spirits. He came to preach the day of the Lord that was the Kingdom of God appearing. (Luke 4:17-19)

Mark 1:14-15, says, "Later on, after John was arrested, Jesus went to Galilee to preach God's Good News. 'At last the time has come!' he announced. 'The Kingdom of God is near! Turn from your sins and believe this Good News!'" (NLT) That was Jesus' message; the Kingdom of God is the Good News. Whether he went to the countryside or into the synagogues, He went about preaching, healing and delivering folk from the bondage of imprisonment. He set people free from whatever had them bound.

This is the awesome news of God's grace! That is to be our message of grace today. The curse of sin was broken at the cross, so we can preach to set the captives free from whatever has them bound. Preach the Good News of the gospel of the Kingdom for the entrance is at the cross and His Life in the Kingdom is forevermore!

July 10th

Power in His Preaching

"Now when John in prison heard the works of Christ, he sent word by His disciples, and said to Him, 'Are You the Expected One, or shall we look for someone else?' And Jesus answered and said to them, 'Go and report to John what you hear and see...'" (Matthew 11:2-4a)

Jesus answered John's disciples' questions with known facts. The Messiah was to preach and do certain things, so He answers, "This is what has been accomplished." Then, he proceeds to list the types of healings that have been performed. The blind receive their sight, people are beginning to see, the lame walk, those who could not help themselves in the spirit are raised to walk with the Lord, the lepers are cleansed, those that are the worst of the sick wherein there is no healing, have been healed. The deaf hear, ears and eyes have been opened to the Gospel of God; people can now hear with open ears to be set free, and the poor in spirit, those who have nothing, have the Gospel preached to them. That was His answer to John's question, 'Are you the One?'

Oh, that we would recognize the power of Jesus Christ and the authority, not only that He had, but that we have seen where He shared His authority with His disciples for them to go and do as He did. Praise the Lord God Almighty for great and marvelous are His deeds to mankind!

The power in His preaching was in the obedience He had to His Father. He spoke only what the Father told Him to speak. He spoke with authority and His actions spoke for themselves. All of the forces of nature were under His command. Any disease or sickness fell at His feet. Any force of the spirit realm moved when He said move. Any force of the realm of the known atmosphere, the wind, the waves, the air, the sea, all listened and obeyed His command.

But the marvelous power of His grace was the most powerful of all, for people had their eyes and ears opened to a message of deliverance that none had ever heard before. He set the captives free from themselves and the power of sin, now that's the power of the One and Only Messiah!

July 11th

More Than a Prophet

"And as these were going away, Jesus began to speak to the multitudes about John…"   (Matthew 11:7a)

Malachi 3:1 says, "Behold, I send My messenger, and he will prepare the way before Me. And the Lord, whom you seek, will suddenly come to His temple, even the Messenger of the covenant, in whom you delight. Behold, He is coming," says the Lord of Hosts."

This reference is attributed to the messenger, John the Baptizer, who had found himself in prison at the hands of Herod Antipas for speaking out against Herod for taking his brother's wife. John was soon beheaded at the behest of the woman's daughter when Herod had vowed to give her anything she wanted. (Matthew 14:1-10)

Jesus' words concerning John were most befitting honor and deep respect. Jesus said of John that he was more than a prophet (v.9), that there was not anyone greater born among women (v.11), that he himself is Elijah, who was to come (v. 14). At the news of John's beheading, in Matthew 14:13-21, Jesus withdrew from the people to be by Himself on a boat, only to come out with such compassion as to heal the multitudes of their sick and then feed the hungry crowds with five loaves and two fish. Jesus had honor and deep respect for a man who was more than a prophet and who was broken for proclaiming the message of the Kingdom of God.

John the Baptist, who baptized in the Jordan River those who repented of their sins, exemplified the dying of the self by baptizing into the river of death and being raised again into new life. Yes, indeed, he was more than a prophet for the spirit of Elijah had come to be the messenger, the forerunner of the Messiah. Have you ever found yourself in the path of obedience to the point where you would be willing to lose it all for the sake of Jesus Christ? I have not found many on that road. At times, I see my own weaknesses and do not follow through in obedience. What does it take for a man to be so lost in Jesus Christ that he will obey the Lord in giving all? That time is coming and now is that the testimony of the faithful ones be as faithful as the man who was more than a prophet.

Revelation 2:10 says, "Do not fear any of these things which you are about to suffer. Indeed, the devil is about to throw some of you into prison, that you may be tested, and you will have tribulation ten days. Be faithful unto death, and I will give you the crown of life."

July 12th

The Prophet Obeys

"Truly I say to you, among those born of women there has not arisen anyone greater than John the Baptist; yet he who is least in the kingdom of heaven is greater than he."   (Matthew 11:11)

It is told in the Gospel according to Luke that an angel appeared to a certain priest named Zacharias that a son would be born to him and his wife, Elizabeth, and that the child would grow up being filled with the Holy Spirit, "For he will be great in the sight of the Lord, and shall drink neither wine nor strong drink. He will also be filled with the Holy Spirit, even from his mother's womb. And he will turn many of the children of Israel to the Lord their God. He will also go before Him in the spirit and power of Elijah, 'to turn the hearts of the fathers to the children,' and to turn the disobedient to the wisdom of the just, to make ready a people prepared for the Lord." (Luke 1:15-17, NKJV)

John bore the fragrance of the Holy Spirit in his life for he was the epitome of self-denial in truth and spirit. What people heard was the way of the Lord. He possessed the fragrance of the anointing of God. Many people today declare themselves to bear that same fragrance of anointing. I question it. For a lot of what I have seen today, the folk claiming the anointing of God do not follow as John did in obedience to the Lord. John exemplified the fragrance of the denial of self, just as Jesus preached and exemplified in His life to His heavenly Father. This is the Presence and Power of the Holy Spirit at work in a life given over to Him.

John's father, Zacharias prayed to the Lord, "And you, child, will be called the prophet of the Highest; for you will go before the face of the Lord to prepare His ways, to give knowledge of salvation to His people by the remission of sins." (Luke 1:76-77, NKJV)

John the Baptist was ordained before his birth to preach the gospel of the Kingdom of God and the repentance of sins. He did all that he was ordained of the Lord to do and Jesus, His Lord, spoke well of him in saying that there was not a man born of women that was greater than him. Jesus spoke, 'yet he who is least is the kingdom of heaven is greater than he.' The least is the greatest of denial and the greatest of denial came in the form of our Savior, Jesus Christ.

It is here that we come to a clearer understanding of what true greatness is in the Kingdom of God. There is One great and that is our Lord God. Jesus humbled Himself and came in the form of a servant. So, no matter what can be said of John the Baptist, John knew himself in his own life before His heavenly Lord, that he was not even worthy to untie His sandals. And, in like manner, neither are we. In our own humble submission to our Lord, we must recognize that He is Lord. John was completely humble to the point of perfect obedience in purpose, task and death. May we be so profoundly obedient in the Spirit, ever-filled in Him.

July 13th

One Way into the Kingdom

"And from the days of John the Baptist until now the kingdom of heaven suffers violence, and violent men take it by force."   *(Matthew 11:12)*

It is imperative that we take individual verses of scripture within their context in order that we would not take the verse out of context to make it mean what we want it to mean so that it fits our philosophies rather than the Truth of God. It has been said of this verse that since 'violent men take the kingdom of God by force', then it's ok to act violently when 'taking' the kingdom of God for ourselves. There is no truth in this concept for it is entirely antithetical to the context and to the nature of God. The inaccurate interpretation of this particular verse has fueled many a crusade and has, because of the false interpretation, revealed who has a clear understanding of the Kingdom and who doesn't. Still today, there are false teachings and beliefs on this verse because men and women ignorantly teach that this kingdom has a present earthly manifestation and that one can violently take the kingdom by force. This is false teaching derived from ignorance that coincides with an internal misunderstanding and immaturity as to the root of violence. Men who preach peace, yet condone violence have an antichrist spirit within.

John the Baptist came preaching, beginning with the Jews first, "Repent, for the Kingdom of God is at hand." Repentance had ordinarily been for Gentiles in order that they might be converted to Judaism, so the baptism was for the Gentiles. The Jews saw themselves as children of God already for their father was Abraham.

In this, they had no need of repentance of anything. The Jews presumed that the Kingdom of God was an earthly kingdom and that the Messiah would come to free them from the Roman rule with an earthly army. Hence, violence would have been the way for the earthly kingdom to come to fruition. The kingdom would have been taken for themselves, by themselves in a violent war, but that is not the true Kingdom of God that John came preaching about; neither was it the Kingdom that Jesus ushered in with His Holy Presence.

The key to understanding the Kingdom of God is to be absolutely certain that this kingdom is a spiritual kingdom and can only be entered by the blood of Jesus Christ. Jesus said that He was the way, the truth and the life and that no man can get to the Father except through Him. He also said that no man could enter the kingdom unless he was born again. All of this and all of the rest of Jesus' teachings were of the spiritual kingdom that does not come with observation, that is, it does not come about by the life and work of men, 'but is within you', placed there by the indwelling Presence of the Holy Spirit. (Luke 17:20-21)

The spiritual habitation of a life given to the Lord will be the habitation of the Holy Spirit, for we are the 'temple of the Holy Spirit'. (1 Corinthians 6:19-20) We enter this kingdom of grace by His grace and by His grace alone. Jesus Christ did all of the work for us on the cross as our substitution for our sins. Yes, we must repent. Yes, must give our lives to Him. And the wonderful exchange of a life given completely to Him is that He takes us and gives us new life in Him. His life, then, is lived through us in the Presence and power of the Holy Spirit. Submission and obedience is preeminent and never violence.

July 14th

All in God's Plan

"For all the prophets and the Law prophesied until John. And if you care to accept it, he himself is Elijah, who was to come." (Matthew 11:13-14)

Jesus confirms that John the Baptist is Elijah, the prophet prophesied to come to usher in the day of the Messiah, "Behold, I am going to send you Elijah the prophet before the coming of the great and terrible day of the Lord. And he will restore the hearts of the fathers to their children, and the hearts of the children to their fathers, lest I come and smite the land with a curse." (Malachi 4:5-6) The angel of the Lord who spoke to Zacharias, John's father, before John's birth, said, "And it is he who will go as a forerunner before Him in the spirit and power of Elijah..." (Luke 1:17a)

This is all a part of the plan of God that had been foretold by the prophets and the Law. Most do not see the plan of God in the Law, but it is there. Everything that occurred in the Old Testament is recorded there for very specific purposes, some known only to God, but are there for God's purposes in leading us all through time to the end of time. What we know of the Old Testament is a foreshadowing of things that were to come and things still yet to come. God knows the end from the beginning. "Now we who have believed have entered that rest, just as God has said, 'So I declare on oath in my anger, they shall never enter my rest.' And yet his work has been finished since the creation of the world." (Heb. 4:3, NIV). "He (the Christ) was chosen before the creation of the world, but was revealed in these last times for your sake." (1 Peter 1:20, NIV) Again, the Lord knows the end from the beginning, "And all who dwell on the earth will worship it (the beast), everyone whose name has not been written before the foundation of the world in the book of life of the Lamb that was slain." (Rev. 13:8, RSV). "Even as He chose us in him before the foundation of the world, that we should be holy and blameless before Him." (Eph. 1:4, RSV)

God, who knows all in His infinite wisdom, proclaimed truth in His word whether it was spoken by a prophet or was written by the hand of Moses, David, or others. God has been speaking for thousands of years and is still speaking today through that same word. God is the same, yesterday, today, and forever. His message of hope, mercy, grace and forgiveness is the message of the eternal kingdom, not written on stone, but written on the hearts of men, that we would come into the fellowship of His grace.

Our Father is omnipresent, always present throughout the ages everywhere. Our Father is omniscient, the all-knowing One, who knows all since before time began. Our Father is omnipotent; He is the One and only all-powerful One who has all power at His command. If you are reading this, and you have given your life to Him, then you are a part of His plan. Thank Him today for allowing you to be a part of Him and thank Him that He has life in you. God loves us with an everlasting love that never fails and never ends. If you care to accept Him, you are a part of His plan and your name is written in the Lamb's book of life. Give Him praise!

July 15th

He Who Has Ears to Hear

"He who has ears to hear, let him hear." (Matthew 11:15)

This saying that Jesus used was used quite frequently enough that He would say it in order that those who were given to spiritual understanding would perceive that it would only be understood with spiritual ears. Those who had not been given the spiritual perception would not hear it in the way of understanding. This principle continues to exist today. The Holy Word can be read, taught, listened to, and proclaimed with a high degree of proficiency of knowledge and still not be understood because it is only understood in the power and illumination of the Holy Spirit. Many people over the centuries have often quoted the Bible as if they wrote it themselves, but their quotes are only head knowledge, not a matter of the heart. For the word to be written on the heart of a man, the Holy Spirit is the only one who can write it there.

Jesus told His disciples, when they did not understand the parables that He taught, the reason He taught using parables. "And when he was alone, those who were about him with the twelve asked him concerning the parables. And he said to them, 'To you has been given the secret of the kingdom of God, but for those outside, everything is in parables; so that they may indeed see but not perceive, and may indeed hear but not understand; lest they should turn again, and be forgiven.'" (Mark 4:10-12, RSV)

Not everyone is going to hear and understand the gospel of the kingdom. Not everyone is going to enter the Kingdom of God, but only those who are given to the life of salvation through the blood of the Lamb. He who has ears, let him hear. Only he who has been given the Spirit of life can grasp the notion of understanding. The writer of the Proverbs was right when he said, 'in all thy getting, get understanding.' (Proverbs 4:7)

"The Lord is not slow about his promise as some count slowness, but is forbearing toward you, not wishing that any should perish, but that all should reach repentance." (2 Peter 3:9, RSV) The Lord came that all might have life and that, to the fullest. He loved the world so much that He gave His Son that as many who would believe, would believe in the Lord Jesus Christ. If you name the Name of Jesus Christ, then pray for your loved ones to come under the conviction of the Holy Spirit. Pray not just for your loved ones, pray for your enemies as well. Pray for those who use you and persecute you. Pray for those in leadership over you. Pray for those in authority. Pray for the day of salvation to dawn in those you see and hear. Pray the Holy Spirit to come and dwell in the hearts of men and women everywhere.

Get out of your comfort and pray for others' ability to hear. The Holy Spirit is the one who convicts the world of sin, of righteousness, and of judgment. Pray for the eyes and ears to be opened to hear the Good News of grace so that the world may know Him in the wonder of His love…pray for ears to be opened!

July 16th

That Which Justifies

"But wisdom is justified by her children." (Matthew 11:19b, KJV)

In the beginning of John the Baptist's ministry, of all of the things the Jewish leaders could say about John that had come neither eating nor drinking, was that he had a demon. Of all of the things those same leaders could say about Jesus, at the time, was that he came eating and drinking and that he was a glutton and a drunkard. The Jewish leaders were already losing their following and were trying to maintain some semblance of leadership, but lacked righteousness, compassion, and truth. They were mean-spirited and jealous. Do you realize the results of jealous and mean-spirited behavior?

We can know through the words of Jesus that we are not to judge others. And, ever how we choose to judge others in spite of the warning not to, we will most definitely be judged. Whatever we send around the corner at someone is going to come back in the same manner when it comes to judging others. I am uncertain what it is about human nature that desires to pretend to know what is in another person's heart. I do not understand why we think we can determine the motives of other people when we haven't even discussed matters of the heart with them. And even then, we are left with a tremendous amount of uncertainty about someone's motives.

Judgment is sure. It is as sure as you are reading these words. What a person is in the matter of the heart, we do not know. Stop acting like you know, you don't. The Jewish leaders, out of their jealous anger, criticized John and Jesus, but didn't know them, nor did they understand their motives or purpose. Are we so adept at understanding that we can know another man's purpose? Can a man know another man's heart? "For who knows a person's thoughts except their own spirit within them? In the same way, no one knows the thoughts of God except the Spirit of God." (1 Corinthians 2:11, NIV)

Jesus says that wisdom is justified by her deeds, her children, the results of the actions and the results of the thoughts inside the man. "You will know them by their fruit," He has said regarding our leaders. Good fruit comes from good trees and bad fruit comes from bad trees. This is not just for leaders, but for all of us. People have a tendency to try you before they understand you. The tendency of some folk is to believe they have a right to judge, but they don't. Do not judge people. Discern in your spirit the end fruit, but if you don't see the fruit yet, wait. If there's something suspicious, pray, you could be wrong. Pray for your friends and pray for your enemies. Pray for your leaders and those in authority over you.

Pray and never cease to pray. The Holy Spirit will illuminate your mind and heart to the type of fruit. Wisdom is justified by her children. Pray for wisdom and be humble in your prayers for you do not know another man's heart. Pray in holy love for others are watching you just the same. Be found in Him and not with the hypocrites.

July 17th

The Reward of the Unrepentant

"Then He began to reproach the cities in which most of His miracles were done, because they did not repent." (Matthew 11:20)

As Jesus had gone about the cities and countryside preaching repentance, the Kingdom of God and performing miracles nothing had been done in a closet. Most of the people, who were in the vicinity of the cities He mentions, had heard of Jesus and His miracles of healing, cleansing lepers, and exorcising demons from people. He mentions the cities of Chorazin, Bethsaida, and Capernaum because He knew who had repented of their sins and who had not. We have to always remember that God knows our hearts and even if we try to fake our religion, we can never fake God. It was Jesus who emphatically stated that the judgment of God is eternal hell.

Yes, there is a definite judgment against those who choose not repent of their sins. When God, in Christ, came preaching for people to repent, He ushered His message in with incredible and never before seen miracles of healing. He states explicitly what other cities in the past would have done, including the horrific sinful city of Sodom, if they heard seen the miracles that had been performed, and that is, they would have repented just by observing the miracles.

People have to realize and recognize when God has arrived in their midst. And when the Holy God arrives in your own city, the first and foremost thing you could do is to repent of your own unworthiness, your sins, your wicked heart. For the cities of peoples to not recognize the arrival of an extraordinary and uncommon visit from God is inexcusable. We are the same. We get so extremely busy and preoccupied that if an angel of the Lord was standing right in front of us, most folk would keep moving on in their self-absorbed lives.

It is so vitally important for us to take the words of Jesus to heart and repent of anything that is not like Him. Change your mind, walk in the Light as He is in the Light. Turn your hearts toward Jesus and keep them stayed in Him. Then, when the time comes for a miracle to occur, you will surely know it's from Him and will be able to glorify Him immediately with the fruits of repentance. Being in the Presence of the Holy One is a miracle in itself in that we are not burned up from the all-consuming fire. Acknowledge the Lord on your knees and bow reverently to His mercy. The cares of this world will very soon fade away, but the miracle of knowing Him lasts forever. Amen!

July 18th

The Revelation of the Lord

"At that time Jesus answered and said, 'I praise Thee, O Father, Lord of heaven and earth, that Thou didst hide these things from the wise and intelligent and didst reveal them to babes." (Matthew 11:25)

When Christ was preaching the Kingdom, He knew then that it was God alone that illuminated the hearts of men to repentance. The revelation of the Lord is from the Lord Himself. No man can come to the Lord, lest the Lord draw Him. "…no one can say 'Jesus is Lord' except by the Holy Spirit." (1 Corinthians 12:3, ESV)

It is the work of the Holy Spirit to convict the world of sin, judgment and righteousness. (John 16:8-13). Jesus was filled with the Holy Spirit so when He preached the Kingdom, it was the work of the Holy Spirit moving on the hearts of men and women to repent. Repentance doesn't come with simple knowledge; it simply is not understood on the cognitive level. As Jesus clearly states, our Father hides these things from the intelligent and the wise. Essentially, those who come to know the Lord in repentance and faith come to know Him by the revelation of the Spirit of God drawing men to Him, not the fanciful preacher, pastor, or bishop. They hear the Good News of grace audibly from these men and witnesses, but it is the work of the Holy Spirit to convict the world of sin and lead men to righteousness. If this fact does anything for the preacher man, it alleviates him of any responsibility of 'saving' people himself, because the preacher man does not have the power to save. Only Jesus saves.

Here we can be thankful that if we name the Name of Jesus Christ, we have been led of the Holy Spirit into new life in Him. He is the One who makes us born again. (John 3). Thank God, then, that your names are written in the book of life for your life begins in the new birth and then…it never ends! You have been given eternal life from Him; it is the gift of God, by faith, not of works, lest any man should boast. (Eph. 2) Bless the Lord at all times and with your mouth give Him praise. He is worthy and He, alone, is worthy. His grace endures forevermore and His loving kindness is forever. This is pure joy in the Holy Spirit for it is He who has made and not, we, ourselves. Praise the Father with me, He is the Lord of heaven and earth, praise His Name forever!

July 19th

The Will of the Father

"Yes, Father, for thus it was well-pleasing in Thy sight."
(Matthew 11:26)

It is the Father's will to whom the way of the Lord is revealed. The way of the Lord and the revelation of the Lord are only revealed by the Lord Himself and in this present time, this way is revealed by the Holy Spirit. Men may preach, witness, teach, cajole, or even try to coerce men and women into believing the way of the Lord, but it is the Lord who does the revealing, convicting, illuminating, and leading people to Himself.

"All things have been handed over to Me by My Father; and no one knows the Son, except the Father; nor does anyone know the Father except the Son, and anyone to whom the Son wills to reveal Him." (Matt. 11:27) The work of the Father, Son, and Holy Spirit is the will of the same. How can we understand the unity of the tri-unity? Can a man understand the will of the Father in completeness? The Son does the will of the Father and the Holy Spirit does the will of the One Who sent Him. And, no one knows anything without the current day revealing of the Holy Spirit. We are indeed limited by what we can know and relate to in the Spirit. "Above all, you must realize that no prophecy in scripture ever came from the prophet's own understanding." (2 Peter 1:20, NLT)

"How wonderful to be wise, to analyze and interpret things. Wisdom lights up a person's face, softening its harshness." (Ecc. 8:1, NLT)

Our Father is so wonderful that He doesn't leave His work completely up to us. We fail Him terribly at times, but He is always faithful to Himself and His Word. That is wonderful indeed. The word of the Lord is more powerful than any two-edged sword and when the word of the Lord gets into us in the power of the Holy Spirit, we catch a glimpse of Him in us and we begin to understand His glory in all matters. In the denying of ourselves and our own understanding, His way is enabled to operate with full vitality. It is our duty to get out of the way for His way to be made known in our minds and hearts first. Selfishness has to go. Self-indulgence into personal knowledge has to go. The hardness of hearts and the hardness of our personalities will melt in His Presence where there is no room for the pride of man.

In our submitting to Him and His revealing Holy Spirit, we see us for who we are and see Him for Who He is in us. It is time to be undone in His Presence and pray to be completely immersed into the Holy Spirit. The way of man is natural, but the way of the Lord is Divine. Seek Him while He may be found, He will show you the Way. If His way is not evident, watch and pray for prayer is your work in Him and to wait on Him is evidence of submission to His way.

July 20th

Come to Me

"Come to Me, all who are weary and heavy laden, and I will give you rest."
(Matthew 11:28)

'Come to Me, voluntarily, willingly, and not under coercion.' Be willing to submit and acknowledge Him as Lord of the heavens and the earth and that includes you and me. Come…stay with Him, not just for a visit, or a visit to a church service… come and stay. Be resolute in your determined appreciation for who He is for He is willing that none should perish and that includes you and me.

This is for all who are weary and heavy laden. This is for the overworked, the stressed out, the worriers, the manipulators and the wasters of time. We have been given so much time to live in this earth and only God knows our limitations of time that He has placed upon us. Don't blow it! Don't let the cares of this world choke the joy out of you or worse, choke you to death. If the seed of the word has been planted in you, go to Him for nourishment, replenishment, and feeding. He is our daily bread and our living water.

Stop the churning consternation of thoughtful worries and trust in Him. He, the Lord of all creation has come to give you rest. Stop saying, 'What if…' Stop the madness of the 'But they said…' Stop the overdose of busyness that you have control over. You do not have control over your circumstances, but God, in prayer, can change you to work through your circumstances in peace and rest. There is no greater power in heaven or on the earth that is greater than Him and yet we seem to rely on our own wits most of the time thinking that our way is the best way and each time we find that it wasn't. Then, we're left with, "Well, if I'd only done this or only done that, then such and such would have happened." What does it take for us to come to the end of ourselves and go to Him for rest?

"I will give you rest" is a promise from God above. We can be certain of God in Jesus Christ that He will do what He says He will do. He is faithful and because He is faithful, the rest that He promises is above and beyond anything that we could ask or think. His rest is internal. He is His rest dwelling on the inside of us keeping us in Him. True freedom is spiritual. True liberty is spiritual abundance in holy peace. The world around us can be going in circles of craziness, but in Him, we don't have to join in the fray. He sets us free to rest no matter what the circumstance.

Rest in Him for His rest is internal and eternal. His rest is free of stress and abounding in joy. Come to Him, He's waiting…

July 21st

The Disposition of the Humble

"Take My yoke upon you, and learn from Me, for I am gentle and humble in heart; and you shall find rest for your souls." (Matthew 11:29)

Jesus had said earlier that no man could truly know Him unless the Father revealed Him to him. Here, Jesus is expressing what He is truly like; He is gentle and humble in heart. We can always listen to Jesus when we want to really know what He was like on the earth. He came as the humble servant willing to die on a cruel cross the sins of the world. Why is it then that we sometimes see church leaders or other Christians who are nothing like what Jesus was in the earth? The disposition of the humble is not the disposition of the prideful or the money grabbers. The disposition of the humble is the disposition of the lowly, the meek, and the servant of the Lord.

This disposition is what Jesus says to take upon your being. Take His yoke, His burden of servitude, but not the burden of service. There are those who would have you be overwhelmed with serving them in the Name of the Lord, sometimes even to death, but that is not what Jesus was saying. There is a huge difference in the disposition of the servant of the Lord and the one who is serving in works.

The servant of the Lord has taken the yoke of the Lord which is His yoke, the yoke that He carries and serves through the vessel of the servant. The other person who dwells in service is simply working for themselves for their own personal gain or someone else's personal gain, thinking that this is the way, but they only get tired and used up for man's glory. This is so, whether it is for their personal glory or the glory of the person they are serving. It's very easy to get manipulated into wrong thinking, so beware of false prophets who want you to work for them in order to fill their coffers for these are treacherous times and abusers of the Word will abuse His followers if they are not fully aware of the fruit of the leader.

Jesus said that He is gentle and lowly in heart. His yoke is easy, that is, not heavy, nor burdensome. The yoke is the yoke of the joining to Him in humble servitude to Him. He dwells within us for His service and it is He doing the work through us, so that we need not grow weary nor faint in His Presence. Humility in servitude is the Divine standard of abiding in Him. He breathes His breath in the power of the Holy Spirit into us and it is His living water that flows through us giving others replenishing life and all the while replenishing us in the process. His life and work are not burdensome. His life in you is peace and rest eternally in Him. He is the carrier of the load of His work and He never tires. So do not fret in Him; be at peace and rest having confidence in Him. He loves you so and abiding in Him is not work anymore than truly loving someone in this earth is work…no, never, but it is a joy to really love someone. He loves us and our response to His love is His love in return. That love is easy, light, and a true joy to behold.

July 22nd

The Purpose of the Sabbath

"At that time Jesus went on the Sabbath through the grain fields, and His disciples became hungry and began to pick the heads of grain and eat." (Matthew 12:1)

As Jesus went about preaching the Kingdom of God, everything He did reflected what He was preaching. Every event recorded has a teaching about the Kingdom of God that we can receive by the revelation of the Holy Spirit. His life was always teaching and no moment was ever wasted on anything that was not of His Father's leading. The preceding word in Matthew 11 was about how His yoke is easy and His burden is light. The word moves from that teaching to Jesus and His disciples walking through the grain fields on the Sabbath day. As they proceed through the grain fields, in their hunger, they lawfully pick heads of grain in order to fill their need to eat. (Deut. 23:25) This was not unlawful according to any of God's laws.

But, according to the Pharisees, Jesus and the disciples had broken the Law, when in effect, they had not, but had broken the oral law of the Pharisees which amounted to a couple of hundred very specific laws that no ordinary man could know, let alone, maintain. Jesus was teaching the ways of God and His intent of the purpose of the Sabbath day.

The purpose of the Sabbath was for it to be a day of rest; that man could work six days and rest on the seventh was beneficial to the workers, as well as, the land and business owners. There was to be no business transacted on that day because the day was to be given as a day to the Lord for rest, worship and praise…a Day of the Lord in honor to Him.

Please take note here that the teaching of the Kingdom of God is spiritual and all of the Words of Jesus are spiritual words. They have to be received with a spiritual heart in order to hear with hearing ears. The word of the Lord gets entangled in men's minds with their words and it is men who convolute the Word with personal expectation and interpretation. Jesus came that we might have life and that, more abundantly. Jesus' life is not about men's words and their overbearing commandments that God did not say or intend. Jesus came to express the Truth in Spirit and the Pharisees oral law had already gone so far off an errant road that they totally misrepresented God and God wanted no part of it. That is why Jesus said that He had not come to abolish the Law, but to fulfill it. Jesus Christ brought the right representation to the Spirit of God and the totality of the Word.

This is our lot as well in that it is the Spirit of God dwelling in us completing His work in us according to His purposes, and not according to the perverted minds of men. Do not be deceived by the works and words of men who do not live according to the Spirit of God. You will know them by their fruit. Worship the Lord in Spirit and in truth in the each and every moment of each and every day; work with accountability and responsibility to your business or employer; rest according to the Spirit of the Lord in right representation to Him. In this, you will know Him and the purpose of the Sabbath will be made real inside of you for He is the Lord of the Sabbath.

July 23rd

The Lord of the Sabbath

"But if you had known what this means, 'I desire compassion, and not a sacrifice,' you would not have condemned the innocent. For the Son of Man is Lord of the Sabbath."   (Matthew 12:7-8)

Religious leaders have a tendency to forget who created what when it comes to the law, commandments, doctrine, dogma, rules, regulations, monetary stipulations, and the list could go on and on with people's expectations of what they believe followers of Christ should do. A true follower of Jesus Christ is a follower of Jesus Christ and has no other loyalty but to Him. Jesus was and is the giver of REST, just as He stated, "…learn from Me, for I am gentle and humble in heart; and you shall find rest for your souls." (Matt. 11:29b)

It is not for us to be so busy with work that we grow weary and tired from the stress of working out a scheme with our work schedule, church schedule, children's school and athletics schedule, leaving no time for family, relaxation, and real rest in the Lord. Jesus came that we might have life and that includes rest! Busyness kills relationships and the first relationship to suffer in the realm of rules, regulations, and busyness is our relationship with abiding in Jesus Christ.

The compassion that our Lord was speaking of is the compassion of holy love, emotional relaxation, relating to our Father and relating to man in favor. Not only does our relationship with our Lord suffer if we stay too busy, our relationship with our spouse and family will suffer because of a lack of energy from misplaced priorities. Jesus said to seek the Lord and His Kingdom first; He is the first priority. Then decide how God is to bless in your relationships, but decide according to the Holy Spirit's leading in your life. Giving time and love to your family is true compassion and a right priority. Being selfless in your compassion towards others is paramount. Too often we're told to sacrifice our time, money, family time, or other things in order to please other people or church leaders to do things for them. Our Lord did not desire for us to sacrifice, but He did desire us to be compassionate.

Jesus is Lord of the Sabbath. Our Lord is the creator of the Sabbath and that allotted time is for rest, worship, relaxation, family, peace, and, again, rest. Learn how to 'be' in Christ. If we can learn how to 'be' in Christ, we will eventually stop all of the doing that really isn't necessary to begin with. Abide in Him, rest in Him, and His wisdom will show you the way in which you should go for His wisdom is always the best so that His purposes are fulfilled in your life and in the lives of your family members. Give the Lord glory and praise!

July 24th

Desiring Compassion

"And behold, there was a man with a withered hand. And they questioned Him, saying, 'Is it lawful to heal on the Sabbath?' in order that they might accuse Him." *(Matthew 12:10)*

We should never be so preoccupied with our misconceptions of others that we deny the love of Jesus inside of us. For many of us, we have been taught so many traditions and rules in our lives that we have a tendency to be more committed to our traditions and religious rules than to human decency. When our Lord stated that He desired mercy and compassion and not sacrifice, we all should have listened to Him for He desires His Spirit to be preeminent in all of life. Read His word for yourself, and pray that the Holy Spirit will illuminate your heart to the truth of His word.

What kind of a man decides the fate of another with made up stipulations and policies that leave out kindness, gentleness, gratefulness, tenderness, and divine love? Surely we can know the fruit of someone who oppresses others with their restrictions, as the religious leaders of the day did. Not even they lived up to all of the laws they created to 'enhance' the Law of God. God is certainly a God of order and authority and there are expectations of His Words that we are to follow and obey, but it is accomplished in the Spirit of the Christ; the holy and divine love of God. Oftentimes, we try to achieve obedience to our perceptions of the Lord at the expense of others, and in so doing, we mistreat and abuse others with malcontent, stress and a rather sulky disposition. This is the power of religion and not the love of God. Be careful of the charges that you make for other people…are we to be ruled by rules or the love of God?

The Kingdom of God does not come with observation, but is within you. If we are born again of His Spirit, then it is His Spirit that dwells within us and the fruit of the Holy Spirit will be exemplified in our actions and speech. Our hearts will be made new in Him, hearts of spiritual love, compassion, gentleness, self-control, kindness, faithfulness, and the like. The heart of God will reside within our hearts as a treasure and we will not be predisposed to choose the letter of the law over the healing grace of another. Grace will take the place of a mean-spirited disposition and the love of God will abound in endless proportions.

Allow the grace of God to take over your life and the Holy Spirit will flow into you and from you in perfect peace. When the time comes, you won't have to ask another person what you should do, but the Spirit within you will lead you to do what needs to be done and say what needs to be said. This is a wonderful place called grace for the life-giver of love will command your days into acts of obedience and love. Then, you will see with the eyes of grace that the man that God has created is of far more value than any other living creature and it is lawful to do good always, especially on the Sabbath. (Matt. 12:12) Mercy commands our compassion to do good to others. He's been so good to us; let Him be good to others as He has been to you.

July 25th

The Healing of the Withered Hand

"Then He said to the man, 'Stretch out your hand!' And he stretched it out, and it was restored to normal like the other." (Matthew 12:13)

We always need to pray to our Lord in seeing that we would see His word as He has inspired it. What the religious leaders saw that Sabbath day was Jesus healing a man with a withered hand in a synagogue, the place of worship and teaching of the Law. Jesus was teaching them that the physical healing of a man was of great value, yes, and it did not matter the time or place that it was done. The religious leaders of the day had placed the Law of God on the people as a burden and a curse and their hearts were restrained against compassion. Jesus thought otherwise.
There are no accidents in the Bible and the events of Jesus' life did not occur by happenstance. Jesus had earlier completed His teaching in the countryside and proceeded to a synagogue on a Sabbath day for many reasons. He was there for worship and for teaching, however, when the man with the withered hand was presented to Him, His loving heart would not allow the man to remain in his condition. The Presence of the Spirit of the Lord desires that we change.

Jesus is still teaching and healing still. He is saying to those who have given their lives to God that the spirit of religion creates dead and lifeless works. As the man with the withered hand, so is religious work without the life of God in it. The hand still exists, but it is no good for purposeful work. The trouble here is to express the intent of God in life here on earth against man's misconceptions of what he has traditionally thought for centuries. What was the purpose of the healing of the withered hand and what did the withered hand represent?

The withered hand represented lifeless work. The Jewish leaders had confounded anyone to work on the Sabbath. Yes, God had given righteous laws concerning the Sabbath, but the leaders created hundreds of laws in addition the word of the Lord. The Sabbath was the withered hand. The Sabbath had become lifeless from religious restrictions.

Too many rules from too many leaders who did not have the heart of God flowing though their veins created a vacuum that suffocated the compassion of God. "But the Pharisees went out, and counseled together against Him, as to how they might destroy Him." (v.14). Man's prideful traditions always trump God in their hearts.

What is it that you do on the Lord's Day? Do you honor the Lord on the seventh day or the first day of the week as is customary for present Christians? Why do you do what you do? What is it that you do that is scriptural and contains the intent of the heart of God in it? These questions are not meant to confuse, but for you to clarify why you do what you do, and only you can do that. The Lord desires compassion and not sacrifice. Remain in His Spirit and He will show you His way that is found only in His word.

July 26th

Jesus Withdrew

"But Jesus, aware of this, withdrew from there. And many followed Him, and He healed them all, and warned them not to make Him known…"
(Matthew 12:15-16)

As the Pharisees went out of the synagogues they took counsel against Jesus for their perception of His disobedience to God in their laws. They sought to destroy Him, but Jesus being aware of this, withdrew from the synagogue, the place of worship and teaching of the Law of God.

Jesus leaves the synagogue and the crowds followed Him for their healing. Have you ever wondered how Jesus healed people? Did He slap them on the forehead and yell at them, 'Be healed!'? Did He touch them in their place of need and squeeze real hard so that whatever ailed them would depart at His squeeze? Did He scream and yell at the demons with a hearty loud voice? Did He wave a wave of His arm and hand over the crowds and all at once they were healed as His arm passed over them? I don't think so. I believe that Jesus looked at every person of need in the eye, one by one, touch by touch, a soft voice for a tender giving of the Spirit of God to another. I do not believe that Jesus had a soft voice, but there is a difference in speaking plainly, directly and softly to an individual that has a tremendous need and having the authority to meet that need in the Spirit. Although the thunder of the Almighty is loud, we are not thunder.

Jesus had to withdraw from the synagogue for the lack of faith, the fullness of restrictions, the mean-spirited leadership, and the coveted lifeless power that the religious leaders so prized. Remember that Jesus was the Son of God, filled with the Spirit of God and the religious leaders did not recognize His Spirit. They unknowingly became the anti-God believing that they were serving God all the while. How confused they were in their pride and self-deception. They thought they were something that God knew they were not.

Who are we and what do we believe about ourselves that only we believe it? Have we deceived ourselves in any of God's word thinking that we are something of

God's plan, but are far from it? Have we ever become an anti-God in someone's life thinking that we were doing God a favor by lording over them with His word without the Spirit of the Word in it? Have we become the man with the withered hand with dead works in need of healing?

"Trust in the Lord with your heart and do not lean upon your own understanding, but acknowledge Him in all your ways and He will direct your paths." (Prov. 3:5-6) Submit to the Lord. Draw near to the Lord while He may be found. Repent of any transgression that you have had against another person. Repent of any way that is anti-God in word or in deed. We are all guilty before the Lord of transgressing against mankind. Seek the Lord, repent, and walk in Him.

July 27th

God's Chosen Servant

"Behold, My servant whom I have chosen; My Beloved in whom My soul is well-pleased; I will put My Spirit upon Him, and He shall proclaim justice to the Gentiles." (Matthew 12:18)

The declaration of the Lord, through Isaiah, the prophet is written here to describe the Lord's chosen servant, Jesus of Nazareth. The Lord's servant is one that the Lord chooses Himself. Jesus was born of the virgin Mary, who was found to be with child by the Holy Spirit. (Matt.1:18)

Immediately after Jesus was baptized by John the Baptist, a voice was heard from heaven saying, 'This is My beloved Son, in whom I am well-pleased.' (Matt. 3:17). "And he saw the Spirit of God descending as a dove…" (Matt. 3:16a). "Then Jesus was led up by the Spirit…" (Matt. 4:1) When Jesus began His ministry, He preached the Kingdom of God 'to the Gentiles' in the regions of Capernaum, Zebulun, and Naphtali, the areas of current day Syria and the surrounding peoples. (Matt. 4:12-17) This is all to fulfill the prophet Isaiah's prophecy of the servant of the Lord's choosing. Nothing that Jesus did was by accident or happenstance, but He was led of the Spirit of God in all things.

Jesus calls us the same and with the same Spirit He calls us to come to Him and take His yoke, His teaching, His love, His obedience, His Spirit upon us and we will never be the same. We can walk on this earth with gift of the Holy Spirit leading us towards the high calling of God upon our lives. The high calling is for every Christian, not just the ones who say they've been called to a specific vocation. Every follower of Jesus Christ has been chosen by Him to follow Him.

"But you are a chosen race, a royal priesthood, a holy nation, a people for His own possession, that you may proclaim the excellencies of Him who called you out of darkness into His marvelous light." (1 Peter 2:9, ESV)

Bless the Lord for His foreknowledge of all things. He is omnipotent; all-knowing. He knows your heart, the number of hairs on your head (Luke 12:7) and you are of far more value than any other creature on the earth (Gen. 1:26, Matt. 6:26, Matt. 10:31). You have been redeemed "with precious blood, as of a lamb unblemished and spotless, the blood of Christ. For He was foreknown before the foundation of the world, but has appeared in these last times for the sake of you who through Him are believers in God, who raised Him from the dead and gave Him glory, so that your faith and hope are in God." (1 Peter 1:19-21)

We have to continually deny ourselves, take up our cross, and follow Him. We are to follow His Spirit in us. In this, He gets all the glory, and whatever He accomplishes through us will always be about Him and never about us.

July 28th

Following Our Lord

"He will not quarrel, nor cry out; nor will anyone hear His voice in the streets… until He leads justice to victory. And in His Name the Gentiles will hope."
(Matthew 12:19, 20b-21)

The plan and purpose of Jesus Christ was for Him to die on a cross for the remission of the sins of the world. He stayed on course throughout His ministry even though the plots and plans of the Pharisees were many and desperate. Throughout His ministry of preaching the Kingdom of God, the healing and deliverance was a part of the preaching, not a separate function. Jesus did not salute Himself, nor did He want anyone to proclaim His designs for He had to keep Himself out of the spotlight in order to fulfill the ministry to its ultimate purpose. He commanded those whom He healed not to mention His name oftentimes after He would heal them. He did not cry His name out in the streets to announce Himself or to defend Himself. His heart was stayed on His Father's will.

When we are called to His course and become followers of Him, it is right representation that we breathe in who He is and who He was while on the earth. We do not have any other standard other than the Word of God that describes Jesus fully. The things that Jesus did, in the Spirit that He did them, is where we find ourselves either following our Lord, or going on our own misconceptions of how we should follow Him, if we ever do. We cannot 'do what Jesus did'. We are not called to do what He did. He completed His purpose in the earth by dying on the cross for humanity and rising again for all eternity. We are not Jesus and only Jesus could do what Jesus did. Here lies the dilemma of thought in the realm we call the natural and the realm He lives in, the spiritual.

Jesus came that we might have life, eternal, abundant, joyful life. This life is lived in the here and now and in the eternal forever. This life that He gives us is a new birth spiritual life. When we submit to Him in faith and are born again in His Spirit, it is His Spirit that we are challenged to abide in because the flesh wars against the spirit. When we abide in Him, He abides in us. It then becomes His Spirit leading us, just as the Holy Spirit led Jesus.

We become true followers of Him when we are being led of His Spirit, not when we are trying to act like Him in the flesh; there is a tremendous difference here in this line of thought, because we cannot 'act like' Jesus. That thought misses the whole point of the Kingdom of God because in that line of thought human Christians are still trying to achieve a spiritual attainment by fleshly means and that doesn't work. Does it?

We do not attain anything by our works. The work of the Holy Spirit is to work in us and we allow Him to flow from us. He does the work. Only the work done in Him will last. He has done the saving, so it is He who does the speaking through us; it is the Spirit's fruit of love, joy, peace, patience, goodness, kindness, gentleness, and self-control that emanates from us when we abide in Him.

July 29th

Demon-possessed, Blind and Dumb

"Then there was brought to Him a demon-possessed man who was blind and dumb, and He healed him, so that the dumb man spoke and saw."
(Matthew 12:22)

The unfortunate soul who was demon-possessed was under satanic influence and was bound up to where he could not see, nor could he talk. I am uncertain if we can even imagine his situation in life. He was brought to Jesus and was completely healed. Before his healing, he had been filled with a demonic spirit that controlled his sight and ability to speak. He could not see nor could he explain. He was completely useless as a man in his present condition. The deliverance and healing by Jesus was swift and effective; He immediately spoke and saw.

For a man to be demon-possessed, he would be possessed by a different kingdom than the kingdom of God, that being the kingdom of satan's domain. Again, as Jesus preached the Kingdom of God, every event that occurred brought significance to the Kingdom being ushered in, not just preached. The domain of satan is carried out by his minions, or demons, and wherever a demon possesses a soul, he has dominion over that soul. This is a Kingdom confrontation and Jesus easily dispossesses the demon. Little by little the forces of darkness are overcome by the Kingdom of Light.

The inability to physically see anything was totally debilitating during that time. The inability to spiritually see anything continues to prevail in people's lives. The Word of God continually prompts us to gain understanding, to seek wisdom, and to see that we may see comes as a gift from the Holy Spirit. The wisdom of man is mere folly compared to the wisdom of God.

The ability to confess the Lord Jesus Christ with our mouths should never be taken for granted. It is a terrible thing to have your words silenced and even worse to not be allowed to speak. To have the mouth closed up seems to have the appearance of having the heart closed up as well. The dwelling of a dark force on someone's life can mean many different things, but in this instance, it meant a total constriction of the ability to communicate. The poor man was shut up and was a slave to his possessor.

Thank God that Jesus Christ came to set the captives free. He came to break the bonds and chains of the people and set them at liberty in the Lord. He came to give sight to the blind and to heal the brokenhearted. Even still, though, the devil rules the air. Paul said, "For our struggle is not against flesh and blood, but against the rulers, against the powers, against the world forces of this darkness, against the spiritual forces of wickedness in the heavenly places." (Eph. 6:12) "Greater is He that is in you, than he that is in the world." (1 Jn.4:4) "Who is it that overcomes the world, but he who believes that Jesus is the Son of God?" (1 Jn. 5:5)

July 30th

The Recognition of the Messiah

"And all the multitudes were amazed, and began to say, 'This man cannot be the Son of David, can he?'   (Matthew 12:23)

The term 'Son of David' referred to the messianic vision from Nathan the prophet to King David, "The Lord also declares to you that the Lord will make a house for you. When your days are complete and you lie down with your fathers, I will raise up your descendent after you, who will come forth from you and I will establish his kingdom. He shall build a house for My name, and I will establish the throne of his kingdom forever." (2 Samuel 7:12-13) The Son of David was a messianic title ushering in the eternal kingdom. When Jesus came preaching the Kingdom of God with all of the miracles He performed, the people eventually realized that this man was the Messiah, thinking He would bring peace to Israel by way of conquering those that ruled over them, namely the Romans. Excitement was beginning to brew. However, Jesus did not come to set up an earthly kingdom, but came to usher in a spiritual eternal kingdom.

That is why it is so very difficult to express the intent of God in regards to the Kingdom of God because for over two thousand years, traditional teaching hasn't talked much about the Kingdom of God in the spiritual sense; so men have set up earthly kingdoms that they can relate to in the flesh. Today, the earthly kingdoms show themselves in a variety of ways. But, Jesus came preaching and teaching the Kingdom of God, spiritual words saying that you must be born again; that you must deny yourself, take up your cross, and follow Him. He taught many, many things by His words and by His miracles.

The New Testament saints gathered together for worship, communion, and fellowship and no matter our personal belief, we are not to forsake fellowshipping with other saints. But nowhere in the New Testament is there any direction for building and maintaining buildings or the giving of extravagant salaries to paid pastors, bishops, apostles, or preachers. Jesus said that the worker was worthy of his support, but He explicitly told His disciples not to acquire gold, silver, or copper for their money belts. (Matt. 10:9-11). Paul told his churches to give to the ministry in honor of the men who taught to help support them. (1 Cor. 9:7-11; 2 Cor. 11:7-9; Gal. 6:6; Phil. 4:15-18) But, by far the majority of the scriptures in the N.T. regarding giving are about giving to help the needy; the pastors and overseers are not the needy. The truth is always in the context. Practices of exorbitant salaries, personal gift offerings to the 'man of God', and indebtedness to banks for building projects reflect the earthly kingdom concept that has effectually hampered the true Gospel of the spiritual Kingdom of God.

Pray that the Holy Spirit leads you to the Truth of Jesus Christ as King over His Kingdom and the Word will become alive in you as you see and hear from the Holy Spirit in the Word that Jesus Christ did come as the true Messiah, the Son of David, the anointed One to deliver us all from sin, the pits of hell, false teachers, and most of all, from ourselves.

July 31st

Kingdom Against Kingdom

"And knowing their thoughts He said to them, 'Any kingdom divided against itself is laid waste; and any city or house divided against itself shall not stand.'"
(Matthew 12:25)

We are getting more in depth now into Jesus' ministry when confrontation and conflict with the natural forces of man abound. Jesus has already won over the temptation of the devil in the wilderness, but the devil hasn't finished his work among the people and so it is the people who are not of God that rise up against that which is God and make accusation. The Kingdom of God is not just a message, but it is a place and the place came in the person of Jesus Christ.

Later in the scripture, in one of the confrontations with a group of Jews, Jesus tells them that He, Jesus, does the will of His Father in heaven. And, they seek to do the will of their father the devil. (John 8:31-47) This is not all Jews, of course, but the ones who had chosen of themselves to go against Jesus and His Kingdom. Beware of what you believe you are going against. When the Kingdom of God is pitted against the kingdom of this world and of the air, make certain of God and which side you are really on. Do not allow others to deceive you into their particular way of thinking. Oftentimes, people choose sides in conflict without demonstrating due diligence in the Spirit to discern what the true Father would have them do.

The teaching Jesus provides, again, is not simple teaching, but a way of life. The Jewish leaders accused Jesus of casting demons out of people by the power of Beelzebub, the devil himself. That particular accusation didn't even make rational sense, so Jesus easily dismantles their argument with the description of a house being divided against itself. Jesus knew the Kingdom of God had arrived in power and His power proved to be preeminent. This power, however, caused bitter resentment among the religious leaders for, again, they are losing ground and credibility with their leadership and their belief system. It was their belief system that was faulty.

Let us all continue in the faith believing in what the Word of God says about itself, rather than what men say it says. This is where the kingdoms of this world lie in wait to deceive even the elect. Trust in the Lord with all of your heart and rely upon the Holy Spirit's leading to lead you in the way of His Truth. Do not walk with Him alone for that, too, can be dangerous because we can easily deceive ourselves. Deception is the work of the enemy. Light illuminates. Let your light shine and do not be afraid to share your faith in Spirit and in Truth. Let Him be the overflow of living water and the house that He has built in you will truly be a house of prayer.

August 1st

The Kingdom Has Come Upon You

"But if I cast out demons by the Spirit of God, then the kingdom of God has come upon you." (Matthew 12:28)

Do we recognize truth when we hear it? What about the times that we think we are right and believe we have always been right in a particular thing, but then are confronted by a person who really knows the truth about the matter? Initially we do not want to concede to the new found truth and only perceive the situation as a confrontation or challenge to see how deep we can dig in our heels to stay the way we are, or to continue to believe what we have always believed. The Word of God says, "Beloved, do not believe every spirit, but test the spirits to see whether they are from God, for many false prophets have gone out into the world." (1 John 4:1, ESV)

Jesus explains His way of expressing the Kingdom of God by way of binding the strongman. "Or how can anyone enter the strong man's house and carry off his property, unless he first binds the strong man? And then he will plunder his house." (Matt. 12:29) The Kingdom of God moves forward and is ever moving. When Jesus dis-possesses the demon-possessed, He was taking back what was rightfully God's creation and setting righteousness up upon the earth. This was the battle scene and the religious leaders didn't even know the depths of the war of the kingdoms. The battle is in the spirit realm, not in flesh and blood realm. For the weapons of our warfare are not carnal, but are mighty for pulling down strongholds, the strongholds of the prince of the power of the air. (2 Cor. 10:14)

The religious zealots of the day could not wrap their minds around Jesus' kingdom for they had always believed in an earthly kingdom rule of God and Jesus did not fit that mold.

Application here is extremely necessary particularly among the married folk. A house divided cannot stand. A family divided will not be able to withstand the onslaught of the enemy for when the time comes to join together to fight together against a common foe, the lack of dependability among the family members will create casualties in the battle. Conflict and confrontation abounds in division. There is endless debate, squabbling, rivalry and the development of stressful consequences. The collateral damage from division is incalculable.

Repent, be moved with compassion, reconcile, forgive, and release. Always allow the abounding love of God to move in your hearts and on your lips to the edification of your spouse, your children and the rest of your family. Build your family up in the nurture of the Lord. Never cease to offer holy love. Be joined in the bonds of Spirit-filled love in the Kingdom of His grace.

August 2nd

There is a Choice

"He who is not with Me is against Me; and he who does not gather with Me scatters." (Matthew 12:30)

We always have a choice in following Jesus, or not. All that we do reflects what is inside our heart. Many times, people say, 'Well, that's not me...' after they've done something or said something. It's as though they are not responsible for their thoughts, words, or actions and someone else is always to blame. It is the irrepressible, 'Not my fault' syndrome that too many people rely on to excuse their poor choice of words, bad behavior, and faulty belief systems. Actions are derivatives of a thought somewhere down the line and when we move under the guise of our selfishness, we move out from under His leading. I did not say that if you are a born again believer that you can walk in and out of salvation. The message of the Kingdom of God is not primarily about your personal salvation... it's about the Kingdom of God. It's about God, not you and me.

The dividing line of actions are made clear here in Jesus' words. If a person is against Jesus Christ, they will effectually be moving in thoughts, words, and deeds that reflect their belief system. If a person is scattering others against Jesus Christ by their deeds, then they are not gathering...they're scattering. Oftentimes, deception is at work in men's minds where they think they're something that they're not. Jesus said that we'll know them by their fruit. We'll know who is with Jesus by the eventual actions of a man by his gathering together in favor of Jesus or his scattering against by his deplorable testimony. People who think that they're a Christian, for whatever reason(s), are sometimes duped by self-deception or ignorance. There are many false teachers in the land who do not know the truth and are incapable of telling the truth. So, when they lead people to their own personal beliefs, which are errant, the person is led astray into an errant belief system, not into Christ.

Throughout the centuries, people have been led to follow men or errant doctrine, rather than Jesus Christ. Jesus forewarned us of this and the warning still holds true today and will until the end of what we call time when the great deceiver will be thrown into the pit of fire.

Be certain of God in Jesus Christ in the power of the Holy Spirit. This is accomplished by His Word. Get with the right fellowship of right believers. The right believers will be rightly dividing the Word of God rightly and not to their own edification. Know the Lord and be filled with the Holy Spirit. The Holy Spirit prays in us when we do not know what to pray. Pray for discernment in the Spirit and follow Him.

August 3rd

It is What it Is

"And whoever shall speak against the Son of Man, it shall be forgiven him; but whoever shall speak against the Holy Spirit, it shall not be forgiven him, either in this age, or in the age to come."   (Matthew 12:32)

We can be eternally grateful to God for His good pleasure to forgive sin, iniquity, and transgression. We can find forgiveness of our sin through the grace of God in Jesus Christ. "For God so loved the world that He gave His only begotten son, that whosoever believes in Him should not perish, but have everlasting life." (John 3:16, KJV) Our Lord is so wonderful that He created a plan for us to be delivered from the penalty and the power of sin.

Jesus Christ was the Son of Man and many things were spoken against Him in His day and many other things have been spoken against Him since. When someone doesn't agree with Jesus Christ, there is still hope for that person to be delivered unto God by the turning to God in submission and seeking His grace knowing that He has the power to forgive. That power to forgive also dwells in us for that same power to forgive is available when men say all manner of things against us, just because we name the Name of Jesus Christ. We can forgive others of their faults against us even in the midst of slander and lie. It is His power to forgive.

It is also His power to not forgive a person who speaks against the Holy Spirit. Do we know exactly what this means in its totality of meaning? I don't. But I do know there comes an appointed time for every man to die and if that man defies the power of the Holy Spirit in his life to submit to the Lord, that person will receive an eternal reward for his decision to not believe. It is the ultimate sin of unbelief and the ultimate penalty is eternal hell. It will not be forgiven in this age, or the age to come. It is what it is.

In this day and time, people are espousing philosophies that there is no God, there is no heaven or hell, there are many ways to God, and Jesus was just a good man or a great prophet, but He was not who He men say that He is. Philosophies of men are just that; philosophies of men. Men and women through the ages have conjectured regarding gods, religion, myths, and fables. Co-existence among peoples and tolerance of all sin will be the ultimate ruination to the end of times. It is its own final reward in the earth.

But true Christianity is not a fable nor does it hold that if you are wrong in this lifetime, you'll still be ok in the next feature. No! If a person holds out until death to defy God, then that person has blasphemed against the Holy Spirit because it is the Holy Spirit that convicts the world of sin, righteousness, and ultimate judgment. (John 16:8-13) Do not wait too late to follow the Holy Spirit. No one knows the hour of their departure from this world. There won't be a 'last call' or a bell to let you know you have one minute to go. Give your life to Jesus Christ and be filled with the Holy Spirit. Then, you can rest in the fact that the Holy Spirit knows your name and your name is written in the book of life. Be certain of God alone, for His grace is sufficient and His judgment is sure.

August 4th

The Fruit of a Tree

"Either make the tree good, and its fruit good; or make the tree bad, and its fruit bad; for the tree is known by its fruit."   *(Matthew 12:33)*

In the context of Jesus' teaching here, it is while He is still speaking to the religious leaders, the Pharisees, about the Kingdom of God and the kingdom of the devil. He has recently released a man from demon-possession, blindness, and the inability to speak, dumbness. Jesus Christ has the ability to come into a person's life and make the person a Spirit-filled follower of God. The Spirit-filled follower of Jesus Christ will bear the fruit of the host, the Holy Spirit. When the power of God comes upon us, He has the power to create in us a clean heart, a new heart, a heart that is born again of His Spirit. He can make any tree good in order to produce good fruit.

The antithesis is to make the tree bad. Bad fruit comes from bad trees and it is awfully hard to hide bad fruit from all of the people all of the time. If a person is of a bad disposition, somebody surely knows about it. It is in all the matter of the heart, the 'what's inside' of a man that matters most.

The matters of the heart we share matter most to us,
What matters most to me I see may not mean much to thee.
What matters most to us we speak, and speak it from the lips;
Our lips reveal what lies inside the depths of sailing ships.

If what my heart so doth profess, it matters most to me,
And what your heart in so confess, it matters most to thee.
Our lips do tell the 'what's inside', the things that matter most;
The hurts, the pain, the sorrow tell, the things we like to boast.

So in your speaking, speaking still, the things that matter most;
Reveal the 'what's inside' of you, revealing the true host.

The fruit of a man is his words, actions, behaviors and disposition. Fruit is revealed through these expressions. The character of a man is revealed in all of this. We may sometimes talk in error or in anger, but not always. If we always talk in error, namely deception or lying; or if we always find ourselves angry, then the fruit is bad coming from a bad tree. Make the tree good by submitting to the Holy Spirit.

August 5th

The Heart Always Speaks

"You brood of vipers, how can you, being evil, speak what is good? For the mouth speaks out of that which fills the heart."   *(Matthew 12:34)*

What does our speech reveal about us? Typically, our speech reveals where we're from, where we grew up, our family ties and upbringing, our education or the lack thereof, our environment, our peers, our ability to communicate, and to some degree, our level of intelligence. Not all of these traits are revealed all of the time because we speak differently under different circumstances to differing people. We may speak one way to our mother and an entirely different way to our policeman. We may speak one way depending on our job, if we're a salesman, for example, and an entirely different way to our spouse when we're angry.

But what is it that our speech reveals about us when we talk to other people? Differing circumstances among differing peoples may generate various ways of communicating, but we are still who we are by what is inside our hearts. We will be to certain people certain ways if we want to present ourselves in a certain light. We will be nice to our employers, but maybe not so nice to our spouse when we get home from work. It really takes a lot of work to be all things to all people, all of the time. Eventually, as we mature, we decide to just be ourselves.

Then, that's when it occurs to us; maybe we aren't as nice as we used to be, when we weren't under so much stress. We have a tendency to like ourselves more than we like others and end up preferring our thoughts to other's thoughts as well. Whatever is in our hearts is surely going to end up being expressed through our mouths. If we are angry, we'll speak angrily. If we're full of joy, we'll express a joyful spirit. Our disposition is our tone of voice. Be careful here, though, that when you hear someone's environmental accent, that you don't mistake it for a bad tone. We are, after all, very different. And, if we are critical of others or demeaning in our hearts and thoughts, it will surely come out of our mouths some way or another.

"When you follow the desires of your sinful nature, your lives will produce evil results: sexual immorality, impure thoughts, eagerness for lustful pleasure, idolatry, participation in demonic activities, hostility, quarreling, jealousy, outbursts of anger, selfish ambition, divisions, the feeling that everyone is wrong except those in your own little group, envy, drunkenness, wild parties, and other kinds of sin. Let me tell you again, that anyone living that sort of life will not inherit the Kingdom of God. But when the Holy Spirit controls our lives, he will produce this kind of fruit in us: love, joy, peace, patience, kindness, goodness, faithfulness, gentleness, and self-control. Here there is no conflict with the law." *(Galatians 5:19-23, NLT)*

August 6th

Accountability for Our Words

"And I say to you, that every careless word that men shall speak, they shall render account for it in the day of judgment. For by your words you shall be justified, and by your words you shall be condemned." *(Matthew 12:36-37)*

A born again believer who truly believes the Word of God trusts the Lord with all his heart and possesses the knowledge of the Word in Truth in the Holy Spirit. With all of that said, it should be pretty easy to walk with the Lord and not mistakes, right? By now, we should be humbled by all of this and should continue to be humbled by all of this because if it was left up to us, we simply wouldn't make it to heaven in our own strength because for most of us, our words would condemn us straight into judgment. Thank God, eternal life is not left up to us. Eternal life is a gift from God and we receive this life by being born again into His Kingdom, His life. We do this in faith believing God has eternally saved us from our sin because of the atoning work He did on the cross. We can do absolutely nothing to deserve the love of God or His eternal salvation. So, if we can do nothing to deserve it by our works, then can we do anything to lose it like saying abominable things to people with our words?

If we repeat what we have talked about that our words emanate from our heart and our words reveal what is inside our heart as well as bear the fruit of whatever is in our hearts, then certainly it stands to reason that our words will either justify us or they will condemn us. We speak what we believe. Our belief system is the internal construct of the heart. If we believe rightly in the Lord Jesus Christ as we said at the beginning of this page, then our words will follow suit, along with our disposition of expressing holy love that only comes from His Holy Spirit. One of Jesus' points here, however, is that people deceive themselves just as the Pharisees had deceived themselves. They believed they were the chosen ones of the children of God, the children of Abraham. Yet, their hearts and conduct was far from God. The fruit of their lips revealed such. They planned to destroy Jesus Christ, the Son of God. They did not receive the Son, so they could not receive the Father. Their speech and conduct revealed their hearts.

Our hearts are continually revealed to others by our words, disposition and conduct. Whatever we truly walk in is who we truly are. God knows all and He is not fooled by anyone. He is the judge for only He knows the hearts of men. We can discern others by their fruit, but Jesus' teaching continues to be clearly made for us to examine ourselves and the examination of others hearts is left up to God. Examine yourself to see if your words match your beliefs. Does your walk match your talk? Be careful in believing that you can lose what you have; the truth is to know God and believe Him until the end. Be faithful unto death. For some, they will lose what they thought they had, but never did, and their words revealed it all the while.

August 7th

A Sign of Unbelief

"Then some of the scribes and Pharisees answered Him, saying, 'Teacher, we want to see a sign from you.'" (Matthew 12:38)

Have you ever wondered how God chose the time of Jesus' arrival on the earth? What was it about this time that the prophecies would be fulfilled of the long-expected One, the son of David, the Messiah? One would have to have a good handle on all of the prophecies that were fulfilled in Jesus' coming to that particular generation to answer that question. Prophecies concerning the location of the birth of the Messiah have been discussed earlier, but what prophecies are when spoken are signs of the future times. Prophecies themselves become signs of greater or horrible things to come and when they do occur, the sign given is the sign revealed. The Pharisees had the 'sign' of the Day of the Lord standing right in front of them and in their blindness; they continued to ask for a sign. Jesus responded to them, "An evil and adulterous generation craves for a sign; and yet no sign shall be given to it but the sign of Jonah the prophet…" (v. 39) Jesus was speaking of Himself in His time in the 'heart of the earth' after His death and before His resurrection. It is the sign of the resurrection. Jesus referred to the heart of the Pharisees and the heart of their generation as 'evil and adulterous', (vs. 39, 45)

The Pharisees wanted proof of Jesus' revelation of who they perceived Him to be. They did not believe in the miracles He had performed already for they stood in accusation of Him calling Him a follower of the devil. What could He possibly do to earn their trust? Absolutely nothing! They did not trust Him; they tested Him and openly rebuked Him. Their speech and their conduct revealed their hearts of evil unbelief. Again, have you ever wondered why God chose that particular generation of time to arrive on the earth?

Oswald Chambers said, "The Bible states and affirms facts for the benefit of those who believe in God." [1] You will believe Biblical facts or you won't. Faith cannot be argued and debated. You either believe in the Way of Jesus Christ, or you don't. Jesus did not come to argue His way into the hearts of men. He rebuked the Pharisees because they simply were not going to get out of the way. In fact, they were the ones responsible for His death. That confrontation had to occur for His death to occur as it did. Our hearts tell on us when we go looking for a sign to prove that God is who He said He is. We believe and walk in our God-given faith, or we don't. There is a difference in doubt and unbelief, and only the man knows his own heart when his doubt becomes belief, if it does at all. Stop asking for signs and learn to abide in Him. Abiding in Him in a complete, loving relationship keeps us in the knowledge of His will.

Be strengthened in the power of His might and not your own. His will is revealed in His Presence. Remain in His Presence and He will be the sign unto you in your heart and you will not have to look for another sign, He will be enough.

August 8th

Completed Relationship

"Now when the unclean spirit goes out of a man, it passes through waterless places, seeking rest and does not find it. Then it says, 'I will return to my house from which I came'; and when it comes, it finds it unoccupied, swept, and put in order." (Matthew 12:43-44)

People go to church services for various reasons. Some folk have been to church only once in their lives; some not at all. Some only go on the holidays of Christmas, Easter, or New Year's Eve. Some go for a while, seemingly cleaning their lives up, and when they think they've had enough of religion, they go back to their old ways of living. Still, some folk go to church services and never skip a beat in their behavior. They're still just as crotchety, mean, lustful, or selfish as they've always been; they just have a new group to share their beliefs with.

So it goes to the man who thinks he's done something religious, but didn't quite go all the way with Jesus. This is where we find Jesus speaking to the Pharisees about their particular situation in their generation. He compares their evil generation to a man who was possessed by an unclean, demonic spirit who was cast away and the man was morally cleaned up, but had no spiritual infilling from the Lord Almighty. He was not born again. So, the unclean, demonic spirit goes and gets seven more spirits more wicked than himself and takes up residence in the morally clean, but spiritually bankrupt man. This was the lot of the perverse generation that put Jesus Christ to death on a cross.

If we want to be complete with God, we have to go all the way. We have to go all in, completely committed, completely true. We cannot fake it with God. We may be able to fool some people, but it is only the Spirit of God that truly completes a man spiritually.

People are searching for truth. They're searching for fulfillment; anything spiritual will do for some folk, as long as it's positive, it's got to be positive and restful, yes…peaceful and positive. They try this and that and that and this. There are many religions, spiritual teachings, philosophies, and belief systems in the world that offer their way to solitude, peace, and wholeness. Jesus Christ said that He is the way, the truth, and the life. No man comes to the Father except through Jesus Christ. We can't just believe that He is the Son of God, even the demons believe. We have to go all the way with Jesus Christ as the Lord of all and that includes being Lord of me and you.

This is complete submission into complete relationship. If any man desires to go after Jesus, let him deny himself, take up his cross, and follow Him. Be filled with His Holy Spirit, abiding in Him, always and forever in a holy, loving, completed relationship. Amen.

August 9th

Real Relationship

"…He said, 'Behold, My mother and My brothers! For whoever does the will of My Father who is in heaven, he is My brother and sister and mother.'"
(Matthew 12:49b-50)

The connection that we have with the will of God and Jesus Christ is that Jesus Christ comes first in the will of the Father. If we believe in the saving grace of God through Jesus Christ, we are in the will of the Father. In this, we become sons and daughters of God. The relationship with our Father, and Christ, as our brother is stated explicitly here. It is not to undermine the Lordship of Jesus Christ as all authority has been given to Him. It is to share the real relationship of a trusted brother, a real friend who understands all that we go through in this life.

In spiritual life, we live, and move, and have our being in Him. In Christ, He is always with us. In Christ, we are abiding in Him, loving Him, obeying His words, and fulfilling the relationship in spiritual truth for that is where the true reality lies. The spiritual life that we have with Him is reality. Everything else is temporal. The things we see, taste, touch, hear, and smell, are the sensory, the temporary things of life. Only in Him do we have the aspect of anything real in this life and beyond.

Real fellowship with other believers is the koinonia (fellowship) in the Spirit with people in agreement with the Spirit of God. We can have all things in common with like-minded believers in Him.

"This is My commandment, that you love one another as I have loved you. Greater love has no man than this, that a man lay down his life for his friends. You are my friends if you do what I command you…this I command you, to love one another." (John 15:12-14, 17, RSV) "A friend loves at all times, and a brother was born for adversity." (Proverbs 17:17, RSV)

Real relationship begins with the heart of God beating in our hearts. Real brothers and sisters, friends and mothers are born of God just as you believe you are. If you truly trust in God, trust in the Spirit that dwells within you. The bond of love that you have with Him can be had with your brothers and sisters in faith. He is not only your Savior, He is your friend. Now go and be a friend to someone else.

August 10th

The Multitudes Continue

"And great multitudes gathered to Him, so that He got into a boat and sat down, and the whole multitude was standing on the beach." (Matthew 13:2)

Everywhere Jesus went, He had no problem drawing a crowd because of His reputation of healing and delivering people. Although He was not always healing folk, He was always teaching and loving people. He was not afraid of people or crowds, but He did have to go to areas where He was not completely submersed by the multitudes of people. Here, it seems differing groups of people follow Him to the seashore and the throng grows to the point where He has to get into a boat, simply to be heard among the multitude. With carefully reading the Word, one could surmise Jesus' preaching style. 'He got into the boat and sat down.' Earlier, He was teaching in someone's house. He would sit and have people come by Him and receive healing or delivering. Although the crowds that were drawn to Jesus were, at times, enormous, up to more than five thousand, He spoke with clarity from a humble, familial position as if He were serving dinner each time He spoke. The breaking of the bread to His disciples was not by happenstance any more than the breaking of the bread to the five thousand was; Jesus was feeding people with the Words of God. I do not believe that Jesus screamed at people while they received and ate His bread, nor did He demand an offering.

Imagine being by the seashore, as Jesus is speaking from the boat, and smelling the wafting smells from the fishermen's boats. This was a fishing district and the fishermen fished at night so that the boats were anchored in the day. The odors of the drying nets and the salt blowing in with the wind would add substance to Jesus' teaching. He was teaching from the point of provision. He was also teaching with the use of parables. Not many understood what He was saying, but did that give them cause to leave? He spoke with authority, but here, His authority was misunderstood and for most, not understood at all. Yet they lingered.

What is it that drives you to Jesus Christ? We have learned that it is the work of the Holy Spirit to lead men to Christ. But what is it that makes you stay with Him? People are drawn to the Lord by the Holy Spirit, but the Spirit of God being the gentleman that He is does not make people do anything against their will. The multitudes followed for their own reasons which were probably multitudinous. What are your reasons for following Him and staying with Him? Do you abide in Him as He commanded, or do you watch from the seashore with a barrier between so that you don't get too close too often so that He doesn't interfere with your plans?

Christ Jesus is our bread of life and our ever constant source of spiritual food. Without Him, I can do nothing and with Him, all things are possible. Do I stay with Him for the possibilities or do I stay with Him for His Presence? He knows for certain. The real family member is a part of the meal and the life of the household. What is it that drives you to Jesus Christ? I guess that it is all in how you view His bread.

August 11th

The Word of the Kingdom

"And He spoke many things to them in parables, saying, 'Behold, the sower went out to sow...Hear then the parable of the sower. When anyone hears the word of the kingdom...'"   *(Matthew 13:3, 18-19a)*

A parable is a story that teaches using allegory (ie., ideas, symbols, concepts) to convey meaning in teaching a lesson. Jesus Christ was the master teacher using parables and He explains to His disciples that He taught using parables, "Therefore I speak to them in parables; because while seeing they do not see and while hearing they do not hear, nor do they understand." (Matt. 13:13) The use of the parable was Jesus' way of teaching what the Kingdom of God was all about. Our Father chose this mode of teaching because He chose this mode of teaching. He chose this way for His reasons. People do not get 'upfront, in your face, confrontational' spiritual words. In that type of expression, people are receiving the person rather than the message and people typically reject the person who is 'upfront and confrontational' with matters of the spiritual heart. Again, Jesus taught sitting down as though He were sitting down together with folk at a dinner meal. He may not have always taught in this manner, but this manner was done enough that we have to take note of it.

The significance of the parable avails the human mind to dependence on a higher cause for resolution and conclusion. As people listened to Jesus' parables, they just didn't get it. People today can read the Word of God for themselves and the same thing can occur...they just don't understand the Bible. One may have knowledge of the Word and remain without understanding. It takes the power of the Holy Spirit to lift the veil of blindness from people so that they can receive understanding, wisdom, and spiritual power from the Words of God. These words are spiritual and those they 'hear' them, hear them in the Spirit.

It is often repeated by spiritual leaders to read and pray and pray and read the Word of God. We must pray for spiritual guidance, understanding, and revelation in the Word. We are not to add to the Word of God by our personal revelation. The revelation of the Word is the revealing of what the Spirit of God is saying in the Word…not some additional clairvoyant, mysticism where we hear some chanting prophecy from some unusual, unknown spirit.

The sower went out to sow seed. The seed is the Word of the kingdom, (v. 19). The sower is God Himself for it is His Word that is being delivered for the purpose of deliverance. We are not the sowers, nor is the seed anything other than the Word of God. This is His work and He is the One who is doing His work. We are His sons and daughters in His Kingdom serving Him and He delights to do His work through us. "The Lord delights in those who fear Him, who put their hope in His unfailing love." (Psalm 147:11, NIV) Delight yourself in His delight and His Word will be a lamp unto your feet and a light unto your path. Delight yourself in Him for He is His Word. (John 1)

August 12th

The Seed by the Road

"And as He sowed, some seeds fell beside the road, and the birds came and ate them up…the evil one comes and snatches away what has been sown in his heart."   (Matthew 13:4, 19b)

As God, in the Holy Spirit, who is the one sowing the seed, which is the Word, we have to take a look at the other facets of the parable. The Word also says, 'How shall they call on Him in whom they have not believed? How will they believe in Him of whom they have not heard? And how shall they hear without a preacher? And how shall they preach, except they be sent?" (Romans 10:14-15a, KJV) If we name the Name of Jesus Christ, we are the preachers sent into the world to give voice to the Sower sowing His seed. "Not to us, O Lord, not to us, but to your name goes all the glory for your unfailing love and faithfulness." (Psalm 115:1, NLT)
We may be the voice, but it is His Spirit that does the convicting of sin, and the delivering of righteousness and judgment to the world. No man should ever take His glory for himself.

The varying soils are the people; the receivers of the Word. Here, there is the soil of the roadside; the hard-worn, stubble that has been crushed a bit by the weight of hardship, having been run over a few times, and broken apart by the impact of the travelers along the way. What people do to other people in their depravity is unlawful and despicable. It typically leaves indelible marks on the victims of people who may fall and crumble under the pressure of that depravity or who will walk in revenge and the lack of forgiveness all of their days. The hard-hearted people of the roadside may also be there for their beliefs, believing that there is no God who could love them as He does or could forgive them for what they have done. The hard-hearted and hard-pressed live in unbelief of holy love and divine forgiveness.

The birds that snatch the Word of the Lord from their hearts are of the evil one, the demonic forces of darkness that desire their own followers to die with them. Hate, deception, and a vengeful spirit plucks love from the soil of the roadside so that that soil may remain lifeless and hard forever. God help us to be merciful to people and not be hard-hearted towards anyone, for He wishes that none would perish. Unfortunately, that is not the nature of man.

We take pause here to be thankful that if we are reading these words, we are reading them because we have taken the time to be fruitful unto Him. He is the One who has saved us from a godless eternity. He loves us so and we ought to love Him in His love and in obedience to His Word. Thank God for His Word. The hard-pressed of life are out there and the proof that we are to go and tell the world about His Kingdom is in this parable as well. We do not know another's heart, hard-hearted or soft as baby, we simply do not know. Our lot is to go and be peace where there is no peace and hope where there is no hope; life where there is no life. Allow His loving kindness to flow from you in the sowing of His Word. Love, forgive, and do not judge.

August 13th

The Seed in the Rocky Places

"And others fell upon the rocky places, where they did not have much soil; and immediately they sprang up, because they had no depth of soil. But when the sun had risen they were scorched; and because they had no root, they withered away…this is the man who hears the word, and immediately receives it with joy; yet he has no firm root in himself, but is only temporary, and when affliction or persecution arises because of the word, immediately he falls away."
(Matthew 13:5-6, 20b-21)

The seed sown among the rocky places depicts the man who might go to church at times and he listens with eagerness to the message. He thinks that life in God is found at the altar, so he goes there or to the preacher and makes a light hearted commitment to God because the Word touched his heart and he thought it was the right thing to do. These folk are altar dwellers periodically going to the altar or seeking out the pastor for their exoneration from their current sin because they just can't seem to get this thing right for themselves.

This man is also the hypocrite who tries to live out a religious life, but can't because it isn't really real for him. He tried it, but it doesn't work, not for him anyway. His old way of life wasn't so bad after all. In fact, He never was that bad a sinner to begin with. Who needs the Gospel? He hasn't murdered anyone. So, he falls away and doesn't even make an attempt to go to church anymore because he doesn't understand how it works. If you live in the United States, this man is most likely your neighbor who stays home on weekends doing his own thing. The church thing just didn't work out for him. He didn't know it was about a relationship.

Receiving the Gospel of Jesus Christ which is the Kingdom of God is receiving and giving. It is the receiving of freedom from a life of sin because Jesus Christ paid the debt and wages of sin on a cross. We have been forgiven of our sin in the power and blood of Jesus Christ. But, the Kingdom of God is in giving, too. We do not earn any reward by what we do, so let's be clear, we cannot earn our way into the Kingdom of God. What we do is give up our rights to ourselves by denying ourselves, taking up our cross and following Him.

The man who lives as the rocky soil is not going to do that. Never did, and possibly never will. He appreciates the Gospel message of what Christ did on the cross, but he isn't going to give up his life for religion according to that way of thinking. That is the problem with some of the preaching of traditional religion; people are getting the wrong message. Somehow, through the centuries the seed has been tainted by man's religion and when many folk hear that word, it simply doesn't work. Again, let's be thankful that the Holy Spirit is leading us towards a right faith in abiding in Him. Giving our all to the Lord was not just for one time. Giving our all was and is for all time. We do not pick ourselves back up once we enter into life in the Kingdom of God. Allow the Holy Spirit to have His way in you in the each and every moment of the each and every day. Walk in the light as He is in the light.

August 14th

The Seed Among the Thorns

"And others fell among the thorns, and the thorns came up and choked them out…And the one on whom the seed was sown among the thorns, this is the man who hears the word, and the worry of the world, and the deceitfulness of riches choke the word and it becomes unfruitful."   *(Matthew 13:7, 22)*

When Jesus came preaching the Kingdom of God, He told the people in the Sermon on the Mount, "...do not be anxious for your life...what you eat, drink, or wear." He talked to them and us about how valuable we are in the eyes of God. He told them that our heavenly Father knows our needs and our first duty to Him is to seek Him and His righteous and all these other things that we need will be added to us. We are loved and cared for by Almighty God who knows our every need. This is life in the Kingdom when we have given all to a God who has already given His all. Jesus told us to cast all of our cares upon Him. We can believe Him at His word and trust in Him fully. Unlike man, He is worthy to be trusted. He, alone, is worthy to be believed.

The man in the story who is the soil with the seed among the thorns is clearly someone who has heard the word, but the word gets choked out from the cares of this life. Too busy, too much to do, obligated to addictions, bills to pay, plans to fulfill, and over-indulgence come to take away the one thing that was the best thing and that is the Word of God. Over-indulgence into things chokes out the truth in matters of the heart because over-indulgence into objects, duties, work, sports, alcohol, drugs, sex, and the like all rob people of the truth. It is the temporal things that we can touch and feel that we think is important, but aren't. The things we cast our eyes upon can become the lust of the flesh and the lust of the eye. Here, blindness leads to death.

Jesus says that 'the word becomes unfruitful'. The implication is that the word is there, but because it gets choked, it isn't able to produce any fruit...fruits of righteousness, fruit of the Spirit. The word in this man is useless, because it is not performing its God intended purpose and that is to glorify God in purposeful fruit to the blessing of others and the glory of God. You may be wondering at this point, 'is this man saved or not?' and my response to that question is 'tradition has taught you to think that way and you need to stop thinking that way!' Life in the Kingdom of God is about life, not judging another man if he is 'saved, or not'. Jesus came that we might have life and that more abundantly.

Pray for others that you know that are choked with the cares and worries of this world. Stress kills people from the inside out. Unbelief is the culprit here. We have to believe that God is bigger than our world of stuff and teach others that the things of this world will come and go, but it is His Word that will last forever and we with Him if our names are written in the Lamb's Book of Life. (Rev. 3:5; 13:8; 20:12-15; 21:27)

August 15th

The Seed in the Good Soil

"And others fell on the good soil, and yielded a crop, some a hundredfold, some sixty, and some thirty. He who has ears let him hear...And the one on whom the seed was good soil, this is the man who hears the word and understands it; who indeed bears fruit and brings forth, some a hundredfold, some sixty, and some thirty." (Matthew 13:8-9, 23)

Jesus makes special care here to describe the major difference in all of the soils and types of men. The good soil, the receptive man, is the man or woman who has been given the ability to hear with spiritual ears and is able to receive the spiritual goodness of the seed, the Word. This man or woman is given the Word and the Word is taken into the heart in abundance. The seed germinates and replicates in the heart of man. The abundant life is the life to the fullest in the heart of man.

This soil, this man, is soil that has been tilled and cultivated. This soil is receptive to the seed and desires all that comes with it; the tilling, the overturning of the soil, the fertilizer, the careful movement of the sower to see that the seed is the right seed in the right soil. There is only one seed here and it is the right seed.

This seed that goes into the good soil is able to go down into the heart of the soil and germinate into the plant that the sower has determined. It is a plant like Himself for He is His Word. He speaks His Word and the ones able to receive it in the heart are joined to it where the seed grows into abundance. The seed in the heart of man is what flows out of the heart of man and is the fruit on the lips and the life of the disposition.

Here, the overflow of living water is spread abroad in our hearts, the heart of the seed in good soil.

The words on our lips and the fruit of our lives become the example for others that as the Gospel of Jesus Christ is inhaled, it is also exhaled in the fruit of the Spirit. The fruit in the parable here is the same fruit in Galatians 5:22 and in John 15:2; it is the fruit of the Spirit. The Spirit is given ability to grow and produce within our hearts and is exhaled in love, joy, peace, patience, kindness, gentleness, faithfulness, goodness, and self-control. Whenever the fruit of the Spirit is exhaled to another of kindred soil, it is replicated once again...some thirty, some sixty, some a hundredfold. The Truth of the Spirit of God does the work. We are His handiwork and vessels of His peace. Speak often of His work in you and out of you will flow fountains of living water to feed the hungry, give sight to the blind, and break the captives free from the bondage of sin. The Lord is good!

P.S. It is not our responsibility to judge soil. It is our responsibility to be obedient. He has told us that there are four types of soil. Pray for others, including your enemies. Pray for those who persecute you or say all manners of things falsely against you for His sake. Bless and do not curse. Exude the fruit of the Spirit of God and He will be the judge of the soil of mankind.

August 16th

The Mysteries of the Kingdom

"And He answered and said to them, 'To you it has been granted to know the mysteries of the kingdom of heaven, but to them it has not been granted.'"
(Matthew 13:11)

The disciples came to Jesus privately after He had spoken the parable of the sower, the seed, and the soil because they did not understand the parable. Not only did they not understand the story, they didn't understand why Jesus didn't simply speak plainly so that all could understand His teachings. "The word *musterion* as used in Scripture means 'the secret counsels of God which are hidden from the ungodly, but when revealed to the godly, are understood by them.'" [1] (Wuest)

Not including Dr. Wuest, but as I continue to read and study, I see many theologians and commentaries depict the disciples as men who lacked great discernment and in our present day declare how easy it is for them to understand the parable. Most of these theologians, however, still do not understand the Kingdom of God because of the religious blindness that is over their eyes and yet, in their minds, believe that they understand all of these mysteries.

Be careful of a man who says he understands all of the scripture. This writer does not, but completely waits on the revelation of the Holy Spirit to the revealed Word of God in prayer, reading the whole counsel of God according to His Nature and reading the right and wrong of what men have said about the scripture in the past. Also, be careful of judging others who do not understand a parable or a specific scripture for Jesus tells us here that understanding will be given to the godly, not to the ungodly. Pray for those who have not yet decided to follow Him, that is our work in interceding.

In Mark 4:13, Jesus responded to His disciples, "Do you not understand this parable? How then will you understand all the parables?" (NKJV) Jesus is patient here with His disciples to fully explain the use of parables and their purpose during this particular season of time. Jesus did not want everyone to understand the mystery of the kingdom of heaven. "For whoever has, to him more shall be given, and he shall have an abundance; but whoever does not have, even what he has shall be taken away from him." (v. 12) The "has' in this context is godly faith…understanding granted by the Holy Spirit. If we have the faith given to us by the Holy Spirit, then

He is the only one who can increase our faith. Faith is the currency of the Kingdom of God. These are all spiritual words and do not concern 'material things' in the context. The teachings of Jesus are guides into the Kingdom.

Perhaps it is for us to reason with the Lord in our own secret place with Him as to whether we shall understand the mysteries of the kingdom. The Holy Spirit reveals to whom He shall reveal. It is not up to us to judge men because they have been given understanding and call them wrong because they seem to know something more than we do. And, it is not up to men of understanding to laud themselves for gratuitous reward because understanding was given to them.

We all need help from our brothers and sisters in Christ for consult, fellowship, teaching, edifying, and exhorting. It is the Holy Spirit who guides us into all Truth. Bless the Lord for all of the understanding that you've been given and share with others the fruit of the Spirit in love. Then, the Lord God is glorified and Kingdom of God is advanced in His glory.

August 17th

They Have Closed Their Eyes

"Therefore I speak to them in parables; because while seeing they do not see, and while hearing they do not hear, not do they understand." (Matthew 13:13)

Personal perspective is an extremely vibrant and lively part of people's personalities. People's perceptions of an idea or an event can vary with each individual and when the perception of an idea is developed, it then becomes the person's perspective on the aforementioned idea or event. Oftentimes, perspectives are viewed as truth to the one holding the perspective. If one person can get another to agree with them on their perspective, then the principle of agreement has entered into both minds and the power of agreement is stronger than the power of perspective. Empowered ignorance is a dangerous thing.

If one person sees a thing one way and another sees it completely different, then who is right? Facts get muddled in thought and personal beliefs get brought in as though they are facts and the consummate relationship to the perceived idea between the thinker and the thought become one and 'voila!' a perceived truth has been created. This is, perhaps, how the people in Jesus' day viewed the coming Messiah. They believed that the chosen one would be a physical military deliverer of the people from their adversaries. At least, that's what the religious zealots believed. The Pharisees couldn't believe Jesus was the Son of God because they just couldn't; their eyes and hearts were closed to that belief. Were they under the influence of a religious spirit? Were they under the influence of the devil? Jesus said that their father was the devil (John 8:44) and that they loved to do the evil things he does.

Who closed the eyes of the people during this time of Jesus' teaching so that they would not and could not understand His teachings on the kingdom? Jesus said, "And in their case the prophecy of Isaiah is being fulfilled, which says, 'You will keep on hearing, but will not understand; and you will keep on seeing, but will not perceive; For the heart of this people has become dull, and with their ears they scarcely hear, and they have closed their eyes lest they should see with their eyes, and hear with their ears, and understand with their heart and return, and I should heal them.'" (Isaiah 6:10; Matt. 13:14-15)

We have to be careful of judging God in the perception that God makes people believe all that they believe. If opportunity has been presented to a person, the person can either agree with the opportunity or disavow it. The time of Jesus Christ on the earth was known before the foundation of the earth. The people's perspectives blinded their eyes to the truth of God and His kingdom. In like manner, we choose what we believe and so do our friends and family. People choose to believe the ways of the world or the spiritual words of the Lord. The ways of the Lord are given to those who will receive the Word in truth, but God doesn't make a man believe against his will. Moral choices are made every day in every human mind. Prayer shifts our thinking into His thinking. We can receive and understand according to our faith and the ever-increasing prayer life of the faithful. Watch and pray is our command. Seek the Lord while He may be found and be ever watchful of what goes into your ears.

August 18th

The Blessing in Seeing

"But blessed are your eyes, because they see; and your ears, because they hear."
(Matthew 13:16)

Oh, the blessedness in sight. To be able to truly see what the Lord has said, it is great! To be able to hear the Lord with understanding, it is tremendous. Oh, taste and see that the Lord is good. His mercy endures forever. What blessed joy there is in seeing truth in His Word and having the spiritual revelation speak to our minds and say, 'This is the way, walk in it.'

Jesus commended His disciples on their God-given ability to hear with hearing ears and see with seeing eyes. The desire of their hearts was made manifest in His sight for they desired to understand and know the One true God. They did not understand all things, and neither do we, but we're on our way, aren't we? We're on His way of Truth, eternal everlasting Truth that has set us free forever.

Although we may not know all things, we know the One who does and He is enough. He is the one who gives sight to the blind and hearing to the deaf. He is the one who enables us to walk with Him. We can do none of this of ourselves. We are blessed, made happy in Him. We will find our completeness only in Him. Again, this is not the material, but the spiritual. The Kingdom of God does not come with observation, saying look here or there, but it is within you. That is where you see and hear the truth, on the inside.

The Holy Spirit is speaking in the still, small voice inside of you blessing you with understanding, peace beyond understanding, and the wealth of God in unspeakable joy. Be the blessed in all the earth and be a blessing to others that He places in your path. We are not meant to bear the Spirit alone, but to bear witness of Him in our hearts to Him. In this, the fruit of His Spirit emanates from our bodies called the temple of the Lord. Jesus said that His house would be a house of prayer, so follow Him in His stead. Be the house of prayer He has gifted you to be. Note that I didn't say go to a house, but you are the house of prayer. Pray, brother and sister, pray, for your intercession for others is heard!

See where you become the salt of the earth and see where you become the light of the world. Hear where you become a river of living water to a thirsty generation. We are to be fountains of living water to a world in need of Him. And just as He spoke to the woman at the well, the time is coming where they neither worship on that mountain or in that temple, but those who worship Him, worship in Spirit and truth. Allow the Holy Spirit to breathe the breath of God in you and out of you for His glory and the glory of the Lord will rise among us all in glorious praise! Amen.

August 19th

The Parable of the Tares among the Wheat

"Another parable He put forth to them, saying, 'The kingdom of heaven is like a man who sowed good seed in his field; but while men slept, his enemy came and sowed tares among the wheat and went his way.'" *(Matthew 13:24-25)*

One day, when I was 16 years old, as I was out on our family's property mowing the lawn, a college-aged Bible salesman came knocking on our door. My mother let him in and talked with him a bit about what he sold. At the time, I had surrendered my life to full-time Christian service to become a minister, and so my mother called me in from the mowing and told me to look at the salesman's books. She told me she would buy one book for me since I was going into the ministry and out of all the books he had to sell I selected the Zondervan Pictorial Bible Dictionary. The huge book contains over 1000 pages of information regarding the Bible and the life and times of the history of the Bible. I honor my mother today for giving me this gift that I have treasured for almost 40 years. In this dictionary it clarifies wheat as "the most common cereal grain. This is the wheat of Joseph's time which bore seven ears in one stalk…today as in the time of Jesus certain varieties of wheat may yield 60 or 100 grains to a head." [1]

This dictionary also defines tares as, "the annual bearded darnel or rye grass that flourishes in wheat fields. It is difficult to tell it from wheat or rye until it heads. After harvest, the wheat is fanned then put through a sieve. The smaller darnel seeds left after fanning pass through the sieve leaving the wheat behind. The darnel is host to an ergot-like smut fungus which infects the seeds. The fungus is a serious poison if eaten by animals or man." [2]

So, in the parable of the sower and of the wheat and the tares, Jesus is telling us that in the time of the sowing, there will be good seed sown that will grow and flourish and produce some 30, some 60, and some a hundredfold. However, 'while men slept his enemy came and sowed tares among the wheat'. The tares look like wheat, but are not wheat. The tares are poisonous and if eaten will kill a human or an animal. Jesus says that during the sowing of the Kingdom, to let the tares and the wheat grow together and in the harvest, the two will be separated because if you separate them now, you will tear up the wheat along with the tares.

We will only know the poisonous tares, or people, by their fruit. The fruit of the Spirit of God his love, joy, peace, patience, goodness, kindness, gentleness, faithfulness, and self-control. The fruit of the tare is poisonous and lethal… "adultery, fornication, uncleanness, lewdness, idolatry, sorcery, contentions, hatred, jealousies, outbursts of wrath, selfish ambitions, dissentions, heresies, envy, murders, drunkenness, revelries and the like…that those who practice such things will not inherit the kingdom of God." (Galatians 5:19-21, NKJV) We will all be known by our fruit. Pray for Truth to be in you and pray for the real fruit of the Spirit of God to be ever-present in your heart and in your mouth.

August 20th

The Wheat of the Field

"And He answered and said, the one who sows the good seed is the Son of Man, and the field is the world; and as for the good seed, these are the sons of the kingdom; and the tares are the sons of the evil one; and the enemy is the devil, and the harvest is the end of the age; and the reapers are the angels."
(Matthew 13:37-39)

It is so wonderful in the events of Jesus with His disciples that when He told His parables and they didn't understand, they could go privately to Him and He would fully explain the meanings of the parts of the stories. Are we as loving to our own children, or students, in that we take special care to fully explain, in love, what the meanings of life in the Spirit are about or any other of the myriad of questions our children or students might ask?

Harshness comes from a brewing spirit of animosity and pride in when we know something and in pride use it against others for our own edification. We demonstrate our own petty jealousy for having paid the price for learning something and now others should pay a similar price to us for the sharing of the said knowledge. Spiritually speaking, teachers and preachers of the Bible are given their revelation by the Spirit of God. I know that I can do nothing of my own self. So, it would seem to me that for me to go to the Spirit and inquire the meaning of something in the Word, just like His disciples did, is very appropriate as a son of the kingdom. If we name the Name of Jesus Christ, we can all go to the Lord for answers to spiritual struggles and know in confidence that He hears us. He wants us to know Him and knowing Him includes Him giving us understanding in the things we do not understand.

If we take the Kingdom of God as seriously as Jesus did, we come to an understanding that those who do the will of the Father are the true sons and daughter of the kingdom. (Matt. 12:46-50) The Father's will is in the scripture and all that is His will is found in Him. Jesus said that if we love Him, we will obey His commands. Truth is found in obedience and holy love is found in Truth. "But if we are living in the light as God is in the light, then we have fellowship with each other, and the blood of Jesus, His son, cleanses us from all sin." (1 John 1:7, NLT) If we are truly in Him, the fruit that we bear will be His fruit.

We must examine ourselves for the fruit of our lips and our disposition reflects our host. Do not be fooled by your perceived religious experience at an altar. If you have not changed into a fruit-bearing son or daughter of the kingdom, then you aren't in the kingdom. "…unless one is born again, he cannot see the kingdom of

God." (John 3:3b) Your internal disposition will reflect your father. Pray to be real, spiritually real, and do not be self-deceived. The Kingdom of God is a treasure and I pray with you for us all to be found alive in Him!

August 21st

Determine Your Disposition

"The Son of Man will send forth His angels, and they will gather out of His kingdom all stumbling blocks, and those who commit lawlessness and will cast them into the furnace of fire; in that place there shall be weeping and gnashing of teeth." (Matthew 13:41-42)

Determine your own disposition and stop judging others according to your own personal belief of who and what you think they are. We must take pause in the Spirit to judge ourselves by His Word in His nature. If we are truly a son or daughter of the kingdom, then let your light so shine before men that your heavenly Father is reflected in you. Do not worry about the other disciples, you, go and take care that you are following your heavenly Father.

Determine your own disposition and stop determining other's hearts by your selfish discernment which is actually judgment. God knows who the wheat and the tares are and in the time of harvest and final judgment, He won't be asking you what He should do with the soul of another. Imagine that…God having to cower to us for our sense of who is a son of the devil or a son of the Father. That is what we are expecting when we take His judgment of others for ourselves and expect Him to do our bidding as if we know all things about another human being. At times, it is quite evident who might be a son of the devil for the sons of lawlessness are made plain by their works. But what about the tares who look like wheat and stand like wheat and are mixed in with the wheat in the field of the world or in the church?

What about the tares in the kingdom that you call church? Are we their judge? Jesus said that we would know them by their fruit. We can ascertain the fruit at times and at other times, we are at a loss of words and proper discernment. We simply don't have all of the facts on other people, but our heavenly Father does. You determine your own disposition and let God be God.

The punishment for the sons of the devil is stated here. Be careful not to glory in their shamelessness or in their punishment. That reveals a certain hatred for mankind that is neither holy nor righteous. Let God be God and you be obedient to the Spirit in holy love to Him and to others that He might bring unto Himself.

He has not left the judgment of who His sons and daughters are up to us, thank God! We need to be the witness unto Him and allow His Spirit to flow to a lost and dying world that needs to know about Him and His Kingdom. Abide in Him for He is His Kingdom and His Kingdom love will flow from you to the world you call your home, your family, your school, your work, and your community. Be the light of the world and light your part of the world with holy love.

August 22nd

The Mustard Seed

"He presented another parable to them, saying, 'The kingdom of heaven is like a mustard seed, which a man took and sowed in his field...'" (Matthew 13:31)

The kingdom of heaven is 'like...' This was Jesus' introduction of explaining what the kingdom of heaven was like. He had not come to set up an earthly kingdom as was hoped for by the religious zealots. His kingdom of heaven was a spiritual kingdom and it still is today. He and John the Baptist ushered in the Kingdom of God by their presence and their preaching. The Kingdom came to fruition with the coming of the Holy Spirit at Pentecost as the disciples prayed in the upper room. The kingdom does not come with observation, but is within you, as Jesus said. He likened the kingdom to a seed, a seed so small, that most would view it as insignificant.

The mustard seed simile is the comparison of that which is considered so insignificant, but which has the ability to grow into a tree large enough for birds to rest in its branches. How long does that take? Time is inconsequential in the kingdom. The significance of the smallness is the way this kingdom works. The kingdom dwells in the heart of a man from the smallest of beginnings as in an embryo and grows into a baby; then to a child and then to a full-grown mature believer. The kingdom is always advancing, always growing, always receiving and always giving. The seed of the kingdom is sown into the hearts of men and women and is nourished by the personal prayers of the receiver. When we pray and abide in Him, the kingdom within is nourished and is fed to grow. It is the seed of the new birth growing within us. Our bodies are His Bethlehem.[1] He is born into us in the work of His Spirit. We do not make ourselves believers by our works; it is the gift of God. It starts with one flourishing man and then goes to another and to another and on and on it spreads.

As we grow into mature believers, others are fed by His Spirit flowing through us. His living water flows out of us to a dry and thirsty generation. His living bread is broken within us to feed the hungry in spirit. Do you see the difference in who is doing the work here? In the kingdom life, He is the one with the provision, the daily bread. The water that we have in us is the water that we shall never be thirsty, the well that never runs dry. In Him, we move and have our very being. In Him, we are transformed by His Presence. In Him, we put on the mind of Christ. In Him, this is the mystery of the gospel, the Christ in you, the hope of glory.

All of who He is He is in us. From the humble beginnings of something as insignificant as a very small mustard seed, the Word grows and matures us as individuals and as sons and daughters of the kingdom together. We are not in this alone for the kingdom of God is growing from the one to the countless. "Rather, speaking the truth in love, we are to grow up in every way into Him who is the head, into Christ, from whom the whole body, joined and held together by every joint with which it is equipped, when each part is working properly, makes the body grow so that it builds itself up in love." (Ephesians 4:15-16, ESV)

August 23rd

The Parable of the Leaven

"He spoke another parable to them, 'The kingdom of heaven is like leaven, which a woman took, and hid in three pecks of meal, until it was all leavened.'"
(Matthew 13:33)

The leaven, otherwise known as yeast, is a powerful microorganism which works to leaven dough into the making of bread. Jesus speaks of the smallest of seeds that they were aware of and now He's speaking of something smaller than the mustard seed and yet everyone knew of its power to make something larger than itself even larger. The intensity and strength of yeast when it is at work in a batch of dough doesn't even warrant explanation to the baker, he knows its value. But to the novice who doesn't know what yeast is, it is that which is used to make bread rise to its potential, otherwise you have flat bread.

The kingdom of heaven is like leaven. Leaven is placed within and works in the internal. It is a growing organism. It works within the dough to make it rise and become much larger and fluffier than it could on its own. Without yeast, bread is lifeless, flat, and can easily become brittle. Do you get the picture?

The kingdom of heaven is within and all of the principles of the kingdom dwell within. The internal power of God moves within us to make us a part of Him and

He becomes a part of us. Once you put yeast into the dough, you cannot separate it later after it has done its work. The leaven makes the dough what it is and the dough has fully absorbed the leaven to make it a part of itself. The dough and the leaven become one. You cannot extract the leaven from leavened dough. Get that! After the dough rises, you can beat the dough and flatten it out if you wish, but you cannot beat the leaven out of the dough. You cannot put the dough through any type of machinery and extract the leaven, it is not only in there to stay, it has made the dough into something else entirely. And that is, if you apply heat and baking time to the now leavened dough, you will have bread…warm, tasty bread good enough to feed others.

Take the bread, break it, and eat it for it is His body, broken for you. In like manner, when His kingdom dwells within us, His glory rises within us so that we can become the bread of life to others. We get broken and torn apart for His glory and yet, He cannot be ripped out of us for He dwells within us and we have become a part of Him as He is a part of us. It is His prayer that we become one with Him as He is one with the Father. (John 17)

Receive Him and be in Him as He is in you. Rest in Him and when you rise in maturity, you will become as broken bread for a very hungry world. Go in peace and be the blessing that He is in you to be.

August 24th

The Prophecy Fulfilled

Listen, O my people, to my instruction; incline your ears to the words of my mouth. I will open my mouth in a parable; I will utter dark sayings of old, which we have heard and known, and our fathers have told us." (Psalm 78:1-3)

At this point in Jesus' ministry, He did not speak to them without a parable which is "a brief narrative which forcefully illustrates a single idea" [1]…the single idea being the Kingdom of God. The Gospel of Jesus Christ was and is the gospel of the Kingdom of God. Matthew quotes the Psalm as saying 'I will utter things hidden since the foundation of the world', (v. 13:35b). The Kingdom of God has always been and will always be. The temporary life of this world as we know it will soon pass away and a new heaven and a new earth will be seen as the eternal dwelling place of the Most High. (Revelation 21:1-3). The things that we see, touch, hear, taste, and smell are the material, temporary things of this world that we relate to. The spiritual kingdom is the eternal reality that is the throne of God. He has always been and will always be.

We have already discussed the purpose of the parables in that seeing people would not see and hearing they would not be able to hear. But to those who open their eyes and open their hearts to receive such a gift as He, He gladly receives them unto Himself. "I tell you the truth, if anyone doesn't receive the Kingdom of God like a child shall not enter it." (Luke 18:17, NLT)

The humility and innocence of a child is the reception of believing and trusting what a man says and believes that he is telling the truth. The child listens with bated breath to hear what the father is saying and desires to do what the father says to do. It is becoming of a child to desire the father's good grace in pleasure knowing that obedience is blissful and ever-believing that truth is in the father's mouth. The child believes in the father's heart. The child believes the father's beliefs. So it is with the Father and the Son believing and being as One. The Holy Spirit we now have imparting the Spirit of God to us who believe in childlike faith, believing that the Son has told us the Truth about His Father's Kingdom.

It is the life of an obedient child to believe, obey, and follow his/her father and mother. It is all so very simple. The type of father or mother that we are to our children goes a long way towards helping our own children to love and have faith in our heavenly Father. We can present a loving father or a stern and hateful father. It is really up to us in what we present to our children and to others on how we personally believe our heavenly Father is to us. The sayings of old, hidden since the foundation of the world reveals a Father who is our Creator, our Provider, Protector, Redeemer, King, Savior, and Friend. He invites us into His abode, His Kingdom that has no end. I want to live there with Him. I pray that you do, too.

What is your prayer today?

August 25th

The Treasure Hidden

"The kingdom of heaven is like a treasure hidden in the field, which a man found and hid; and from joy over it he goes and sells all that he has, and buys that field." (Matthew 13:44)

Covered in rock, asphalt, pavement, and trees
Layered over with mortar, brick, wood, and steel.
Layered over with more wood, more steel and carpets galore,
Covered with layers of what men think it is.

Fabric and steel and painted glass;
Cloaked in suits and robes and ties and hats.
Relaxed now a bit, but all the same;
The place of the treasure hidden.

For it is nowhere seen
At times, not even here.
The souls of men still wane
In search of the treasure hidden

For naught they search, they search amiss
In search of the treasure hidden
Still mocked, alone it is
The treasure still unseen.

As in the hour of breath to breathe
In search of the treasure hidden
Breathe in, breathe out and look inside
The place of the treasure hidden.

The place of the treasure hidden is the place that men go searching to find peace and rest. Jesus told us to "ask, and it would be given to you, seek and you will find, knock and the door will be opened." (Matt. 7:7, KJV) The world and the prince of this world have blinded many to the truth of the Kingdom.

Religion and man's religious attempts to make the Kingdom what they think it ought to be, hides the Kingdom from others' opportunities to find it. But here, Jesus forewarns us that the kingdom is like a treasure hidden in a field. You have to seek it; go after it; it's not going to be sitting out in the open for all to see. It's not a church building nor is it a material, temporal thing. The Kingdom of God is not just a place but it is the person of Jesus Christ. He is the King of His domain and the Lord of all creation. In the humblest of hearts, continually submit to Him and give up all that you are and His grace will cover you and fill you with the treasure that you have so longed for…His Holy Spirit of grace, glory, and life.

August 26th

The Pearl of Great Value

"Again, the kingdom of heaven is like a merchant seeking fine pearls, and upon finding one pearl of great value, he went and sold all that he had, and bought it." (Matthew 13:45-46)

The merchant who seeks fine pearls has a very good idea what he is looking for. He doesn't want a reasonable facsimile, he wants the real thing. His eye is on the prize of the best and he will not cease from searching until he has found the nothing but the very best. What he was willing to do, however, is what most men fail to do and that is when he found the pearl of great value, he went and sold all that he had so that he could purchase the pearl for his keeping.

We have to take a look at the merchant…he knew what he was looking for and a substitution would not suffice. There are many false prophets gone out into the world and there are many false teachings as well. We have to search the Word of God for the Truth in the Holy Spirit. Read the Word every day for yourself and pray the Holy Spirit to guide you into all Truth.

The merchant, upon finding the pearl of great value, went and sold all that he had so that he would be able to purchase the pearl. When we are presented with the Gospel of Jesus Christ, we have to give up all that we are in order to become born again in His Spirit. It is the work of God, but it will not happen for us unless we relinquish our own wills unto Him and humble ourselves in His Presence. The old religious clichés of inviting Jesus into our heart and in a matter of 8 to 10 seconds, we become saved, is not exactly what the scripture says. It is not the amount of the time that is wrong, it is the presumption that we can take a piece of Jesus into our lives and then walk away. Absolutely not, we must be born again! Easy believism is cheap grace and not grace at all.

Be willing to give up all, just like the merchant was willing to do. We give up all that we are and receive all that He is, bless the Lord. Current teaching has the gospel skewed from a one way reception of Jesus in your heart and then you supposedly go and live your life for Jesus. Again, that is not what the Word says.

Jesus pictures the Kingdom of God as the greatest of all values. We only obtain at the juncture of giving all that we are. Jesus said, "And calling the crowds with His disciples, he said to them, 'If anyone would come after Me, let him deny himself, take up his cross, and follow Me." (Mark 8:34, ESV).

Be willing to give all, surrender all, and deny all, especially the things that you think are the best of you, and go…follow Him.

August 27th

The Good Fish and the Bad Fish

"Again, the kingdom of heaven is like a dragnet cast into the sea, and gathering fish of every kind; and when it was filled, they drew it up on the beach; and they sat down, and gathered the good fish into containers, but the bad they threw away." (Matthew 13:47-48)

The Truth of the Word of God is oftentimes difficult to understand and for those who think that everyone is going to heaven, then that same Truth can be a terribly hard pill to swallow. Jesus came that men might have life and that life more abundantly. Our Father wishes that none would perish, but that all would come to everlasting life. The Word never promises that all are going to heaven, and Jesus makes it very clear through His parables and teachings that all are definitely not going to be in the kingdom of heaven. Who decides? God does, not us.

In this parable, the sea is the world of men and women. The dragnet is the preaching of the Gospel. How will they know if they do not hear and how will they hear without a preacher? At the end of the age, the good will be separated from the bad. How do we know good from bad? Jesus has told us that it is by our fruit. The fruit of the Spirit of God is love, joy, peace, patience, goodness, kindness, gentleness, faithfulness, and self-control. You must be born again to inherit these qualities of the Spirit-filled life. Otherwise, you will not inherit the kingdom of God.

The fish obviously represent the peoples of the world and according to this parable and other parables, there are only two types, the good and the bad. Please do not take this parable unilaterally and make it to mean that 'good' people will be gathered into the kingdom as if to say that 'if I do good things for people, then the Lord will see I'm a really good person, and He'll let me live with Him in heaven.' That is not what this parable is saying. Jesus said that only the Father is 'good'. In that case, none of us would make it on our own merit or goodness, because none of us are righteous in His eyes. His goodness only comes from His Spirit and He is the only one who can make our 'tree' good by totally making us a new creation in Him. The ultimate penalty, or judgment, by the Lord is His judgment alone.

The real Christians will be separated from the fake hypocrites and the rest of the world who simply did not believe and abide in Him as Lord. Also, the real Christians will not be sitting in the judgment seat at the time of the judgment, any more than they are supposed sitting in the judgment seat of anyone now. The disciples of Jesus Christ are supposed to be about our Father's business of making disciples with the Good News of the Kingdom. We are to be His voice in the wilderness, crying out for others to walk in the way of the Lord. He is the one true judge. What is it to us if someone is perceivably blessed, or not? You, you follow the Lord and teach others to do the same.

August 28th

We Never Stop Learning

"Therefore every scribe who has become a disciple of the kingdom of heaven is like a head of a household, who brings forth out of his treasure things new and old." (Matthew 13:52)

If you've read the Bible for any length of time, you realize that the more you read, study, and pray through the scripture, the more the Word speaks to you by the power of the Holy Spirit. It is the work of the Holy Spirit to illuminate the word into our understanding. We can learn something new every time we read the same passages. We also learn according to our level of understanding. If the Holy Spirit has taught us one thing about a specific passage and we refuse to obey in that Word, we will fail to move on from that point in the Spirit. We are given what we are able according to our faith and, in like fellowship, what we are willing to obey.

The scribe who becomes a disciple of the kingdom of heaven is the one who lives in the word and writes it out plainly for others to understand and read. He is the one who abides in the word and writes it out with explanation so that old things are learned and new things are derived from the old and the learning never ceases. The power of the Holy Spirit is at work in the Word. The Word is living because of the Spirit of God.

There are few vocations greater than a scribe who abides in the Lord and is able to break bread with people in generosity by sharing the Word in Spirit and Truth. The word becomes fire in the bones of the scribe who generates the vibrancy of the Kingdom in words for others to understand. It is an unending quill of servitude to His Master in writing out what His Master says.

This scribe who becomes a disciple of the kingdom of heaven is likened to a head of a household who willingly shares the great things of the Lord with his children. The kingdom father who serves his children in teaching them and admonishing them in the Lord is the father who is blessed by the fruit of the Spirit in and on his children.

The love of the Word of God is seen in the heart of the disciple and is exacted in the hearts of believers everywhere. The children of God desire His Word. The disciple of the kingdom of heaven is the purveyor of all that is good and worthy to be spoken. The likeness of the kingdom is endless and provoking. Our hearts are drawn to His kingdom in the power of His Word. It is not just any scribe that will do, but it is the scribe who is the disciple of the kingdom of heaven who is the true head of the household. Seek the Lord where His Kingdom abounds.

August 29th

Believing Unbelief

"And He did not do many miracles there because of their unbelief."
(Matthew 13:58)

When Jesus had finished the parables and the teachings He went back to His hometown and taught in the synagogue. Even though they were astonished at His wisdom and whatever miracles He might have performed there, He just couldn't break through their belief that this was the carpenter's son and who could believe that a carpenter's son could perform such miracles. Does it take great effort to not believe what is looking at you in the face?

All that Jesus did, He did for many reasons. He went back to His hometown not only to show His hometown people how powerful their lack of faith is, but it stands even today that through their unbelieving testimony, that the lack of faith is pivotal in the possibility of the power of God to move in a community. Jesus showed us, unequivocally, that unbelief is a very powerful presence even in the Presence of God. He was also giving them the opportunity to believe and they showed us how simple it was to not believe. It takes a simple amount of belief to not believe something just as it takes a simple faith to believe in Jesus Christ. Miracles, events, teachings, wisdom, and things taking place that they had never seen before stood as stumbling blocks rather than precipitous inspiration to believe. Jesus did say that unless we have the faith of a child, we would not see the kingdom of God. A child can believe an adult word just by the word alone. The innocence of the child's thinking reflects the matters of the heart.

In like manner, the unbelieving spirit reflects the spirit of the heart of the man who chooses his own way to believe what he wants to believe. Even the miracle of the new birth being born again is prevented by a simple belief that it is either unnecessary or not received by unbelief. Either you believe Jesus Christ or you don't. Jesus did not fight with anyone about the kingdom. You either believed Him, or you didn't. The power of our own belief is illuminated here. It is a two way reciprocal relationship that when He speaks, we need to believe what He says, just like it is when He says I will be in you, you die to be in Him. There is nothing about the Kingdom that is one-sided. It takes the power of God to do His work and the open hearted faith of a child to believe He is who He says He is and He can do what He says He's done…and that is give you a new life and save your soul from the penalty of sin.

The power of God is all-powerful, but He is a gentleman and if you want to die with your sin, He will let you. He never begged anyone to believe that He was the Son of God. The marvelous aspect of believing in Him is that the faith to believe actually comes from Him; that is, it comes to hearts receptive of His faith and glory. Open your heart and be receptive so that He will fill you with His grace and give you life forevermore.

August 30th

The Effect of Conscience

"At that time Herod the tetrarch heard the news about Jesus, and said to his servants, 'This is John the Baptist; he has risen from the dead; and that is why miraculous powers are at work in him.'"   *(Matthew 14:1-2)*

We do not perfectly know if Herod the tetrarch believed in people rising from the dead, even though he stated such. How could a heathen Roman ruler who was a murderer and an adulterer believe in a spirit moving from one body to the next if it was not his conscience driving him to the internal to reflect on what he had done to John the Baptist? He knew that he not only had taken John's life by beheading him, but he knew he had taken his brother's wife. The conscience of a man in sin is awakened by holiness and he had certainly been confronted by the Holy Spirit at work in John.

Now, Jesus' renowned power was prevailing in the region and Herod hears of the work of the Holy Spirit in the body of Jesus of Nazareth. Herod just doesn't know that it's the work of the Holy Spirit; he thinks it's the spirit of John the Baptist. Jesus knows what Herod would do to Him, so He leaves that district for other cities. Still, we have to examine the work of conscience in a man in sin and the power of holiness when holiness comes knocking on the door of the sinful man's heart.

If we name the Name of Jesus Christ, it is so vital for us to recognize the work of the Holy Spirit in our lives. It is the work of the Spirit to convict the world of sin, judgment, and righteousness. At times, we could preach, nag, or complain until we are exhausted and then preach some more and the prevailing body of sin simply doesn't get what it is they've done. But when God in the Holy Spirit through a submitted vessel arrives, then the spirit of the man of sin is quickened. This is not to say that repentance is immediate or even forthcoming, for Herod did not repent of his sin, but I have known men, including myself, that have repented when confronted by the power of the Holy Spirit.

It is not up to us to judge men, but it is our duty as a vessel of the Lord to rightly represent the Holy Spirit and allow Him to do His work in other's lives and leave the results and the judgment up to Him. Sometimes, the best thing we can say to a man of sin when the time of confrontation arises is, "The Kingdom of God has come upon you. Repent!" And then, go and pray for that soul's repentance. This is the power of God in the work of the Holy Spirit in the Kingdom of God. It's all about Him and nothing about us. Freely you have been given, so freely give.

August 31st

The Need to Be Alone

"Now when Jesus heard it, He withdrew from there in a boat, to a lonely place by Himself..."   (Matthew 14:13a)

Now when Jesus heard about John the Baptist's death from John's disciples, Jesus goes to be alone on a boat. This passage is also found in Mark 6:32, Luke 9:10b, and John 6:1. Although the other gospels say that the disciples were with Jesus, it doesn't mean that Jesus wasn't alone on the boat by Himself. Jesus retreated to contemplate the loss and death of His cousin, and the Father's servant, John the Baptist. We cannot ever forget the impact of the work of John, nor could Jesus fail to understand what John's death meant in the timing of Jesus' ministry. Another aspect of the Lord's work had culminated in John's death, for John had spoken the words, "He must increase, but I must decrease." (John 3:3, ESV). Only Jesus knew what those words would mean. It was time to reflect on the life and ministry of John in honor of him.

When our Lord would go to be alone, He would always pray. It is recorded often of our Lord that He would go to a mountain, or go to a solitary place and pray. Here, the location is a boat to get away from the bustling crowds and the thoughts of a worried tetrarch in Herod. It was not time for Jesus to die and whether there was any concern for Herod's thoughts of John rising from the dead; Jesus would have no part of that.

We cannot underestimate our need to be alone with our Lord. We have to go to the secret placed often, unimpeded by the company of family and friends. We have to have large amounts of time to be with our Lord in prayer. Prayer is being with Him and listening in meditation in His Presence. Many folk believe that prayer is asking for things and that may sometimes be the case, but it is not our motivation. His Presence is to be our motivation in prayer, whether we are alone in our closet or alone in His Presence in a room full of people. We can pray privately or we can pray with others publicly, but we cannot pray faithfully publicly if we have not prayed faithfully privately.

It is time to be on our knees alone with Him. Sit privately with Him in your secret place. Everyone's secret place is different, but everyone's secret place involves the Presence of God in holiness and power. God still moves and His Spirit rewards those openly who seek Him privately. The reward is the blessing of the Presence in time continuance. We do not leave Him in the secret place, He promises to go with us where we go and we know that in the Kingdom of God, wherever He is, we are and wherever we are, He is.

Father, we thank you for allowing us to be a part of You. You are so wonderful to us and we continually submit to You in Your Presence. We pray Your peace be upon us this day, oh Lord our Rock and our Redeemer. Amen.

September 1st

The Reward of Following the Lord

"...and when the multitudes heard of this, they followed Him on foot from the cities. And when He went ashore, He saw a great multitude, and felt compassion for them, and healed their sick."   *(Matthew 14:13b-14)*

We do not know how much time elapsed from when Jesus departed to the boat to be alone and when the multitudes heard about where he had gone. Word of mouth passes quickly, sometimes to our dismay it passes too quickly. The multitudes did not have technology to move information around regarding Jesus' status, however, word of mouth has always been man's greatest proclaimer of what is happening in the local community.

The multitudes followed Jesus wherever He went, it seemed. They were many and tired, having no made of transportation other than their feet. If they traveled any distance to get to Jesus, it would take longer to get back to their home. Their reward for following Him to His place of rest was that they, too, would find rest in Him. His compassion on the multitudes was always evident. His compassion always involved physical healing as well. The compassion of the Holy Spirit is revealing to those in need. People in need of emotional, physical, mental or spiritual healing can always find their need met in the compassion of the Holy Spirit.

It is a wonder at how some folk view the masses of people at times. Some say, "There's just too many people, I don't want to go there…" Leaders, looking at their Sunday congregations, see only needs and are bothered by their needs, but welcome the offerings. To note: Jesus did not require monetary offerings for meeting the needs of people in healing and teaching.

We have to learn from the events in the scripture because they help us in our present. The ever constant reward of following Jesus is, first of all, His Presence. He is where He is and we can depend on Him to be faithful to Himself and His Word. Secondly, wherever He is, there is healing. He heals our hearts first, second, and third. He heals our minds. He heals us of our diseases whether you believe that, or not. Some are healed miraculously in an instant and others are healed over time. But Jesus did not heal everyone He met, nor does He do that today. Whatever He did then, He can do today. Beware of those who say, though, that He will heal every one of their diseases. He didn't do it then and I have not seen Him do that today. Perhaps His healing takes different forms in the human body, but let's keep the main focus of His Presence at heart and not just what we can get from Him.

The reward of the faithful follower is Jesus Himself. He told us to seek, ask, and knock. He did not tell us how many times or when to stop. In fact, if He didn't tell us when to stop, why we would ever stop seeking, asking, and knocking? Draw near to the Lord while He may be found and you will not be found lacking in any good thing.

September 2nd

The More Than Enough Blessing

"But Jesus said to them, 'They do not need to go away; you give them something to eat!"   (Matthew 14:16)

Imagine seeing the multitude of people seemingly everywhere. It is said that there were 'about five thousand men who ate, aside from women and children.' (v.21) When the response came back from the disciples that they were able to locate five loaves of bread and two fish, Jesus implored them, 'Bring them here to me.' (v.18) Remember, Jesus is always teaching whether He's teaching or healing or delivering or feeding. He takes the five loaves of bread and the two fish and looks up toward heaven and blesses the food and then breaks the loaves. What does it mean that He blesses the food? I do not believe it means what we have been taught and what we have taught our children; that being, simply thanking God for our food.

That is as simplistic a teaching as there is, but I believe that Jesus 'blessed' the food because that what the Word says He did. It doesn't say that He gave thanks to the Lord for the food as we have been taught to say 'our blessing' before we eat. No, that is not what Jesus did. He blessed the food, broke it and it multiplied!

The scenario is this: there are more than five thousand people, possibly as many as ten thousand, sitting hungry waiting to be taught - 'fed'. Jesus takes what was there, the five loaves and the two fish. He looks up to heaven in agreement with His Father and 'blesses' the food. The blessing of the food caused it to be multiplied to the 'more than enough'. It is the power of God revealed over again just like the widow woman and the jars of oil in 2 Kings 4:4-6, where the widow woman is given a 'more than enough' supply of oil to pay all of her debts and then some. It is the same as the 'more than enough' supply in Exodus 36:7, when the people brought supply for the sanctuary and Moses had to tell the people to stop, because they had already given 'more than enough'.

It is the same 'more than enough' in the daily manna that was given to the people of Israel in the Exodus. It is the same 'more than enough' blessing that Paul received from the Philippians in abundance and ample supply. The same 'more than enough' blessing that in the parable of the prodigal son in Luke 15:17, where the son realizes that in his father's house, there is 'more than enough' and to spare. This is the power of God at work in the blessing of the 'more than enough' which requires whatever to be given to be broken and dispersed to meet the needs of the many.

Be willing to be the bread of life as He was the Bread of Life for you. In this, we become broken bread to share the Bread of Life with others. He was broken for us, bruised for our iniquities, and the chastisement of the people fell upon Him. It is the blessing of the power of God that as He was broken for the sin of the world, the world is blessed from His brokenness in us. His Spirit is all-encompassing and all-empowering and the blessing of the 'more than enough' continues forever.

September 3rd

Preparation for Prayer

"And immediately He made the disciples get into the boat, and go ahead of Him to the other side, while He sent the multitudes away." (Matthew 14:22)

I have often wondered if Jesus slept much because when He was not out about doing good, healing, and teaching, the Word often says that He would go and be alone to pray. Immediately after supplying the multitudes with the 'more than enough' blessing of broken bread and fish; He sends the disciples away in the boat and the multitudes away to their dwellings. It is said that what they picked up after everyone ate was twelve full baskets of food…this was after He fed the five thousand plus people. (v. 20) Everyone was well fed, however, Jesus needed to retire to prayer to replenish His Spirit after the blessing.

"He went up to the mountain by Himself to pray; and when it was evening, He was there alone." (v. 23) We cannot underestimate our need to be alone with our Lord to pray. If Jesus did it as the Son of God, we, too, need it more so than He. I am finding that it is He who grows within me in the times of reliance and prayer. My faith grows in Him when He grows in me. He is the builder of my faith and without Him I am alone and without a plan. The same is true if I decide to move on without Him, which is what most of us have done when we get ourselves into trouble; we've moved without Him moving in leadership.

Prayer comes first, not our plans and then the request of blessing. When we present our bodies to Him as a living sacrifice, we are still living, just as Isaac was on Abraham's trip to the land of Moriah. We present our bodies to Him as our reasonable act of worship. He takes us and breaks us for His purposes. Don't cry when He decides what He wants to do with you. If you have given your life to Him, let Him pray the prayer of blessing over your broken life that the blessing of the 'more than enough' covers you in abundant everlasting life. Then and only then will you be able to join with Abraham and call that place…The Lord Will Provide. (Genesis 22)

He is fed in us as we pray from spirit to Spirit. He witnesses to Himself within us as we pray. And He prays within us even when we do not know what to pray. (Romans 8) It is up to us to send the noises and the multitudes of the busyness from work and life away so that we can clearly hear His voice and recognize His Spirit within us.

Prayer with Him gives Him the opportunity to guide us into understanding and lead us in the way in which we should go. Jesus did this, how much more so should we who stay in desperate need of holiness, righteousness, and faith. By His Spirit we live, and love and have our being. Stay in His Spirit, abide in His grace, and the more than enough blessing will be in you forever.

September 4th

Go To the Mountain

"And after he had sent the multitudes away, he went up to the mountain by Himself to pray; and when it was evening, he was there alone."
(Matthew 14:23)

"And after bidding them farewell, He departed to the mountain to pray."
(Mark 6:46)

"And it was at this time that He went off to the mountain to pray, and He spent the whole night in prayer to God." (Luke 6:12)

Jesus was the Son of God. He was God incarnate. He was divinely God and divinely human. He bled and died as the Son of God and the Son of Man. He prayed to His heavenly Father. How much more so should we who are made just a little lower than the angels go to our heavenly Father and pray in Jesus' Name.

Jesus told us to pray in secret. He told us to go to our room and pray in the secret place. Jesus went to the mountain, to be alone with His Father. Jesus prayed for His Father's words and His Father's will. He said that He only said what the Father had Him say and that He only did what the Father had Him do. How about you? How about me?

Our mountain is to be our place to pray. The place to pray must be alone. We will pray aloud at our dinner table with our family. We will pray with our spouses. We will pray aloud with our children in the mornings before school or events, and we will pray aloud with our children at bedtime. We will pray at all times, in unceasing prayer. We will pray aloud in public worship and confession. We will pray aloud in public, yes; to be heard by the public, no.

But you, when you pray, go to the secret place, and your heavenly Father will hear you. Pray and read His word and read and pray His word. Get to the mountain to be with Him. He is His will and as you know Him, you will know His will. Praying is getting into alignment with Him. Know Him today in the each and every moment you breathe in His breath and go out and allow Him to change your world today!

September 5th

Fearlessly Facing the Storm

"But the boat was already many stadia away from the land, battered by the waves; for the wind was contrary. And in the fourth watch of the night He came to them, walking on the sea."   *(Matthew 14:24-25)*

In all that Jesus did, He was always teaching us. He wasn't teaching us to take everything literal, if that were the case, then every disciple would be able to heal people, multiply bread and fish enough for five thousand people, and we could literally walk on water. Always looking within the context of the scripture, we discover spiritual truths over and over again, and at times, discover new truths that we have never seen before. The Word is alive because the Holy Spirit is alive in the Word to speak to us about the Word for today. These truths are spiritual and must be received in the Spirit.

"A stadion was about 600 feet"[1] and the boat was many stadia away. The boat is being battered by the waves. It is being tossed and thrown, but not overturned. The wind was causing the storm and the wind was contrary, it was moving in contrary directions of varying speeds and lifts. It was as though the force causing the winds to cause the seas to rage were purposely attempting to overturn the boat of the disciples for their ultimate death. What was the force that raged against the disciples' boat? Even though we know from the story that the boat was not overturned, in the moments of the storm, the poor disciples didn't know what was going to happen.

About the fourth watch of the night, which was between three o'clock until six o'clock in the morning, Jesus is seen walking on the water towards the boat. They think it is a ghost and become extremely frightened. Imagine that! Then they cry out in fear for what they believe is happening to them. Have they sunk in the midst of the storm only to see the dead walking on the water? Have the dead come to life from the raging of the storm? What would you be thinking if you were out in the middle of a raging storm at sea and your boat was being tossed about from the wind and the waves, and then in the middle of the storm and the night, you see a figure walking on the sea? Be honest! They might have been thinking that they were next!

"But immediately Jesus spoke to them saying, 'Take courage, it is I, do not be afraid.'" (v.27) All it takes is for us to hear His voice, 'It is I, do not be afraid.' Our problem is that we get so stressed out from our storms that we don't even look for Him or open our ears for His voice to speak until we are more than halfway through the horrible experience we're going through. We do not know the forces that are trying to kill us at times, but we can know that He is always present. We do not know what manner of spirit is attacking us from without or within, but we do know that He is able to conquer any fear, any doubt, any trouble and any storm in our lives.

The storms will definitely come and they will rage and Jesus will be there in His own miraculous way right along with us. Acknowledge Him in all of your ways and see His purposes come to pass even in the midst of the contrariness of the wind and the waves in your life. He is Almighty and He is Immanuel, God with us!

September 6th

A Stroke of Courage

"And Peter answered Him and said, 'Lord, if it is You, command me to come to You on the water.' And He said, "Come!" And Peter got out of the boat, and walked on the water and came toward Jesus." (Matthew 14:28-29)

What will it take for us to be driven out of our boat? What will it take for us to see that in us is no good thing and it's time for us to be rid of ourselves to have all that He is. He's walking on the water towards you and calling your name, saying, 'Come! Follow Me." Get out of your boat, yourself, and get into Him. The waves are crashing, your body is beaten, and is being tossed all about, and yet, you don't want to give up what you hold dear…and that is yourself!

Selfishness is the one thing most pastors don't preach about because they believe that sin is the only problem. The sin may certainly influence from without, but it's what's in your mind that is the majority of your problem. Get out of yourself…get out of the boat and let Him take over.

Our own selfishness keeps us in sinking ships. It's our selfishness that looks at the storms of life and asks for deliverance from the storm, but not deliverance from ourselves. Most of the time, we are our own worst enemy. Get out of the self and into Life. Jesus said that if any man desired to come after Him, he needed to deny himself, take up his cross and follow Him. For what would a man give in exchange for his soul…even the whole world? Would you take the whole world in exchange for your soul? But Jesus said if we would lose our lives for His sake, we would have the life that only He can give.

Peter stood looking out into the water cresting high with waves and said, 'Lord, if it's You, call me to come to You!' We do that at times as well, and bargain with God in the midst of our troubles and in the middle of our deliverance, we say, 'Lord, if it's You???' Then we get delivered from the 'whatever' and off we go to sink again because we couldn't keep our eyes on our deliverer. Troubles beset everyone, but to the ones who go out in courage, just as Peter did and say, 'Lord, I know it's You, I recognize your Spirit, You're here to deliver once again and I praise You and thank You for it!'

Don't criticize Peter for being overtaken by the waves. Learn from him that if we can keep our eyes on Jesus, then in the power of the Holy Spirit, all things will be possible even in the midst of the most terrible storm you could go through. Yell out to Jesus, keeping your eyes on Him and say, 'Jesus, I come!' and He will receive you with open arms!

September 7th

Increase Our Faith

"But seeing the wind, he became afraid, and beginning to sink, he cried out, saying, 'Lord, save me!' And immediately Jesus stretched out His hand and took hold of him, and said to him, 'O you of little faith, why did you doubt?'"
(Matthew 14:30-31)

The courage that it took for Peter to get out that boat in the midst of the storm and literally walk out onto the sea was inexplicably extraordinary. It is beyond my imagination. But what we see as courage was in reality faith. It was courage in the flesh, but faith in the heart, and faith is greater than courage. I believe it to be both faith and courage; but when Peter began to sink into the sea; Jesus did not have to pull him out of the water because of his lack of courage but because of his little faith. It was faith that encouraged him to step out onto the water and it was the amount of faith that was the tipping point on whether he remained on top of the water, or sank as he did. Faith, in the Spirit, can be measured. The Holy Spirit is able to determine our level of faith. We see what we see as tangible objects; the things that are temporal, the ordinary things of life. When someone does something extraordinary, we try to attach words and physical symbols to the instance so that we can somehow identify with a particular event of extraordinary activity. Faith is intangible to us, but a tangible thing to the Holy Spirit; it is unseen in the natural. We cannot account for our faith and take a measuring rod to it and determine the amount or level of our faith, but the Holy Spirit can. The Holy Spirit knows for certain what we can only know when we are tried. Faith is measured on the inside and not by the size of our bank account or our position in life.

Faith walkers are tried every day and every day an amount is added to their coffers. Faith comes from hearing and hearing from the Word of God. The Word is God Himself and in our current dimension, it is the work of the Holy Spirit. We do not create or manufacture our own faith. The apostles cried out to the Lord, 'Lord, increase our faith.' (Luke 17:5)

It was Jesus walking on the raging sea that said to Peter, 'O you of little faith.' How much faith does it require to walk on water? Personally, I do not know anyone with that amount of faith, and I have been in churches all of my life. Again, never criticize Peter for having 'little faith'. He walked on a stormy sea and you do not know anyone who has done that in 'faith'. Another thing that gets repeated wrongly is that teachers will say Peter had a lack of faith. Faith is measured in amounts and the little that Peter had was more than any man I have ever known.

Faith comes from the Holy Spirit. We do not believe on our own accord. The faith that we have was given to us. (2 Cor. 9:10; Rom. 10:17; Gal. 5:22) "The wind blows where it wishes and you hear the sound of it, but do not know where it comes from and where it is going; so is everyone who is born of the Spirit." (John 3:8) The dwelling place of God is the Kingdom of God…it is His domain. He is His Holy Spirit and the way into Him is by His Spirit. Pray in the Spirit that the Lord will increase your faith for it is the faith that He has given you that enables you to understand, obey, love, and move about in His Kingdom. Do not fear for it is He who is doing the testing for the more increase in Him. (1 Peter 1:7; 4:12; James 1:2, 12)

September 8th

Revealing Power

"And those who were in the boat worshipped Him, saying, 'You are certainly God's Son'"   *(Matthew 14:33)*

The revealing power of God humbles men of faith to their knees in worship. It is one thing to hear about God and His creative power and quite another to know God for yourself and see His work with your own eyes. When Jesus and Peter got into the boat, the storm ceased. They were able to see deliverance from the storm, but more importantly, they were able to have a private account of the miraculous power of God with their very own eyes. They saw Jesus walk on a raging sea and lead Peter to do the same thing. They saw that it was He Who had the power to walk on the laws of nature and it was He Who had the power to give faith to Peter to do the same thing. It was the power of God at work to control the weather to calm the sea. They recognized His authority as God in the flesh and could do nothing but fall to their knees in worship.

How often are we struck by the power of God and recognize that it is He Who has performed this mighty work and it drives us to our knees in worship and adoration? If you've never found yourself in that atmosphere, then wake yourself up to the power of God. Pray that He will open your eyes to His mighty works. He is still at work in lives today. Get out of yourself and into the Spirit to see the Spirit's working power to change men's lives, to heal the sick, to heal the brokenhearted and restore sight to the blind and hearing to the deaf.

Anytime you get a revelation from Him, marvel not at your own intellect or discernment, but marvel at the work of the Holy Spirit speaking to you. Anytime you hear or see the healing of someone, marvel not at the handiwork of a specialist or doctor, but marvel at the handiwork of God. Anytime you see a man change from his evil ways and repent to God and to his wife, marvel not in criticism of his old ways, but marvel at the handiwork of God.

Give God the glory for the mighty works that He performs every day in people. God is to be glorified for His wonderful works and power. Do not underestimate the power of God to work on your behalf today as you pray for a lost family member or an erring son. Pray, always pray for others and intercede that the Holy Spirit will move in their conscious to come to Him or come back to Him. The possibility of God's power can move mountains of problems and we need to recognize Him when He performs His work and give honor to whom honor is due. Worship Him now for His power to move in your life and change you completely into a son or daughter of God. He alone deserves our praise and adoration. Never take credit for His handiwork and the faith that He has given you will be increased all the more to see more of His glory at work.

September 9th

Recognizing Power

"And when the men of that place recognized Him, they sent into all that surrounding district and brought to Him all who were sick; and they began to entreat Him that they might just touch the fringe of His cloak; and as many as touched it were cured."   *(Matthew 14:35-36)*

People who live in want and need see things more readily than those that have their needs met. While a man of renown, who has many material things, may desire the more that life has to give him, the poor and needy gravitate towards the one who has the power to give them the very basic things in life. Rich, healthy folk simply do not 'need' Jesus. They may find Him somewhere along their path when they are confronted by the Spirit, but even Jesus said that it was hard for a rich man to enter the kingdom of heaven. (Matt. 19:23)

In Gennesaret, the need for healing was astronomical among the folk who lived there and the surrounding region. Word of mouth was the way news was spread for people to come to Jesus' location wherever He might be found. But the true passion of the people was their recognition of Jesus' power. The recognition of Jesus' power is the entry point of faith. Where there is no recognition of God, there is no faith.

The belief was so strong there that all the surrounding district of peoples gathered for their health needs to be met. They believed and they were rewarded according to their faith. They believed so strongly that if they could just touch the fringe of His cloak, then they would be healed; and they were.

My spirit here is interrupted with what has happened to us. There has been so little experience of the power of God in people's lives today, particularly in the United States; that most have come to believe that the power that was expressed in the days of the Bible was only for then and not for now. But, the Bible doesn't say that. The only people who do say that are people who have been taught that by some unfaithful creature who has created and perpetuated a lie from hell. Just because you think you have not experienced this kind of faith and this kind of healing does not mean that it does not exist. The existence of a thing exists in the minds and hearts of people.

Faith is a fact. Even though faith is not an outward tangible object, we believe that it exists in our hearts and it does, whether some other person of unbelief believes it or not. Faith exists just as any other scientific fact exists. One cannot argue faith; either you believe it exists or you don't. The people of Gennesaret believed in faith that Jesus could heal them of any of their diseases, even to the touching of his cloak. Again, what has happened to us?

Has it been the hundreds of years of traditional religious thought to cover the power of God under a veil simply because a group of men hundreds of years ago stopped believing? Recognize the power of God. Jesus is the same, yesterday, today, and forevermore! (Hebrews 13:8) That is a giant clue to those who preach that the power of God was for then and not for now. Believe in God by what God says about Himself and not what men try to teach you by their doctrines. Recognize His power and you will be amazed in ever-increasing faith in Him.

September 10th

The Doctrines of Men

"Then some of the Pharisees and scribes came to Jesus from Jerusalem, saying, 'Why do your disciples transgress the tradition of the elders? For they do not wash their hands when they eat bread.'" (Matthew 15:1-2)

Where the recognition of Almighty God abounds, faith abounds, and where faith, the God kind of faith abounds, the power of God moves mightily in majestic power. Healing, release, forgiveness, and freedom abound in God faith.

The opposite is also true. Where men dare to tread against the Spirit of God believing their unbelief, the recognition of God is absent. Hence, where there is no recognition and acknowledgement of God, there is no faith. Where there is no faith in God, the power of God lies dormant. (Matt. 11:20; 13:58)

And so it is with the Pharisees, both of yesterday and today. The Pharisees are the prideful religious folk who dwell in whitewashed tombs thinking that it is their works that get them an audience with God. They think they can earn their way into His Presence and teach others to obey their rules that not even they can obey completely. Where there is self-sufficiency, there is no faith. Self-anything prevents the want-to-be believer from entering into a real life of faith. The doctrines of men in their religious turpitude dispel truth from its hinges and replaces truth with a lie. Where there is no recognition of God in truth and spirit, there is no truth, and where there is no truth, there is no faith. In the system of religion, men dwell on their doctrines rather than worship the Lord in faith. Remember that the power of God brings men to their knees in worship of Him. A man who refuses to worship Him, does not know Him in faith, but only by what other men have said about Him. "But all these things they will do to you on account of my name, because they do not know him who sent me." (John 15:21, ESV)

"The Kingdom of God does not come with observation, neither will they say, see here, or see there, but the Kingdom of God dwells within you." (Luke 17:20). The fruit of the Spirit of God will flow from the Spirit-filled believer and works of obedience will follow the faith that resides in the holy heart saved eternally for God. Other men try to do the work of God for God, but in their own power and do not have the faith that comes only from God.

The faith inside a man is measured only by the Spirit. It does not come by washing your hands, but by the washing of your heart by the Word of the Holy Spirit. The Kingdom of God has come upon you. You must be born again! Otherwise, you will not see the kingdom of God. (John 3:3)

September 11th

Traditions and Hypocrisy

"This people honors Me with their lips, but their heart is far from Me. But in vain do they worship Me, teaching as doctrines the precepts of men."
(Isaiah 29:13/Matthew 15:8-9)

When God said to honor our fathers and mothers, and 'He who speaks evil of father or mother, let him be put to death' (v. 4), He meant it for always and all times. Just because we may have been taught that as a part of the ten commandments as a child, it doesn't mean that when we become 18 years old, or 68 years old, that we outgrow the commandment. We never outgrow God's Holy Word, no matter how old we get. With that said, we never get too old that we are not to honor our fathers and mothers. The Pharisees didn't quite get that. They thought that with all of their regimented additional laws that they had created it somehow exonerated them from obeying God's original Word. So, it would make them 'look' better in the eyes of men to give their tithes, offerings, and monies to the Temple in outward shows of religiosity, but leave their fathers and mothers to go hungry or homeless in the process.

Traditions and religion never trump God's Word, the nature of God or God Himself. If a church leader is leading you or others to negate the Word of God or the love of God, which is His nature, in order to fulfill their man-made traditions, then it is time to honor the Lord by obeying Him in the totality of His Word. Jesus called the Pharisees 'hypocrites' for their service to their traditions at the expense of their own fathers and mothers. Where is the love of God in that?

It is what is in our hearts that reveals who we are and who is ruling our destiny. Our mouths, disposition, and our money reveal who our real lord is. Bad fruit comes from bad trees and good fruit comes from good trees. We have to have a heart that desires the Lord in all matters of life. Make the heart good by denying the self and going on to completeness in Him.

It is in the each and every moment that we continually need to submit to our Lord. Whenever a question arises, get used to communing with Him so that you clearly hear His voice say, 'This is the way, walk in it.' We learn to hear His voice by reading, studying, and praying His Word. In His Word, we learn His nature and His nature is always that of holy love. Let His holy love be your driving force from within as His Spirit dwells within you. Abiding in Him and Him abiding in you is life in the Kingdom of God. Know His Word! Know His Spirit! Breathe in and breathe out the Word of the Lord and He will prove Himself faithful and add faith to your life in the Spirit.

September 12th

The Defiled Man

"...Hear and understand. Not what enters into the mouth defiles the man, but what proceeds out of the mouth, this defiles the man."   *(Matthew 15:10b-11)*

Jesus was saying here what we see quite plainly today, that the ceremonial washing of the hands does not 'spiritually' clean a man. Jesus was always referring to the internal and the within. The Kingdom is within and the heart is within. What comes out of the mouth, whether it be a word or a dispositional attitude; it emanates from the within the heart.

Oftentimes, we really do not want to admit this about ourselves. We look and listen to other people and we quickly jump to conclusions about them because of their words, their tone of voice, or their disposition. We form judgments of others against them if we don't like them and we form judgments in favor of other folk that we believe we like at the time; and all the while, we say it was what they said, or how they said it. Basically, people judge others based on their personal likes and dislikes forgetting that they're not supposed to be judging others at all. A judgment that comes from the mouth, just because you believe it was expressed nicely is still an unlawful judgment. You see, it's not just the ugly, mean things that defile a person; it's also the judgments, the criticism, the haughty behavior, the prideful gestures, and the clickish nature of a selfish human being trying to belong to other selfish folk in a group. All of these things and more emanate from the hearts of men and women.

None of us are exempt when it comes to possessing an unjust heart. "The human heart is the most deceitful above all things and beyond cure. Who can understand it?" (Jer. 17:9, NIV)

The criticism of a hypocrite is undeniably wounding and yet the hypocrite doesn't realize that their heart is cruel and they simply refuse to admit it. The Psalmist knew his heart when he pleaded with the Lord, "Create a clean heart in me, O Lord, and renew a right spirit within me." (Psalm 51:10, KJV)

Jesus said, "But the things that proceed out of the mouth come from the heart, and those defile the man. For out of the heart come evil thoughts, murders, adulteries, fornications, thefts, false witness and slanders." (v. 18, 19)

This is an internal check time for you, not for your spouse or your neighbor, your brother or sister, or your co-worker. This message is for you as you read these words. Check your spirit by checking your words, tone of voice, disposition, and attitude. We all have bad days and we all say things we shouldn't, but the time has come for the Kingdom of God to come upon you and for you to repent of all these things, turn and walk away from the evil heart that lies within. The fruit is in your mouth and you're not fooling anyone anymore for you now know the Truth and the Truth can make you free if you will deny the self, take up your cross, and follow Him in the each and every moment in the each and every day. You must be born again! And, if you believe that you have been born again, then why do you continually find yourself saying things that are defiled from the heart?

Being born again is how you have a newly cleansed heart, not just a washed heart from a bad day, but a totally new heart living in His Spirit forevermore. You are responsible for yourself before the Holy Spirit of God. It's time to be clean. Allow Him to make you clean right now…

September 13th

The Cleansed Heart

"But the things that proceed out of the mouth come from the heart, and those defile the man." (Matthew 15:18)

The things, or people, we talk about are the things that we have thought about in our hearts. We ruminate on our inclinations, the things we hold dear. Eventually these things will come out of us whether it comes from our mouths in words, our hands in our writings, our attitudes in our facial expressions, or the tone in our disposition. Whatever is in is bound to come out at some point in time. Whatever is in us is either good or bad. Good fruit doesn't come from bad trees any more than bad fruit can come from a good tree. Again, we all have our moments of indiscretions and moments of anger, but it certainly should never be our normal way of communicating or place of dwelling. The Word speaks about the things that we practice; the things that we constantly do. If the things that we practice in our speech patterns are out of line, then we need to check our hearts that our hearts are in line with the Spirit of God. Some folk think that they can act any way they please because they think they are 'saved'. The words of Jesus Christ bode differently than that opinion.

The cleansed heart of a man is cleansed by the work of the Holy Spirit. This work is mysterious in nature because no man knows how the Holy Spirit accomplishes the miracle of the new birth in a man or woman, we just know that we have been changed into His likeness and that is something that we cannot do for ourselves.

"…but when the goodness and loving kindness of God our Savior appeared, He saved us, not because of deeds done by us in righteousness, but in virtue of His own mercy, by the washing of regeneration and renewal in the Holy Spirit, which He poured out upon us richly through Jesus Christ our Savior, so that we might be justified by His grace and become heirs of hope in eternal life." (Titus 3:4-7, RSV)

When Jesus Christ died on the cross to save the world from sin, He died with the sin of the whole world upon Him. He was our sacrifice. He died once for all and that work was finished over two thousand years ago. If you believe that, and that He was risen from the grave to sit at the right hand of the Father, then that is the beginning of seeing and knowing just how awesome He really is. God, in Christ, loved the whole world so much that He gave His Son for us that we might have life and that more abundantly. That event was a one-time event that changed all of time, past, present, and future. The world is saved from sin; the majority of folk, though, simply do not know that, or they have chosen not to believe it for innumerable reasons.

The conquering of sin was the first thing that had to be done in order that we would have the opportunity to be free from the power of sin and the wages of sin. Jesus said, 'You must be born again.' (John 3:3) Believing that He has conquered sin for you and me is first; believing with our total being so much so that we give up who we are to become a part of Him and He transforms our heart first by the work of His Spirit. The cleansed heart becomes the transformed life abiding in the grace that He affords us. Pray right now for the Holy Spirit to transform your heart and rule in your heart as His will becomes certain to be done in the earthen vessel that bears your name.

September 14th

Increased Faith

"Then Jesus answered and said to her, 'O woman, your faith is great; be it done for you as you wish.' And her daughter was healed at once."
(Matthew 15:28)

The exchange of conversation between the Syrophoenician woman and Jesus is an exchange of information and need. She has the need of her daughter being delivered from demon-possession. She is not a Hebrew and Jesus points out that He was 'sent only to the lost sheep of the house of Israel'. (v. 24) She does not relent, but presses forward in faith for the sake of her child. She knows for a fact that Jesus can deliver her child. He continues in His directive of maintaining His focus on the people of Israel and not on Gentiles of any persuasion. She counters in perseverance and is persuasive when it comes to this one point: she had faith. Faith is an object of true consistency in the spiritual Kingdom of God. Spiritual faith can be shared, added to, multiplied, accepted, increased, used, spoken, and measured in the Kingdom of God.

People cannot see, touch, taste, hear, or smell faith. In the natural realm it is an invisible intangible. People who have faith know they have it. People who do not have faith don't really know if they do or not. People who do not have faith, spiritual faith, don't know what they don't know. That is why it is so easy for a person who lacks faith to simply move on from a Gospel message; they just don't get it and they really don't care.

That's why a real Christian doesn't need to badger and cajole a person without faith. Prayer is the work of the faithful that God would move in the hearts of the faithless that they would be convicted by the Holy Spirit. Then, upon conviction of the Holy Spirit, the heart door is moved from complacency to decision; to eventual acceptance or rejection. Faithless people do not pray; they need the prayers of the faithful.

The Syrophoenician woman had great faith and displayed it in a desire to get close enough to Jesus to have a conversation. Not only did she have the conversation, she was relentless in her reasoning, logic, and expression of faith. What we see as a reasoning argument for provision, Jesus saw as a revelation of faith. Many times, I have heard similar arguments of prayer before God with similar needs, but the person doing the arguing and demanding before God becomes insolent in order for their needs to get met by God. Patient perseverance in reverence displayed in humble faith is received well by our Almighty Holy Lord. Prideful insolence is what is sometimes displayed, however, and some folk call that faith. Prideful insolence is arrogance and out of order before an Almighty God. Being overtly loud with your hope for a thing before God is not faith; it's just being loud.

We have to possess the faith and nature of God in order to relate to God in reverent prayer. Humility is evident in God's eyes and ears. Reverence for His Almighty power is enjoined in respect and adoration in the heart and its motives are clear to God. Stammering, repetitive demands emanating from a reckless pride is not faith at all. On the other hand, weak, unbelieving and undeserving self-deprecation is equally undeserving of being called faith. Asking Almighty God a request without expectation is an example of asking amiss; wavering and doubting are not in the seed of spiritual faith. It is pure faith in pure motives from a right heart that God responds to when He decides to respond ever how He chooses. God, alone, is God. Pray for increased faith.

September 15th

Expressing Glory

"…the multitude marveled as they saw the dumb speaking, the crippled restored, and the lame walking, and the blind seeing; and they glorified the God of Israel."
(Matthew 15:31)

When the multitudes came to Jesus, they brought their lame, crippled, blind, dumb, and many others and laid them at His feet. The will of man will submit to Holy power in faith when its need is greater than its pride. The able brought the unable to Jesus in faith and He healed them. We have to see the power in intercession here. Stop looking at folk with disdain, who are simply unable to get to Jesus on their own. Many people need the intercession of the faithful in order to be able to get to Jesus faithfully. Faithless people do not pray because they do not have faith and because they do not have faith, they need someone with faith to take them there.

When the unable are led to the Lord by the faith-filled able, then the wonders and miracles of God are certainly going to take place. When the wonders of Almighty God transpire with the needy and unable, then we can't do anything but give glory to God. There are those who would receive the glory of God unto themselves in times of wonder, but Jesus gave all glory to His Father always and the people did what Jesus did. At times, when we see a man of God taking God's glory for himself, he receives it gladly and pridefully because that is what he believes. Somehow, he believes he is responsible for the wonders of God and by this is culpable of being led astray. Not so with Jesus!

Always recognize the Presence of God in your life. It is easy to give God glory for all things and through all things when we recognize in faith that it is God Who is Lord and Provider. God knows all and there is no thing that He does not know. He knows our hearts and our weaknesses; He knows our every need. He is our Healer, our Sustainer, our Savior, our Lord, our Omnipotent King, and our ever-present Provider.

The Kingdom of God is within you if you name the Name of Jesus Christ. See where He has provided sight to your spiritual blindness and Light to your darkness. Hear where He has provided health and wholeness to your spiritual hearing in that you know His voice when He speaks. Thank Him that He makes you to walk upright in righteousness and that He has provided a right and straight path to walk upon. Give Him glory that He has delivered you from the power and penalty of sin and made you to sit in heavenly places in Christ Jesus. Give glory to God! Give all the glory to God and Bless His Holy Name!

September 16th

For Those Who Remain

"And Jesus called His disciples to Him, and said, 'I feel compassion for the multitude, because they have remained with Me now three days and have nothing to eat; and I do not wish to send them away hungry, lest they faint on the way."
(Matthew 15:32)

Those who remained with Jesus in all of His teaching for three days waited for His provision in the natural. Either they were there for the original feeding of the five thousand and saw with their own eyes the provision that day; or they had heard about it and they were not going to leave without that food provision that they knew He could provide. The compassion of our Lord concedes to their need and, again, He sits them down and provides yet another miracle with seven loaves of bread and some fish and feeds the hungry crowd. They collect the leftovers into seven large baskets and then He sends the multitudes away.

Jesus recognized their faith in that they knew emphatically that He could provide for them physically. He was the ultimate Provider in health, healing, deliverance, spiritual blessing, and even physical food. But, He sent the multitudes away. He was not there to become their natural provider and leader of deliverance from their natural enemies. He was not there to feed the hungry crowds even though He had the power and compassion to do so. He was not there for their every whim. And, in like faith, neither is He here for us to be our natural provider, our meal maker, our natural healer, or our provider of our every whim. And yet, that is how He is presented even today in churches that preach their version of a natural god providing our natural whims to the masses. Jesus Christ's words are spirit, He said that Himself. (John 6:63)

Jesus had compassion on the people and provided because He had the spiritual power to multiply that which, in the natural, became leaven, and in the spiritual became the 'more than enough'. The spiritual power that Jesus possessed acted like leaven in the natural bread. His Almighty spiritual power can do the 'whatever' it is told to do in the natural. Spiritual power is a tangible object in the Kingdom of God. Spiritual power is not seen, heard, or felt in the natural; it is spiritual emanating from the domain of the Spirit. Spiritual power is. Faith is.

They both abide in the Kingdom of God. Jesus Christ was the conduit for that power. No other man can claim that possession. All power and authority has been given to Him, Jesus Christ. To us in the natural, it is akin to breaking leaven and every time it is broken, it multiplies. So it is with the Word of God. That's why He is referred to as the Bread of Life that was broken for us.

It was that Spirit power that the apostles walked in when they went out and the spirits of this world were subject to them. They received what Jesus alone gave them. Then, and only then, did they possess what Jesus possessed, the power to deliver, to heal, and the power to share. The Gospel of the Kingdom of God expresses that same Spirit power because our Lord has sent His Holy Spirit into this world to act on His behalf. Receive the Holy Spirit and see the wonders that take place in your life. I know this to be true and you will, too.

September 17th

The Power of Leaven

"And the disciples came to the other side of the sea, but they had forgotten to bring any bread. And Jesus said to them, 'Watch out and beware of the leaven of the Pharisees and Sadducees." *(Matthew 16:5-6)*

As Jesus was discussing the Pharisees demand for Him to show them a sign which would represent God being with Him, Jesus expresses to His disciples to watch out for and beware of the leaven of the religious leaders. Jesus had shown His disciples the power of leaven as He multiplied the bread and fish for the five thousand and the four thousand. No, this is not literal leaven. These are spiritual symbols for spiritual words. Do not get caught up in the natural as Jesus' disciples did, we should know better by now.

The power of leaven is the power to work from within. The Pharisees' leaven was religious ideas and philosophies that were the foundations of their oral laws. Ideas, ideologies, and personal philosophies all integrate to create belief systems for individuals. It is the erroneous idea that leads men astray. It is the wrong interpretation of truths that debilitate the mind into wrong beliefs. Erroneous beliefs such as creating further oral laws, of which the Pharisees and Sadducees were masters of, gave erroneous authority to the men rather than people honoring God for His handiwork and His commands. Men create ideologies in order to further their own thoughts, thereby giving them authority over the peoples' religious mindsets. So many laws were created that the people could not understand them all, nor could they obey them. This gave the ruling party advantage and privilege before the people and they implied that the advantage was before God as well. This is what Jesus came against…their false authority built on false foundations of false beliefs, and the people couldn't or wouldn't do anything about it. But Jesus, having authority not based on men's philosophies, bore the authority of God Himself.

Men of renown with charismatic personalities sell people on half-truths that are not truths at all. The wicked deceiver works his best when he can tell a little truth, or a little scripture, but interpret it according to how he sees it and not according to the nature of God or the context of the Word. Vain repetition of errant theology has a tendency to make it sound real, but no matter how many times a lie is repeated, it is still a lie. Men try to get into people's hearts with emotions, false promises, deceptions, and half-truths. And, just as Jesus told us, we need to watch out for and beware of the leaven of false prophets, religious hirelings, deceptive soothsayers, and sometimes…complete ignorance of what the Word of God really says.

It is absolutely necessary that we know Jesus Christ in a very personal relationship in the Spirit and have Him teach us, "Thus says the Lord." The bread was not about the bread, it was about the leaven. Know the Truth of God's Word and the lie, and the men that tell them, will not have their way with your heart.

September 18th

Who Do You Say that He Is?

"Now when Jesus came into the district of Caesarea Philippi, He was asking His disciples, 'Who do people say that the Son of Man is?'" *(Matthew 16:13)*

The disciples responded and said what some folk had said. Some believed that He was John the Baptist, Elijah, Jeremiah, or one of the prophets. Then He asked them what they thought and Peter immediately responded with, 'You are the Christ, the Son of the Living God.' (v. 16) Jesus tells Peter and the rest of the disciples, 'Blessed are you, Simon Barjona, because flesh and blood did not reveal this to you, but My Father who is in heaven.'" (v. 17)

Much later after Jesus' resurrection, the Apostle Paul wrote, "So I want you to know that no one speaking by the Spirit of God will curse Jesus, and no one can say Jesus is Lord except by the Holy Spirit." (1 Corinthians 12:3, NLT). The Apostle John wrote, "This is how we know if they have the Spirit of God: if a person claiming to be a prophet acknowledges that Jesus Christ came in a real body, that person has the Spirit of God. But if someone claims to be a prophet and does not acknowledge the truth about Jesus, that person is not from God. Such a person has the spirit of the antichrist, which you have heard is coming into the world, and indeed is already here." (1 John 3:2-3, NLT)

The key here is that no one comes to the knowledge of the saving grace of God without reading the Word for themselves or someone sharing the Word of God with them in some fashion. The story of Jesus Christ is found in the Word. The Holy Spirit speaks through the Word, which is living and sharper than any two-edged sword. The Holy Spirit speaks through people who know the Word and speak the

Word to others so that the Spirit bears witness to others by convicting the world of sin, of righteousness, and of judgment. (John 16) Peter's knowledge of Jesus being the Son of God, Messiah was made know to Him by God.

We do not call Jesus our Lord without the Spirit telling us that is who He is. He is Lord of all and yet all do not know Him as Lord. This brings us to, 'What do you call Jesus?' Who is He to you? Is He your Lord and Master? If so, do you treat Him as your Lord? Is He your Savior? If so, do you understand what He has saved you from and is saving you to? Is He your friend? Jesus told His disciples, 'I call you friends.' (John 15:15) Jeremiah knew the Lord as friend. (Jeremiah 3:4)

Who do you say that He is? There will come a time when every knee will bow and every tongue will confess and say, "Jesus is Lord". (Phil. 2:10-11; Rom. 14:11) Submit to Jesus Christ as Lord and know Him in the fullness of His grace in the each and every moment that you breathe. Breathe in His Spirit and breathe out His Word. His Word is Truth for He Is the great I AM.

September 19th

Upon This Rock

"And also I say to you that you are Peter, and upon this rock I will build My church; and the gates of Hades shall not overpower it." *(Matthew 16:18)*

Jesus Christ told Peter, which in the Greek is *Petros*, that upon this rock, in the Greek *petra*, He would build His church. Jesus Christ is the sole builder of His church. No man has been given authority to build His church and no man has been given any authority of which it is built upon and that includes Peter. Jesus Christ is the *petra* on which the church of God is built. There is no other foundation for the Kingdom of God to be built for the Kingdom of God is only found in Jesus Christ. It is the work of the Holy Spirit to lead men into conviction of their sin and it is the power of the Holy Spirit that leads men unto righteousness and ultimate judgment. No man has ever been given that power or authority. The church of Jesus Christ is His body; He is the head, the chief cornerstone, and all authority in heaven and in earth has been given to Him. Bless the Name of Jesus!

We have been afforded such a great opportunity in this dispensation of time to be set free in His Spirit. We are no longer under any bonds or chains of demonic or man's designs. Even though there is still sin in this world, we know that we are free from the bondage of it and we no longer have to sin. We are not only set free from the penalty of sin, we are set free from the power of it. Sin no longer has dominion over us. We live in the dominion of the Christ, the Kingdom of God.

It is not the truth when someone says, 'the devil made me do it'. People do what they do out of influence at times, but it is always a choice. The battlefield is in the mind of your choices in the each and every moment. If we have been washed in the blood of Jesus Christ and having been born again, we are under the autonomy and dominion of Jesus Christ. In Him, we live and move and have our very being. The gates of hell, which is anything not like the Christ, shall have no power or dominion over us. We cannot be overpowered by the prince of the power of the air. In all of our getting, get understanding in this! Christ has already won the victory at the cross; we do not have to wait to die to go to heaven to have victory, we have victory in Jesus in the here and now. In Christ, we are more than conquerors because in Him, He is our refuge and strength.

Bless the Lord at all times and at all times let His praise be in your mouth. Give honor and glory to the Lord our God that He prevailed over all darkness for our benefit. He has built His church and will continue to build His church through the power of His Holy Spirit. Thank God that He is all-powerful and that no weapon formed against us shall prosper. Bless His Name forever!

September 20th

The Keys to the Kingdom of Heaven

"I will give you the keys to the kingdom of heaven; and whatever you shall bind on earth shall be bound in heaven, and whatever you shall loose on earth shall be loosed in heaven." (Matthew 16:19)

The keys to the kingdom of heaven (the Gospel) were the keys, not as in a door-lock, but the principles, which were the doctrines of grace and mercy. Whatever they preached in the power of the Holy Spirit, was from the Holy Spirit. Whatever they bound, the sayings of the things that were not in due course of the Kingdom, they were bound. Whatever was loosed in the due course of the Gospel was loosed; that which was permitted, clean, doctrinally sound, right practices and doctrines. These were the keys to the Gospel…the right message of repentance, for the Kingdom of God was at hand. Grace, peace, mercy, truth, and the love of God were all a part of this Gospel which was being loosed into the world.

These keys were not keys that locked and unlocked physical doors, but keys that unlocked minds and hearts to God's truth of the narrow way. The binding and loosing was not about giving Peter, or any man of God, the authority to forgive men's sins, no, only God, in Christ, forgives men's sins. Man has no authority on this earth to remit sin.

Whatever we bind on earth or loose on earth is bound or loosed in heaven. These are the matters of the heart in agreement. The power in heaven is loosed in the earth by the freedom that is gained in the power of the Gospel of the Kingdom of God. Freedom is set free and no man can bind freedom when it is set free in the heart of a man. Nor can any man add burdens to his freedom by adding the doctrines of men to the Gospel of peace. (Gal. 4:8-9; Gal. 5:1) Whatever you set free in this earth by your preaching the Gospel of Jesus Christ is free in heaven. Whatever you loose by the power of the Spirit will be loosed in heaven. Man on earth has no authority in this regard as well. Man has no authority to bind anything or loose anything by the speaking or commanding of words. This binding and loosing has to do with the purpose of the Gospel of the Kingdom of God in the power of the Holy Spirit. The power in the binding and the loosing is in the Person of the Holy Spirit at work in the earth and in the heavens. He, the Holy Spirit, is the constant.

"For the kingdom of God is not about eating and drinking but of righteousness and peace and joy in the Holy Spirit." (Rom. 14:17, ESV) Do not add burdens to yourselves by adding restrictions and laws. The law of love is where we are bound to Him and loosed to love in His love. It is the teaching that we either get bound up in or loosed free from. Let no man add to the words of Jesus Christ regarding His Gospel of the Kingdom of God. "So if the Son sets you free, you are truly free." (John 8:36, NLT) Walk in freedom for you have been loosed not only in heaven above for your future, but in the here and now to walk out what He has put inside of you and that is His Holy Spirit of love and grace.

September 21st

His Purpose Revealed

"From that time Jesus Christ began to show His disciples that He must go to Jerusalem, and suffer many things from the elders and chief priests and scribes, and be killed, and be raised up on the third day."   (Matthew 16:21)

It was the plan and purpose of God for Jesus Christ to come to this earth to suffer and die for the sins of the world. "And all that dwell upon the earth shall worship him (the beast), whose names are not written in the book of the life of the Lamb slain from the foundation of the world." (Rev. 13:8, KJV, Cambridge Ed.) It is a mystery of God for Him to know all things from the beginning, but in faith we believe this was how He knew all things and was able to express it through the years in the mouths and the writings of the prophets.

"For just as Jonah was three days and three nights in the belly of the sea monster, so shall the Son of Man be three days and three nights in the heart of the earth." (Matt. 12:40)

With Jesus Christ, there were no coincidences, no accidents, no lack of forethought, and no mishaps. Everything Jesus did was planned and it was His purpose to die on a cross at the hands of the Roman rulers under the direction of the Jewish religious leaders. His purpose was to be the sacrifice, the one man dying for the many, to save the world from the penalty of sin, which is death; and the power of sin, which is inevitable for all humanity. Without Christ, we are powerless to not sin, but in Christ, we come to realize that the power of sin has been broken over our lives and we do not have to sin. "So you should also consider yourselves dead to the power of sin and alive to God in Christ Jesus." (Rom. 6:11, NLT)

Being alive to God in Christ Jesus is the purpose of dwelling in the Kingdom of God. When we abide in Him, we are dwelling in Him by the power of the Holy Spirit dwelling in us. We are in the mutual relationship, being in Him and Him being in us. When we walk into His Kingdom, we are walking into Him and when we are walking we are we walking with Him for He is with us and will be in us. "Because the truth is in us and will be with us forever." (2 John 1:2, NLT)

Jesus told His disciples what was going to happen to Him so that they would know what was going on. If they had known all of the scripture, they would have soon come to realize that this had been prophesied in ages past, but no one thought about it that way, as Peter subsequently proves. We have to take Jesus at His Word. All of His Word is Truth and is profitable of us to heed. His purposes were sure then and they are sure today for us.

As we abide in Him, He abides in us, and the open reward of the secret place is sure. Remain in Him in faithfulness, even as He is faithful. Know Him in the secret place of abiding in Him in the each and every moment of your life. Allow the faith that He has placed inside of you to grow to full measure, pressed down, and then to overflowing exuberance.

He is the fountain of living waters where we never run dry. Drink Him in and let the overflow of His Spirit flow out of you to a world that needs to know Him.

September 22nd

Becoming a Stumbling Block

"But He turned and said to Peter, 'Get behind Me, Satan! You are a stumbling block to Me; for you are not setting your mind on God's interests, but man's."
(Matthew 16:23)

If the plans and purposes of Jesus Christ were to do as He said 'to go to Jerusalem, suffer many things, be killed and raised up on the third day', then His purpose on the earth was to serve the purpose and will of His Father in heaven. All that Jesus did on the earth was the plan, purpose, and will of His Father in heaven. Prophesies had been foretold, but His disciples were not privy to all of these prophesies for they were not religious leaders, nor students of the Law.

Many of the disciples were fishermen by trade and were at the mercies of their peers for the information of who they believed the Messiah to be. Many of the zealots of that day believed the Messiah of the Hebrew people would be a physical deliverer to deliver the people from Roman oppression just as Moses delivered God's people from the Egyptians. Here, Jesus is telling them the truth about His purpose and this purpose comes from God, the Father, not man's inclinations or interpretations.

Jesus speaks to Peter, the one who just said by the power of the Holy Spirit, "You are the Christ, the Son of the living God" and says to him in his error of purpose and interpretation, "Get behind Me, Satan!" The reflection here is that man, Jesus' disciples, and all who have followed Jesus since, is an imperfect being incapable of knowing truth in its entirety, even when He hears it first hand from Jesus' mouth.

We are a peculiar lot, for we can hear Truth from the mouth of our Lord, and just like the religious leaders of the Jews, we want to interpret what He said our way and if our way doesn't make sense to us and others, we'll add our interpretations of His Words to make us feel better. By the time we're through with our interpretations, we are left with becoming the stumbling block to the human race.

We become like Peter in that we like to tell Jesus what we think His purpose is and was and then tell other people what we think He was saying. In all of this, the leadership of the church throughout all Christendom and throughout all time has placed stumbling blocks of errant teaching to the world at large. By far, the majority of what is taught in churches today is man's interests and not God's.

It is so vitally important to read the Word of God for ourselves within the context. Always read entire passages together…paragraphs, entire chapters, or even entire books in one sitting. The divisions within the books were created by men for easier reading. However, the divisions of chapter and verse create the sense of separateness and compartmentalization that was not intended in the Holy Writ. The punctuation and the subdivision of chapter and verse are there for our convenience, but essentially create the possibility of errant interpretation due to over-organization.

The Holy Spirit will speak to you when you get serious about Him and His Word and just as He said years ago, "But you have received the Holy Spirit and He lives within you, so you don't need anyone to teach you what is true. For the Spirit teaches you everything you need to know, and what he teaches is true-it is not a lie. So, just as he has taught you, remain in fellowship with Christ." (1 John 2:27, NLT)

September 23rd

The Cost of Discipleship

"Then Jesus said to His disciples, 'If anyone wishes to come after Me, let him deny himself, and take up his cross, and follow Me.'"   (Matthew 16:24)

God's purposes for His own Son have been made very clear. When Jesus expresses these plans and purposes, He then details the purposes of His disciples in this saying. This is the pathway to discipleship in Jesus Christ; it is the pathway to the Kingdom of God; the way is narrow and few there are that find their way in it. Everything that He said was for us to follow and heed. We do not get to pick and choose what we will follow and what He intended for other people in some other time period. His Words will always be Truth and no man has the authority to deny some words and choose others to live by.

"If anyone desire to come after Him"…the desire comes first. We are led to the Lord by an unction from the Holy Spirit. It is the power of the Holy Spirit to convict the world of sin. Men's mouths will speak the wonders of Jesus Christ, but it is the Holy Spirit that woos men and has the power to give faith. We become His mouthpiece to speak and write about faith in believing in Jesus Christ. Still, a man's desire to know Him in personal relationship is from the Holy Spirit.

"Let him deny himself"…deny who you know yourself to be; not just the bad part of you, or the parts you know that are prone to sin. We have to lose ourselves from ourselves in order to be brought into Him. It is a mystery of how He comes into our lives in the power of the Holy Spirit to become born again. (John 3:3)

But this denying of the self, as Oswald Chambers puts it, is denying the claim to the rights to ourselves. [1] We have to lay ourselves down in submission to Him as Almighty God.

"And take up his cross"…we do not take up the cross of Christ, no, only Jesus Christ could do what Jesus did. We cannot be 'like' Jesus, or 'do what Jesus would do' for only Jesus' purposes and plans were for Jesus. We have our own cross to pick up after we deny ourselves. Too many folk throughout time have been told to pick up the cross of Christ, but were never told to deny themselves and pick up their own cross. That's what religion teaches and is a stumbling block to true faith. Jesus has a plan and purpose for your life…specifically. By denying ourselves and picking up our own cross, we are submitting to Him to guide us into His Truth. He then reveals His purposes in our lives.

"And follow Me"…by following Jesus Christ, we have laid down the worst of us, the best of us, the plans of us and the future of us. We lay it all down at His feet and reckon ourselves dead to Christ. When we become dead to ourselves, we become alive in Him. Following Him is not just a one-time experience, following Him, is in the each and every moment of now and forevermore. Desire, deny, take up your cross and follow Him now, He's waiting.

September 24th

Denying the Self

"Then Jesus said to His disciples, 'If anyone wishes to come after Me, let him deny himself, and take up his cross, and follow Me.'" *(Matthew 16:24, NASB)*

Jesus gave this message directly to His disciples. This message still stands today, albeit it is not preached often enough. If you name the Name of Jesus Christ and claim to be a disciple of His, then you have to commit to the denial of yourself for now and all eternity. Please understand that Jesus was not talking about things. He did not say to deny yourself of things and come and follow Me. No! He said to deny yourself.

But how do you do that? If you know and have been practicing this daily, then you know and I encourage you in the faith. But if you have never made entreaty to the idea of denying yourself before God, today is the first day to begin.

The desire to go after Jesus and follow Him is first. If there is no desire to be with Him and serve Him, then you need to pray for that first and check to see if the truth in you exists. The desire and love for Him has to be so great, that as Jesus said, you cannot love anyone greater than you can love Him, otherwise you are not fit to be called His. (Matthew 10:35-39)

Following Jesus Christ into His Kingdom, again, is desiring Him more than anyone, or anything known to your mind and heart. Secondly, denying the self that you know you are is being willing to submit all that you are to Him. His Holy Spirit comes to you and makes you a new creation – born again new. He makes you into a new you with life in Him. (Matthew 16:25) But you have to give up the old in order to enter the new.

Third, take up your cross daily. Daily submit to Him, commit your ways to Him, acknowledge Him, and He will become to you the Light to your path, your Shepherd, your Door, your Way, your Truth, and your Life. Then, following Him becomes your nature and not your chore. He said to take His yoke upon you and that His burden is easy and His yoke is light.

Trust in Him today with your very life and He will make you brand new in Him. Love Him with all of your heart, your soul, your mind, and your strength. The new you is in Him, stay faithfully in Him, following Him, for this is the beginning of what denying the self is all about! Seek first the kingdom of God and His righteousness and all these things will be added to you. (Matthew 6:33)

September 25th

Letting Go

"For whoever wishes to save his life will lose it; but whoever loses his life for My sake will find it." (Matthew 16:25, NASB)

One of the greatest powers on earth is the will of man. Men and women are made in the image of God and He made us with the strength to overcome, to make decisions, to desire, to want, and to will among a myriad of other possibilities of strengths and in our humanity, our weaknesses. He made us with a human will. We can decide to do almost anything we set our minds to. Some say, if there's a will, there's a way.

We do have a choice. We can do what we want to do, or we can submit to Him, and do what He wants to do in us. When we are met by Jesus Christ, He bids us to come and follow Him. But in following Him, we do not do that successfully by doing that our way. We must submit and relinquish all that we are, giving up our rights to ourselves, and allowing Him to take over our being. He makes us a new creation in Him as we enter into His rest in His kingdom. In His Kingdom, He is King, not me and not you. In His Kingdom, He is Lord over all that is. Oddly enough, He is Lord over all that is anyway, but in the dwelling place of grace, we recognize and freely acknowledge His Lordship.

Outside of His Kingdom, the people believe they are in charge, even though so much of their lives is completely out of their control. Strange thinking, don't you think?

If you are willing to lose your life for His sake, then He promises to give you the life that He has to give in His Kingdom, being made righteous and holy, because He is holy and righteous for it is Christ Who becomes our righteousness. "…who has blessed us with every blessing in the heavenly places in Christ, just as He chose us in Him before the foundation of the world, that we should be holy and blameless before Him." (Eph. 1:3-4)

In letting go of you, you get to have new life in Christ. This new life does not come any other way. In letting go of you, you are repenting of you, not just your sin. If you find that your Christianity has not worked for you, it is not Christ's fault, get rid of your selfishness and allow Him to be Lord of your life.

Deny yourself first and deny yourself daily, even if you're the only one doing it. Jesus Christ became the standard to show us the way. He is worthy because He has accomplished this thing called 'giving all'. Let Him do the same in you, today!

September 26th

The Reward of Exchange

"For what will a man be profited, if he gains the whole world, and forfeits his soul? Or what will a man give in exchange for his soul?"   *(Matthew 16:26)*

Have we come to an honest evaluation of ourselves yet? Have you arrived at any conclusions about your own life in Christ? Would you consider yourself a true disciple? Would you consider yourself born-again, a new creation in Him? Has there been real substantive change in your life since you first began a relationship with Jesus Christ?

Jesus said that those who worship Him, worship Him in spirit and truth. We have to be honest with ourselves about Jesus Christ. Are you spending time with Him in prayer? Are you getting to know His word in meditation and study? Do you have a

One on one relationship with Him as your Lord? Are you abiding, living, in Him? Please be honest with yourself, and do not attempt to deceive yourself any further if you cannot answer these questions affirmatively. If you have answered all of these questions affirmatively, then what are you doing to help others get to where you are? He told us to make disciples, are you obeying His word?

If you will give more than a moment to think about your family, church friends, your co-workers, your acquaintances, and the people on the street, you know in your heart that the majority of people have given their lives to things, entertainment, sports, and the plethora of other gods that saturate the gateways to our minds. Real people give up their lives every day for something, anything that will make them happy or happier, and/or take them out of their miserable existence. What have they received in exchange for souls?

You see, you have exchanged your soul for new life in Christ; that is your abundant and eternal reward. Please take the time now to pray for the folk around you and the lives they think they live. Do not judge them, pray for them, and pray for Jesus Christ to become Lord over all.

September 27th

Lose Your Life for Life in Him

"For whoever wishes to save his life shall lose it; but whoever loses his life for My sake shall find it. For what will a man be profited, if he gains the whole world, and forfeits his soul?" (Matthew 16:25-26)

If any man desire to go after Jesus and follow Him, he must deny himself first. The denying of the self is the losing and loosing of the self. In the last fifty years, there has been an entire genre of books written and created called self-help books. In the Kingdom of God, there is no self-help because in the Kingdom, the self is denied, crucified, and died to. If a professing Christian is reading a book in order to promote 'self-help', they're actually moving in a realm unrelated to Jesus Christ. Self-help is a genre that is antichrist for it promotes the building up of the self, rather than the denial of the self, which Jesus requires for follow-ship.

Jesus doesn't need followers who have a better way of following Him than how He has prescribed. That is what some Christian self-help gurus portend; which is false teaching. The follower of Jesus Christ must be willing to lose themselves for Him. In the losing of ourselves for Him in Him, we get new life in Him; we get onto the right road with Him. The 'born again' life doesn't come any other way. We cannot become a new creation in Christ by staying who we are and improving. He doesn't make us better...He makes us new! In the submitting to Him, we are regenerated into a new creature, old things pass away and all things become new. This is the life that is found by losing it. When we lose our lives for His sake, for the follow-ship of Him, we find new life in Him. New life in Him is being in His Presence in His Kingdom. He is in us and we are in Him in new life…His life.

In the temptation of Jesus Christ by the devil in the desert, it was about Jesus being here on the earth as the Son of God, but the devil tempted Him to do His work the devil's way. Jesus could not and would not have any of the temptation for Jesus did not and could not sin. But the tempter tempted anyway. Jesus laid His life down from glory and entered the earth. He laid His life down at Calvary and entered the earth. He was raised from the dead to prove that He had the power over death, hell, sin, and the grave. That same power can come to us to give us life forevermore in Him, but we have to give all that we are to Him. He takes what we are and makes us a new creation in Him.

There is nothing in this world that is worth taking that is worthy of our souls. When men choose their way or the world's way of doing things, that is basically what they're doing. They are giving up their souls in exchange for the world's way of life. Not so with the true believer and follower of Jesus Christ. The true disciple gives up his life for His sake and the reward for that is abundant, ever joyful life in Him, now and forevermore. Did I say happy, no, for the joy that He gives is internal and eternal. The circumstances of life will throw us around at times, but be of good cheer, He has overcome the world beginning with your eternal soul.

September 28th

A Future Judgment

"For the Son of Man is going to come in the glory of His Father with His angels; and will then recompense every man according to his deeds." (Matthew 16:27)

Jesus foretells of a future and certain judgment in accordance with His context. He tells us and His disciples that in order to follow Him as a true disciple, desire comes first, then denial, then taking up our own cross, and following Him. There is a two-fold eventuality here. First, the reward of the true disciple who had given up their all to be in Him in love and grace is the reward of eternal life in glory with the Father.

Secondly, the other eventuality is that there will be those who decided that an object, a goal, money, finances, wealth, fame, or just themselves and their sin was enough not to give up in exchange for new life in Him. Jesus asked the question, "What will a man give in exchange for his soul"…even up to the whole world…is anything, any pleasure, any person, any self, or any sin worth keeping in exchange for new life in Him? As we have seen in our lives, people in all walks of life stay who they are in order to remain who they are in order to keep what they've got on the earth.

The earth will soon pass away and all that remains in it will pass away as well. The recompense that Jesus brings is the judgment for a man's deeds. If the person has chosen self over life, then their reward will be what Jesus has said, they will be thrown out.
 "There will be weeping and gnashing of teeth, for you will see Abraham, Isaac, Jacob, and all the prophets in the kingdom of God but you yourselves cast out." (Luke 13:28, NLT)

To remain in Him is to be with Him forever. Remaining in Him in His Kingdom is where He lives and has dominion. God is love and in the context of the Holy Word, God is Holy Love. There are too many definitions of what people think love is and unless the definition includes holiness, then the definition misses the mark of God's intention and God's love.

 When we remain in Him, we remain in His love and the love that He possesses, possesses us. It is this holy love that brought our Savior into the world and it is this same holy love that saved the world from its sin. The holy love of God is what constrains us and makes and molds us into Him. As Paul stated in 1 Corinthians 13, even if I give up all my possessions to feed the poor or give up my body to be burned and have not love, I am nothing.

So, please get this…Jesus is not talking about giving up things to show others how religious we are. It is not about giving up our lives in the flesh, so that we do the work of the Lord ourselves. The Kingdom of God is about denying the self, all that we are and all that we ever hope to be and giving it all to the Lord in humility and submission. We become broken and spilled out vessels in His Presence and the only way we become anything from that point is to be born again by His Holy Spirit. Dwelling in Him is dwelling in His Kingdom of Holy Love. Then, the love of God pours out of us to a lost and dying world. Nothing in my hands I bring and nothing to this life I cling says the songwriter. Make us new in You, O Lord, that we would remain in You forever. Amen.

September 29th

The Son of Man in His Kingdom

"Truly I say to you, there are some of those who are standing here who shall not taste death until they see the Son of Man coming in His kingdom."
(Matthew 16:28)

This particular passage is also in Mark 9:1 and in Luke 9:27. There are many interpretations regarding this passage and some commentaries disavow practically all of the known interpretations of this particular passage. However, when taken within the context of Jesus Christ referring to His being the Son of Man coming with His angels to recompense all according to their deeds and then moving into the Transfiguration to show Peter, James, and John a glimpse of what the Kingdom was like, then it would be fitting to apply this future prediction of Jesus to the forthcoming glimpse of Peter, James, and John at the mount of transfiguration when one uses the other Gospels of Luke and Mark within the context.

What a man sees on this earth in relation to His Lord is minute compared to a glimpse of Him in His glory. There are those who say that's all that this event precluded, it was just a glimpse of glory, but I beg to differ. Jesus was telling His disciples that a few of you will see the Son of Man, who is the Son of God in the flesh being born of a man, in His Kingdom. The Kingdom of God is the invisible spiritual kingdom and dwelling place of the Most High God. It does not come with observation in that we can say, 'Here it is, or there it is!' And, because we cannot see it, it does not mean that it does not exist, nor do we not know in totality its current and future location. Jesus was speaking of the soon transfiguration on the mount with Elijah and Moses.

Jesus was also pointing to the differentiation, once again, that His Kingdom is not of this world and it is not made up of things that this world has to offer. In fact, the whole world is not of greater value than a man's soul in inheriting the kingdom. Jesus knew the value of a man's soul for He had come to die for them and He knew the value of the whole world for He had created it.

Man's value, to Him, is incalculable, but man, in his ignorance will place a value on his own life by choosing some worldly good, place, or thing over the value of following God. That makes absolutely no logical or practical sense, but men and women do it every day by their choices in who they will serve. People serve themselves and the gods of this world every day over the denial of self and service of our Lord. Unfortunately, even though it makes no practical or logical sense to follow the ways of the world rather than Christ, we have an innate tendency to follow our selves first, unwittingly being influenced by the myriads of influencers that we allow in our lives.

Our true Master is who we truly serve. Only the individual knows for certain if they have absolutely given their lives to Christ. The proof is in the fruit. The one we serve will be the one who gets the most out of us and the one who comes out of us. Pray that the Holy Spirit move in all of our lives that His fruit be bearing fruit in our lives, our mouths, and our disposition. Let the mediations of our hearts always be on Him and let the praises of our mouths always be about Him for His glory and His glory alone.

September 30th

The Transfiguration

"And He was transfigured before them; and His face shown like the sun, and His garments became as white as light. And, behold, Moses and Elijah appeared to them, talking with Him." (Matthew 17:2-3)

Jesus has taken Peter, James, and John to a mountain and just as He had earlier said, there would be those who would not taste death until they saw the 'Son of Man coming in His kingdom'. Mark 9:1 says, 'until they see the kingdom of God after it has come with power.' Luke 9:27 says, 'until they see the kingdom of God.' Jesus predicted what was about to occur and by this prediction, He has told us what it was that the three disciples saw that night on the mountain. It was a glimpse of the glory of the Kingdom present in visible glory.

Whether this glory is always about us, that is, around us, I do not know, but the glory of the Lord does rise among us in holy worship, "Arise, shine, for your light has come, and the glory of the Lord has risen upon you." (Isaiah 60:1, ESV) In the Exodus, the glory of the Lord settled on Mt. Sinai. (Ex. 24:16) Isaiah states that the glory of the Lord will be revealed and that the people of the Lord will see it together. (Isaiah 40:5). Ezekiel saw the glory of the Lord revealed, "So I arose and went out into the valley, and behold, the glory of the Lord stood there, like the glory that I had seen like by the Chebar canal, and I fell on my face." (Ez. 3:23, ESV). The glory of the Lord has been revealed at various times to His prophets. It was just as glorious, or even more so, when Jesus appeared in it with Elijah and Moses. Here, though, we get a vivid picture of the glory of the Lord in His kingdom. The invisible became visible once again for the three disciples to see. Glory surrounds our Lord and as is fitting as the Kingdom is, it is full of the glory of God.

Our God, who knows no time or space, is outside of what we know as time and space. He is ever-present regardless of time or space. He was before the foundations of the world; He is now; and He will be forevermore. He is everywhere throughout time in His omnipresence. We try to place our finite minds around the infinite and we fail to put words to that which is and yet invisible to the human eye. The human experience is fallible to the spirit and so it is in faith that we move towards the mark of the high calling of God whether we completely understand it or not.

I have seen angels dance in glory. The invisible has become the visible by my eyes at times and I am covered in the truth of what I have seen. Isaiah saw the Lord, high and lifted up and the train of His robe filled the temple. (Isaiah 6) What Peter, James, and John saw that night is testified to in truth in Matthew, Mark, and Luke. They saw the glory of the Kingdom in visible glory. Jesus showed them what was and still is…it is simply hidden for a time and a season.

The Kingdom of God is at hand and is much closer than you think.

October 1st

Learning to Be in His Presence

"And Peter answered and said to Jesus, 'Lord, it is good for us to be here; if You wish, I will make three tabernacles here, one for you, one for Moses, one for Elijah.'"   (Matthew 16:4)

Have you ever been someplace that was so spectacular, mere words could not describe the experience, and mere words were insufficient to even speak; leaving silence as the reward of the moment? This was that moment for the three disciples, during and after the transfiguration, for even when Peter was speaking these words a bright cloud overshadowed them and a voice spoke from the cloud, saying, "This is My beloved Son, in whom I am well-pleased; listen to Him!"

This was not the time for Peter to be talking, let alone planning some traditional evidence of a tabernacle of rocks that signified the location of the event. Peter should have been bowing on his knees during the transfiguration rather than waiting until the voice came from the cloud.

They had just witnessed the glory of the Kingdom of God and yet Peter opened his mouth to speak, which is what most of us usually do when the glory passes by us. We want to talk about it, record it, give it a name, and traditionally hold our hearts to it in as an annual celebratory event.

What we absolutely need to learn is how to 'be' in His Presence. In my own life, I have learned to be desperately humbled. I see the hand of God and sense Him more than in a moment or in a flash of worship. I am learning to be still; quieted and quitted from work in His Presence. Peter wanted to talk, create and work when he should have been bowing in glory with a quieted spirit. I do not castigate Peter for his actions, for I have done worse in His Presence. We cannot look down on the disciples at any time, ridiculing them for their perceived slowness, inadequacies, or religious demeanor. Jesus came to abolish religious thought with the truth and it takes spiritual revelation to get that. Unfortunately, pride will willfully and defiantly stand in His Presence.

The Presence of the Glory of Almighty God is more powerful than one can imagine and yet it is unrecognizable to the unseeing eye. When the invisible becomes the visible, no one can stand and confront holiness face to face. "And when the disciples heard this, they fell on their faces and were much afraid." (v. 6) Our problem remains with us in that 'God is with us' in His Holy Spirit and dwells among us in the ones who name the Name of Jesus Christ. Yet, many have been taught that He is 'way up there somewhere in the heavens' and that is not what the New Testament says, but clearly teaches the Truth, which is, He is 'in' us.

We can learn to 'be' with Him when we recognize where He is. He is above in the heavens and we are seated with Him at His right hand. (Eph. 2) He is with us and abiding in us as we abide in Him where we are. (John 15, 16, 17) Learn the Word of where He says He is in this new dispensation of time. Don't believe me; believe the Word that Jesus taught, "I am with you always, even to the end of the age." (Matt. 28:20b)

There should never be a time when we are not aware of His Presence in our lives. He is here and His Kingdom dwells within you.

October 2nd

Arise, and Do not be Afraid

"And Jesus came to them and touched them and said, 'Arise, and do not be afraid.'"   (Matthew 16:7)

The recorded Word expresses various times of when God's people were engaged by the glory of God. The Hebrew people with Mt. Sinai were afraid of the Presence of God in His glory, as were the shepherds who stood watch over their flocks by night when a host of the heavenly angels came upon them and 'they were sore afraid'. Here, the three disciples marveled at first with Jesus, Elijah, and Moses in the transfiguration, but when the bright cloud appeared and the Lord Almighty spoke, they fell to their knees in humility and fear.

In the various times of Biblical theophany, "which is a visible appearance of God" [1] in the form of a vision or a human; men become afraid and then are told, 'Do not fear.' Surprisingly enough, when the humans are told by the Lord, 'Do not be afraid,' the response is quite calming and reflective. It would seem almost immediate that the disciples' disposition changes when Jesus says don't be afraid. As they are coming down the mountain, He also tells them, "Tell the vision to no one until the Son of Man has risen from the dead." (v. 9) Jesus didn't desire a tabernacle of tradition to be built nor did He desire for them to be awestruck in immovability; they simply left where they were and Jesus didn't make a big deal out of it.

Not so with us and our traditions. We have been taught to reward our experiences with repeated do-overs every year with our personal experiences with God regarded as the 'best event to happen to us ever.' With traditions and experiences of the past, we 'trade' our present for our past experiences. In deep reflection of the past experiences, our present becomes useless because nothing could ever take place in our lives like 'whatever happened.' What I want us to see is that the Holy Spirit dwells in us now; in the each and every moment, not just that one-time event that happened to you 18 years ago, or 18 minutes ago. If that is all you have, an experience that you really believe was God, some 18 to 28 years ago, and you haven't talked to God since, you have proven that you do not have a true relationship to God who supposedly transitioned you to whatever you have become today. Jesus Christ is alive and the relationship that we have with Him is inseparable and unforgettable, not because He was God 28 years ago, but because He is God with us right now.

The Kingdom of God does not come with observation, but is within you. We believe Jesus Christ at His Word. When we became born again, that was a one-time transition into new life, like being born as a baby. We then feed from Him and live with Him as our daily bread and He grows in us in like manner. Prayer is feeding the God in us to levels of maturity in the faith. This is how our faith, as a seed, grows. Constant, abiding faithful communion with Him is how we 'remember' Him and recognize Him daily. Do not be afraid to be with Him. Do not allow your past, your sin, or even your past spiritual experiences to rob you of His present Presence. Do not fear, but revere. Be alive in Him and rejoice today…even this very moment.

October 3rd

Elijah Has Come

"And He answered and said, 'Elijah is coming and will restore all things; but I say to you, that Elijah already came, and they did not recognize him, but did to him whatever they wished. So also the Son of Man is going to suffer at their hands.'"   (Matthew 17:11-12)

As Jesus and the disciples were coming down the mountain, Jesus tells them not to tell anyone about the vision of the transfiguration until He has risen from the dead. (v. 9) He had already told them earlier that He would have to suffer many things and be killed. They are putting all of this together in their minds and remember that the scribes preached that Elijah would have to come and restore things in order to pave the way for the Messiah. Jesus confirms the prophecy and tells them that Elijah has already come. They presume correctly that Elijah had come in the form of John the Baptist. (v.13) The progression of time continues rather rapidly, it seems, through reading the Word of the Gospels. Many words spoken that are not contained in the Word leave us with excerpts of time unspoken, but the Word of God has in it what we need to know in order that we might be led to God Almighty through the inspiration of the Word given. What we know now, we know because holy men wrote down what the Holy Spirit led them to write.

Like the disciples, we try to piece this thing together to make it work in our minds, but we have been given the Holy Spirit which brings us to the incredible value of faith. We were not there when all these things took place and even though we see from hindsight, many people still do not get it or understand the Gospel of the Jesus Christ because of the history involved in its expression.
We have what we have in the Word, but the majority of what we know concerning the Word is what we have been told by others. We have been taught by preachers and teachers of the faith and hopefully, we have been taught right in the Spirit. But, tradition tells me that most of us weren't taught right, because we were given religious teachings from hundreds of years ago or even some few years ago that men have made up according to their traditions of thought.

Has anyone ever tried to explain how John the Baptist was actually the spirit of Elijah in the flesh? The Word says it is so. Has anyone tried to explain how the transfiguration occurred on the mountain? Jesus said it was a vision. Jesus' Gospel was also the Kingdom of God, yet men of renown have preached that the Gospel is many other things, oftentimes completely unaware of or ignoring the Kingdom of God. We have to move forward in faith with what we have been given in the Word, and in faith, believe what Jesus says about Himself and His Gospel.

The simplicity of the Word in faith is supernatural, but with the guidance and revelation of the Holy Spirit, we can know what is going on, unlike the disciples who 'were in the moment'. Thank God for His Holy Spirit who guides us into all Truth and we can know this Truth to be made free forever in Him. John the Baptist paved the way; He was Elijah in the flesh. I don't know how, but in faith, it just doesn't matter, does it? God planned it that way and we can be thankful for the obedience of faithful men who are willing to lay their lives down for God no matter what happens to them.

October 4th

The Littleness of Faith

"Then the disciples came to Jesus privately and said, 'Why could we not cast it out?' And He said to them, 'Because of the littleness of your faith; for truly I say to you, if you have faith as a mustard seed, you shall say to this mountain, move from here to there, and it shall move; and nothing shall be impossible to you.'"
(Matthew 17:19-20)

We should always bring our children to the Lord for healing and wholeness. It is the parents' responsibility for their children's spiritual well-being. This isn't just when they're sick; for they need to come to know Jesus and be welcomed into the Kingdom of God. Jesus strongly desires that we bring our children to Him and that we raise them in the nurture and admonition of the Lord and that we earnestly pray for our children. Never let a day go by that you do not pray for your children; it is our responsibility first and foremost to bring our children to Jesus in prayer.

As we have learned about faith, that it is a gift given by the Lord in the regenerating power of the Holy Spirit, we have to understand that when Jesus refers to faith as a mustard seed, it begins very small. The seed of faith is within us and it needs to be fed. The way that faith grows is by the careful feeding of us in prayer. If we do not pray, our faith does not grow. When we pray earnest prayers in faith, we are asking God to do something for us or for someone else. The more we see God perform His mighty works, the more our faith grows. The more our faith grows in prayer, the more we know to go to Him for and in all things.

Our faith grows by trial and testing as well. When we get to the end of a rope, we pray and seek the Lord. However, if we were already in the Lord in prayer, we might not find ourselves at the end of a rope. Many times we grow inadvertently in faith because, we try God by walking away from Him for a while and then in a moment of need, we see He is there with us and our faith in Him is magnified and fed. Trial, testing, and suffering teach us to rely upon Him. Just as Jesus was tempted in the desert and did not succumb to the wiles of the devil, we do not have to succumb either. We can tell the devil where to go and in the power of the Spirit, he will flee from us. When we find ourselves or our loved ones suffering, we can believe that God, in Christ will deliver us. Faith must grow. If it doesn't, it remains 'little,' just as Jesus described the disciples' faith.

Again, we do not have the right to rebuke the disciples for the littleness of their faith. When was the last time you drove a demon from a person possessed? Did you have the discernment that was the problem and not some perceived health issue? When was the last time you prayed and a very sick person regained their health and was healed? Just how little is our faith these days?

Faith is a tangible object in the Kingdom of God. It is as a tiny seed that can grow to the point that it can be a tree. The faith given by God is the God-kind of faith that can say to any problem, 'Be gone from here…just like a mountain…and cast it into the sea!' But, it takes prayer and fasting, the relinquishing and denying of the self, to see this kind of faith in action. Pray and never cease to pray and be with Him.

Depend on Jesus in abiding in Him and your faith will grow in being with Him. He is faith full and the faith He gives is powerful.

October 5th

The Walk of Obedience

"And while they were gathering together in Galilee, Jesus said to them, 'The Son of Man is going to be delivered into the hands of men; and they will kill Him, and He will be raised on the third day.' And they were deeply grieved."
(Matthew 17:22-23)

Jesus Christ' obedience to His Father's will is so significant that without His learning obedience through suffering, we would not be truly alive today. We have probably heard 'the old, old story at how a Savior came from glory to save a wretch like me' so many times that we gloss over it as old news. We want to get to a part that we haven't heard before, or didn't quite understand, in order to make our relationship with Him relevant. We like to talk about what we learned that was new as though our revelation that we just received was 'new' and no one had ever been taught that before. We think we are special, even though the old, old story has been around for over two thousand years. Even this particular work that you are reading is not special; it is a grave attempt to be obedient to the Truth.

Jesus Christ learned obedience through suffering. He came to die. His disciples did not understand that when they were with Him, even though He told them repeatedly what was going to happen to Him. At first, they rejected the idea that He would have to die. Over time, however, they began to receive all of His teaching and that included His purpose in life and that was to die. I am uncertain if they understood His purpose in death; no one can speak for them, but they didn't really get it until after He had been resurrected and after they had received the Holy Spirit at Pentecost.

Obedience to our Father is paramount. Jesus was the standard in living out obedience. Only He could follow the Father as He did and only He is the one who has followed the Father as He did. Other men have tried and have either been obedient in moments or died trying. Jesus' obedience to His Father's will always underscored the events in His life. All that He did was under direct influence and obedience to His heavenly Father. His obedience was the plumline of His life. He had to obey in order to accomplish His purpose in life and in death.

At times, we grow very weary of attempting to obey God's Word. That is religion in action. Honestly, we cannot obey all of God's Word, that's why Jesus came to show us not a better way, but the only way to follow the Lord…and that is to deny ourselves. Paul said, 'I die daily…' The ableness, or ability, to deny ourselves comes from desiring Him so much that we want Him instead of ourselves at the helm of our lives. Then, He empowers us by the work of the Holy Spirit to submit, follow, walk, and run in the Spirit.

With the amount of faith that He has given you, let Him build on that faith in faithful abiding and obedience to Him. He is the giver and foundation of our faith; He is also the builder. Let Him increase your faith in humble obedience to Him. Those that refuse to learn obedience in suffering in Him remain little in their faith and live on the road of complaints and murmuring, which is an outward expression of rejecting obedience.

October 6th

Pay Your Taxes

"But lest we give them offense, go to the sea, and throw in a hook, and take the first fish that comes up; and when you open his mouth, you will find a stater. Take that and give it to them for you and Me." *(Matthew 17:27)*

The tax collectors of the poll tax had come calling and confronted Peter in the street. When they asked Peter if his Master paid the poll tax, Peter impulsively responded, 'Yes!' Jesus, knowing what had transpired in the conversation asks Peter if He was even required to pay that tax, and Peter had to admit, 'No, only strangers are required to pay that tax.' Then Jesus gives Peter the strangest command and that was to go fishing for money out in the sea. The two-drachma tax was being exacted upon them and the stater had a value of four-drachma; [1] the more than enough supply. The obvious witness here for us all is for us to pay our taxes when they are due, lest we create a stumbling block for the tax agents and for our own personal testimony.

Sometimes the obvious is too obvious in the regards of our testimony not being tarnished when our taxes come due and we pay them on time. However, there is much more here than simply paying our bills on time. Jesus hears our conversations and our Lord knows our thoughts before we think them. When we commit ourselves to something, let it be in the Father's will. We will know His will by remaining in Him. If we have to have a crash course on making a decision according to our Father's will, we can best be assured that we are already not in it. Remaining in Him is the way to not be in doubt of a road taken.

The wonderful aspect of preaching the Kingdom of God is that it leads us to a place. The Kingdom is the person and place of Jesus Christ. If we can envision being invited to go to a place that has been purchased for us and all we have to do is to give up ourselves for this eternal Kingdom, then it's time to walk out of ourselves and into Him. When we walk through the blood-stained Door, we enter into His rest. We enter into Him. It is there that we find all of our spiritual provision, for this is a spiritual place of abiding and living in Him. He supplies all we need according to His riches in glory. These are spiritual words for a spiritual life.

Please do not let a preacher tell you that God is going to give you money from a fish to pay your taxes and then you go fishing rather than going to work. Jesus was using literal events to teach us obedience, supply, the more than enough, faithfulness, His ability to hear and know what we need, and even the things we think we need, but really don't. All of these were enjoined in this sequence of events. They literally happened to teach us the more than enough supply of living in His Kingdom. And just as Jesus told Peter to go to the sea and put a hook in the water and pull out that first fish, open its mouth and find a stater in it, to more than enough pay our taxes… so it is with us today, that if we will abide in Him absolutely, then He will tell us what we need to do in order to fill that supply that we need in our hearts. He knows what you need. Abide in Him and see His glory in the filling of it. Allow Him to increase your faith to meet your every need.

October 7th

Greatness in the Kingdom

"At that time the disciples came to Jesus, saying, 'Who then is greatest in the kingdom of heaven?'" (Matthew 18:1)

When praying, Jesus loves for you to speak from the heart in Him to Him and with Him:

Praying like a pro is for pulpiteers and rascal ears, it makes them feel much better.
To be a pro in praying is to grow the heart in leather.

All covered in the pride of life and seeming good 'tis true;
But praying like the pro is not in Spirit, nor in Truth.

Beware the altered hues of praying men out loud;
He does not hear the loudest ones for loud is for the crowd.

He hears the thoughts and words we say in secret or in tears;
My heart does faint and faint does now to breathe His breath so clear.

It is in the pride of life that men ask questions in order to be seen or heard. It is the depth of pride that causes us to feel as though we deserve a reward simply for receiving a gift as though we are somebody deserving even more. To be chosen by the Lord is to be wonderful indeed, but when the disciples went to asking for the 'more', they found their answer in the form of a child.

Jesus' response to them that day about greatness in the Kingdom taught the disciples and us a most valuable lesson that too many folk would rather soon forget. The lesson is this: "Jesus called a little child to Himself and said, 'Truly I say to you, unless you are converted and become like children, you shall not enter the kingdom of heaven.'" (v.2) Jesus did not respond to their query of greatness, but to the absolute of child-like faith in the Kingdom. There is no pride in the Kingdom of God. Pride is a stumbling block that men seek when they do not understand what they're seeking. We have to hear that we must be converted, born again, having received the new birth of true life in the Kingdom. We must be born again and that is only accomplished by the power and work of the Holy Spirit. We do not become better; we become new.

When we are born again, we become like little children with little faith. Just as baby children are when they are first born, in being totally reliant on the parent for their care and feeding, so are we. When we are converted, we become the new creation that Paul talked about. This process can only begin with humbling ourselves before Almighty God. Jesus says that whoever humbles themselves as a child; then he is the greatest in the kingdom of heaven. (v.4)

October 8th

Stumbling Blocks

"…but whoever causes one of these little ones who believe in Me to stumble, it is better for him that a heavy millstone be hung around his neck, and that he be drowned in the depth of the sea." (Matthew 18:6)

Jesus moves from the answer to the disciples' question of greatness to the bottom line of us all and that is our children. We were all children once and whether our upbringing was a pleasant one or not, we are still responsible for our children to bring them up in the kindnesses of the Lord. We are to know the Lord ourselves for ourselves, of course, but we are not here simply for ourselves. The children of our families and the children of our communities are always the primary responsibility of adults everywhere.

Children cannot take care of themselves; they need adults to care for them in every way, especially spiritually. Food, clothing, and shelter are the basic necessities of life that we need to give to our children, but the need so much more and we need to protect their future with spiritual leadership and guidance just as much as we would feed them food every day. Your children will always be your children, regardless of their age and maturation. Your son will always be your son and your daughter will always be your daughter. Take the most wondrous care of the children that our Lord has given you to manage.

Jesus gives a warning here that has not been heeded throughout time. 'Whoever causes one of these little ones to stumble' is the admonition and warning because everything we do around our children is teaching them how to be. We will be either teaching good things or horrible things by the way we talk and behave around them. We teach them in how we treat them and in how we treat our spouses.
Children know when we are being a hypocrite. Their pleasant innocent spirits when they are very young see the obvious of what we oftentimes fail to see…and that is how we talk, what we say, and the tone of our disposition gets scrutinized in the most innocent of ears and eyes. There is not much that goes unnoticed in the eyes of a child.

Our walk must match our talk in the home, at church, in public and in private. We cannot get away with secret hypocrisy with our children. We may be able to fool our friends and co-workers in public for a while, but whatever we really are gets acted out at home where we think we are safe, but we are only fooling ourselves if we play the hypocrite. Let Jesus Christ change you from the inside out and you will be His light in your home and in your public arenas.

A stumbling block to a child is one who leads the child away from the right representation of the nature and love of God. If a child is fearful and frightened by men because someone abused the child in some awful way, then Jesus declared what would happen to that person. Child abuse will not go unpunished in His Kingdom Light. Whatever is done in darkness will be brought into the light. Watch out for your children and the children in your community. Allow the Holy Spirit to fill you with His love and guidance. And the love of Jesus Christ will guide you into all Truth and protect the innocent in their present and in their future. Be obedient to the care of the children. We have to commit to their loving care, nurture, spiritual teaching and covering.

October 9th

The Inevitable Stumbling Blocks

"Woe to the world because of its stumbling blocks! For it is inevitable that stumbling blocks come; but woe to that man through whom the stumbling block comes!" *(Matthew 18:7)*

The stumbling blocks are those things that cause others to sin. They are the "offenses, displeasures, and snares"[1] that entrap all of us at one time or another to cause us to do just about anything within the depravity of man. These are the stumbling blocks that we put in others' way to cause them to resent, become angry, to dissipate, to backbite and murmur, or to think or do even worse things already mentioned. Offenses are going to come, and none of us are exempt from offending other people.

One example of this is someone who thinks they are above reproach and lives a pretty perfect life and there's no way they could ever offend anyone, let alone cause another to sin. When pride goes before a person of reckless self-assurance, the fall of another is surely going to come. Leaders in the faith must be aware that they are culpable of offending those of little faith; beware lest you fall into a trap of running people off from the fellowship. Jesus does not look highly on those who walk in offending others because of their positions.

There are other more dastardly sins as well that are aroused in the hearts of people from lust, pornography, and the dark forces at work to entice people to lose their virginity to fornication or when they're married, causing another to commit adultery. Repeated advances of sensuality do not go unnoticed and neither do acts of unkindness, hatred, and the inducement to incite violence on another. These are examples of stumbling blocks that some create for others and even themselves. Jesus says 'woe' to those from whom the stumbling block comes.

It is better to realize our ways of personality and how we move on the earth and deal with ourselves honestly than to come up short some day and recognize that we caused another person to sin because of how we lived, what we said, or how we treated people. People tear up other people's marriages every day and get other people fired from their jobs because of lust, jealousy, lies, and covetousness. Guard your heart lest you think that you are immune to the deceptions of the evil one. Even the best of believers can be tricked by their own self-deception or pride and dive into something that they should never have considered.

If you find that you have caused another to sin, repent of it, recognize the depth of what you've done. Go and apologize. Many times people create stumbling blocks for others and they do not realize the depth of their egregiousness. Saying, 'I'm sorry' is oftentimes not good enough, there has to be true repentance and a sense that this will not happen again. Watch and pray that you be not tempted.

Pray, brothers and sisters, pray that we will not be offenders of the faith, causing others to be offended by Jesus Christ because of how we have treated them. Express holy love in and through all things and walk in the light as He is in the light and you will not satisfy the deeds of the flesh which create a multitude of sins.

If you have been offended, talk to your brother, do not let the sun go down on your anger. Live in peace and let the brotherhood of peace surround you wherever you go and in the each and every moment abide in Him in His Presence. Amen.

October 10th

Watch and Pray for the Children

"See that you do not despise one of these little ones, for I say to you, that their angels in heaven continually behold the face of My Father who is in heaven."
(Matthew 18:10)

We were all children once and we most likely knew who liked us and who didn't. Couldn't you always tell the teachers who didn't like being around children. To them, it was just a job and they really did not want to be around a classroom of children. We've also seen other adults that grow weary of children too quickly to the point of despising the little ones and calling them names; treating them with disdain and disrespect. Child abuse starts out this way and goes further down a road of contemptuousness towards children when left unchecked.

Love is to abound in our hearts so much so, that even the most unwholesome child can be taken care of in our care. We are to love and nurture children as though they are our own; or, as though they are children of our heavenly Father. Jesus says their angels are before the Father's face. The knowledge of this should cause some to reckon themselves dead to their sins of how they have treated children in the past and be renewed in the fellowship of love and care for all little ones. The idea, alone, of a child being a child of God, our Father, would need to be taken into deliberate consideration in how we treat His children for He knows for sure already. Do you really want the Father God after you for the way you treated His child? Treat your children well and see to it that the children in your community are cared for in love and not abused.

Daily we go to our Father and pray being built up in the faith that He has given us. Not everyone is able to work with children and this is not a demand that all must be able to do that. But we all must walk in the disposition of holy love. His children need us to do that for them, just as we needed loving parents, teachers, guides, and mentors in our lives when we were growing up. I'm uncertain what it is that makes older people forget that they were children once. We cannot forget our childhood for the sake of the children of our future.

Pray for your children every day. No matter how old they get, keep praying for them as intercessors before a Holy King. Life gets too busy for some, and we should be aware of our opportunities to care for our own and others' children to lead them, keep them, and cover them in the Holy Spirit. Pray now for the children in your life. Pray for them by name and do not forget to pray in holy love.

October 11th

The Proportion of a Mistake

"…it is inevitable that stumbling blocks come…" (Matthew 18:7b)

Committing a mistake in the eyes of another causes an eruption in the heart of the viewer. Whatever is in the heart of the person who views another who sins, or simply commits an error, will come out of his/her mouth and reveal their true disposition. It will either be a disposition of love, faith, and forgiveness or a heart of judgmental criticism watching and waiting for a fall. Surely someone else's sin, or careless error, will find you out in your heart of hearts. A sickening judgmental spirit lies in the heart of the hypocrite waiting to pounce on the believer in prosecutorial persecution for a mistake committed.

Whether the one has sinned a little or great sin is not the question here. Here, the matter of making a simple error in judgment, taking a wrong turn, spilling milk, leaving something undone or done wrongly, but correctable, is the true matter of state here. Spiteful spouses have watchful eyes waiting for their turn to rebuke as do children of judgmental parents who have been criticized all their lives for simply being a child.

The reward of a judging spirit is a judging spirit. It is inescapable and transcends time and space. When a judgmental crack is opened in a person, be certain that whatever they dish out will surely come back to them in multiples. We reap what we sow and eventually sow what we reap because all we have is what we have sown in others and what we have sown in the recesses of our minds. Too many old people are left alone because they spent their lives criticizing others and now the others have no desire to be with them. Judgmental spirits breed alienation in the present and in the future. Few people desire to be around a seemingly perfect nag.

Watching and waiting for another to fall is a symptom of a heart gone wrong or a heart that was never right to begin with. Only God and that person know his/her heart. All we have is fruit to determine whether the inside of a man is good or bad. If the fruit is love, joy, peace, patience, goodness, kindness, faithfulness, gentleness, and self-control, then that fruit emanates from the heart of the Holy Spirit. If the fruit is judgmental, backbiting, complaining, murmuring, sorcery, fornication, lying, stealing, hate, or murder, then it is of the evil one waiting to accuse.

Good fruit comes from a good tree and bad fruit comes from a bad tree. Somehow, in the refusal to see the simplicity of Jesus' teachings, we get ourselves bound to other people who possess bad fruit and the result is stress, turmoil, criticism or worse and we allow ourselves to be driven down a bad road of contempt. Can there be any good on a bad road?

Release yourself and others from a contemptuous spirit and see the Light of Jesus Christ in His holy love. Be the Light in the world and do not become the switch that turns light into darkness. Know the Truth of a dark spirit and live at peace in Light recognizing good fruit when you see it and bad fruit when it knocks on your door. Release, forgive, and holy love in His Holy Spirit.

October 12th

He Searches for the Children

"Thus it is not the will of your Father who is in heaven that one of these little ones perish" (Matthew 18:14)

Jesus spends careful time with teaching His disciples about how much little children mean to the Father. He tells within the context that their angels are continually before the face of our Father. He says that if an adult causes one of these little ones to stumble, that is to fall out of the Way, that they deserve a millstone tied around their neck and cast into the sea. He speaks of cutting your eye out if your eye causes you to stumble or cutting your hand off if it causes you to stumble; but it is all in regard to being a stumbling block to little children. We have to take what we are, do, and teach around children extremely seriously. We cannot abuse, misuse, or lead children astray and think that it's going to be ok with our heavenly Father. Quite the contrary!

In the analogy of the shepherd who has 100 sheep and one of them has gone astray, the shepherd goes and searches for the lost sheep and rejoices over it more than the 99 who did not stray. Jesus is relating this analogy to children and their importance to the Father in the Kingdom. It is not the will of the Father that one of His little ones should perish. Woe to that man or woman who causes one of these little ones to stumble.

In all of life we find ourselves teaching in everything we do. When children grow to be adults, it is the adults who are doing the teaching by their very lives. Everything that is said or written, mannerisms, dispositions, attitudes, all teach towards the belief systems of little children everywhere. No adult is exempt from this grave opportunity.

A man's work may be in any field or endeavor and yet, ultimately, his work will affect a child somewhere down the line. The man is responsible for his work and ever how far it goes down the line towards the effects it will have on humanity; it will eventually reach to influence a child in some way. It's not just the parents and teachers who are culpable of the wrong and the right; it is every single or married adult in their personal belief systems that will eventually affect a child by their belief systems.

People do not know what they do and how deep the depths are of their personal belief systems on children. We are a series of moral choices and every moral choice we make will eventually affect a child to lead them to Light or to lead them in the way of the world.

It is so vitally important here to be in Jesus Christ in Spirit and in Truth. Our testimony of the spiritual good and the right is out for all to see, even when we think we are at home alone…we are never alone. Know the Lord Jesus Christ and abide in Him. Spiritual new birth life is first, then growing into maturity. When our hearts are in His order and nature, then the children will be led to Him according to His order and nature and not to some vain belief that leads them astray to some offering of the world and utter destruction. Watch and pray for the little ones!

October 13th

Appropriate Fellowship

"And if your brother sins (against you), go and reprove him in private; if he listens to you, you have won your brother." (Matthew 18:15)

The inevitability of stumbling blocks to come has been addressed by Jesus. We all have sinned and fallen short of the glory of God. There is none righteous, no, not one. We have all sinned and we all usually find ourselves committing acts of sin against God because we are in a body of flesh that wars against the Spirit of God. Even though we may find ourselves in periodic acts of sin, we know now that we do not have to sin. The power over sin is in the Holy Spirit and we do not have to succumb to the outer influences that war against His nature residing in us. Still, we do succumb and offend our neighbor in the process.

None of us are exempt from this unfortunate experience called life in this world. Because Jesus knows our hearts and nature and our propensity to offend, He teaches us what to do when someone sins against us personally. We are to go to our brother and explain the sinful offense and reprove him in private, between him and you alone. However, what we normally do when someone sins against us, or even someone we know, we take the person's sin and tell other people 'what that person did to me or said about me'. This is not to be, for that is the case of gossip and immaturity. That is unlawful in the Kingdom of God for Jesus speaks directly to us and cautions us about what to do in the case of being sinned against by your brother.

Let's be perfectly clear here that Jesus is explicitly talking about the sin of another against a brother or sister in Christ. He is not talking about someone who gets offended at a person just because they 'think' someone did something to them, but they really didn't. A person has to take offense upon himself and typically the more immature in the faith, and sometimes completely faithless people who think they have faith, are at fault here because they are always getting offended at somebody for any reason. This is not what Jesus is talking about here. He is talking about sin, not petty fault finding in people who get offended by others as a result of their personal immaturity. Grow up and mature in the Spirit of God. Jesus Christ was wounded, beaten unmercifully, and murdered on a despicable cross and what I have seen in most church goers is the ability to hang on to themselves and their pride and take offense at almost anything. The easily offended person is shameless in the sight of the blood of Jesus Christ and should repent of their selfishness and egregious pride of life thinking that the Lord's church is all about them.

If your brother or sister in Christ has sinned against you, go to that person alone, and discuss the offending sin between the two of you. Is an apology required? Jesus doesn't say. What is continually repeated in the New Testament is for us to let love abound in our hearts and to make it a point to forgive. Jesus did not speak to a required apology, but He did speak to the issue of agreement. When we go to our brother, we present the sin of the brother to the brother. If he hears (agrees with you that he committed that sin), then you have gained your brother. Do not put words into his mouth and do not expect to hear your specific required apology. Allow the Holy Spirit to work in his heart and the conviction of the Spirit will do His work His way.

October 14th

Heavenly Direction

"But if he does not listen to you..." (Matthew 18:16a)

The idea of one person talking to another in the expression of a grievance is that the offended party speaks explicitly with the sinning offender regarding the specific sin. We are to speak privately and plainly in what we believe has been done against us. This way, the person accused of committing the sin is confronted with his sin and is not attacked personally as in a personality squabble that simply arises from situational conflicts between two egregious parties.

The ability to communicate the grievance is so important here. The sin must be revealed, not skirted around because of possibilities. When the person who is being confronted 'hears' the grievance, that person has heard to the extent that a decision is rendered almost immediately. The decision in 'hearing' is that the sinning brother either agrees with the victim or disagrees. If the person agrees, then you have gained your brother and you wait on him to act out that 'agreement' in how that person's nature is typically revealed. What we desire to see is the fruit of the Spirit of God in love, patience, goodness, etc. What we desire is reconciliation first, second, and third!

If the offending brother does not 'hear' or listen…then agreement of the sin will not be substantiated. Jesus gives us clear instructions to further our cause by taking two or more with us again to the brother and speaking the sinful offense clearly to the brother. At times, after careful thought, a brother will relent and agree that the sin transpired and the passageways of fellowship are renewed. However, if the offending brother does not 'hear', that is, agrees with the assessment of the two, or more, then Jesus says to take the sinning brother to the body of believers and let them decide what to do in the case of the sinning brother.

Again, this is not a case of mutual personality offenses that are born of silly immaturity, but a real case scenario of blatant sin against a brother or sister in Christ. Love covers a multitude of sins and forgiveness of offenses is directed to us by our Lord. He is our Lord and seeks reconciliation. The purpose of all of this is reconciliation. We do not stand in judgment of others, but are submitted to Him in love for He first loved us. His direction is clear, though, that when a sinning brother sins, and refuses to listen, hear, and agree that he has sinned; then when he refuses to even listen to the church, the church has the mandate to treat him as an outcast. Do you throw him out of the church? Jesus doesn't say, but He does say that he is to be treated as one who is not fellowshipped with. Fellowship denotes agreement. True Holy Spirit koinonia is agreement in the Holy Spirit. Where there is no agreement, there is no koinonia, or true fellowship.

Watch and pray that you do not fall into temptation and watch and pray for others that the Spirit of God will confine us all to His love and agreement in Spirit-filled fellowship with Him and with our brothers and sisters in Christ. Life in the Kingdom is that we are as He is…Holy Love.

October 15th

Binding and Loosing

"Truly I say to you, whatever you shall bind on earth shall be bound in heaven; and whatever you shall loose on earth, shall be loosed in heaven. Again I say, if two of you agree on earth about anything that they may ask, it shall be done for them by My Father who is in heaven." (Matthew 18:18-19)

The binding and loosing here has to do with our relationships in Christ in agreement. Our words are so vitally important; I do believe that we underestimate the value and weight of our words, testimony, decisions, contracts, and vows that we make before the Lord every day. At times, we speak words that demean, debilitate, and destroy others and do not think another thing about it, because we said it in secret to another who happened to agree with our assessment of another person. How destructive we can be at times with our cursing, even when done privately and unwittingly we come into agreement with a dark, divisive spirit.

The power of the tongue is in the power of agreement. Jesus explains to us that if two of us agree on earth about anything, that includes the thought that a man has sinned against another and the church agrees together that he has, then that man is an outcast in earth and in heaven. The Lord will hear the prayer of a repentant man because it is the Lord who is doing the convicting. If a man persists in his sin and remains in it, then his prayers of anything but repentance go unnoticed. How weighty our words and decisions are before a Holy God. We cannot take lightly our spirit in joining with His Spirit. Truth prevails in Truth; so stay on the road of the straight and narrow.

Jesus' admonition to the value He places on the power of agreement is exciting to those who like to ask for things. Seemingly, some folk believe that if they can get another person into agreement with them, they can go and ask God for anything, because that's what He said, right? Not really. Context is always within the context of the words within the verse, the verse within the paragraph, the paragraph within the chapter, the chapter within the book, and the book within the covenant, old or new, and the nature of God Himself. Within the context, the power of binding and loosing is in the power of agreement with the brothers and sisters in Christ who have fellowship with one another concerning certain things. These are the things that Jesus just spoke about, but they are also the things that are of like nature to the context.

It is not in the context for two like-minded people to stand holding hands praying together to God that God would fill their bank account with money. I have seen similar requests made to God under the presumption that God is required to fulfill their demands because they decreed and declared it in loosing favor to their finances. This is out of order and not what He was talking about.

Jesus words are spiritual words and must be reckoned with spiritually. Spiritual blessings are spiritual in nature (ie., love, joy, peace, faith, etc.). Nowhere does Jesus promise that He will fill your physical bank account with money because you demanded it of Him. Seek first the Kingdom of God and all these things will be added to you. Get into agreement with the Spirit of God and the fellowship of God and man will be in agreement in one with Him in His Kingdom.

October 16th

The Presence of the Lord

"For where two or three have gathered in My name, there I am in their midst."
(Matthew 18:20)

The power in agreement is in the Presence of the Lord. Oh, the joy that floods my soul with the sound of His voice. He is all-powerful at all times. When His saints gather together in His name, He is there in the midst, in the middle, in the atmosphere in and among His people. Oh, the wonder of His name and the magnificence of His Presence!

Our hearts are made glad in Him together! Our souls burst with singing and shouting, "Hallelujah!" It is such a wonderful joy to be in His Presence and to be with others; in fellowship with others, He is all the more. His Spirit inhabits the praises of His people. The atmosphere of the earth is air. The atmosphere of heaven is glory. The atmosphere of the Christian is God Himself!

It is crucial to our understanding that living a submitted life before Him in the continual denial of the self is the pathway to breathing in His Kingdom. His Presence is in His Kingdom and His Kingdom is in His Presence. It is as walking into a room that you know where He abides and you go to that room where you know He is and you stay there and you don't want to leave. Imagine a group of people who know and believe what you believe in the Spirit and being with them abiding in Him. You are all in the same room together in Him; there He is in the midst. He is about you and He is in you. He is your connection with your brother and sister in Christ.

Your words in the midst are important. Let the words of your mouth and the meditations of your heart be acceptable to Him for He is your Rock and Redeemer!

Let Truth prevail and let His Spirit rise among you. Then, you will see the glory of the Lord and the words of your mouths will be in agreement in Him, so much so that what you then bind on this earth is bound in heaven where He is and whatever is loosed in the midst of Him is loosed in agreement in heaven. There, in the midst of His people, and here, with just you and Him there is oneness in Him; just as Jesus prayed in John 17, that they might be one as You and I are one.

Isn't it wonderful that we live with such a wonderful Savior who loves us so much that not only did He die for us to save us eternally to be with Him; we can be with Him today in Him and with others who live in His Spirit? All glory and honor and praise belong to Him who sits on the throne…not just the throne in heaven, but the throne in my heart! Then I shall see that day in maturity in faith with complete agreement in Him when I realize that the throne in heaven is His Kingdom's throne in my heart.

October 17th

Forgiveness is not Abstract

"Then Peter came and said to Him, 'Lord, how often shall my brother sin against me and I forgive him? Up to seven times?' Jesus said to him, 'I do not say to you, up to seven times, but up to seventy times seven.'" *(Matthew 18:21-22)*

As Peter is listening to this discourse on offenses, stumbling blocks, sins against one another, and the ways to deal with each other in reconciliation, he approached Jesus with the same question that we would probably ask and that is, 'How many times must I forgive before it is enough?' We always want to know our boundaries and limitations whether it be for our saving grace or for our knowing our standards in giving or for knowing our standards in forgiving. They all seem to go together, don't you think? We want limits and rules and laws fixed so that we know when we've broken a law or when someone else has or when we've done enough.

The roads that we take to new places are often fret with turns and trees that we've never seen. When we are led to places not of our own accord, we desire a map, an exact map in which to navigate where we are going. But even the maps sometimes seem to lead us astray, because we didn't read it right and so we took a wrong turn rather than following our instinct. God has placed within us Spirit-filled believers a 'due north', the way in which we should go and it is the way in which we should not depart; it is the path that He has chosen for us, the pathway to forgive others as He has forgiven us. His Holy Spirit deems it so.

He has forgiven us for all and all that we are and all that we have done. His forgiveness is great and greater than our transgressions and yet…we desire a map to forgive because forgiving is a Godly thing to do and when we get offended by sinful men, we don't want to be so godly. We become transverse, crossed, and unwilling to move forward because they did…whatever it was they did to us. "Forgive…me? Forgive him?" "Yes, that is what I said." "How often, even this time?" "Yes, especially this time."

Forgiveness is not abstract in that we do not know what it means or how to do it. It is not abstract in that it could mean this or it could mean that, no, it is not that difficult. Forgiveness is simple; it is the obedience to Him that is difficult. It is the denying of the self once again in His holy love that we make difficult and trying when we would rather choose our way of dealing with life's circumstances that He allowed in the first place.

Don't make His love and forgiveness out to be an unchartered territory in your life. You want to go to new places in Him. Follow His paths that He has laid out for us and even if the way seems dark and the trees seem to be covered in something we do not recognize, they are His trees that He has planted by the river of Life that bear the fruit of love, grace, mercy, and forgiveness. Allow the unrecognizable and the difficult to become the fruit of your mouth and the fruit of your spirit in Him today. He leads us on the pathway to peace and that pathway is paved with forgiveness. Forgive and never cease to forgive and the abstract and unrecognizable will become clear in holy faith and holy love.

October 18th

Forgiveness in the Kingdom

"For this reason the kingdom of heaven may be compared to a certain king who wished to settle accounts with his slaves." (Matthew 18:23)

Forgiveness in the Kingdom is the Lord's forgiveness that He gives and expects that His people do as He does. The parable of the unmerciful servant details how great our Lord's mercy is to us in that we owe a debt to our Lord that is so great; we are unable to pay it. Jesus' use of "the 10,000 talents owed by the slave is equivalent to 30,000,000 denarii."[1] "One denarii was a day's wage."[2] The slave who owed so much could not pay back his debt and the king who was rich in mercy and forgiveness forgave the debt and did not send him and his family to prison to pay what could not possibly be paid. Then, the slave turns on a debtor that had that owed him a hundred denarii, (v.28), and refuses to have mercy on him, but throws him into prison in order to exact payment for that man's debt. Where mercy was offered, it was not received in its heart; therefore it was not offered to another. The king, then, throws the initial slave into prison for exacting an unforgiving spirit upon his fellow man.

This is as the Kingdom of God is. When Jesus suffered and died on the cross, His work was finished just as He said. The payment for the sins of the world was exacted from His sacrifice for us. The payment was made by His life given for all men for all time. All sins have been forgiven at the cross of Jesus Christ. Jesus does not keep dying on the cruel cross each time you sin and ask for forgiveness, no! All sins throughout all time have been paid for. The sins of mankind cannot be paid for by man, so it took a great Savior in Jesus Christ to make that payment for us. Acknowledgement of this is not believing and receiving. Many have only acknowledged the fact.

If you believe this by the convicting power of the Holy Spirit, then what happens in your faith is that the faith that He gives you in your heart is exactly the belief that your payment for your debt has been paid, once and for all, over two thousand years ago. When you realize this in the Spirit; that He paid a debt so great that you could not pay it, He comes to you and regenerates you in His mercy. This is receiving Him and accepting Him in what He has done for you and all mankind. You then live a changed life in Him. Regeneration is by His Spirit alone. Simply believing in the payment and transaction is not regeneration.

The difference in what the unmerciful slave did and what the Spirit-filled believer is this: the unmerciful slave acknowledged the pardon, because the pardon was made on his behalf, but, he did not receive the pardon in his heart, he was unchanged, so he was unable to impart the same pardon, or forgiveness to another. It is as James said, 'The devils also believe and tremble…' The unmerciful slave acknowledged the pardon, but it was not imparted to his being…in his heart there was no transfer.

This is like the man who goes to a church service and stands at the altar and says, 'I believe what Christ did for me!' and then he goes his way unchanged and still treats others as he always did, yet believing the preacher who told him he was saved, but he wasn't. The Kingdom isn't about getting a ticket; it's about being changed and remaining in Him forever. As He is, we become. He is holy love and so are we. He is forgiving and so are we.

October 19th

Forgiveness is From the Heart

"And his lord, moved with anger, handed him over to the torturers until he should repay all that was owed him. So shall My heavenly Father also do to you, if each of you does not forgive his brother from your heart." (Matthew 18:35)

If forgiveness is from the heart of God and imparted to us in belief and change, how does the change occur? How does the transaction of belief turn into a regenerated heart and how do we know? Carefully watch the work of the merciful king with the unmerciful slave and you will see the adverse of what is not permissible in the Kingdom of God.

The unpayable debt of the slave was excused and the slave walks away only to find a debtor to himself with a payable debt as an opportunity of revelation of a life-change into what the merciful king was all about. The unmerciful slave whose debt had been exonerated had not received the spirit of the forgiver; he received the idea of the payment made, but did not internalize the idea into a true belief. If he had, he would have come to an understanding of what had just transpired in his life.

But he didn't understand what had happened to him; he only cared about himself and his particular lot in life. He owed "the equivalent of 30,000,000 denarii",[1] in which "one denarii was one day's wage"[2]; it was an unpayable and unsustainable debt. He was only concerned for himself, not his king, or his king's goods or welfare; he lived for himself. Although the king realized this, the king maintained his nature and forgave the slave of his debt. But in the transaction, it was the spirit of the king that was being transacted and not the debt. The debt represents the wall between the king and the slave. The king excused the wall in his spirit and made the slave free in his kingdom. The freedom to be free in the kingdom is tested in spirit by an opportunity. When the opportunity arose by the slave who owed 100 denarii, the original slave failed the test of the revelation of the heart. The spirit of the king had not transacted into the spirit of the unmerciful slave, therefore the unmerciful slave remained in his unmerciful state with the original amount being owed and the original punishment being exacted.

And so it is with lives today who want to say they are Christian because they say they 'believe'. Has the person changed by the Spirit of our Holy Lord by regeneration or has the person merely 'believed' in the idea of a payment made? The proof in knowing the Truth about the real Christian is in the fact that only God can forgive as He forgives and if the person has the Spirit of God dwelling in them, then the Spirit dwelling in them will be there to forgive when forgiveness is needed, which usually is every day. Remember, the freedom to be free in the kingdom is tested in spirit by an opportunity. If the Spirit to forgive is not there, then the person thinks they are something they are not.

The temple of the Holy Spirit is able to forgive and love as only He is able to love. There must be a transaction of transference of the Spirit of God into a man who submits himself to His Spirit. Unless that is done, that man will remain owing his payment on the sin he has committed because of his own inability to truly receive in his heart and the proof will be in the fruit of the man's life. Salvation is about the impartation of the Holy Spirit into the life of the true believer. If that has not occurred, then the man only believes in the idea of salvation and really isn't in the kingdom. It's time to be real.

October 20th

Marriage

"…and He said, for this cause a man shall leave his father and mother, and shall cleave to his wife; and the two shall become one flesh? Consequently, they are no longer two, but one flesh. What God has therefore joined together, let no man separate." *(Matthew 19:5-6)*

People get married for a variety of reasons and have many more definitions about love than they do about marriage. People do marry for love and out of love because they think they fell in love, but is love enough? Is the kind of love that is talked about in the motion pictures the same kind of love that God talks about when He talks about Himself? Does married life today resemble anything that God intended when He established it in His holy covenant? Marriage is between one man and one woman, just as God has established it. Let it remain forever as it is to be in His eyes and not in our own.

The man shall be called the husband and the woman shall be called the wife. And, the two of them shall cleave to each other in such a manner that they become one. However, this oneness does not just simply happen because the man and the woman deem it so. There must be agreement. Not only do the man and woman need to agree with one another, the man and woman in agreement need to agree with God Almighty. Here, it is the Spirit manifesting Himself in the marriage to where the two become one flesh and it is God Himself that joins them together. Any other formula or design is not marriage, but simply a union of sorts outside the design of God among two distinct people. True marriage was established by God and it is only true marriage when it is ordained by God.

Marriage is and is ordained by God when it is established in the heart of a man and woman according to His design and not the designs of men.

The perfect union in what God has joined together is that which God intended regardless of creed, culture, time, or space. It is not up to man or woman to separate or re-define what God creates. What God had joined together is joined in Spiritual oneness with Him. Any attempt to separate that union is not of God, but from the evil one. Keep the marriage bed undefiled; that not only includes the flesh, but also includes the mind. How many marriages dissolve into two distinct vessels when the mind is attracted to fantasy, lust, selfishness, or covetousness? Troubles in marriage always start in the heart where one or both begin to ease into personal and selfish gratification to the point where only one or none of the parties is satisfied with the relationship.

Romantic love is not Holy love. Holy love is of God and is born into lives who are born of His Holy Spirit. Again, it is the Spirit of the marriage that makes the union and it is the Spirit of God that makes it continue. Anytime two people are together, there is going to be the opportunity for divisiveness, differences of opinion, or demonstrations of self. In the Spirit, we are directed by His Spirit to walk in His Spirit and not fulfill the desires of the flesh. Husbands love your wives. Wives, respect your husbands. Both submit to one another in holy love and holy love will be of God leading in your marriage. Submit to the Lord and allow Him to be Lord in your own individual lives and in the one life that He has created you to be together. Amen.

October 21st

Divorce

"He said to them, 'Because of your hardness of heart, Moses permitted you to divorce your wives; but from the beginning it has not been this way.'"
(Matthew 19:8)

The oneness in spirit that comes from the Holy Spirit is what joins the man and woman together in marriage, love, and union. The divorce issue needs to be addressed early on in the engagement period between a man and a woman because if it isn't addressed thoroughly, the one spouse will not know what the other spouse is thinking about the issue. If two people get married and the divorce idea remains open to either party in the marriage, it's like getting into a submarine with the hatch open and diving under water. The submarine is bound to sink. Divorce is a division of the spiritual union of marriage. When the two become one flesh, the two become one in spirit. Divorce rips that spirit apart and causes damage to both parties and if there are children, the children will be torn as well even though the revelation of the tear may not reveal itself until many years hence. Jesus clearly states that the only reason one may divorce is because of immorality…adultery. (v.9)

Jesus' response to the Pharisees here reveals what men were up to in that era. Men were divorcing their wives for any petty reason; some just because they didn't want to be married to that particular woman anymore. God's Word in Deuteronomy 24:1-4 details the rights of the certificate of divorce.[1] If a woman was put out of the house, then legitimately it would have been for the reason of adultery and would require stoning, but being that the woman was merely put out, then the certificate was needed to prove that she had not committed adultery, but was merely divorced and free to marry another.[2] Jesus said that it was because of the hardness of their hearts that they were given liberty to create these 'certificates of divorce'.

Hardness of heart is the stony, unloving, unreceptive, and unforgiving heart. It is the kind of heart in heartless people who desire their own way in everything at the expense of the heart of their spouse. Although Jesus restricts this to the men of the age, in today's era, both men and women are fully culpable of having a hard heart against their mate. The mate is for life, but the hardness of unloving, unforgiving spirits abound in today's society and the typical case of the hard heart is to blame the other spouse for all of the problems in a marriage and that is hardly ever the case.

Continually, we are reminded to submit to the Lord in the each and every moment, guarding our hearts in Christ Jesus, putting on love and light in a very dark world. Marriage between a man and a woman can be awesomely delightful and it can be as deadly as poison. It is always in the matter of the heart where the Holy Spirit is desired to reside. Allow the Holy Spirit into your life and into your marriage if you have not already and submit one to another in Holy love to Him.

Rest in peace in your home in His beloved rest and the peace of God will deliver you. Remaining faithful to Him trusting in Him through all things and for all things is where the right road in the Kingdom relies. Trust Him and it will be much easier to trust your spouse with your very life and love and give your husband or wife honor above yourself.

October 22nd

Bring the Children to Jesus

"But Jesus said, 'Let the children alone, and do not hinder them from coming to Me; for the kingdom of heaven belongs to such as these.'"   *(Matthew 19:14)*

Have you ever wondered why it is that some people seem to know what the Lord wills and they take it upon themselves to judge who gets to heaven and who doesn't? Why is it that some people think they have the authority to make judgmental decisions about the souls of men? It is now as it was with Jesus' disciples when the people, being pure in their needs of Jesus, decide to bring their children to Him so that He can lay His hands on them, bless them, and pray for them. The disciples take unauthorized authority to become the deciders of the children's fate. They prevent them from getting to Jesus.

In all of our getting, get understanding. Jesus is very explicit here about bringing children to Jesus, for such is the kingdom of heaven. The people were after the spiritual blessing and we should take heed to the people's desire and desire all the more for our children. Jesus is loving and open and kind to receive these little ones and He still is. Always be open to bringing people to Christ for Him alone to bless. Man is not the one who holds the blessing over men; it is God and God alone.

If you name the Name of Jesus Christ, do not get so caught up in busy work for Him that you neglect even the smallest of ones in getting to Him. I am not referring to baptizing babies, of which there is no scriptural substantiation; I am referring to bringing children to Christ and teaching them the ways of the Kingdom of God. The teachers cannot get in the way of the teaching of the Kingdom. Life in Jesus Christ is not about you and your selfishness, in fact, it is the polar opposite; it is all about Jesus Christ. Bringing people to Jesus Christ is not about your decisions; it's about availing ourselves to the work of the Holy Spirit, for it is His work of convicting of sin, of judgment, righteousness, and faith. The little ones are not receiving your faith, no matter how large or small it may be. They are to receive from the Holy Spirit a blessing that will last them an eternity. Do not get in the way of that blessing by your impertinence. When the father leads his child to Christ, the father leads up to a point and then steps out of the way so that the child can see the True Father in all of His glory. That's what we desire, yes? We desire that our children and the children of our community see the Father in the power of the Holy Spirit. Then, and only then, will we be able to say, I've begun my task, but only just begun. For the child to enter into His grace is just the beginning of a lifetime of sanctified learning in Him. Teach your children well and lead them into the way of the Kingdom of God, for the kingdom can and will dwell within them, just as it does for you today.

October 23rd

The Message of the Kingdom

"Jesus said to him, 'If you wish to be complete, go and sell your possessions and give to the poor, and you shall have treasure in heaven; and come, follow Me.'"
(Matthew 19:21)

The story of the rich young ruler is in Matthew 19:16-22, Mark 10:17-22, and Luke 18:18-23. It is the consummate question asked by the many who think that obtaining life is about doing something for God or for someone else. The obvious from this statement is that, "No, you cannot 'do' something for God or for someone else in order to obtain eternal life."

The rich young ruler complimented Jesus as a 'Good Teacher' as he asked, 'What good must I do to obtain eternal life?' As Jesus explains first that only One is good and that is the Father God, He speaks about being good and then tells him he needs to keep the commandments, listing a few. The rich man replies that he has done those things, and inquires that there must be something else to do. Jesus tells him to go and sell all that he has, give the money to the poor, and come, follow Him. Just as Jesus had continued to preach, "If any man desires to come after Me, let him deny himself, take up his cross, and come, follow Me." (Matt. 16:24) The message of the Kingdom is there in a passageway: desire Him, deny the self, take up your cross, and follow Him.

Many teachers want to make much to do about the man's money for he was very rich, which was a part of what made him sorrowful in his departure from Jesus, knowing he did not obtain the eternal life that he sought. But if we get caught up along with some other teaching about making it mandatory to sell all of your possessions, which was only for this man to do, we miss the teaching of the Christ. Jesus Christ knows us through and through. He knows our prayers before we ask them. The Lord knows the number of hairs on our head. He values us with great value and so it was with this young man. It didn't matter to Jesus that this man was rich or that he was a member of the ruling body of Jews; those things mattered to him and they matter to other men. To our Lord, those things are not important.

He came to give us Life, eternal, right now, abundant kind of Life. The trade is this: give up all that you have and all that you are for Him, in this we are repenting and denying and desiring and He will give you what He came here to give you and that is - Life! This is Life in the Kingdom of God. We enter in only by His grace because it is only by His blood that cleanses us in the process. In the giving up of ourselves, we are desiring Him, denying the self, taking up our cross, and following Him. There is no doing of works in this process.

We cannot earn eternal life in heaven and we cannot ever do enough good works to merit His favor. That includes the giving of money to hucksters on the Christian cable networks or to your favorite bishop who desires yet another love offering. We cannot pay Him for His grace or His love. Love the Lord, your God with all of your heart, all of your soul, all of your mind, and all of your strength. And love your neighbor as yourself. The only way you can do this is to allow Him to do it through you. Give in, give up, and get on with Him in His Kingdom according to His Holy Spirit love at work in you forevermore. Amen!

October 24th

Entering the Kingdom

"And Jesus said to His disciples, 'Truly I say to you, it is hard for a rich man to enter the kingdom of heaven.'"   (Matthew 19:23)

Humans place their trust in what they believe to be real or true. What is true for one is not true for another. We tend to trust the things that supply our needs and perceivably give us happiness. Whatever those things are, they are different to each and every person. However, a rich person has something that the not-so-rich, or the poor, do not have. The rich have hope based on assets, whether it is from a wealthy bank account, real estate holdings, a profitable business, power and prestige, or an inheritance that has come or is soon to come. The rich have hope based on assets. That hope has to be protected, grown, and secured. They have security in that hope. Therefore, they have a built-in foundation of attachment to the things that give them their hope and their security. If they have to give that up, there would be too much uncertainty on whether they could attain wealth to that level again; so, they must hold on to it tightly.

When Jesus comes calling and preaching the Kingdom of God, what is He preaching? "Repent, for the Kingdom of God is at hand!" "If any man desire to come after Me, let him deny himself, take up his cross, and come, follow Me." It isn't difficult to see and understand that any man who has based all of his hopes and security on his personal or business wealth finds it practically impossible to enter the Kingdom of heaven. Jesus, though, doesn't say it's impossible, He says it is 'hard for a rich man', not impossible. The funny thing about how we hear what we hear is that the disciples were then astonished and said, "Then who can be saved?"

Their astonishment may have well have been a crushing blow because they were thinking in the flesh, in the natural. This thinking was that everyone, then, if they desire eternal life must go and sell everything they have and that rich people can't enter the kingdom of heaven. Jesus did not say that, nor did He imply that. That is simply how some people hear what they think they hear, but it isn't what Jesus said.

Jesus words are always spiritual words. He concludes with looking at them and saying, "With men this is impossible, but with God all things are possible." (v.26) We cannot take the view of our views and say that God said what we're thinking. Not everything we think or everything we believe is the truth. With God, all things are possible. We are not the judge of who enters the kingdom of heaven, God is. Our lot is to go and preach the Gospel of the Kingdom and allow the Holy Spirit to do His work to set men and women free. God knows the hearts of people and where they are when they get preached to. Nothing surprises Him. We need to be obedient to God and allow Him to work through our lives for the sake of other lives who need to know Him. Thank God for His Life in you and thank Him for allowing us to be with Him in His Kingdom.

Oswald Chambers says, "It may be hard for a rich man to enter into the kingdom of heaven, but it is just as hard for a poor man to seek first the kingdom of God."[1] We have to give up what we know in order to gain that which only He can give. Allow the Holy Spirit to do His work in your life and know that the grace He has afforded you, He affords to whom He desires. Let Him be God and you follow in loving obedience.

October 25th

The Present and Eternal Reward

"And everyone who has left houses or brothers or sisters or father or mother or children or farms for My name's sake shall receive many times as much, and shall inherit eternal life." (Matthew 19:29)

After this discourse, Peter asks Jesus, 'We have left everything and followed You; what then will be there for us?' (v.27) This is all after Jesus telling them that unless you have the heart of a child, one of tenderness, dependency, and lacking in self-assertion, you will not enter the kingdom of heaven. He tells them that it is extremely difficult for the rich to see the kingdom of heaven to the point that it would be easier for a camel to go through the eye of a sewing needle than for the rich to enter the kingdom.

What then is in it for them, the disciples? They have left all for His name's sake, for His message, and for Him. Is there something there for them?

Jesus wastes no time in His reply and tells them that whatever they left behind, no matter what it is, they will receive it a manifold (Greek), a hundredfold (KJV, RSV), or a hundred times (NIV) more than what they left behind. Every time I walk into a true fellowship of believers, I'm walking into a family of brothers and sisters, fathers and mothers, and all of God's children together. We see Him clearly in His little ones and when we are together, the true koinonia of His Spirit is in the midst of us. Any time we are invited to the home of a believer, we are in the home of one born of His Spirit and we have that kindred spirit to call our own in Him.

I do not worry for my own children who are growning up in the Lord and serve the Lord in fellowship with like-minded believers. They have me as their Dad, yes, but they also have other elders and father and mother types in the spirit who are there to help guide them in love in His way. They have other brothers and sisters now in multiples that we could only dream of at home. Thank God. Our Lord's abundant life is for the here and now. His Kingdom dwells within us and within every like-minded believer. This is true wonderful fellowship in Him.

Eternal, everlasting life is not only future, but is present, perpetual, ongoing, never-ending. It is Life from the beginning. It is also something that we really find hard to grasp, so we've listened to our teachers tell us that it is for heaven when we die, inexplicably eternal in heaven when we die. But, that is not what the concept means. Again, it is past and future, perpetual, ongoing, and never-ending. It is a very present state of being in Spiritual Life that is only found in Him. Jesus told us to abide in Him and He will abide in us. When we are regenerated, we are given new birth life in Him; we are born again.

This life that He gives is imparted to us in the Holy Spirit and it is a right now kind of life bearing the fruit of the Holy Spirit. Eternal life is in Him and only in Him. The Kingdom of God dwells within you. He, by His Spirit dwells within you. Jesus equates 'life' with the 'kingdom of heaven/God'. (19:17, 23-24). "And this is the testimony that God gave us eternal life, and this life is in His Son. He who has the Son has life; he who has not the Son of God has not life." (1 John 5:11-12, RSV)

October 26th

The Lord is Gracious

"Is it not lawful for me to do what I wish with what is my own? Or is your eye envious because I am generous? Thus, the last shall be first and the first last." (Matthew 20:15-16)

"For My thoughts are not your thoughts, neither are your ways My ways, says the Lord. For as the heavens are higher than the earth, so are My ways higher than your ways, and My thoughts than your thoughts." (Isaiah 55:8-9, RSV)

Again, do not ridicule the disciples for their selfish thinking when they asked, 'What then will there be for us?' (v.19:27) If we are honest with ourselves, we think the same way with the same thoughts most of the time. We have to work at being selfless because we live in a mortal body of flesh. Our current culture of extremism is also at play because the extremes are all about the self and what every human can do on their own for themselves.

Jesus likens the kingdom of heaven to the first being last and the last being first. He is referring to time, something that our Lord is not restricted to. From the time of the disciples to our current day, many believers have come to Spirit-filled relationship with Him. Just because the disciples were first in order in time did not mean that everyone who followed them would be in a pecking order of grace with the last remaining folk at the end of the age getting morsels of heaven while the earlier folk in time relished in the luxuries of heavenly bliss. That is not so in the Kingdom. When a person comes to grace in believing, receiving faith, being changed from within with the heart of the Spirit of God, they are breathed into the Kingdom of God, just like all who have gone before and all who will follow them. Grace is grace for all and for all time. There are not portions of grace in the kingdom of God. What the first receives, the last receives.

How we think as mere mortals has to be dealt with. Our thoughts are clearly not His thoughts, and most of us know this, yet we continue on our binges of expectation thinking somehow we deserve a little extra for how hard we tried in doing something good for God. We do not enter His grace on any of our merit nor retain it for anything that we might do when living in His grace. It is His Spirit that does all of the work in leading us, convicting us, welcoming us, and He does the same through us for other believers. We all receive the same wonderful grace from the most wonderful generous Lord.

Our Lord is King and worthy of all our praise. He is worthy of all our thanksgiving, our obedience, and our humble worship. Smile an everlasting smile in Him today knowing that your life in Him is born from Him and He is faithful to His promises. Remain in His love and grace and allow that same love and grace to flow through you today.

October 27ᵗʰ

His Purpose

"Behold, we are going up to Jerusalem; and the Son of Man will be delivered to the chief priests and scribes, and they will condemn Him to death, and will deliver Him to the Gentiles to mock and scourge and crucify Him, and on the third day He will be raised up." (Matthew 20:18-19)

Jesus Christ was born of the Holy Spirit; born of a virgin, and walked this earth as a sinless man in the flesh. He was known as the Son of Man, being fully man, and was known as the Son of God, being born of God as was God in the earth while He was here among us. "And the Word became flesh, and dwelt among us, and we beheld His glory, glory as of the only begotten of the Father, full of grace and truth." (John 1:14)

Jesus Christ was the ultimate teacher, the standard of teaching in the embodiment of mind, spirit, and flesh. He walked out what He taught unlike so many of us who have strived to follow in His steps. He was the lover of souls, the healer of mankind, the deliverer of many, and the friend to His friends. Yet, in all that He was, He was all the more the Messiah, the chosen One, the anointed One, the long-expected One, the Deliverer, Redeemer, the one and only sacrifice for all mankind…He was and is the Savior of the world.

Jesus strove with His disciples to keep their minds stayed on His purpose. Every time He shared His purpose which was spoken in verses 18-19, He was keeping the main thing the main thing. He knew His purpose for His purpose was from the foundation of the world. (Rev. 13:8). He knew His purpose and He His purpose was in the will of the Father. He learned obedience through suffering and obedience to His Father was never questioned. He was born to die and to die in a very specific way at a very specific time for all of mankind from the foundation of the earth to the end of the age.

He knew the specifics of His purpose as well. He knew who would hand Him over to the Gentiles. He knew who would sell Him out and who would deny Him. He knew He would be beaten, mocked, scourged, and crucified. He knew that the chief priests, the religionists, the scribes would condemn Him to death. He knew

His own people would not receive Him and His message because they just didn't know Him. (John 1) Yet He remained faithful and obedient to His task and purpose.

Whatever your purpose is here on this earth, it is up to you to get to know the Father and remain in Him. We all have different tasks and purposes in this earth while we are here, but our constant connection together is His Holy Spirit. Getting to know Him is first. When we know Him as He is and remain with Him as He is, we will know our Father's will and be in it because we will be in Him. Abide in Him and He will abide in you. His Kingdom is life in Him paid for by His life.

October 28th

Our Plans

"Then the mother of the sons of Zebedee came to Him with her sons, bowing down, and making a request of Him. And He said to her, "What do you wish?" She said to Him, "Command that in Your kingdom these two sons of mine may sit, one on Your right and one on Your left."" (Matthew 20:20-21)

It seems as though every time Jesus relates His purpose to His disciples, one or more of them tends to relate their thoughts on His purpose, but from their point of view and not God's. As we know, our thoughts are not His thoughts and our ways are not His ways, so it was with Jesus' purpose on the earth and the disciples' plan while they were with Him. His thoughts and plans were higher and nobler even to making a provision of eternal life for the whole world and almost each time He spoke about it; they seemed to counter His purpose with plans of their own. Isn't that just like us?

We have the uncanny ability to read the Word of God, yet read it for ourselves the way we see it and the way we want to understand it according to our personal beliefs and expectations. Just as Peter asked, "What's in this for us?" the sons of Zebedee, James and John, allow their mother to auspiciously ask Jesus to have her sons sit in the places of authority in His kingdom. What they were asking for was favoritism, because they saw themselves as the favorites of Jesus. Being a favorite, then, must traslate into favored position, authority or material blessing, right? That's what the current self-proclaimed apostles and bishops preach.

The Lord's favor comes to those whom He knows personally who are obedient to Him. God is no respecter of persons...He doesn't have favorites which is the vain philosophy of the seeker of gold rather than being a seeker of God.

Whenever Jesus relays heavy spiritual thought, the disciples counter that with thoughts on the much lower road of gratification, selfish indulgence, and distractions galore. Never think to demean the disciples for their impertinence because we typically act none the wiser. We believe what we want and expect the Word to match our beliefs of what we have been told.

When was the last time you sat down to pray, got distracted and didn't even pray? When was the last time you went to fellowship in worship and anger with your spouse, your children, or your fellow church friend(s) kept you from entering into real spiritual worship? When was the last time you sat down to read and pray and some errant thought swept through your mind and then your time with the Lord elapsed and you just moved on full of thoughts, but empty in heart?
Our ways are not His ways, and our thoughts are not His thoughts.

"Finally, brethren, whatever is true, whatever is honorable, whatever is just, whatever is pure, whatever is lovely, whatever is gracious, if there is any excellence, if there is anything worthy of praise, think about these things." (Philippians 4:8, RSV)

Give honor to the Lord with your heart and not just your lips. Let our walk match our talk with a heart full of obedient humility and a willingness to submit fully to His will. The world will shoot arrows of thoughts to you, but stand in the fullness of His grace with the shield of faith and it will quench the fiery darts of the evil one. Keep your mind stayed on Him in His kingdom. Know where you dwell for it is in Him that we have Life forevermore!

October 29th

The Desire for Authority

"You do not know what you are asking...You know that the rulers of the Gentiles lord it over them, and their great men exercise authority over them. It is not so among you, but whoever wishes to become great among you shall be your servant, and whoever wishes to be first among you shall be your slave."
(Matthew 20:22a, 25b-27)

The desire for authority is the desire for power. The desire for a seat by the King is the desire for recognized autonomy. Most types of men desire authority over other men. People want to be in charge and that idea is not relegated solely to men. The desire to be the leader, particularly when you didn't have to work for the position, is a desire of exploited pride and elevated selfishness and it doesn't matter if a person thinks it's for a spiritual cause, or not, pride is pride and selfishness relegated to authority to abhorrent in the eyes of God.

The closer that Jesus got to Jerusalem and the fulfillment of His purpose, the more the disciples explored the idea of greatness, throne-room seating, authority, and leadership position. They wanted to be higher than the next disciple and position jockeying was a constant thought on the horizon. What they continued to fail to recognize was the spirituality of Jesus' words. His words were spirit and they were true. They liked the true part, but received His words in the flesh with tones of material reward that they could relate to. Again, this is what we do when we read a passage of scripture and try to make it fit our personal applications and self-gratifications. We want what we want in the natural realm and Jesus repeatedly made it very clear that that was not what His Kingdom was about.

The disciples also interpreted the kingdom as an earthly kingdom or a spiritual kingdom with earthly ramifications. They believed in Jesus' words about the kingdom, but they interpreted it according to their ideas of what they knew and believed a kingdom was. Another aspect of authority is what Jesus spoke to in how the Gentiles lord their authority over people. There is a great deal of enigmatic power when it comes to authority and they saw how incredible the power of God was in Jesus' life and in the experiences they had when He had given them authority to heal and deliver people. They equated power with authority, along with their ideas of worldly realms and not in spiritual leading.

Jesus corrects their ideas with the truth, that the real leader is the servant of all and the real power and authority was in being a slave to the many. He later washes their feet to help prove the point. The Kingdom of God is a spiritual kingdom that is entered into by becoming a new born baby via a new birth and having the childlike innocence and dependency upon our King, rather than being conquering warriors who kill people to earn their rights, privileges, and seats of honor.

Seats of honor in the Kingdom go to the chief servants, not the chief dictators. Leadership in Christ is serving all in the needs of the fellowship with a servant's heart, not the heart of a marketing salesman who has sold everyone on his ability to manipulate. or hs power of positve persuasion in positive positivity. The King of kings cannot be manipulated and doesn't believe in that type of leading because that is spiritual abuse.

Jesus talked about having the heart and faith of a child. Jesus said that the chief servant will serve, not be served. Today's American religion has turned the Word upside down to make it mean the opposite of what Jesus proclaimed. False teachers lead by ignorance and the ignorant are none the wiser. Humble yourself and you'll find the position of power is on your knees in Him.

October 30th

The Truth in Leadership

"...just as the Son of Man did not come to be served, but to serve, and give His life a ransom for many." (Matthew 20:28)

The truth about spiritual leadership is found in the very person of Jesus Christ. The truth about spiritual leadership is seeing Jesus Christ as the only standard in His body of believers. He taught us all how to be born again and that is to follow His Spirit's guidance. He first denied Himself, humbling Himself in the form of a baby in Bethlehem. He first descended from the throne to the manger and was birthed among the beasts. That is leadership! He was led as a baby and grew as a child in the nurture and admonition of the Lord of heaven. He did all that He did under the guidance of His heavenly Father and pronounced that nothing that He did was of Himself, including laying His own life down in submission to His Father's will... that is leadership!

The problem that the disciples had and the problem that we still have today with spiritual leadership is that the disciples' standard was found in the Jewish ruling body and the examples they saw in Roman rule. They saw a literal king's throne and them sitting around the edges. When it came time to serve, though, they realized that there were no thrones, but only hard work, persecution, alienation, and ultimate sacrifice in death. John was the only original disciple to not be put to death in some gruesome way. Their leadership was found in their suffering and obedience to their Lord and Master. So, in effect, they did learn to serve and slave for Him at the expense of their lives and the furtherance of the Gospel.

Not so with us today, particularly in the United States. Spiritual leadership is viewed from the seat of a pulpit, a video screen, and a guaranteed salary. Today's spiritual leadership consists of men and women of renown who flaunt their authority over people with the flick of a pen, sometimes not even doing the honor of a conversation, because they are too busy being overly important. Their perceived authority has bought them relegated and limited power that they have learned to abide in because even a little power over men's minds and wallets is better than none. They use the Lord's money to pad their wallets, their lifestyles, and magnificent buildings that only the manna of men can afford. Not all, but many live as wicked hirelings rather than abide in the sanctity of the Spirit. Years ago, I had a pastor to offer me a small sum of money if I would write him out a sermon to preach the next Sunday; he just didn't have it in him to do it himself. No!

True Holy Spirit led leadership is for the fit and the prepared, not the favored favorite.

The Christ standard of spiritual leadership is found in the final words of verse 28, "and to give His life a ransom for the many." Thank God there are a few men and women who do not fit the unspiritual, contemporary view of spiritual leadership for they are more in tune with His Holy Spirit than they are with the spirit of the prince of the air. These are men and women who give of their lives and resources for the souls of men for the sake of the Gospel risking their relationships, time, and futures on a hope that God, in Jesus Christ, will deliver people from the power of sin and death.

October 31st

Spiritual Blindness

"And as they were going out from Jericho, a great multitude followed Him. And behold, two blind men sitting by the road, hearing that Jesus was passing by, cried out, saying, 'Lord have mercy on us, Son of David!'" (Matthew 20:29-30)

Each time Jesus goes from town to town, He usually has a crowd about Him with specific needs. As Jesus walks along the way with the crowds in tow, there are two men who are blind sitting by the roadside. For Jesus to continue to teach His disciples about humility in the Kingdom, rather than greatness and servant hood rather than reward, there are two blind men in need of sight. The people were spiritually blind to the ways and means of the kingdom of heaven. There were no coincidences in Jesus' life and opportunities. If the Lord engineers our circumstances, then certainly, the Lord had engineered His own. The disciples and the people had spiritual blindness that they had need of healing; and so here presents the two men by the road in need of their sight.

It is the Lord who has mercy on us in our times of blindness either because we cannot see, or we simply refuse to see. The determining factor is the quality or state of the soil. Is the soil redeemable and useful or is it wasted uncultivated ground? Jesus, the Son of David had come first to the house of Israel to heal the sight of the blind. He came to set men free who had been spiritually blind from birth; to open the eyes of the ones who could not see, but were so loved that mercy found the desperate cries of the sons and healed their beleaguered state. Jesus healed the two of their blindness because that's what they said they needed. They needed their sight, not a seat; they needed to see and not a throne. It was only a matter of time that the disciples would really 'get it' in understanding of what His kingdom was all about. It was not about personal authority and thrones, swords and warriors, and killing for the blood of men. No, this kingdom was far greater than what men had ever seen and far more vast than the eye could ever imagine.

This Kingdom is about a King who loves in mercy and has compassion on His royal sons and daughters. It is about a Kingdom where men and women are set free from every chain that binds and every need is fulfilled. This Kingdom is a kingdom of peace and rest, where no sorrow is shed and no lack goes unfulfilled. It is a place where burdens are lifted from the hearts of men to show them a lighter way to live and a loving way to be. This kingdom is a spiritual, heavenly kingdom in thought, word, and deed. It is a place of worship, adoration, and praise of its Creator and King.

Yes, this kingdom is the Kingdom of God, bought with the blood of its King who died that all who truly believe might have life in it and that to the fullest. He had ushered in His own place of rest to offer it as the reward itself, the place of peace. This kingdom has the power to heal the wounded heart and to bring the dead into life by a spiritual new birth. This place of perpetual power is the place of the living God, the God Most High; the everlasting Kingdom of God.

November 1st

Preparation for the King

"...Jesus sent two disciples, saying to them, 'Go into the village opposite you, and immediately you will find a donkey tied there and a colt with her; untie them, and bring them to Me. And if anyone says something to you, you shall say, 'The Lord has need of them,' and immediately he will send them.'"

(Matthew 21:1b-3)

All that Jesus did was in accordance with His Father's will. His Father's will is found in Him, the Father. Jesus was able to daily abide in His Father thereby knowing what His Father was directing Him to do. Humble, submissive obedience to the Lord works that way. Jesus walked in His Father's anointing. He smelled of it, spoke it, lived it, and died in it. All that He did, He did in preparation for the ultimate sacrifice; to lay down His life as a ransom for many.

The act of riding into Jerusalem on the back of a donkey was first prophesied in Zechariah 9:9, "Rejoice greatly, O daughter of Zion! Shout aloud, O daughter of Jerusalem! Lo, your king comes to you; triumphant and victorious is he, humble and riding on an ass, on a colt the foal of an ass." (RSV). Preparation for the King had already been made by God who birthed the colt and the donkey for Jesus to use at that time and place. These are not coincidences. These are prophesies fulfilled.

The disciples obey their Lord and bring the colt and the donkey to Jesus. They laid out their garments for Him to sit on the donkey, which was befitting a royal rider, which gave Him honor by giving Him the clothes off their backs. They honored Him then as the people subsequently did by spreading their garments on the road for Him to travel into the city.

Preparation for a King incudes honor befitting a King. That's why we humbly bow before His Presence. Who stands in the Presence of a King?

True humility goes before true honor. Pride goes before a fall. Men of renown are not men of honor, but of pride. They stand when they should kneel; they gawk when they should be bowing. Arrogant men may seem to cast a bow now and again, but it is with one eye on the prize that they seek. Not so with Jesus Christ. He was always humble and the act of riding into the city was an act of humility and not an act of prestige as some teachers teach.

The preparation that we make before Him to be with Him is only known by Him for He knows our hearts. Reverence and humility are actually insufficient terms to how our hearts are to be in His Presence. The weight of His glory is too heavy for mortal man. Bowing is insufficient. When His glory appears, the ability to breathe is constricted. His atmosphere of glory is different than what we know and we have to adjust what we know to be real and true under the breath of His Holy Spirit. The Presence of the King requires preparation. We do not enter into Him as proud men, but as men of lowly estate. And He is always and forevermore the King and not ourselves.

November 2nd

Honor to the King

"And the multitudes going before Him, and those who followed after were crying out, saying, 'Hosanna to the Son of David; Blessed is He who come in the name if the Lord; Hosanna in the highest!' And when He had entered Jerusalem, all the city was stirred, saying, 'Who is this?' And the multitudes were saying, 'This is the prophet Jesus, from Nazareth in Galilee.'" (Matthew 21:9-11)

Giving honor to Jesus Christ is what the disciples and the people did, at least the ones who knew what they were doing. The people ushered Him in by taking branches of palm trees and laying them in His path as a presentation of victory, eternal life, or peace. The palm branches played a significant part in His path for it rightly represented Who He truly was…the Prince of peace.

What drove the people, however, to do such an act of honor towards Him? This all was not a staged pre-planned event like many of our current church services of today. The people were always around Him and following Him, so when the donkey and the colt are brought around for Him to sit on; for certain, the word quickly spread.

Amazingly enough, the word about Jesus was always spread by word of mouth. People talk and everyone within an ear's shot pretty much knew what was going on. Gossip is one of the most popular aspects of human life. No matter what age of time or culture, people are going to talk. For that reason, it is difficult to give the people too much credit here for it was this same people shouting 'Hosanna' who were the ones just a few days later shouting, 'Crucify Him!' Word of mouth spread in both instances and proves that no matter what the news, good news or bad, word of mouth is the mode of transportation for many events. The people's mouths spoke what they believed, "This is the prophet Jesus, from Nazareth in Galilee." The best retort some Pharisees had for those statements were, 'Can anything good come from Nazareth?' Jesus was actually born in Bethlehem, but raised in Nazareth. There was no celebration here by the Sanhedrin, the Pharisees and the Sadducees. They waited with bated breath in jealousy and gritted teeth.

Have you ever been so stressed out with another that your teeth grinded together seething in anger? Perhaps not, but I don't believe the Pharisees could have said no to that question. Imagine being there in the celebration with the majority of the people welcoming Him into the city with honor and peace; and still others on the periphery biding their time and gritting their teeth in hatred all the while plotting and planning to kill the King.

Jesus was approaching the time of His purpose. He had come to die. Not many knew this for if they were aware of that, there would have been a battle among the people, some to save Him from His purpose, still others to help it along before its time. And so it is today, even still there are those who are trying to save the name of Jesus for their religious purposes and others still trying to bury His Name in the ground. Not much has changed, but His Gospel of the Kingdom of God is alive and dwelling in the lives that name His Name. The precious name of Jesus is to be highly exalted for He is highly exalted among the heavens.

Rejoice forevermore for the Prince of Peace has come and no man will ever put Him down in the grave again!

November 3rd

Jesus Entered the Temple

"And Jesus entered the temple and cast out all those who were buying and selling in the temple, and overturned the tables of the moneychangers and the seats of those who were selling doves." (Matthew 21:12)

As Jesus enters the outer courts of the temple that day, He peruses the grounds in views as an owner would peruse his personal holdings. He knows what He sees when He sees the money changers, those hired to profit off of the exchange of changing the Roman coins into Jewish coins for the sake of giving their tithes and offerings to the temple.[1] Jewish coins were only used in the temple as described by the Pharisees; so when the people came in with their Roman coins, they had to do a mandatory monetary exchange.[2] These money-changers made their money off of the exchange and split the profits with the Pharisees who hired them.[3] There were also those who sold doves, pigeons, oils, salt, etc. for the purposes of the sacrifices because many of the people had traveled long distances and could buy these 'sacrifices' at the temple entrance. Additionally, there were people who would use the temple as a short-cut passageway to get from one end of the city to the other. The rules were that no one could use the temple in that manner, but the rules had been relaxed, permitting all sort of folk with all sorts of items to pass through the temple on their way to some other place.[4] (Mark 11:16). Jesus would not permit these people to use the temple as a short-cut passageway, so He blocked them from doing so.

In the midst of what Jesus saw that day was the egregious failure of men to recognize His heavenly Father. Jesus makes a whip of cords (John 2:15), and proceeds to whip the money-changers, turning over their tables and the tables of the sellers of doves. He drives all of them out of the temple teaching them and exclaiming, "It is written, 'My house shall be called a house of prayer.' But you have made it a den of robbers." (Mark 11:17).

Jesus drove out the cursed abuse of profiteering. The Lord's temple was to be a house of prayer and a place to worship the Father in Truth. There was to be no business going on there for it was set aside to be a holy place with holy offerings lifted to God, not to men. This was God's house and as is later revealed in the scriptures, we are the temple of the Holy Spirit. (1 Cor. 6:19) We should never allow bartering and the trading of goods going on in our hearts. Our lives have been bought with a price with Jesus' blood and no man should ever have the opportunity to buy our souls for a price. Our hearts should be hearts of prayer inhabiting the Holy Spirit giving honor and glory only to Him. What is the Lord's should be kept for Him and not sold as a prostitute would sell her body. The purity of the soul cleansed in His blood should not be offered to idols for worship or for pleasure.

When we have been indwelt by the Holy Spirit, our bodies should remain with Him while we are on this earth kept clean from the darkness that prevails over the minds and hearts of men. Continue with the Lord in prayer and remain steadfast in Him knowing He keeps you in His care and loves with His everlasting love.

November 4th

A House Divided

"And the blind and the lame came to Him in the temple, and He healed them. But when the chief priests and the scribes saw the wonderful things He had done...they became indignant..." (Matthew 21:14-15)

As Jesus continued His presence in the temple, He was followed by the people in need of healing. He healed the blind and the lame. While He was doing this, the people's children were crying in the temple saying, "Hosanna to the Son of David." Hosanna relates to "the Messianic salvation"[1] expected of the one who was to come. Psalm 118:22-26, speaks about the chief cornerstone, the stone that the builders rejected, and the honor of the one saying, 'blessed is He who comes in the name of the Lord."

The chief priests and scribes know and hear of all that was being done that day by Jesus and they are so angry with Him that they come to Him in their anger and ask, 'Do you hear what they are saying?' Jesus responds, "Yes; have you never read, 'Out of the mouth of babes and sucklings thou hast brought perfect praise'?" And leaving them, He went out of the city to Bethany and lodged there." (v.16-17, RSV)

A house divided cannot stand. Either the people will serve the one or they will serve the other. People cannot serve two masters. Jesus came with the Spirit of God and threw out what was never supposed to be there in the first place and that was the profiteers and the robbers. He opens the temple to the people in need of healing from their blindness and their lame. He makes it possible to them to see and to walk. The people praise the Lord in the temple for His mighty acts of kindness upon His people and all the while the people are being healed and praising the Lord, the chief priests and scribes are preparing for battle.

I hope that you get the whole picture here because that is what the confrontation looks like between religion and the Kingdom of God. Religion is a substitute for the real Spirit of God. Religion profits off of the people at the expense of their hearts. Systematized religious leaders take from the hearts and the backs of the people and leave them hungry for the Lord and spiritually blind with no God to walk with because of all of the rules they have imposed upon the people and the loyalty that they demand. Religion comes between God and His people and robs them of their spiritual heart so that they are only left with making a pittance of a sacrifice at the approval of men. People are left blind and tired at the hands of religious leaders and then the religious leaders complain if their system is messed with. They can't stand Jesus and Jesus knows it. Jesus will not hang around stiff-necked religion that suffocates the life out of people and attempts to profit off of the offerings given to God. God is not in that and Jesus leaves the temple as proof.

The same religious deception has been going on since that time and people have been none the wiser. Jesus came to set people free and yet the deception comes from the dark spiritual force under the guise of religion to blind the hearts of people. Guard your hearts and minds in Christ Jesus and continually submit to Him and Him alone. He is your rest and your perfect peace. Only Him will I trust and only Him will I serve. Do not allow man to divide your heart with blessings that he actually cannot give you. The Lord God is the reward of the faithful and His Kingdom will reign forever and ever and ever! Amen.

November 5th

The Barren Fig Tree

"And Jesus answered and said to them, 'Truly I say to you, if you have faith, and do not doubt, you shall not only do what was done to the fig tree, but even if you say to this mountain, 'Be taken up and cast into the sea,' it shall happen.'"
(Matthew 21:21)

As Jesus and His disciples where returning to the city the next morning, they come across a barren fig tree that had leaves, but no fruit. Jesus was hungry and proceeded to curse the fruitless tree by saying that no longer would there be any fruit. The tree withers and dries up from its roots. (Mark 11:20). In Matthew Henry's commentary, he implies that this curse is related to the fruitless lives of the religious in the Hebrew state.[1]

From what Jesus had had to deal with concerning the chief priests, scribes, and the rulers of Pharisees and Sadducees, He was dealing a blow to their future which was to come by 70 A.D. with the destruction of Jerusalem by the Romans.

However, in Jesus' explanation He doesn't give an answer to their question, 'How did the fig tree wither away so soon?', He succinctly points to the power and authority of faith-filled prayer.

Faith-filled prayer is prayer prayed by a person filled with faith given by God in the Holy Spirit. As we've learned, faith is a tangible object in the Kingdom of God. It is in Him that we live and move and have our being. (Acts 17:28) So the faith that Jesus is referring to here is the God-kind of faith that only comes from God in faith. That is how powerful His faith is and it is the same faith that He gives to us when we dwell in Him. He told His disciples that they were of 'little faith'. Faith comes from Him and grows as a seed grows in the ground.

This is the same faith that when the disciples continued in the faith, it was the faith that was healing people and drawing people to the Lord. This faith was coveted by Simon the sorcerer, (Acts 8:9) but he did not possess the faith. The faith given by the Lord is given in our submission to Him and He is our faith. Faith is not a substance to be used for ourselves any more than we can take God and wield Him as a sword to do our bidding. Some folk believe that is what decreeing and declaring is all about and that is false teaching. Faith only comes from Him and is in Him as we are in Him. Faith is not a magic box or wand to wave to get what we want as some profess to teach. Faith is the Holy Spirit having grown in us to move as He moves and when we speak in faith, we are speaking from the location of His Holy Presence flowing from us into the world for His will and His glory.

Jesus was our standard in teaching us and our Master Teacher in showing us that in faith, His God-kind of faith that only comes from Him, can move mountains. Imagine, the mustard seed planted in the ground and as it grows, it moves the earth in its growth pattern spiraling up out of the ground to reach the sun. That is His faith in you that He has planted in you. His faith, when nourished by prayer and Presence, grows within you and me to spiral up towards the Son. Then, mature faith can say to whatever mountain or problem that has come into your path, 'Be cast into the sea!' Dwell in Him and grow the faith He has inside of you and as you grow and mature in Him, speak the faith out loud and watch the Lord's power work for His glory.

November 6th

Kingdom Faith

"And all things you ask in prayer, believing, you shall receive."
(Matthew 21:22)

Dwelling in Him is abiding in Him. Abiding in Him is abiding in faith because we dwell in Him by faith, but it is not something we have conjured up ourselves, no, this faith comes from Him and is in Him as it is in us. Faith is the current of Him being in us. Faith in the Kingdom of God is Him and is the treasure that we seek. We are given faith to believe and when we believe by His faith and His faith becomes our own. It starts out as a seed as He is birthed in us and is grown through prayer, fasting, prayer, and Presence. He is fed in us by the constant communication of prayer with Him in His Spirit. "The apostles said to the Lord, 'Increase our faith!' (Luke 17:5, ESV). He is the One who has given us our faith and He is the One who increases it and causes it to grow. "And the Lord make you increase and abound in love for one another, and for all as we do for you." (1 Thess. 3:12, ESV). The love of the Father comes from Him and the increase of His love dwelling in us is only increased by Him as well.

This is why it is so vitally important for us to abide in Christ Jesus. If you have given your life in submission to Him, He dwells in you by the power of the Holy Spirit. As you die to yourself, you are baptized into His death and are raised into new life in Him…into His Kingdom of Life. Dwelling in Him is abiding in Him. Feeding on Him in His word is feeding the life inside of you and that life inside of you is there by faith. As John the Baptist said, 'He must increase and I must decrease.' We are not the same person and we do not stay the same person.

He grows in faith within us. So, when we pray, believing, it is not we who are doing the declaring, we are simply declaring Him in the earth. When we dwell in Him, we dwell in His will and whatever we are asking, we are asking according to His will. We simply put our mouths to what He wants in the earth and declare it!

If we have a proper placement and position in Him, we understand that it is not us who is declaring a thing or even asking a thing, but it is Him in us in faith proving His will in us to accomplish His will through us in the words we speak and the actions we take. We become His mouthpiece, His hands, and His feet in the earth. There should never be any pride in us that we could do such and such, because we understand that it is always Him doing the work. We by faith, we move by faith, we work by faith, and we live by faith…all in Him. He is our dwelling place and how lovely are the dwelling places of the Lord Most High!

Praise be to the Father that in Him we see a glimpse of Him moving in us to speak in faith, believing that whatever we ask, we ask in Him in faith, knowing that whatever we ask when we dwell in constant communication with Him, we receive.

To the errant, this may seem to place constrictions on their asking, but to make it very clear this is all about Him and none about us. This is all for His glory and none for us. When it is all about Him and none about us, we can then see Him and only Him in His glory. Lord, increase our faith!

November 7th

True Authority

"And Jesus answered and said to them, 'I will ask you one thing, too, which if you tell Me, I will also tell you by what authority I do these things.'"
(Matthew 21:24)

Of all the teachings, healings, deliverances, and miracles that Jesus had performed none had been so exacting against the religious as when He drove out the money-changers the week of the Passover so that the ruling priests and scribes were financially affected. Once again, they come to confront Him regarding His authority. They had questioned Him before about authority and declared that He cast out demons by Beelzebub, which didn't even make sense for it would reveal a house divided. The religious rulers always desire comfort in being left alone to do as they please so that they may increase in wealth and power as the expense of the people. The bottom line of this was that Jesus' impact on them was becoming too confrontational and they were on the losing end currently and they simply had to put an end to it. They had to confront Him with what they believed they had and that was their perceived authority. No one questioned their authority except Jesus and perhaps John the Baptist, but He was dead.

It is, after all, that ruling classes of people, particularly in the religious realm, desire their authority to rest on their heads so that they can control the teaching and the movement. As long as they maintain the sense of authority, they can teach what they will and no one can question them regarding it. This is where the chief priests, scribes, and Sanhedrin lived…in their own religious authority…thinking that they were of God and God's representatives. But when true authority walked on the earth in the form of Jesus Christ, they recognized the lack of power they truly had among the people. The God-kind of authority came with the God-kind of power and even still they resented it all the more and declared it unworthy of their acknowledgments.

They tested Jesus unwittingly as tools of a spirit to unseat that which is unconquerable. Jesus asks them a question in order to answer their question on authority and from whence He came. They refused to answer Jesus' question for if they had, they would have proven themselves out of the order of God; they merely remained silent at the proposition of following the teaching of John the Baptist and the authority that he came in as a prophet of the Lord.

All authority has been given to Christ Jesus and He is the unconquerable conqueror. He has already won the victory over sin, death, hell, and the grave. Although the religious rulers put Him to death, they were simply the tools of God in achieving His plan of saving the world from the wages and power of sin. Their rebellion against God became the pathway of His suffering and it was in His suffering and death that He was made able to become the living resurrection that represents the Life we now have in Him. He is the resurrection and the Life and the life we now live we live in Him. "For if we have been united with Him in a death like His, we shall certainly be united in a resurrection like His." (Romans 6:5, ESV) True authority is only found in Jesus. Blessed be that wonderful Name!

November 8th

It's About the Kingdom

"...Jesus said to them, 'Truly I say to you that the tax gatherers and harlots will get into the kingdom of God before you. For John came to you in the way of righteousness and you did not believe him; but the tax gatherers and harlots did believe him; and you, seeing this, did not even feel remorse afterward so as to believe him.'"   *(Matthew 21:31b-32)*

John the Baptist's message was one of repentance and acceptance that the Kingdom of God was at hand. It was the perceived lower class of folk who were duly recognized as the sinner par excellence class that were most of John's believers in his message of repentance. Humility before a Holy God is fully recognized by God. Jesus recognized this about the tax gatherers and harlots that had received John's message. I do not strike a problem with these people's salvation for it would be heretical to ponder against what Jesus has already spoken regarding these people and their ability to 'get into the kingdom of God'. This actually hones in the point that John's message and Jesus' message was the Gospel of the Kingdom of God. There is no plausible argument worthy of mentioning for Jesus' words are sufficient in all things.

We trust in a Holy God who is worthy to love in holy love and worthy to perform His holy acts of kindness and compassion upon whom He delights in. He delights in submission, humility, and the giving up of ourselves. When we recognize Him as the One and only true God in repentance, humility, submission, and the denial of ourselves, He recognizes us and comes to us to sup with us as He sees fit. He is the only Almighty and He is the only one to choose the pathway to His Kingdom paved with the sacrifice of His only begotten Son. If Jesus says that they will 'get into the kingdom of God', it would be best to believe Jesus rather than any other teacher out there who would like to explain this all away. The Gospel of Jesus Christ was the Kingdom of God and it still is today!

The men who stood in the way of the Kingdom were the religious hypocrites who believed they served and represented God as His sons in the earth. If any man wanted to come to the Lord, they had to come through them and their teachings. They put themselves in the way, thereby creating an authority known only to themselves and substantiated only through their interpretations of the Law. And so it is today, even still. Men of renown who create their own authority saying, 'God said it…God willed it…God has ordained it in me…'

Always look to the real servants of God who do not put themselves in the way of the Christ, but wholeheartedly preach the Gospel of Jesus Christ and then get out of the way so that the Lord can speak, convict, judge, and make righteous in the way that only He can do it. Men cannot save other men, only the Holy Spirit can bring a man or woman to Himself. The Holy Spirit accomplishes His work in His way, in His time, and in His breath of Life. Submit to the Lord in all things and allow His Spirit to move through you that His work is accomplished in the earth. Yes, He uses preachers like you and me who will acknowledge Him in His holy work to lead others to Him and not to ourselves for any gain or any presumptive power of authority over the ones we lead to Him. Only He is Lord…always and forever!

November 9th

The Sons of Disobedience

"Therefore I say to you, the kingdom of God will be taken away from you, and will be given to a nation producing the fruit of it."   *(Matthew 21:43)*

Jesus speaks two parables here to His disciples and to the religious rulers. The first He tells of the two sons who were told to do a specific things by their father. The first son agrees to obey, but subsequently does not. The second son, disobedient in heart to begin with, ultimately relents and proceeds to obey his father. It was an easy choice for the rulers to see who was obedient and who wasn't.

Then, Jesus tells another parable about the landowner who goes and buys some land, creates a winepress with secure walls and sets up workers to work the winepress for profit. When the wealthy landowner sends one slave after another after another to recoup his profit from his land, the workers beat or kill the slaves sent by the landowner. Alas, after many failed attempts to recoup his money from the workers, the landowner decides to send his own son, thinking they will honor his son, but no, they kill him, thinking they will inherit the land. Jesus left the decision up to the religious leaders to decide what judgment the workers deserved for their unjust and disobedient ways of life. Here again, Jesus clearly depicts the Kingdom weighing in the balance against the mighty forces of the religious hierarchy and the rulers are not amused, but were set on seizing Jesus to destroy Him. It was the will of God that the will of the people disallowed anything to be done against Him.

In both parables the sons and workers of disobedience are clear to see. It wasn't until after the second parable, though, that the religious rulers had had quite enough of Jesus and His teaching. The sons of disobedience would prove their fruit by Jesus' words and they simply could not help themselves. Jesus had shown them a mirror of themselves and when they looked into the mirror, they saw themselves for who and what they were. They were disobedient, dishonest, murdering thieves. Even though they saw how Jesus depicted them, they were still not repentant, but even more steadfast to remove Jesus from their midst. Their hatred for Jesus was beginning to show on their faces and in their actions.

It is so even today with the sons of disobedient, no matter who they might be. Disobedience sets its heart against God and rather than repent of its dark heart, it seethes with even more hatred towards what is real and true in the Spirit. A real son of disobedience is a terror to deal with and requires much faith and prayer before going up against him. Always watch and pray and beware that the sons of disobedience still exist today to go against the righteousness of God.

It's not only unrighteous men that we contend with, but as Paul stated, "We are not fighting against flesh and blood enemies, but against evil rulers and authorities of the unseen world, against mighty powers in this dark world and against the spiritual forces of evil in the heavenly places." (Eph. 6:12, NLT) As we contend with people who war against God mildly or aggressively, know that it is of the influence of the evil one and remain steadfast in courage knowing that "…greater is He that is in you than He that is in the world."
(1 John 4:4b, NLT)

November 10th

Parable of the Marriage Feast

"The kingdom of heaven may be compared to a king, who gave a wedding feast for his son."   (Matthew 22:2)

Jesus continues to speak to the chief priests and the Pharisees another parable that has been called the parable of the marriage feast. We have to remember that Jesus is talking to the Pharisees and other religious rulers, so the message is for them specifically and for us to gleen from especially concerning the nature of God and our responsibility to be fully clothed in Christ.

The story is about a king, God, who desires to give a wedding for his son, Jesus, and those to whom would be invited to join his table for the feast. This parable is not about the bride of Christ for in this parable the bride is not spoken of, only the guests to the marriage feast. This parable is about the invitation to a feast and who was originally invited, but refused for a various number of reasons. Those invited eventually killed the slaves who were inviting them. Subsequently, the king decides to kill the murderers and burn their city to the ground for killing his slaves; then he decides to open the invitation up to the entire countryside, basically letting all who are willing to come, come.

When the king comes into the midst of all those who were seated for the marriage feast, there is one there who does not have on the appropriate clothing attire for the occasion. This person, the hypocrite, becomes the focal point. He gets thrown out into outer darkness where there is weeping and gnashing of teeth, the place we know as hell. Jesus concludes with, 'For many are called, but few are chosen.'

The original invitation is to be with God as He desired men to be, not as they desired to be themselves. The invitation was for His people, Israel, but they beat, stoned, and killed the prophets along the way, and in no uncertain terms turned a deaf ear to His prophets, including John the Baptist and Jesus Himself. The focus shoots straight through to the one who had entered the feast not properly clothed. He was the one who had showed up thinking he was something he was not. He was the hypocrite who came as one thing, but the king knew him by his clothing, as He does all of us by our fruit.

In the Lord's heart, it is the hypocrite that is truly despised. These are the deceivers who present themselves to be something they are not. They deceive and are perhaps self-deceived. Self-deception is a terrible trait for one may seem to be noble minded in his own mind, but everyone is not fooled by his pride. People who know Truth are not deceived by the self-deceived for they wear their thoughts on their sleeves for all to see, but they don't see it themselves.

It is so vitally important that we are real with ourselves. We have to stop lying to ourselves attempting to fool ourselves into thinking we're something that we're not. This goes beyond being honest internally to being Holy Spirit filled Truthful so that we can go to God with a clear conscience knowing ourselves for who we truly are in His sight. Allow the mirror of His Word to penetrate to your innermost being with His searchlight of Truth. Our eternity depends on it when we cry to the Lord, saying, "Search me, O God, and see if there be any wicked way in me…"

November 11th

Render to God What is His

"And He said to them, 'Whose likeness and inscription is this?' They said to Him, 'Caesar's.' Then He said to them, 'Then render to Caesar what is Caesar's; and to God the things that are God's.'"   *(Matthew 22:21-22)*

Matthew 22:15-22, depicts the continued attempts of the Pharisees to trap Jesus into heresy or, here, into sedition, whereupon He would be speaking traitorously against Caesar. Jesus implores them to get a coin and He asks them one question in order to make His point, 'Then render to Caesar what is Caesar's and to God what is God's.' The Pharisees marveled at Jesus and left Him for another more opportune time to entrap Him yet again.

I marvel, too, at Jesus' words and ponder exactly all the things that are God's. If Jesus would have us render to God what is His, then have you pondered all that is His? I know that I am His and I know that my family, my wife and my children are His. I know that the house, cars, and things that we possess are His, including all the finances that He entrusts us with. I know that I'm not really an owner of anything, but just a manger of what He has given us to manage. So, to render to God what is His becomes not so much a matter of pondering, but a matter of obedience.

Just how far we are willing to go with Him is how far we realize that we really are not in control of much, because He is in control. We don't engineer our circumstances, He does; we simply respond and react and sometimes counter our circumstances to make our lives better, but often we make them worse by how we respond to every day circumstances that are out of our control.

We are not totally lifeless, incompetent puppets in all of this, for we are His handiwork, wonderfully made in His image. He loves us with a holy everlasting love and by this, if we name the Name of Jesus Christ, we have given over our lives to Him in submission to Him. The task is for us to acknowledge this daily in denying ourselves truly before Him in His Presence. Daily, I recognize that I dwell in Him and Him in me. And, with that being the case, the Almighty God of all that is, is with me and I am His. I love being His child.

Render to whomever the whatever is due them. It may be that we owe debts, then pay the debts, and pay the taxes on time when they're due. Pay the monthly bills when they're due. But in all of this, render to God what is God's and in so doing, you will find yourself becoming unencumbered by the world's distractions and the multitudes of opportunities to give to the world what is in reality God's in the first place. When you find yourself spending money that is His, you give to 'the whoever or the whatever' instead of giving to God.

Over spending to indebtedness is killing our nation and our families and we did not get this way overnight. Stop the madness and inquire of God what is His in your life. Submit to Him as your Lord and Master and you will eventually see that all that you see is His and you'll stop giving to the world what rightfully belongs to Him, your very soul.

November 12th

He is the God of the Living

"But Jesus answered and said to them, 'You are mistaken, not understanding the scriptures, or the power of God. For in the resurrection they neither marry, nor are given in marriage, but are like angels in heaven…I Am the God of Abraham, and the God of Isaac, and the God of Jacob? He is not the God of the dead but of the living.'"   (Matthew 22:29-30, 32)

The Sadducees (v.23) did not believe in an afterlife, hence, they could not believe in the resurrection. They viewed the possibility of a resurrection from their religious point of view. They implied that the way we are here is the way we are in heaven, and if there is a resurrection, all things would translate from our worldly state of understanding to our heavenly home. Not so, says Jesus who tells then that they are mistaken, not understanding the scriptures, or the power of God.

When Paul was talking about the resurrection, and our heavenly bodies being completely different than what we have here on earth, it was just as what Jesus was saying when He said there would be no giving of marriage; that we would be as angels in heaven. In 1 Corinthians 15:49-51, Paul states, "Just as we have born the likeness of the earthly man, so are those who are of the earth. And just as we have born the likeness of the earthly man, so shall we bear the likeness of the man from heaven. I declare to you, brothers, that flesh and blood cannot inherit the kingdom of God, nor does the perishable inherit the imperishable. Listen, I tell you a mystery: We will not all sleep, but we will all be changed…" (NIV) The current religious look at the beliefs of the Sadducees who were mistaken in their understanding of the scripture and translate that thought line over to Paul's writings and say that the Kingdom of God is the resurrection and can only be 'inherited' in the future resurrection.

If that thought line is true, then Jesus would have been wrong when He told us, "Neither shall they say, lo here! Or lo, there! But the kingdom of God is within you." (Luke 17:21, KJV) Certainly Jesus has never been wrong, and in the context, neither is Paul. It is what we do to the scriptures by our taking verses out of their context that is wrong and we make it to mean what we want it to mean. The religionists have not understood the kingdom of God. They saw it clearly in the natural that when it came, God would set up an earthly kingdom. Then, in the resurrection, the kingdom of God would be as it was on earth.

The Truth is that Jesus came with the Kingdom of God, Himself, as the King of His Kingdom, but His kingdom has always been a spiritual kingdom, not an earthly one. So, in our understanding, we see that this spiritual kingdom dwells in us by the grace of God and we do not have to wait to die and go to heaven to enjoy His wonderful Presence. Just as Jesus said, the 'spiritual' Kingdom of God dwells within you and as we continue in His grace abiding in Him, we understand that being 'in' Him is being in His Kingdom. Honor the Lord in His Holy Presence; honor His righteousness and thank Him for it is He who allows us into His Presence today to be with Him and Him in us, in His Kingdom of Life! He is the God of the living!

November 13th

The Great Commandment

"And He said to him, 'And you shall love the Lord your God with all your heart, and with all your soul, and with all your mind.' This is the great and foremost commandment. The second is like it, 'You shall love your neighbor as yourself.' On these two commandments depend the whole Law and the Prophets.'"
(Matthew 22:37-40)

Jesus responded to the lawyer's question with Deuteronomy 6:5. Of all of the commandments that He could have regarded as the greatest, it was the commandment to love the Lord your God with all that you are. If you love the Lord your God with all that you are, then all that you are is His. All that you have is His, your heart, that is, your spirit that He has placed inside of you; your soul, that is, the natural personality and individual that you are; your mind encompasses your thoughts, beliefs, and possessions of ideals. Among all of this, there isn't anything else to give Him for none of this is about things, but is about who and what we are internally.

If all that we are is His, then what is His is His, indeed. Jesus then says, the second is likened to it and that is to love your neighbor as yourself. If all that we are is His, then all the love we have is for Him. The loving of ourselves is for Him as well and that same love we give in honor to Him, we give to others, our neighbors. This is the deep love, a holy love that only comes in the spirit. In this, there is no separation. We are His and our love is His. When we love others, it will be with His love for what we are is His.

This is why there is absolutely no response from the lawyer or the Pharisees on this answer. Everything in the Law and the Prophets would hinge on this type of love, His Holy love, because all would be His. The Pharisees just didn't think that way. Besides, they had too much to lose in loving that way; they stood to lose their prestige, power, and authority if they loved that way for they would no longer be in charge of all things religious and God would be getting all of the love and the glory and not themselves. How can a man love God and love his neighbor as himself; they simply could not grasp that concept, they were too full of pride and saw the commandments as 'doing' things and not 'being loving'. That is the essential problem with religion.

When we enter into His grace, His grace enters into us. When we come to understand that there is nothing we can ever do to warrant His grace and love, we will stop all of the 'doing' things to earn His love and we will rest and relax in Him, rather than working for Him. When we are overwhelmed in His understanding of how greatly He loves, His love will fill us to overflow and flow from us to love our neighbor as we have loved Him, which is all that we are. The world will know us by our love, not by our intellect, our knowledge of scripture, or our building of our own kingdoms. The world will know His love by how we love them. That is the only way.

November 14th

The Truth Comes to Life

"And no one else was able to answer Him a word, nor did anyone dare from that day on to ask Him another question." (Matthew 22:46)

As Jesus had been continually approached by the scribes, priests, and lawyers to answer their questions about the Law, it was usually in context to their oral law, which they seemed to know best. They knew their interpretations best, rather than the literal written Law of the Lord and the specific words that He had spoken through the prophets which revealed our Lord's heart. They knew what they knew and it was what they knew that actually created their stumbling blocks for themselves. When they are all together as a group, Jesus asks them a question, and in that setting, they had to answer the question, they couldn't say, 'We'll get back with you tomorrow.' They simply could not answer Jesus' question of how is it that King David would say in the Spirit and call Him, Lord, and then He, the Lord, would still be called the 'Son of David'. They had absolutely no clue as to the answer to that question. Although the prophets spoke in this manner, and David, himself was considered a prophet as well, the course of the matter would be that one would have to know the nature of the Lord in order to know how He could be Lord, King, Messiah, and Son of David all as one and still be the same person. They actually had not thought through that one.

What they didn't know was that the Son of David was standing there asking them the question. What they didn't realize was that the same God who was in the beginning was with them in the present. They did not comprehend the idea that God, who knows no time or space, could be standing right in front of them in the form of a carpenter's son from Nazareth. They could not comprehend that the Author and Finisher of our faith was the one undergoing the testing. He was not only the Author of our faith, but He was and still is the Author of His Word, the Word become flesh and dwelling among them.

They, in their religious fervor saw God who sat upon a throne up in the heavens someplace and they were His representatives in the earth. They had no clue that the Father of all was standing there in the Presence as a Son and it was God in the flesh taking to them.

The Pharisees had taken the word of God for themselves, hidden it from the people and had created another word to take its place, their oral laws. They were the self-created substitutes that stood in the way of the Almighty God and so they took their place among the murderers and murdered the Son whom the Father had sent to deliver His people and His Kingdom. What they also didn't know was that the

Son did deliver the Kingdom, He delivered in a message in and from Himself; He ushered in His Holy Spirit, and He continues to deliver us today by delivering the Gospel of the Kingdom to the world.

God bless the Holy Name of Jesus Christ, for we can now see that He was His Father's Son, born of flesh, born of a virgin. Yes, the Kingdom of God was ushered in in all of His glory, the glory of the only begotten of the Father. The Word became flesh and dwelt among us, bless the Lord! (John 1)

November 15th

The Seat of Hypocrisy

"Then Jesus spoke to the multitudes and to His disciples, saying, 'The scribes and the Pharisees have seated themselves in the chair of Moses; therefore all that they tell you, do and observe, but do not do according to their deeds; for they say things, and do not do them." (Matthew 23:1-3)

It's amazing at times at how we learn things. We can learn by reading, listening, watching a video, watching a teacher perform a task; we can learn things on our own by trial and error and we can learn things by watching how not to do something. We can also learn by watching others make their mistakes so we don't have to. Finally, we learn from people who have lied to us as we think we have been told the truth, but haven't and we learn our lessons the hard way, by being taken advantage of.

In Matthew chapter 23, Jesus Christ goes on the offensive for a door has been opened to Him to teach the multitudes of the ways of the Pharisees and scribes, the teachers of the Law. They have had enough of Jesus for now and leave Him to the masses, only to go and plot their next move against Him. Matthew 23 is very telling on the religious leaders and as we continue to learn, not much has changed in over two thousand years.

Jesus says that the leaders have seated themselves in the chair of Moses. This is a symbolic chair of authority, grand leadership, and spiritual oversight of the Law of God. Moses was that kind of a leader. They see themselves as ones having the authority of God over God's people. They teach and deceive and lead by deception and hypocrisy. They teach the Law, but do not do it themselves. They teach more than the written Law so that they can do as they please because they have already attained. They teach and do their oral laws, the doctrines of men, but do not do what God had first ordained. They were the consummate hypocrites with all the rights and privileges of the authority of God, but they did it their way. They had usurped the chair of Moses by their 'divine' right, calling, and monetary payments. They believed they were God's representatives, but were false teachers of the first degree. Have you ever known anyone like that? If you have, you're not alone, because false teachers and hypocrites continue to exist today in all forms of life; particularly in religion…it seems to be a breeding ground for the breed.

Our case is not to go hunting for the hypocrite, because he or she is usually standing in the mirror. Jesus said to judge not, so that is one responsibility we do not have to undertake. We need to look at ourselves for any wayward thinking, judgmental behaviors, or cross-eyed stares that we may have against other people when we are thinking we're something that we're not. Hypocrisy hits all of us at some point and it is up to our own selves to see it in ourselves by the mirror of God's Holy Word. Stop looking at other people to judge them whether they go to a church or some other organization. Do not do as the hypocrites and do not do as the hypocrites if you find yourself being one. Get off that road and get on the road of denying the self, that's the first place to look. Self-reliance leads to self-deception and it's all about you at that point. Learn from Jesus and the others of what not to do and what not to be like. Be real in Him. He is our life and our salvation. Be grace!

November 16th

The Greatest Among You

"But the greatest among you shall be your servant. And whoever exalts himself shall be humbled; and whoever humbles himself shall be exalted."
(Matthew 23:11-12)

Jesus continues here with specific directives for leadership among the people. He has spoken about not being a hypocrite, that is leading by false representation by telling your followers to do things you are either unwilling to do or not planning on doing yourself. Our Lord despises hypocrisy. It is not real living, or real leadership, but is a lie. It is from the father of lies because it ultimately leads people away from the Truth of the Word to a man or woman.

Jesus specifically describes some facets of true Spiritual leadership in His Kingdom. He is explicit when He says: "But do not be called Rabbi, for One is your Teacher, and you are all brothers. And do not call anyone on earth your father; for One is your Father, He who is in heaven. And do not be called leaders; for One is your Leader, that is, Christ." (v.8-10)

Religion continues to teach the opposite today and anyone teaching the opposite of Jesus Christ is "anti-Christ teaching". Jesus' teachings have to do with true, Spirit-filled, Spirit-led leadership in the Kingdom of God. Religion has continued in the practices of the Pharisees and the scribes. Religion teaches the opposite of Jesus and desires seats of authority, labels, positions, monetary reward and control over the hearts and minds of people. It didn't miss a beat with the exception of the early church in the first one hundred years. Then, religion got its foothold in the Lord's body and the church hasn't been led properly since then.

Yes, religion has its stranglehold on the church, but it doesn't mean that everyone is going to hell. What we have to do is receive the Gospel of Jesus Christ and that is the Gospel of the Kingdom of God. In the Kingdom of God, the greatest among you is your servant. He might get paid, he might not, that depends upon the need, and not the greed. If there is greed, then it is not real. The fruit is on the tree, folks. Good trees bear good fruit. Good fruit is the fruit of the Spirit. Again, love, joy, peace, patience, goodness, kindness, gentleness, faithfulness, and self-control are all fruits of the Spirit of the Living God. The Holy Spirit will exemplify these fruits through the heart and mouth of the Spirit-filled believer.

The transition of the Lord's body moving from religion to the Gospel of the Kingdom of God is going to be trying, but churches are already doing so and teaching that which Jesus taught and attempting to undo two thousand years of religious stronghold. The church of today needs correction in accordance with the Truth of God. There is a light and dark difference between the church and religion.

The leadership doesn't want to lose its pay or its buildings. But, the Truth must be preached in order to bring all things to pass to the glory of God and our Savior, Jesus Christ. Submit to Him, not to me or to any man. Submit to Him for He alone is your righteousness, not me or any man. No man that you know has saved you and no man or woman can. It's about abiding in Jesus Christ and in Him, alone. Bless the Lord with your life, your soul, your all. Only in Him shall we see the day of salvation come to our house and our world. Only in Him can Truth, grace, and Life be ever-present. in you now and in your future.

November 17th

The Kingdom of Heaven

"But woe to you, scribes and Pharisees, hypocrites, because you shut off the kingdom of heaven from men; for you do not enter in yourselves, nor do you allow those who are entering to go in."   (Matthew 23:13)

The kingdom of heaven is heaven; it is a specific location. But where exactly is heaven? Is it in the heavenlies far above us so far that we cannot see? The kingdom of heaven is a place for those who are chosen to enter to enter. Jesus speaks woe upon the scribes and Pharisees for their hypocrisy and false leadings and teachings led people away from the kingdom of heaven.

The kingdom of heaven, according to Jesus, is a present and ever-present reality. He says, "the Kingdom of God is within you." (Luke 17:21) Jesus says that the hypocrites shut off people from entering in and do not enter in themselves. So, it was a present reality then in the Presence of our Lord Jesus. For the hypocrite, what is on the outside matters, not the inside hidden places.

For the hypocrite, appearances mean everything and the weightier matters of justice, mercy, and faithfulness are neglected. (v.23) Jesus spoke of the hypocrites maintaining outward appearances to appear clean and worthy of our Lord's favor, but neglected the internal where He said they were unclean, (v.26), whitewashed tombs, (v.27), full of hypocrisy and lawlessness, (v.28), serpents, a brood of vipers, and sons of murderers, (v.30-33)

Religion has its privileges and its privileges are for the leaders first and only the followers who pay homage to their kind of leadership are rewarded according to the favor of the leader and not the favor of God.

Jesus came to honor and glorify His Father. All that He did, He did according to His Father's purpose and specific will in His life. He is our standard of leadership in the Spirit. All leadership in the Spirit leads people to the Father, not to themselves. Jesus openly and explicitly spoke to bringing people to honor and glorify the Father. He did not come to glorify Himself, but on the contrary, humbled Himself as the servant of all mankind of all time. That is Spiritual leadership and only He can fit that mold and purpose. When we enter into the ever-present kingdom of heaven in Him by His grace, we enter into a place in Him and Him in us. Again, where is the kingdom of heaven? Re-read the Gospels. Re-read the Word of the New Testament again to see it for yourself. Religion would have you listen once again to their sound of the old; the sounds of the scribes and the Pharisees, saying, 'Listen only to me, I'll show you the way…"

Invariably, people will listen to the old tradition of religion and be kept from entering in even still. The whitewashed tombs continue to exist today. The spirit that seemingly prevailed to kill Jesus and the message of the gospel of the Kingdom of God persists, still killing hearts, still hampering, still twisting the Truth into an old, old story of doing things their way, the way of the hypocrite. The way of the hypocrite is succinct. It is the art of recognizing God and dealing with Him with outward appearances, believing that as long as I say I am a thing, I am that thing; then, I can move on with my life the way I see fit. Jesus said, "Do not do as the hypocrites." Be truth!

November 18th

The In and The Out

"You blind Pharisee, first clean the inside of the cup and of the dish, so that the outside of it may become clean also." (Matthew 23:26)

When Jesus accused the scribes and the Pharisees of preventing people from entering into the kingdom of heaven, He talked about two distinct places. These two places are the inside of the man and the outside of the man. The Kingdom of God is within you. When we abide 'in' Him, He abides 'in' us. "Believe me that I am in the Father and the Father in me; or else believe me for the sake of the works themselves." (John 14:11, RSV) "Truly, truly, I say to you, he who believes in me will also do the works that I do…" (v.14:12) Believe Jesus, yes! And the demons also believe Jesus. (James 2:19) The demons do not 'believe "in" Jesus', they do not call Him their Lord and obey Him as His disciples. You have to be "in" Him to believe "in" Him. For Truth to be "in" a man, he has to be "in" Christ. The True believer doesn't simply outwardly say he believes, but the True believer is "in" Christ in his believing. He is in a place and the place is the Kingdom of God.

Many religion teachers teach people that all they have to do to become a Christian is simply believe. Do you understand how errant that is? Religionists boil Jesus and the New Testament down to one word, 'believe'. Again, even the demons believe and tremble (James 2:19), but they are not heart-changed, born again, denying the self, true disciples. The demonic forces serve their father, the father of lies; that is just one fruit of their spirit. I pray that you are seeing the major difference here. Jesus preached the gospel of the kingdom, that which is dealing with the inside. Religion preaches the external and doesn't really know how to deal with the internal. It is an unworthy substitute for the Truth of Jesus Christ even though now it preaches Jesus Christ as a Savior. Religion eventually rolls the external into doing something to earn your salvation, or to keep it. The doing of things is the outside, washing the outside of the cup so that it looks clean, but inside, at home, or in relationships, it is abusive, using, and undermining in order to get its own way. Religion is the way and spirit of the hypocrite. It is not real and true, nor does it lead to the real and true. It hinders people from entering into Truth. All religion, whether it be a version of Christianity or otherwise, always leads to doing something in order to receive peace or to maintain it. In Christ, He is our peace for He dwells within us. (Ephesians 2:14)

"Jesus answered him, 'If a man loves me, he will keep my word, and my Father will love him, and we will come to him and make our home with him. He who does not love me does not keep my words; and the word which you hear is not mine but the Father's who sent me." (John 14:23-24, RSV) "Remain in me, and I will remain in you. No branch can bear fruit by itself; it must remain in the vine. Neither can you bear fruit unless you remain in me." (John 15:4, RSV)

November 19th

The Time and the Place

"O Jerusalem, Jerusalem, who kills the prophets and stones those who are sent to her! How often I wanted to gather your children together, the way a hen gathers her chicks under her wings, and you were unwilling. Behold, your house is being left to you desolate."   (Matthew 23:37-38)

If you've ever wondered why our Lord God sent Jesus as His only begotten Son to Jerusalem at this time in the earth and this location on the earth, perhaps this lends a clue to the answer. Throughout their history, the people of Israel have consistently rejected their leadership in their ultimate rejection of their Holy Father. They are His chosen people, His children, and He is their Father, their shepherd, their provider, and protector. He led them in faith by their father Abraham for they are his seed. He has always provided for them and protected them in His way and not the way of the earth. They have rejected and/or murdered His prophets that have spoken for Him on His behalf. And now, here is the Son, the son who was sent in specific kingdom parables, and they choose to kill Him as well, just as the kingdom parables depicted.

Time has taken its course and the city of our Lord, Jerusalem, the Holy City, the City of Peace, is the chosen place that our Lord selected to confront sin, spiritual forces of darkness, and the spirit of religion in one place and one time. As you re-read the holy scripture with a mind towards the kingdom, watch Jesus' movements and our Father's direction first attacking sin, then the outward signs of bondage, blindness, deafness, lameness, and the palsy, which is the representation of the dark spiritual forces. Jesus moves on from the repentance of sin and the release of the captives from demonic possession to confronting what had taken over the hearts and minds of God's people and that was religion and religious leadership. How ironic that the City of Peace would be the place of confrontation between a Holy God and the gods of sin, demons, and religion, the greatest form of hypocrisy.

Religion had cloaked the City of Peace into thinking it was something that it wasn't and so bondage took over the minds, hearts, and bodies of the people.

"He opened the book and found the place where it was written, 'The Spirit of the Lord is upon me, because he has anointed me to preach good news to the poor. He has sent me to proclaim release to the captives and recovering of sight to the blind, to set at liberty those who are oppressed, to proclaim the acceptable year of the Lord…he closed the book…and began to say to them, 'Today this scripture has been fulfilled in your hearing.'" (Luke 4:17b-21, RSV) The time and the place is taking its course all coming together towards the main event of all time when the confrontation of all the dark forces work together against the Holy One, the Son, the only begotten of the Father. Jesus proves that death in dying is the way to True Life. He bore out that victory so that, in the literal sense, we do not follow His literal death, but follow Him in denying all that we are, giving up the bad, the sinful, and the very best of us in order to receive Him in His heavenly spiritual Kingdom; the ever-present Kingdom of God, the true place of peace!

November 20th

The Prophecy of the Temple

"And He answered and said to them, "Do you not see all these things? Truly I say to you, not one stone here shall be left upon another, which will not be torn down."   (Matthew 24:2)

As Jesus walks out of the temple immediately after pronouncing the woes upon the Pharisees, scribes, and religious leaders, He is met by His disciples and they are inquiring about the temple. Jesus responds with the prophecy of the literal destruction of the temple[1] in question.

In 70 A.D., the Roman government and its soldiers had grown weary of the assaults from the Jewish zealots, the freedom fighters fighting for the Hebrew's freedom from Roman domination.

In just a matter of months, the Romans had conquered the city through military maneuvers, starving the rebellious, and taking building by building until all of the city was under their control and/or demolished. The historian Josephus said that the temple foundation, as well as, other stone structures were uprooted and overturned so that one might not even know where the location of the buildings existed. The destruction was so severe that over 1.1 million Jews were killed, over 97,000 captured and the city lie in such waste that you couldn't tell a city had existed there. The Romans ultimate victory was complete by 73 A.D. with the siege, mass suicide of over 970 Jews, and destruction of Masada, a fortified plateau above the city of Jerusalem.[2]

Jesus was speaking literally regarding the destruction of the temple and yet the disciples continued to ask Him about when these things were going to occur. Jesus would speak literally of some things and spiritually prophecy of others, but all that He said ultimately was spiritual prophecy; some of which has transpired and others are still yet to come to pass in this realm.

Learning to read the Words of Jesus and trusting Him in His words is a part of the Life that He gives us. In the Spirit, He speaks words of Spirit and that is how we come to understand what He is saying to us in that moment and for all time. We can go to His words and learn something new each time; His word is active, living, and breathing because His words are activated in the Holy Spirit. Without the revelation of the Holy Spirit, we cannot know Him, nor can we understand Him and His word. This propels us to consider those who do not know Him and to stop our judgment of them in their lack of understanding. It is the work of the Holy Spirit to convict the world of sin and if someone we know lacks the conviction of the Holy Spirit then all they hear from us is condemnation rather than communication.

The things that people see, the Temple, the church buildings; these are things that have and will continue to pass away due to our own doing, the doing of others, or just plain time. Eventually all things will pass away with the exception of what is done in Him. He always is and will always be, so what is done in Him will remain as He is. We do not place our trust in buildings, jobs, other people, the government, preachers or teachers. We place our trust in the only begotten of the Father, Jesus Christ. It is in Him that He gives us faith to more than believe and confess, for it is in Him we believe and confess with our total being. Faith comes from Him… Lord, increase our faith!

November 21st

The Fruit of the Misleading

"And Jesus answered and said to them, "See to it that no one misleads you. For many will come in My name, saying, 'I am the Christ,' and will mislead many.'"
(Matthew 24:4)

Jesus goes on to talk about what will happen throughout time with the talk of wars and rumors of wars, talk about the end of time, nation and kingdoms rising up against each other, but, He says that these things are the beginning of birth pangs. He is cautioning them to think on the differences in the natural realm versus the spiritual realm. In our natural world, we will have wars and nations have risen and will continue to rise against other nations. All are egregiously searching for that ultimate authority over their surroundings first, and then on to other fields of autonomy. Man wants to protect himself from other men and man's first inclination in doing so is to conquer his foes before his foes conquer him. This sense of protectionism is always with the individual to the group to the state to the nation and beyond. When the sense of protection and security is found, then taking over other lands has always been on the horizon.

The fruit of the misleading, however, in the spiritual sense, comes from the self. Self always desires its way and in desiring its own way, it will seek to destroy or eliminate that which is not like itself. That's why Jesus warns that many will fall away and give up one another and hate one another. (v.10) The misleading leads to leaders who do not walk in Truth, but rather walk in their idea of truth, usually conjured up within the confines of personal doctrine obscuring the Truth of the Gospel with their version of what suits them and their internal belief systems.

The doctrines of men have taken over the Gospel of Jesus Christ, the Kingdom of God, and replaced it with a hierarchical system of men lording over other men what they personally believe to be their truth. Authority over men is always at stake and power over the minds of men in these errant doctrines of systemized church and religion. "And many false prophets will arise and will mislead many." (v.11) False prophets have existed in early Christianity since the days of the Acts of the Apostles. False prophets have false beliefs that they propagate as truth and turn the Gospel of Jesus Christ into obscurity so that their ideas are furthered and their money pouches are increased. Systematized religion fits into the fruit of the misleading, false teaching and errant theology because the misleading is unending to the fruit of itself; which is, men preaching their version of their gospel hiding the truth from the masses. Doctrines and rituals become the substitution for Christ and stands in the way of people getting to Christ in Truth. Ask yourself, "Why am I performing this ritual at church? Where did it come from, Jesus or man?

Get your own Bible and get back to re-reading the Word of God for yourself. Peter said that we are all a royal priesthood, (1 Peter 2:5-9) Paul states such in Galatians 5:27-29. Whoever is born of Christ is in Him and has no need of a mediator, for Christ is our one and only mediator. Are you placing your trust in Christ or in another man or woman or a system?

Apostles, prophets, pastors, evangelists, and teachers are certainly Biblical leaders. (Eph. 4:11; 1 Cor. 12:28) Allow the Holy Spirit to lead you in the Truth to a fellowship who knows the Truth of the Kingdom of God, Jesus' Gospel; for it is His Gospel that is to usher in the Christ Himself in the end. (v.14)

November 22nd

Enduring to the End

"But the one who endures to the end, he shall be saved."
(Matthew 24:13)

Again, I say to you, trust the Lord Jesus Christ at His Word. He is the Word that became flesh. His word is truth. Abiding in Him is not a suggestion. When He said that unless a man is born again, he cannot see the kingdom of God, (John 3:3); that was not just a suggestive idea that we could ponder and if we decided not to be born again, then we'd be ok. No, that's not what He said. Always get back to what Jesus said; not what men have said that he said through the centuries in watering down a false version of their handed down perceptions of truth. You have to be in Him, first, to remain in Him and the corollary is the same. He has to be in you in order for you to be in Him. Remaining in Him is remaining in the vine, for He is the vine and we are the branches. (John 15)

We must continue with Him in Him. (1 John 2:6; 1 John 4:13; Rom. 2:7; 8:25; Rev. 2:10-13) Remaining faithful to Him, His fellowship, His word, and His abiding grace is absolutely necessary to enduring to the end. Certain preachers preach an easy belief, a cheap grace, wherein the believer is said to be a believer if he only believes…in about 8 seconds. That is false doctrine and leads many astray from the Truth. This remaining in Him is not a sort of works mentality either in that because we have been freely given grace, then we have to work to stay in it. No, we cannot work to attain faith, nor work to retain faith. (Eph. 2:8-10)

This remaining in Him is simply that: remaining in Him. His yoke is easy and His burden is light. I cannot unbecome being born again; it is for all eternity. The reckoning in remaining is this – we have to know what we're doing when we're being brought into Him. We will not understand it fully, but we will know, because it is revealed by His Holy Spirit. A person who has been introduced into the Kingdom of Light by His Holy Spirit knows and is transformed by His Spirit into a new creation into a place of peace and rest in Him. We become changed from the inside and over time, we exhibit the fruit of His Holy Spirit and loose the fruit of darkness away from our being.

Simply believing a fact of scripture is not 'knowing' God in a permanent relationship. That is simple head knowledge where no transaction has been made. There is no Biblical support for the idea of 'once saved, always saved'. That idea is not in the scriptures and is usually propagated by preachers and teachers who do not fully communicate the Gospel of the Kingdom of God, but a gospel of heaven minded 'believers' who are getting a ticket to heaven for when they die; and their usual and customary state of being is to remain as they are until they die, because they have this 'ticket to heaven'. This is another fruit of the misleading. These are the folk who are incapable of walking in the light because the light is not in them and they don't understand why they keep doing the same old things.

Follow Jesus' words of being born again, abiding in Him, and enduring to the end. There is no fear in Truth, only in doubt. The One who is faithful gives faith to those who submit to Him and the beautiful exchange of our becoming a new creation in Him creates the desire to endure.

November 23rd

The Gospel of the Kingdom

"And this gospel of the kingdom shall be preached in the whole world for a witness to all the nations, and then the end shall come." (Matthew 24:14)

John the Baptist came preaching, "Repent, for the kingdom of heaven is at hand!" And so did Jesus Christ. (Matt. 3:2; Matt. 4:17, NKJV) The gospel of Jesus Christ was and still is the Gospel of the Kingdom of God. Everything Jesus did points to the Kingdom; all of the events, healings, and miracles illustrated the power and majesty of the Kingdom. The Kingdom had entered the earth through the Person of Jesus Christ yet this Gospel has been hidden, cloaked in religion since before 100 A.D. When man joined his version of the gospel with Judaism, it became something extraordinary in the minds of men for it was then that man could capitalize on its features all the while capitalizing on its authority and power. Man used the hierarchy of religion to gain a stranglehold on the hearts of men so that they could contain what was never theirs to contain.

Leaders became priests and overseers became bishops. The church became organized in buildings and led by men who used the word of God for their own gain. House fellowships became directed by the city bishop and if another man was called bishop, he had to submit to the stronger man. The larger the city; the stronger the city overseer bishop became. All the funds of the fellowship began to flow upward towards the hierarchy and the main grounds and buildings that could house the Christians over the organized services.[1]

No more to the flow of the Holy Spirit and the leading of individuals and hearts of men. No, it had to be organized and sanctioned by men; chosen men who chose who belonged and who didn't. If you weren't a part of the sanctioned system, you weren't a Christian, so they determined. Men choosing men and women who believed as they believed and would not accept anyone who refused to believe in their beliefs. They became the substitute; the intermediary of the Christ…the representers who created their own doctrinal statements and creeds of faith so that the populace had to submit to them rather than the Christ who'd paid the price for their sin. And so has the church become a substitute for the Christ, rather than accepting their lot of being His body, they have become its head. It is the blind leading the blind into a ditch for all eternity.[2]

Throughout Christendom, the gospel has taken on different meanings at various times. To some, the gospel is merely grace. To others, it is social and cannot be without social love. Still to others, it is 'Jesus Christ and Him crucified!' all the while their preachers pummel their fists onto their pulpits of rage and clamor. And some still teach simple homilies, while keeping their flocks submitted to a worldly hierarchy that submits to no one and prays to everyone just so they don't miss the mark someplace. These are only manmade versions and portions of the Truth.

Jesus' gospel of the Kingdom of God is the gospel that is to be preached in the whole world for a witness to all the nations. The Kingdom of God is at hand. Be born again of His Spirit and deny yourself before Him, then take up your cross, and follow Him. Abide in Him forever. Amen!

November 24th

The Coming of the Son of Man

"But of that day and hour no one knows, not even the angels of heaven, nor the Son, but the Father alone." (Matthew 24:36)

Many fine teachers try to teach the end of days and all that must transpire in order for it to come to pass. Jesus said Himself that the first thing that must happen is that this gospel of the kingdom would be preached in the whole world for a witness to all the nations, and then the end will come. (v.14) With all of the events that preachers try to assemble in the end of days manifestation, one might eventually figure out that the first things must come first before any other event will transpire. Being that Jesus Christ admitted that the only One to know the end of day's timetable was the Father Himself, it would behoove us to admonish and reprove any man who makes a claim to knowing the 'when' of the end of days. Foolish men follow fools who try to become something that they're not. No one knows, not even the angels, nor the Son, the day and the hour of the day of His return.

It is our duty to remain in Him and follow Him in His word. We are commissioned to preach the gospel of the kingdom, making disciples of all the nations, baptizing them in the name of the Father, the Son, and the Holy Spirit, teaching them to observe all that He commanded us; and that with a promise; that He would be with us always, even to the end of the age. (Matt. 28:19-20) We are not called to be end of day prophets and seers. We are commissioned to preach the gospel of the kingdom. The problem is that hardly anyone has been preaching the gospel of the kingdom just as Jesus prescribed.

Almost two thousand years ago men decided to preach something other than the prescription and so, here we are two thousand years later and the majority of what we've had is many converts to religion, false teachings, blindness, and misleading heresies. All of which Jesus Christ forewarned us against while He was preaching to the worst hypocrites known in His era of time…religion par excellence via the Pharisees and the Sadducees. He Himself was a Jew who came to preach the gospel of the kingdom to the Jews first, so there's nothing wrong with being a Jew. They were and are God's children; but, they are not the only ones now. God's children are His sons and daughters by grace, through faith in Jesus Christ. Those are the sons and daughters of God and brothers and sisters to our Lord and Savior, Jesus Christ.

Continue to abide in Him and Him in you. Remain steadfast and courageous in His Kingdom. I do not know at what time or season that you will be reading this, but this is for your specific encouragement to remain in Him. The kingdom of God is at hand and now the gospel of the kingdom will be preached as a witness to all nations. God is blessing in His kingdom. His kingdom come, His will be done on earth as it is in heaven. Where He is, you are and where you are, He is. Be in Him now and forevermore and we shall reign with Him forever, Amen!

November 25th

Be on the Alert

"Therefore be on the alert, for you do not know which day your Lord is coming... For this reason you be ready too; for the Son of Man is coming at an hour when you do not think He will." (Matthew 24:42, 44)

Like the loving Lord that He is, He forewarns us to take special care that we, in our remaining in Him, be as He is, and not as we selfishly choose to be at times. At times, we decide to pick ourselves back up and love our selfish ways more than His ways. Often, we prove that His ways are higher than ours because we refuse to put on the mind of Christ, and selfishly walk our own paths. Then, when realize that we've gone prodigal, He watches and waits for us in our despairing, despicable self to return to our Father on bended knee. Assuredly, He reminds us that we are His sons and daughters and not slaves, the ones who have no birth in Him. We are born of His Spirit, dwelling in Him, being enriched in His glory.

In this, remaining in Him takes on new meaning. It means that while we remain here on earth, we persevere in Him, not letting go of our faith, but having our faith grow in steadfastness, suffering as He suffered, and yielding to His will, and not our own. We are to be busy being in Him; not busy working for Him, but allowing His Spirit to work through us while we are here. That is the only way His fruit goes on display, when we submit to Him, trusting Him with every ounce of our lives.

To be on the alert is to watch and pray, just as He told His disciples in the garden so that they, and we, would not fall into temptation. Be alert to stay awake in Him so that He continually has the advantage of flowing through us to others who need Him; that is the flow of the kingdom. The kingdom is not about possessions, money, authority, or fame. The kingdom is about Him and His desires in the Spirit on the earth. His kingdom is unshakeable and will last forever. Be on the alert for those who need to be there with Him!

Intercede for others. Learn to pray for your parents, honoring them all the days of your life. Learn to pray for your spouse, the one our Lord has given you to cherish in holy matrimony. Once you loved that person with a romantic love, now you can love that spouse with a holy love that you know only came from Him. Pray for your children and your brothers and sisters. Never forget to pray for your children; they are your offspring in the earth; love them with an everlasting holy love. Intercede on behalf of those whom our Lord has placed in your paths of work, school, and community. Pray for others. It will unleash the Holy Spirit in your life to lovingly care for them and that includes your enemies.

Never cease to pray for others; so, go and pray now for all of the ones the Lord has placed in our path and you will learn to love with the holy love of God that comes down from "…the Father of lights with whom there is no variation or shadow due to change." (James 1:17, ESV)

November 26th

The Faithful and Sensible Slave

"Who then is the faithful and sensible slave whom his master put in charge of his household to give them their food at the proper time? Blessed is that slave whom his master finds so doing when he comes." (Matthew 24:45-46)

So many believers take Jesus' promises as faith facts to suit themselves, especially when it comes to naming a blessing for doing something that they should be doing out of love and honor rather than the expectation of a reward. There actually is no additional blessing attributed here in this passage; it is simply a declaration of how things are in the kingdom when a slave of the King is faithful and sensible in all that he does in the kingdom. Jesus' words are real and true; He is faithful to His word. We get hyped about His faithfulness, knowing in our own pitiful self-pity, that we just can't measure up to Him in faithfulness, so we use that as an out in order to respond or react to others selfishly, indifferent, angrily, or worse.

As James says, my brethren, that should not be. Blessing and cursing should not come from the same fountain. (James 3:10) What the Holy Spirit has placed inside of us is Himself. What comes out of us should be Him. If something other than Him is coming out of you, then reconcile yourself to the Truth of God's word and fully examine what it is that is flowing from you in any given situation.

We are in a fleshly human existence and I am not proclaiming perfection here, but I am also not relinquishing holiness either. What is born of the Spirit will reflect the Holy Spirit's autonomy and as we mature in the faith, we respond with more Holy Spirit fruit than we did when we were first born in Him.

But brethren, if you've had no change since that day of your perceived 'new birth' or your perceived day when somebody prayed over you and you said, "I believe!" then you are not who or what you thought you were led to be. If there's been no change, then it's time to get on your knees and submit to the only King in glory and repent of what you are, where you've been, and where you're going. Repent of yourself, your sin, and your internal selfishness. Pray that the Holy Spirit will convict you of your sin, of judgment, and His righteousness. Pray for His Holy

Spirit to change you from within, making you a new creation, giving you that new birth that only comes from Him. Repent, submit, deny yourself, and desire Him above all for all times.

Jesus clearly and unequivocally states that the evil slave of His is the one who doesn't really believe that Jesus will come at an hour when he least expects it. So, the evil slave of God beats his slaves, mistreats others, and 'parties like a rock star' thinking that "I have my ticket to heaven, now I will go and do as I please!" "Not so", says Jesus. He will take that slave 'of His' and cut him in pieces and assign him a place with the hypocrites where there will be the weeping and gnashing of teeth.

It behooves us all to learn and trust in the right gospel, the gospel of the kingdom that requires faithfulness to the end and not ignorance and arrogance that ultimately leads to eternal death and destruction. Amen?

November 27th

The Importance of Keeping Watch

"And while they were going away to make the purchase, the bridegroom came, and those who were ready went in with him to the wedding feast; and the door was shut." (Matthew 25:10)

When Jesus says, "Then the kingdom of heaven will be comparable to…" He is making an illustration to the aforementioned teaching. He was speaking specifically to watching and being on alert as a faithful follower and devoted disciple at all times because you do not know the day or the hour of His return. We do not know the day or hour of His return, nor do we know the day or hour of our particular departure from this earth. We do not know when we will die. Therefore, we must not only be ready, we must remain ready and on alert. I must confess that if He had come back at some points in my life, He would have found me so encumbered with myself and reproach, I know where I'd be right now; but He didn't and so I abide in Him in the fact that I have this moment this day to live graciously in Him filling my heart with the possession of Him and only Him. The faithful slave is the faithful follower; the constant on-alert disciple.

We have to be leery of men's designs and teachings. Men, for some time, have taught 'once saved, always saved', that is a manmade concept and not Jesus

Christ's. What men teach and say is in the Bible needs to be reviewed while they are preaching. At times, they're teaching what their fathers' taught them and constant unabated repetition of false doctrines and teachings get handed down through the generations. Read Jesus' words for yourself. Encourage your pastors and teachers in the Lord and rightly divide the word of God along with them rather than ignorantly believing everything a man or woman says.

Jesus talks about faithful and unfaithful servants and slaves. The faithful ones remain faithful until death and obtain the kingdom. The 'faith-full' slave will remain in faith and the 'faith-less' slaves will be unfaithful. The unfaithful ones do not inherit the kingdom. It is so simple and yet what other men teach is most times, outright lies based on a 'ticket to heaven' or a 'hope and a prayer'. I must admit I am shocked by some men's beliefs that are so flippant at times, that it seems as though they believe there isn't really a heaven or hell in the great beyond, but there really is. And the kingdom of heaven, in this parable, is for the virgin, the disciple dressed in Christ's righteousness, who although all grew weary in well-doing, only half of them kept their oil 'grace, Holy-Spirit filled' lives filled with constant Presence that was real and true; unlike the other five who believed, but had only made an outward appearance of a profession of faith, but were inwardly empty. All ten thought they would make it into the kingdom wedding feast to meet the bridegroom, but only five were totally prepared and ready to go in when the bridegroom was made ready. The others were not totally filled with preparedness and at the time of His Presence weren't there, so they were locked out.

A note of caution here: Many of the traditional writers of commentaries talk about the omission of the 'bride of Christ' here as if to imply that Jesus wasn't talking about the church, therefore this teaching couldn't apply to the church and the possibility of some folk making it 'in' and others not...it would ruin their manmade concepts. Listen to Jesus! Jesus was specifically speaking to the idea of His disciples being on alert, faithfully filled to the brim with His Presence in constant abiding in Him. If men's teachings do not stack up to what Jesus said, then they want to interpret it as something else and, again, that's false teaching. Be ready! Be filled to overflow! Be faith-full and remain in Him!

November 28th

True Abiding in Him

"And the other virgins also came, saying, 'Lord, lord, open up for us.' But he answered and said, 'Truly I say to you, I do not know you.'"
(Matthew 25:11-12)

Years ago I was reading an article of a prominent evangelist where people write in and ask him questions and a person wrote in and asked the question, "What would be the most frightening verse in the scripture for you?" He responded with the verse, "I tell you, my friends, do not fear those who kill the body, and after that have no more than they can do. But I will warn you whom to fear: fear him who, after he has killed, has power to cast into hell; yes, I tell you, fear him!" (Luke 12:4-5, RSV). I agree with the evangelist, but at the time and it still is, the most frightening passage in the scripture for me is, "On that day, many will say to me, 'Lord, Lord, did we not prophesy in your name, and cast out demons in your name, and do many mighty works in your name?' And then I will declare to them, 'I never knew you; depart from me, you evildoers.'" (Matt. 7:22-23) In that passage, Jesus is speaking about servants of the Lord who thought they served the Lord, but they did not have a relationship of abiding in Him. He never knew them. They knew "about" Him, His word, and worked works in His Name, but He never knew them.

The point Jesus made then in Matthew 7, He is making again when speaking directly about being always on alert. We have to have a relationship of knowing Him and Him knowing us in the great exchange of being born again. The Truth of abiding in Him is the mutual reciprocal relationship of being in Him and Him in us. Knowing in spiritual terms is more than just having head knowledge or believing an idea. Knowing is going all the way; the totality of the being is immersed into Him. Confession is not simply mouthing words as some men teach, no, it is the total giving over of the self.

We try to think as Westerners, Western Hemisphere thinkers, the basic American way. God does not think like we think here in America. We have to learn to have His thoughts and subject our minds to His mind, the putting on of the mind of Christ. When Jesus says, "Believe!" that means more than getting the idea straight and say it with your mouth. Belief and confession in the Word is the giving up of all there is to our lives. My total belief system becomes His. I am submitted and changed by His grace.

The power to love and abide in Him in the each and every moment comes from Him. If you were told that you were 'saved' by some preacher who prayed an eight second prayer and you do not spend time with Him in worship, prayer, meditation, abiding in His Presence, and simply being with Him, then, if I were you, I'd find another preacher who could lead me into His Kingdom grace by being born again. At the end of your time on earth, you do not want the Lord of Creation to say to you, "I never knew you, depart from Me!" Jesus promised in John 14:23, that if we would love and abide in Him, obey His words, then He and the Father would come and make their home in us. Now that's you knowing Him and Him knowing you. That's where I want to be, always with Him. The blessing is in Him, not in things.

November 29th

The Parable of the Talents

"His master said to him, 'Well done, good and faithful slave; you were faithful with a few things, I will put you in charge of many things, enter into the joy of your master.'"   (Matthew 25:21)

I had a preacher friend ask me a question regarding this parable, "How does money translate into authority?" I asked him what he meant. He said, "The servants were given talents, money; and the ones who traded well made the master more money. In fact, they doubled his money. How does that translate into the master giving them authority over his possessions, because authority was their reward?" I pondered his question and didn't answer him right away because I knew he believed that money was the currency of the kingdom. I was not able to give him a right answer because he was on a wrong road to begin with.

Faith is the currency of the Kingdom, if there is such a thing as currency in the kingdom, because it is faith that we are given, not money. Faith in the kingdom is a measured and tangible object in the spiritual kingdom. Faith comes from the Holy Spirit of God. It comes to us as a seed in the new birth. Faith can grow from being a seed. It can be measured by God and it can be multiplied as in leaven.

The stewards were given talents, about $1,000.00 in value, each according to their abilities. One was given five, one was given two, and the other was given one. The first two traded in business transactions and they both doubled what they were given. The third squandered his opportunity and hid the talent for various reasons known only by him and the master. The first two, after the master's return, were rewarded with authority of the master's possessions. They knew that what they were given was not their own. They didn't do anything to deserve the opportunity and all they had done was be faithful with the master's possessions and increase what he had allowed them to manage. They were faithful to the master. Not so with the third steward, he not only had no increase, he hid what he had been given, so as not to lose it; and so as not to work for someone who would take the profit at his on personal efforts. He had no gain, no effort, no service, and no faith in his master's business. The only thing he had knowledge of was how he perceived his master operated. What he thought he had been given was taken from him.

The kingdom of God is as this in that when we are born into His Spirit, we have been given faith by Him and that faith gets exercised every time we move, breathe, work, serve, and abide in Him. Our faith, even as small as a mustard seed, can grow exponentially according to our own ability to faith in Him. It is His faith that He has given us, not our own; we don't own anything. His faith in us goes to work in us growing Him in us and as we move and serve in Him, He is able to flow from us in fruit, growth, and the replication of seed faith flowing from our mouths. He is His faith. His Spirit is the one that flows from us as a fountain of living waters. The faithful steward of God, abiding in His kingdom grace, knows that it is Him doing the work, the speaking, the saving, the convicting, and all is His possession, including our very souls. What we have, then, in faith, grows and the more will be given…more faith.

Jesus words are spirit and, once again, He used natural words and references of talents (money) to teach a spiritual truth. Be faith-full in what He has given you and by faith, share what He has placed inside of you to the world around you. It's as simple as opening your mouth and allowing Him to transact His Spirit to the one who needs to hear Him. He does the work through you, the faith-full abiding disciple of grace.

November 30th

Receiving the More

"For to everyone who has shall more be given, and he shall have an abundance; but from the one who does not have, even what he does have shall be taken away." (Matthew 25:29)

Our Lord is faithful in all that He does and says. It is His nature to be faithful for faith is His creation and faith is His gift to us. It is a part of Him that He imparts to us in the regeneration process known as being born again. It is the sole work of the Holy Spirit; we can't do anything to deserve it or earn it. His faith full stewards have been given their faith by Him and there is no other means by which we can obtain faith but only by Him and in Him. He is the author and finisher of our faith.

It is not our faith, as in our own personal possession, but is a gift from God. The faith we receive from Him grows inside of us as the tiny mustard seed and can grow as powerful as to say to a mountain, "Be cast into the sea!" (Matt. 21:21) His faith inside of us is to grow, manage, use, and be allowed to flourish all under His guidance. He does the work in us and He is the One who continues His good work. He knows His faith and He knows whom He has placed His faith in.

Over the years, I have heard preachers preach, "Place your faith in Jesus Christ!" Well, if faith comes from God alone, then that is fairly impossible to do because we do not have any faith to begin with! That's just simple ignorance speaking. All faith comes from God for all is His possession. The songwriter penned nothing in my hands I bring, and only to His hands I cling. We are His sheep, His sons and daughters, His stewards, His slaves. We are all made free in Him by faith… His faith. So, to everyone who has, more will be given, and he shall have an abundance…of faith!

On the other hand, "…the one who does not have, even what he does have shall be taken away. And cast out the worthless slave into the outer darkness; in that place there shall be weeping and gnashing of teeth." (v.29b-30) The one who does not have is the one who 'believed with a head knowledge' about God. Most of the civilized world has heard about God, but not everyone has been given faith by Him.

However, if we look closely at this parable and at another parable of the seed and the sower, we may catch a glimpse of the Truth of the word in the Kingdom. In the parable of the sower and the seed, the sower is the Father, the seed is the word/faith, and the soil represented the types of folk out there who are able (according to their ability) to receive the seed/word/faith. The soil that was able to receive the seed/word/faith was able to multiply the word/seed/faith within itself. The seed always comes from the sower and is reproduced into multiples in good soil. In the bad soil, the seed is rejected, left by the wayside, suffocated by stress and turmoil, or simply gone unused by neglect. That seed is taken away from the soil that rejected it for it did not impart the word/seed/faith into itself. It was given, but ultimately was rejected, not received or neglected. That is the danger in one preacher telling another man that he's saved just because he believed in an eight second prayer. The preacher does not know what is inside the man, only God and that man knows what is on the inside. That is the blind leading the blind. That is why Jesus specifically taught us to make disciples, not go out and save people. If we make disciples, then we will know the person who we're teaching because we will have been in a relationship with the person who needs spiritual leadership and guidance.

The souls of men are too important to leave to an eight second prayer only to leave them to themselves and the prospect that they're something that they're not. Woe be to that preacher who leads the little ones astray by not taking the time to obey the Lord in making disciples rather than making converts to the positive realm of cheap grace.

Faith in Jesus Christ is only found 'in' Jesus Christ. That's where the regeneration takes place. We do not cause our own new birth; it is the supernatural process of being in His faith in Him. It is a relationship in Him.

December 1st

Inheriting the Kingdom

"Then the King will say to those on His right, 'Come, you who are blessed of My Father, inherit the kingdom prepared for you from the foundation of the world." (Matthew 25:34)

The ubiquitous kingdom advances when those who are blessed of the Father with faith utilize that faith into the loving care of those around him. Jesus has said that when He is seated on His glorious throne, He will separate the nations as a shepherd separates the sheep and the goats. The sheep are His; the goats have another road. The deciding points of our Lord were those who were blessed of the Father who fed the hungry, gave drink to the thirsty, gave invitation to the strangers, visited the sick, and the imprisoned. Those who are blessed of the Father have the blessing of faith, Presence, abiding holy love, and the direction of the Holy Spirit all within them. They are led to care for these people in Spirit and in Truth because they have the heart of the Father abiding in them. The feeding of the hungry or the poor not only relates to the material foods that we share, but it is also the sharing of the faith to fill the void in spiritual lifeless souls. The faith that He gives us must translate into multiplicity with other people. We are not given faith to be monks and hermits keeping what we've been given for ourselves. We share His faith spiritually, materially, emotionally, mentally, and physically. If we have absolutely given all to Him, then all is His to use as He sees fit.

It is when we're given opportunity and we refuse to share whatever it is that we're challenged with that the idea comes back to haunt us, "I should have helped that person out; maybe I was the only Christ they were going to meet today." You see, there are ministries and programs that feed people and house the homeless and visit the sick, elderly, and imprisoned. But they are all not God in the earth. If you find yourself reading this, you can pretty much count on that our Lord has led you to these pages to remind you to share what He has placed inside of you or whatever He has given you to manage. We are His hands, His feet, His voice, and His touch in the earth. So whenever we love, hug, visit, or feed someone in His nature, His nature proceeds from us to the other folk who need Him. Those are our opportunities of grace faithing…sharing His grace, sharing His faith, and sharing bread or water in holy love.

Allow the ubiquitous kingdom, His ever-present and future inheritance, to be shared with others who need His love. Your future is certain in Him. Your present is waiting. Release, forgive, give, and share His grace today with each opportunity that you have in Him. "And if anyone who gives a cup of cold water to one of these little ones because he is my disciple, I tell you the truth, he will certainly not lose his reward." (Matthew 10:42, NIV) Eternal life is the reward and the kingdom is eternal. (v.46) This Life is ever-present, today in us; in our future inheritance, in Him, where we will always be in His glory. Give God praise!

December 2nd

Exercising Faith

"Then He will answer them, saying, 'Truly I say to you, to the extent that you did not do it to the least of these, you did not do it to Me.' And these will go away into eternal punishment, but the righteousness into eternal life."
(Matthew 25:45-46)

When the righteous exercise the faith that they have been given by Jesus Christ, they exercise it in allowing Him to have His way in them. Faith comes from the Holy Spirit of God; it is not something conjured up within ourselves. Faith exercised is faith shared out of the overflow of the Spirit within us to a world of opportunities that are constantly around us. Faith exercised is feeding the hungry and giving drink to the thirsty. Faith exercised is visiting the sick and the imprisoned. This is not mere social service, which social services can provide, but a Spirit-filled, Spirit-led opportunity to help others in Jesus' nature. He healed, He delivered, and He fed others in the nature of His Father for it is His nature to feed, give drink, and visit the sick and the imprisoned. Faith in Christ is the Spirit doing His work through us to a lost and hurting world.

The goats, the ones on His left, were the ones when given opportunity turned their face towards another way in order not to see the need. Here, we see that the eternal punishment is for the ones who refuse to help in times of need. But, is that the reason for the eternal punishment? Just because you didn't help in times of need? Emphatically, no! The reason Jesus tells us in this parable of the sheep and the goats is that only He knows what is inside a man or woman. He knows if the seed of faith, which is Himself, is living on the inside of that person. If the seed of faith, the Word in the flesh is there, the evidence will be a life lived in the will and nature of the Father. In this, the needy will be seen and helped. The adverse is positively true as well. If a person does not have the faith of God living on the inside of them, then it simply won't matter. The evidence will be there…they will not help the least of these. Ultimately, the goat-spirited person will be helping themselves for themselves.

Social needs have always been with us. Even Jesus told His disciples that the poor you would always have with you. (Matthew 26:11) As a faith-filled disciple, we are admonished to help the needy when we are given opportunity. However, when a person decides that their helping the needy according to their own belief system includes helping women have abortions so that they can murder their unborn babies, the insides of the goat is open for the world to see.

People invariably reveal what is on the inside of them. If you really believe that feeding a helpless, homeless dog with one hand and killing an unborn baby with the other hand is your way of social justice or your form of Christian thinking, then I challenge you to read the Word of God in where you will end up with that belief. Abortion is murdering unborn babies.

"Jesus said, 'Truly I say to you, to the extent that you did not do it to the least of these, you did not do it to Me.' And these will go away to eternal punishment." (Matt. 25:45-46a)

December 3rd

He Already Knew

"And it came about that when Jesus had finished all these words, He said to His disciples, 'You know that after two days the Passover is coming, and the Son of Man is to be delivered up for crucifixion.'" (Matthew 26:1-2)

The time has come for the last remaining days before the crucifixion of the Christ and Jesus reminds them again that His time is quickly drawing near. He was born to die and He knew it. I am uncertain if anyone can imagine His resolve to submit to His heavenly Father throughout His entire life here on earth. He knew what was going to happen, but He had not experienced it in the flesh as of that time.

The disciples didn't really 'get it' in all that He had repeatedly said about His upcoming betrayal, scourging, and death by crucifixion. There is no mention of the disciples' response to Jesus' prophetic telling regarding His immediate future. Luke 22:3, records Judas' response, for that is when Judas goes to the chief priests and officers on how they might betray Him to them. Jesus already knew all these things for in His Spirit, the book of the Revelation reveals, "And all that dwell upon the earth shall worship him (the blasphemous beast), whose names are not written in the book of life of the Lamb slain from the foundation of the world." (Rev. 13:8, KJV). He knew from before the beginning of time and creation.

David wrote in Psalm 22, "My God, my God, why have you forsaken me? (v.1) "…all who see me mock me; they hurl insults, shaking their heads: 'He trusts in the Lord, let the Lord rescue him. Let him deliver him, since he delights in him. I am poured out like water and all my bones are out of joint. My heart has turned to wax; it has melted away within me. My strength has dried up like a potsherd. And my tongue sticks to the roof of my mouth; you lay me in the dust of death. Dogs have surrounded me; a band of evil men has encircled me, they have pierced my hands and my feet. I can count all my bones; people stare and gloat over me. They divide my garments among them and cast lots for my clothing…" (Psalm 22: 1, 7-18, NIV) He already knew what would happen to Him and inspired David to write out the prophecy.

It took a man who knew God's heart to hear what the Spirit was sensing, saying, and revealing for a time yet to come. And yet, as disturbing as these words are, they became the script for the day of the cross.

Yes, He already knew He was taking the curse of sin upon Him, "And if a man has committed a crime punishable by death and he is put to death, and you hand him on a tree, his body shall not remain all night upon the tree, but you shall bury him the same day, for a hanged man is accursed by God…" (Deuteronomy 21:22-23a, RSV) Isaiah prophesied, "He shall see the travail of his soul, and shall be satisfied; by his knowledge shall my righteous servant justify many; for he shall bear their iniquities….because he hath poured out his soul unto death; and he was numbered with the transgressors; and he bare the sin of many, and made intercession for the transgressors." (Isaiah 53:11-12, KJV)

Jesus already knew; His time had come to die.

December 4th

A Precious Gift

"Now when Jesus was in Bethany, at the home of Simon the leper, a woman came to Him with an alabaster vial of very costly perfume, and she poured it upon His head as He reclined at the table." (Matthew 26:6)

The gift that this woman placed on Jesus' head was supposed to have been very expensive. It was pure nard, a rare and costly perfume of fragrance and oil, and she breaks the flask and pours it out onto Jesus' head. As we read the passage of verses 6-13, we see Jesus' view of what she had done as being a 'good deed to Him'; "For when she poured this perfume upon My body, she did it to prepare Me for burial." (v.12) Whether the woman knew exactly what she was doing as Jesus put it, we do not know; but what we do know is that she obeyed the Holy Spirit's leading in her life and out of compassion, love, and adoration for Jesus, she pours out, most probably, her most costly possession.

She gives to Him the best that she had in her life and that was something that she held dear and was very expensive as well.

There's always so much to learn in the scriptures, but here we simply have to stop and examine our own selves and see exactly what we've done to give to Jesus to celebrate Him and thank Him for what He is constantly doing in our lives. I am at a loss here for her gift cannot be replicated. He did not receive the burial ointments with His grave clothes for His resurrection prevented that from occurring. This was a one-time gift given to Jesus and the woman was chosen to give it. She obeyed in love. What have I done in my life with Him and for Him that exemplifies such adoration and love? It's not service, or giving money at church, no, it's something far more meaningful and extravagant than that. What is it that I do or have done that even comes close to what she did that day?

Or, have I sat on the sidelines, like the disciples in the room that night and, in rebuke and anger, declare that the gift was wasted; that we could have sold it to feed the poor. Or, we make something ritualistic and religious out of it and try to repeat it in the flesh, but have no spiritual idea of what we're doing. How many times have you seen someone give something to Jesus? I know that when we 'do unto the least of these, we're doing unto Him,' so is that what this is about?

The fruit in the room that day revealed the hearts of men as they are. The disciples were selfishly frustrated with what she did, but only Jesus knew her heart. Giving to Jesus a very precious gift was what she was told to do that day. It was her gift to her Lord for a very special time.

Take the time now to lay yourself at His feet and ask Him what He desires of you. Wait there, with your heart given to Him and He will tell you in no uncertain terms what He desires from you. I really believe that, for the most part, we are unable to comprehend the depth of what she did that day, but lying at His feet in adoration and giving to Him is the first to place to start to understanding and connecting to a precious gift so richly given. I give Him my life.

December 5th

The Other Kingdom at Work

"Then one of the twelve, named Judas Iscariot, went to the chief priests, and said, 'What are you willing to give me to deliver Him up to you?' And they weighed out to him thirty pieces of silver."   *(Matthew 26:14-15)*

Even though we continue to pray and pray and read and pray to continue faithfully in the faith, we have to realize that until Jesus comes back, the kingdom of darkness is always plotting its next move. As glorious as it was to see the adoration of the woman who poured out the perfumed oil upon Jesus' body to prepare Him for burial, there was the reason for the burial and that was the death on the cross. In order for the death on the cross, there had to be betrayal with thoughts of murder. These thoughts are imparted by the evil one and enacted upon those whom receive his thoughts to do his work. His is the other kingdom at work until he is thrown into the eternal abyss never to be heard from again.

"For you yourselves know full well that the day of the Lord will come just like a thief in the night. While they are saying, 'Peace and safety!' then destruction will come upon them suddenly like birth pangs upon a woman with child; and they shall not escape. But you, brethren are not in darkness, that the day should overtake you like a thief; for you are all sons of light and sons of day. We are not of night, nor of darkness, so then let us not sleep as others do, but let us be alert and sober." (1 Thess. 5:2-6).

If we will focus our faith in Him, on Him, by watching and praying as He told His disciples in the garden, then when the fiery darts of the evil one are fired at us, we'll be ready to quench its power over us. It's the one who simply doesn't believe that the dark forces need to be reckoned with who falls prey first. There's absolutely no reason for us to be ignorant of the evil one's deceptive and destructive ways. All the while people are worshipping our Lord in honor, the evil one is at work to deceive and destroy that which He is building up. The thief came to steal, kill, and destroy and he has multiplied his thoughts against Christ particularly through the internet today in errant and wicked philosophies, human trafficking, pornography, and ideas that prevail over the hearts and minds of men, women, and children across the globe.

Never cease to pray for others in intercession. Pray for your family, yes, and friends, and those who are in charge over you. Pray for them and never cease to pray for your children and the children of your community, by name. Adoring hearts in worship of the Holy One pray and watch and pray that we are not tempted or fall into dismay. Love Him with your whole heart and know that when a good man fails, he is not forgotten by our Lord. Pray and do not judge. Be alert and sober for you do not know the time or hour when our Lord will call your name. Be vigilant and never cease to pray!

December 6th

The Bread and the Wine

"And while they were eating, Jesus took some bread, and after blessing, He broke it and gave it to the disciples, and said, 'Take, eat; this is My body."
(Matthew 26:26)

The disciples eating the Passover meal together signified agreement with the feast of the Passover lamb which was celebrated every year in remembrance of the house of Israel being passed over by the death angel in the plight of the slavery in Egypt many years hence. The meal consisted of the paschal lamb, a lamb without blemish and unleavened bread; a bread intended to be their mainstay for their future journey out of bondage. As the disciples completed their meal, Jesus prepared something else for them to eat that would reveal a far greater depth of His purpose and how He would ultimately leave them, but would always be with them.

Jesus takes the bread and blesses it, meaning He took the whole loaf and set it apart for God to use. He breaks off pieces of the bread to give to each disciple for them to eat. He says, "take, eat, this is My body." This was not His literal body that He spoke of, but was consistent with all of Jesus's words in that His words were 'spiritual' words and relayed significant meaning into the heavenly spiritual realm. He then takes a cup of wine and, after giving thanks, says, "Drink from it, all of you; for this is My blood of the covenant, which is poured out for many for forgiveness of sins." Again, it is not His literal blood, but the wine conveys the symbol of His blood shed, which will be the covenant for the forgiveness of sins.

The eating of the bread, as His 'body' and the drinking of the wine as His 'blood' convey the truths that Jesus speaks to His disciples immediately following the partaking of the bread and the wine. Jesus had already told them that, "...the kingdom of God does not come with observation: neither shall they say, Lo here! Or, Lo there! For, behold, the kingdom of God is within you." (Luke 17:20b-21, KJV) In the Gospel of John, He teaches them further after they leave the supper about the spiritual aspect of being 'in'. Jesus tells Phillip, "Believe Me that I am in the Father, and the Father in Me..." (John 14:11)

These are all spiritual words and never do they convey the natural body and blood of the Christ as in one church's view of transubstantiation, which is a manmade idea.

He tells His disciples, "If anyone loves Me, he will keep My word; and My Father will love him, and we will come to him, and make our abode with him." (14:23) He also says, "I am the vine, you are the branches; he who abides in Me, and I in him, he bears much fruit; for apart from Me, you can do nothing." (John 15:5) The constant abiding in Him in the each and every moment is the grace that He affords us to remain in Him. As we celebrate taking the Lord's bread and the cup, we are reminded to remain faithful in taking Him in. His body was broken for us for each of us to receive. His blood was shed for the forgiveness of sins of the whole world for all time.

When we spiritually receive Him, we receive His Spirit and take Him into our being. We remember what He did for us in the breaking of His body and the shedding of His blood by celebrating His bread and the cup. Daily, though, we remember what He did by abiding in Him and Him in us. In Him, we have fellowship and communion with Him. "To them God chose to make known how great among the Gentiles are the riches of the glory of this mystery, which is Christ in you, the hope of glory." (Col. 1:27, RSV)

December 7th

A Promise Made

"Peter said to Him, 'Even if I have to die with You, I will not deny You.' All the disciples said the same thing too." (Matthew 26:35)

Our commitments made at the altar can be made out of need, fervor, emotion or manipulation from a preacher or they can be made from a conviction of the Holy Spirit. When we are at the altar, we have a tendency to make promises to God that are, oftentimes, not kept. The altar is supposed to be the place of sacrifice. The mere existence of your being placed on an altar would signify your imminent death. The altar is the place of permanent sacrifice, the place of dying. Jesus went all the way for us and yet we mock Him each time we take a gander at the altar in our church facilities and think that 'if I can make down to the altar, I'll get saved; He'll make things right; I'll get healed; or a myriad of various thoughts and prayers that get thrown up to God so that He will make our lives easier to bare. If you decide to make a decision at an altar, let it be Holy Spirit driven and not man driven.

I do not dare mock Peter's commitment to Jesus here at the Mount of Olives. Peter was the embodiment of sincerity when he made his promise to His Lord that night. Most preachers will simply talk down about Peter and his promise made, but not kept because of the truth; he denied the Christ three times before the rooster crowed, just like Jesus said he would. Peter still had not learned to listen to Jesus' prophecies about himself. He had more faith in himself than what Jesus said was about to occur; that they would all run. Aren't we like that at times?

The fact remains that there are few of us throughout time who have been forced to go to the death for Jesus Christ. The numbers of the martyrs are in the millions by now and that number will continue to grow towards the end of time. However, how we live today is really the truth of our existence in Him. Every day, in the each and every moment, we make decisions to either deny ourselves or deny our Lord. Any choice for our self is a choice to deny Him. We have to see the disciples and Peter, specifically, in a compassionate view as opposed to a judgmental view. Many folk in their teaching and preaching judge the disciples as though the teacher would have performed better given the circumstances. But the disciples' circumstances were only for them and not for us. We cannot say what we would do. We can only speak to our present condition and that is, 'What will I do today to remain faithful in Him?'

We are a culmination of a series of moral choices, constantly being bombarded with thoughts, decisions, receptions, words, and actions. It is what we do with Jesus in the each and every moment that proves our worth to Him. He always is. But are we always with Him? To the church at Smyrna, John wrote, "Do not fear what you are about to suffer. Behold, the devil is about to throw some of you into prison, so that you will be tested, and you will have tribulation for ten days. Be faithful unto death and I will give you the crown of life." (Rev. 2:10, ESV)
In the future, that test is going to come. But, for now, your test of faithfulness is what you do when you're alone, visiting in another city where you think no one knows you and, yes, in the each and every moment we have in the day. Will you deny yourself or will you deny the Lord? Be faithful unto death. Learning to deny the self takes every day practice. Be faith full and fully aware that Jesus told His disciples to watch and pray that you are not tempted. That includes us.

December 8th

Worlds Apart

"And He came to the disciples and found them sleeping, and said to Peter, 'So, you men could not keep watch with Me for one hour? Keep watching and praying, that you may not enter into temptation; the spirit is willing, but the flesh is weak." (Matthew 26:40-41)

As Jesus and His disciples enter the garden of Gethsemane, He says to some, "Sit here while I go over there and pray." He takes Peter, James and John further into the garden and specifically tells them that He wants them to watch with Him because His soul is deeply grieved, even to the point of death, for He already knew all that was about to happen. Jesus goes a little further into the garden and prays, 'My Father, if it is possible, let this cup pass from Me; yet not as I wilt, but as Thou wilt.' (v.39) Jesus prays in fervent desperate prayer and is obviously grieved at what is about to transpire concerning his own life. The disciples fall asleep. The flesh and the spirit are two different worlds.

Jesus was filled and anointed with the Holy Spirit. The Holy Spirit had not yet manifest in the disciples lives, so all the power they had, had to be found in Him. This is not an excuse for the disciples' behavior, but it is the truth of the matter in this instance. The Spirit that dwells is willing to be active in Him for He never sleeps and never slumbers. He always is. Not so with our flesh.

In the flesh, we can be here today and gone tomorrow. In the flesh, we are weak, we sin; we give up and give in. The flesh wars against the spirit. The things that we see, taste, touch, hear, and smell are the actual fleshly things of life that will not last. The flesh needs to eat and needs to sleep. But, what about Jesus, didn't He need to sleep? That is the difference in the flesh and the spirit and what leads us in our lives. In the Spirit, we are led to Life.

The Holy Spirit guides us in the way that we should go. The Spirit is willing, but the flesh that is constantly needy is faithfully weak. That was Peter's life in those moments, that even though he promised His Lord he would go with Him to the death, he denied Him in the flesh. Here, we need the promise of the Spirit; for Him to abide in us. He provides our faith for He is our faith. He is the Author and Finisher of our faith. He is the faithful giver of every good and perfect gift coming down from the Father of lights.

Keep watching and praying in the Spirit with your spiritual eyes opened wide that you do not enter into temptation. We are battered with so many thoughts every day that we have to realize that most thoughts are not from the Holy Spirit, unless we are faithfully abiding in His Spirit. When we realize that we haven't been praying and watching, we see where we get off His path of righteousness and onto something far less that was not meant for us. We constantly take the paths that are not meant for us because we refuse to go to Him, stay in Him, and watch and pray in Him. That's when a lot of folk go to praying and searching for God's will as though they can receive something from Him. It's as if we could pull the moon towards us so we can touch it. Many folk want to stay where they are as they are and think they can get God to move on their behalf.

Watching and praying in the will of God is remaining in Him where He is, in His Kingdom of Life. That part of remaining, watching and praying requires a bit of effort on our part. Prayer is our work so that we can work out what He has worked in. Go to prayer right now…

December 9th

Thy Will Be Done

"He went away again a second time and prayed, 'My Father, if this cannot pass away unless I drink it, Thy will be done.'" **(Matthew 26:42)**

Although Jesus' spiritual world was a world apart from that of the sleeping flesh of the disciples, He still had to suffer anguish in His own flesh and body from the thoughts of what was coming, thoughts of the sin of the world, and thoughts of being completely alone. I cannot begin to imagine the agony He had while being beaten, mocked, scourged, and crucified on a tree. I also cannot begin to imagine the thoughts He had in anticipation of the horrible events that were about to unfold. This gives us pause here in the event that another person is going through something that we've never had to go through, it's not the time to pat them on the back and say, "Cheer up, everything's going to be all right!" Do not presume, in your arrogance, that you know what someone else is going through when you don't. Jesus told His disciples to watch and pray, lest they enter into temptation; the same goes for all of us at all times in intercession for others and when we have friends who are going through agony that we cannot even empathize with.

Jesus came to do His Father's will and all that He did was according to His Father's plan. Jesus, the Son of God, prayed to His Father. He was the standard for us to be praying; to go the mountain, the secret place, or wherever we are to pray to our heavenly Father, saying, 'Thy will be done in this earth, as it is in heaven.' Jesus said, "I do as the Father has commanded me, so that the world may know that I love the Father." (John 14:31, RSV) "Jesus said to him (Philip) 'Have I been with you so long and yet you have not known me, Philip? He who has seen me has seen the Father...'" (John 14:9, RSV)

The holy love that our Lord had in serving His Father was purity in oneness. Can we comprehend the oneness with the Father? Jesus prayed for His disciples and for all of us just after the Passover meal in John 17, for all of His followers to be one in Him as He is in the Father. Being one means moving as one. In Him, there are no externalities to influence us to move away from His faith. That is the marvelous aspect of dwelling in Him in His Kingdom. Being in Him is a very definite place and the place is the Kingdom of God. We don't have to wait to physically die and go to heaven in order to dwell in Him. Jesus desires us to abide in Him in the here and now, don't wait until you die to abide in His love and grace, be with Him now.

God's holy and perfect will is Himself. Although His perfect will is that none should perish, many will perish in His permissive will. Although His perfect will declares no sickness, disease, or death; His permissive will allows it for that is our current domain. Watching and praying for His will and abiding in Him draws us into Him; into that perfect will.

Yes, the flesh will die, for the flesh is weak, but our spirit will join with Him in oneness, just as Jesus prayed and that is the place that I want to be...one with Him, just as He prayed for us to be.

December 10th

The Betrayal

"At that time Jesus said to the multitudes, 'Have you come out with swords and clubs to arrest Me as against a robber? Every day I used to sit in the temple teaching and you did not seize Me. But all this has taken place that the scriptures of the prophets may be fulfilled.' Then all the disciples left Him and fled."
(Matthew 26:55-56)

Jesus' betrayal was spoken of first by the prophet's words from long ago. Some of these are:

Zechariah 11:12, "Then I said to them, 'If it seems right to you, give me my wages; but if not, keep them.' And they weighed out as my wages thirty shekels of silver." Psalm 41:9, "Even my bosom friend in whom I trusted, who ate of my bread, has lifted his heel against me." (RSV)

Isaiah 53:7-9, "He was oppressed and he was afflicted, yet he opened not his mouth; like a lamb that is led to the slaughter, and like a sheep that before its shearers is dumb, so he opened not his mouth, by oppression and judgment he was taken away…" (RSV)

Zechariah 13:7, "'Awake, O sword, against my shepherd, against the man who stands next to me,' says the Lord of hosts. 'Strike the shepherd, that the sheep may be scattered; I will turn my hand against the little ones.'" (RSV)

Of all of these disturbing prophecies that foretold of the Christ's betrayal, there was one that told of the consequences of the betrayal between God and His people. The prophet Zechariah speaks of breaking, or annulling the brotherhood between Judah and Israel, between Himself and His people. (11:14)

The prophet also spoke of putting people that are left of Him through a refiner's fire. (13:8-9) And, he also said, "And if one asks him, 'What are these wounds on your back?' he will say, 'The wounds I received in the house of my friends.'" (13:6, RSV)

All through Judas' betrayal of Jesus, in Matthew 26, it seems as though Judas knows exactly what he is doing. Yet, the question he asks of Jesus is quite profound in v. 25, 'And Judas, who was betraying Him, answered and said, 'Surely it is not I, Rabbi?' He said to him, 'You have said it yourself.'" Judas knew what he was doing, yet he was blinded by greed, the love of money, his own personal zealousness for the cause of the country, and the impact of the possession of devil in his life while the dark realm was seeking a way to kill Jesus. (Luke 22:1-4)

The completion of the betrayal in the garden honestly takes my breath away for it was men who betrayed Him, including one of His own. The prophecies foretold it, yet it was consummated and completed by willing men. It is the will of men to do as they are led and, as scary as it may seem, we, too, find ourselves, at times, doing things to other people that are just as ignoble. We betray confidences, telling other people 'what we know that they don't know.' We betray our spouses when we lust at other people with our eyes. We betray our employers with theft, shorting hours, playing hooky or playing sick.

We betray our friends with other friends, at their expense, just for a minor gain in camaraderie, but all we're doing is gossiping. We betray family members with hopes of ultimate gain when the parents die so that we won't get left out in the final will. There are severe consequences to betrayal and the ultimate loser is ourselves when we betray people and most especially, our Lord. We cut ourselves off from relationship with Him when we betray people for He always knows. Betrayal begins in the heart of man for some inward personal gain; there are no secrets with our Lord.

December 11th

Before the High Priest

"But Jesus kept silent. And the high priest said to Him, 'I adjure you by the living God, that you tell us whether you are the Christ, the Son of God.' Jesus said to him, 'You have said it yourself; nevertheless I tell you, hereafter you shall see the Son of Man sitting at the right hand of power, and coming on the clouds of heaven.'"   (Matthew 26:63-64)

It was in these statements that Caiaphas, the high priest heard blasphemy; and so he led his co-conspirators to a conviction of death in the over-night trial of Jesus Christ. They were so overwhelmed with hatred and resentment for Jesus, that their physical bodies were in torment to torture Him. They were all co-conspirators and their group had turned into a devilish mob with mob-like behavior. They were shouting, "'He is deserving of death!' Then they spat in His face and beat Him with their fists; and others slapped Him, and said, 'Prophesy to us, You Christ; who is the one who hit You?'" (26:66b-67)

The influence of the evil one is quite evident here. This is not a courtroom proceeding between two parties, it's not even a courtroom; it's a temple hall, supposedly the place of prayer. No, this conspiracy is really not even among men, it is a conspiracy to commit murder by the evil one himself. He always uses men or women to consummate and complete his desires in the earth. In all of this, he had willing vessels filled with hate, bitterness, and wrath unto death. How can a man hate so much as to kill another man? But this mob had turned into the act as quickly as it was declared in the atmosphere. They had been plotting all along, but now, now, was their chance to end this man's disruption in their pitiful little lives. And the evil one, who is the inventor and influencer of the religious spirit, is at his best in secret gatherings to conspire against one man, the Son of Man who was ready to pay the penalty of the sin of the world.

Please remember that these men were the upper crust of the religious and it was only these men who tried and punished Jesus unto death. Religion is but a substitute for the true relationship that we can have with our Lord. And, religion still today fights for its rights over your soul, your dollars, your mind, and your children. If religion can keep you satisfied with the substitute that it is, then why would you ever need a relationship with Jesus Christ? Anything that comes into conflict with a person's relationship with Jesus Christ is anti-Christ. That includes anything that can act as a substitute as well. The only people that Jesus Christ had conflict with was the religious ruling class, the system and structure created by men for their own personal gain under the guise of worshipping and honoring the Lord. That same system and structure is alive and well today.

Focus the faith that the Holy Spirit has placed inside of you on Him. After all, it is His faith that he gave you to trust in Him. He has done all the work at Calvary and He has done all the work in making you a new creation. He is the forgiving and loving One. Trust in Him with all of your heart and lean not upon your own understanding, but acknowledge Him in all of your ways and He will guide your paths. The true Church, the living body of Christ is alive as well. Trust in the Lord that His Holy Spirit will show you the difference between His body of believers and the systems that so easily beset us.

December 12th

Denial of the Savior

"And Peter remembered the word which Jesus had said, 'Before a cock crows, you will deny Me three times.' And he went out and wept bitterly."
(Matthew 26:75)

Again, I say, I do not mock Peter for doing what the Lord had prophesied that he would do. Peter was self-deceived. I have been there myself. He thought he could do anything around his Lord. That included protecting Him, serving Him, obeying Him, and honoring Him. He never saw himself doing anything dishonorable to His Master, but saw himself as the one who would lay his life down, if need be, for the cause of his Rabbi. But Jesus knew him all too well, just as He knows us as we really are. None of us can ever mock Peter's public denial for we have all done the same, or worse, at times.

In fact, hardly any of us, in the United States, that is, have ever been confronted with our lives and had to state whether or not we follow Jesus Christ. That day is coming, but as of this writing, it has not occurred here. Peter could have lost his life that night if he had confessed himself as a disciple of Jesus Christ. God did not have any intention of Peter losing his life in that hour, it was not his time. What Peter had to let go of was that inordinate affection with his personal pride. When Jesus said if any man desire to come after Me, let him deny himself…that means denying the self, not just the bad sinful stuff we do, but the entire self. That includes the good, better, and best of myself; it all has to be given up in order to walk in unity with Christ.

The teaching had to be taught and it was Peter's lot to be served. The teaching that no matter how attentive we are to Jesus, no matter how obedient we may think we are, no matter how close we think we are to His Presence, if we find power in anything that we are, we are doomed to fail. Peter was in the top three leaders with James and John, the sons of Zebedee. Remember, it was their mother that wanted Jesus to have them sit on His right and left when His kingdom thrones were set. There is nothing like being in the top three in leadership, but in Christ, none of that matters. No personal power is admitted into His Kingdom. If any person believes that they have anything to do with His purposes, then His purposes are not going to be fulfilled as He has planned. It will be an alternative substitute that looks and sounds like the real thing, but is far from it. The total denial of the self is weighing in the balance. No amount of religious service can earn you the right to sit at His table.

Let Peter's denial be our standard of teaching that no matter who we are, what we've done, or where we think we may line up to proximity to Jesus, none of it matters to Him. It is how He says it has to be done. Give up all and go all in. Stop teetering on the rail or standing in the doorway thinking you've got to this one thing to set matters straight for the Lord. We are in the Lord's body, not our own. It is His work, not our own. It is His Life that is lived, not our own.

"Do you not know that your body is a temple of the Holy Spirit within you, which you have from God? You are not your own; you were bought with a price. So glorify God in your body." (1 Corinthians 6:19, RSV) Glorify Him as He glorified His heavenly Father in submission to Him and to Him alone.

December 13th

Conspiracy to Commit Murder

"Now when the morning had come, all the chief priests and the elders of the people took counsel against Jesus to put Him to death; and they bound Him, and led him away, and delivered Him up to Pilate the governor." (Matthew 27:1-2)

It is of a sad estate to make a continuance of the conspiracy to murder Jesus, but that is what the religious rulers did and so we make our way to Calvary. In order for Jesus to die on a cross for the forgiveness of the sins of the world, someone had to put Him to death. The Romans had no fault in Him as we shall soon see, but it was the religious rulers that did have extreme prejudice against Him, extreme enough to kill Him. The time and the place had been set and so the players play their ways upon the stage with vim and vigor, a ghastly sight to behold. The co-conspirator in Judas had second thoughts, however, and tries to give the blood money back to the chief priests. They have nothing to do with accepting the money back, but go and buy the Potter's Field for the price of the thirty shekels of silver. Meanwhile, Judas, in his remorse, goes and hangs himself on a tree. This had been prophesied by the prophet Zechariah 11:12-13.

What is it that we do with our lives when we perceive that evil is triumphing over good? Do we hide our heads in the sand as the ostrich, or simply look away as the Levite did when he saw the man beaten and decided to look the other way? It is attributed to Edmund Burke the saying, "The only thing necessary for evil to triumph is for good men to do nothing." What is it that you have done in your past when you have seen evil at work in someone's life? Did you stand idly by and allow the work of the evil one to have his way. Do you not know that you are here on this earth for a purpose and that is to be salt and light in a very dark world?

Where is it that we get the strength to stand up and say, "No more!" to the prevailing darkness in the land? We cannot sit idly by and allow destruction to happen to others when we could say or do something about it. Raise yourself up out of the prayer closet and let the Lord have His way in you! Stop doing nothing. Start by praying and get up and get on with the Lord. It may be that you get throttled, but get on with the Lord in His work. Do not allow the sad state of our demise in this nation to tell you it's time to quit. Never! It's time to get up and get a move on with the Lord moving forward in faith. Jesus Christ is the only answer for the prevailing evil in our nation today. Get to know Him and dwell in His Holy Spirit. Then, allow His Holy Spirit to have His way in you today and forevermore. Be strong in the Lord and never, ever give up hope!

December 14th

He Answered Not a Word

"And while He was being accused by the chief priests and elders, He answered nothing. Then Pilate said to Him, 'Do You not hear how many things they testify against You?' But He answered him not one word, so that the governor marveled greatly."   (Matthew 27:12-14, NKJV)

How many times have we stood to defend ourselves and it was all for naught? How many times have we argued our points and it was, again, all for naught? When we will learn to deny our mouths from speaking in defense of our positions when, if we would allow the Holy Spirit to rule in our hearts, we would realize that speaking is not the thing to do in the moment?

For the most part, we lack spiritual discernment in when to speak and when to remain silent. Jesus remained silent before His accusers; it was the Father's choice. We are not always to remain silent and we are not always to defend ourselves. What we are to do is to listen to the Holy Spirit within us and yield to His dominion. If we remain silent, then it will be because He deemed it so. If we speak, then we speak in His Spirit with Him answering the questions in wisdom. There is not much more to say here because the revelation comes from Him and the part that we play is obedience.

Our lot is: Will we obey the Spirit of God and remain silent when we are to remain silent and when we are to speak, we yield to His infinite wisdom on the matter and allow His honor to speak through us? The choice to obey is always ours. And, in the heat of an ornery debate or accusation, silence is truly golden in the ears of a Holy God. Vengeance is His, He will repay for any injustice done on this earth. However, the payment for the injustice may not occur until the villainous meet the Lord Most High at the judgment seat. Obedience in faith requires trusting Him in and through all things. Trust Him to see you through.

December 15th

The Conspiracy Continues

"But the chief priests and the elders persuaded the multitudes to ask for Barabbas, and to put Jesus to death." (Matthew 27:20)

As the chief priests send Jesus to the Governor Pilate, Pilate doesn't want anything to do with Him, so he goes through the motions with the religious leaders and ultimately finds himself before a mob of people who had been convinced by the rulers that Jesus was a blasphemer and a heretic worthy of death. The same people, who had earlier that week thrown palm branches down welcoming His presence into Jerusalem, were now chanting as mob conspirators, "Crucify Him! His blood be on us and on our children!" The conspiracy to commit murder had moved from the temple chambers of the religious rulers to adding Judas, the disciple, to inflaming the city of Jerusalem with chants of death. Then, the Romans were charged to carry out His death on a cross. The whole city was responsible for His crucifixion, which is why the whole city was held responsible in its own destruction in 70 A.D.

Conspiracy may go unnoticed by authorities or by the public, but no conspiracy ever goes unnoticed by an all-knowing God. People get used all of the time without their knowledge in times of evil preparations. It is even more heinous when people know exactly what they're doing and no one says anything about it. Common folk like to cover for each other and oftentimes they cover for their leaders. I was in a situation one time where I was set up by one in order to be attacked by another. It was all in order to get me to leave a place when all they had to do is say, "It's time to go," but that would have been too easy. They had to involve the evil one in a plot to remove me from what I did not care. The conspiracy continues over and over again in people's lives because they choose to allow the evil one to direct their paths. When I was in the middle of the attack, it was as though I was looking into the eyes of the devil himself with him saying, "do not ever come back into this building again, or I'll bash your head through that wall!"

That is how conspiracy works. It takes willing participants to participate in doing just about anything to another person, all in the name of something else. For the most part, conspirators usually protect one another in the beginning, but one by one, they break their code and move on to other ordeals. It is a challenge to live in this world and not be touched by the conspiracy of evil for it is lurking about us in dark places.

Again, pray, pray, pray for your children. Pray for your spouses. Conspiracy comes to break up families and homes. That is the biggest conspiracy going on today. Pray for your family and pray with your family. Stop acting out at home in selfishness and start denying yourself before the Lord. Lead your family to understand the Kingdom concepts of denying the self and submitting to Him in the each and every moment. As Oswald Chambers puts it, "give up the claim to the rights to yourself."[1] Watch and pray that you do not fall into temptation, for he goes about as a roaring lion seeking whom he may devour. Remember this, greater is He that is in you than he that is in the world. Go in peace!

December 16th

The Scourging

"…and weaving a crown of thorns, they put it on His head, and a reed in His right hand; and they kneeled down and mocked Him, saying, 'Hail, King of the Jews!' And they spat on Him, and took the reed and began to beat Him on the head." (Matthew 27:29-30)

"Pilate addressed them once more, desiring to release Jesus; but they shouted out, 'Crucify him, crucify him!' A third time he said to them, 'Why? What evil has he done? I have found in him no crime deserving death; I will therefore chastise him and release him.' But they were urgent, demanding with loud cries that he should be crucified. And their voices prevailed." (Luke 23:20-23, RSV)

"Then Pilate took Jesus and scourged him. And the soldiers plated a crown of thorns, and put it on his head, and arrayed him in a purple robe, they came up to him, saying, 'Hail, King of the Jews!' and struck him with their hands." (John 19:1-3, RSV)

"But he was wounded for our transgressions; he was crushed for our iniquities; upon him was the chastisement that brought us peace, and with his stripes we are healed." (Isaiah 53:5, ESV)

The scourging included being tied to a post and beaten with rods to a prostrated Jesus. The intention was to inflict as much severe and excruciating pain as possible. Then the beating included a three pronged whip made of leather and tipped with bone and metal for the purpose of tearing the flesh and bringing as much agony as was bearable to any man. Most men died from the torture and the loss of blood. The Romans used the scourging as a general purpose for the indignity of slaves and men sentenced to death.[1] This was the initiation prior to a crucifixion. Pilate believed that the use of the scourging would bring the Jews satisfaction for he did not believe Jesus deserved being put to death. He was overruled by the anguish of the mob and eventually succumbed to their devilish desires.

"Yet it was the will of the Lord to bruise him; he has put him to grief; when he makes himself an offering for sin, he shall see his offspring, he shall prolong his days; the will of the Lord shall prosper in his hand; he shall see the fruit of the travail of his soul and be satisfied; by his knowledge shall the righteous one, my servant, make many to be accounted righteous; and he shall bear their iniquities." (Isaiah 53:10-11, RSV)

Jesus was in the will and the hands of the Lord. He was bruised, beaten, scourged, and torn for our transgressions. Our sin is that bad in the eyes of God. Take time to bow now in His Presence and remove from yourself the sinful thing from your midst. Repent and sin no more. Do not put Him to shame again in your life. Walk in newness and walk in freedom knowing that you do not have to sin anymore. Submit to Him; submit only to Him. Thank Jesus for what He did for you by living in Him now and forevermore. Amen!

December 17th

The Crucifixion

"And when they had come to a place called Golgotha, which means Place of the Skull, they gave Him wine to drink mingled with gall; and after tasting it, He was unwilling to drink. And when they crucified Him, they divided up His garments among themselves..."   (Matthew 27:33-35)

"The soldiers therefore, when they had crucified Jesus, took his outer garments and made four parts, a part to every soldier and also the tunic; now the tunic was seamless, woven in one piece. They said therefore to one another, 'Let us not tear it, but cast lots for it, to decide whose it shall be'; that the scripture might be fulfilled, 'They divided My outer garments among them, and for My clothing they cast lots.'" (John 19:23)

With the prophecy already given of what was to happen to the Messiah, who takes away the sins of the world, it leaves no doubt as to the world's response of a man tortured to die on a cross as they traded and gambled for His clothing.

The world is no different today. People continue on their journeys going about their business trading, buying, and selling. People give, take, barter, and work. Some are lazy and never work, while others run amuck in their lives with such busyness they make an ant look sluggish. Duties, distractions, opportunities, and desires loom in the moments capturing minds, hearts, and imaginations as butterflies in a net. This is the world as we have known it. People are busy, lame, destructive, constructive, hungry for more, and starving for attention. Some still are lazy and simply do not care about anything but waiting on their personal welfare to be taken care of by someone else or some government entity.

The physical realm as we know it is constantly moving as the world turns on its axis. The sun rises and sets yet another day and most people rush to their graves hardly giving a thought to the spiritual realm going on about them. Yes, we are spiritual beings inhabiting a physical body and it takes a spiritual person to recognize there is far more to our universe than our next meal or the clothes on our backs.

What was looming that day on Calvary was not just a man hung on a tree for anyone to see, there was something far greater in the spirit realm occurring and the dark forces had done their worst. Thank God in heaven, even the worst of the devil and his minions are never enough for the greatness of our God. He alone is most powerful and the power He exemplified that day was the power to lay His own life down in the form of a cross for the purpose of paying the price for the sin of the whole world. His purposes were being completed and the devil had performed his worst on the very best that God had to give, His only begotten Son.

We can live today in the new birth of Life because of Jesus' obedience to death on the cross. Do not neglect so great a sacrifice that was paid for you and me. Submit to Him today and live!

December 18th

Between Two Thieves

"At that time two robbers were crucified with Him, one on His right and one on the left." (Matthew 27:38)

"And one of the criminals who were hanged there was hurling abuse at Him, saying, 'Are You not the Christ? Save Yourself and us!' But the other answered, and rebuking him said, 'Do you not even fear God, since you are under the same sentence of condemnation? And we indeed justly, for we are receiving what we deserve for our deeds; but this man has done nothing wrong.' And he was saying, 'Jesus, remember me when You come in Your kingdom!' And He said to him, 'Truly I say to you, today you shall be with Me in Paradise.'" (Luke 23:39-43)

If we look closely at the two thieves we see there is a world of difference in their spirits as is revealed in their attitudes on the cross. They were both thieves, yet their spirits were different in how they viewed Jesus as the Son of God. The one thief feared God. He had a conscience that spoke to him of his wrongness. The other thief did not. He understood that he was a condemned sinner and understood that he was receiving his just reward. He understood that Jesus had done no wrong and was suffering unjustly. He believed Jesus was who men said that He was; a King with a kingdom, and a spiritual King at that. The other thief had no clue for he was not under any conviction by the Holy Spirit.

This thief confessed his sin publicly and when he said, 'remember me when You come into Your kingdom,' it was the audible recognition of the heart being transformed by a Holy God. He had turned his eyes on Jesus and Jesus turned His eyes on him and declared, 'Assuredly, I say to you, today you will be with me in Paradise.' Jesus recognized conscious confession and repentance. Jesus recognized the fear of God and the just condemnation of sin before God.
The thief had:
a)   Acknowledged God.
b)   Confessed the fear of God.
c)   Confessed his own sin and just condemnation for his sin.

d) He acknowledged the justness and rightness of Jesus. He saw Him as blameless.

e) He confessed his belief in Jesus as a King with a spiritual kingdom.

f) He had submitted to Jesus with a humble heart. This submission is the reflective act of repentance and when Jesus recognized his spirit, He gave him entrance into the Kingdom.

g) The concurrent action of a Holy Jesus and a penitent sinner is the spiritual act of conversion and proves that this event can take place in a manner of minutes, but it must take place with the Holy Spirit present with a penitent sinner. The Holy Spirit does the convicting, the converting, and the comforting. The penitent thief did more than simply 'believe'; it was what he believed and how he openly submitted with his dying breath in Spiritual knowledge given by the Holy Spirit as to who Jesus was, the King of the Kingdom of God. All of this must take place in regeneration.

Father, help us to be willing to know and understand Your Truth.

December 19th

My God, My God

"Now from the sixth hour darkness fell upon all the land until the ninth hour. And about the ninth hour Jesus cried out with a loud voice, saying, 'Eli, Eli, lama sabacthani?' that is, 'My God, My God, why hast Thou forsaken Me?'"
(Matthew 27:45-46)

From twelve o'clock noon until three o'clock in the afternoon, darkness fell upon the land that day. It is unknown if darkness fell upon the whole earth during that time, but what we will concern ourselves with is what the Word says. The darkness that fell for those three hours while Jesus was suffering and dying with the sin of the world upon Him exemplified the darkness of sin upon the earth and how it had to be dealt with and that was with the spotless, blood sacrifice of Jesus Christ.

John the Baptist saw Him as, 'The Lamb of God who takes away the sins of the world.' (John 1:29) It was during this darkness that it is said He took the suffering and the sin of the world upon Himself. "Namely, that God was in Christ reconciling the world to Himself, not counting their trespasses against them, and He has committed to us the word of reconciliation…He made Him who knew no sin to be sin on our behalf, that we might become the righteousness of God." (2 Cor. 5:19, 21) "…knowing this, that our old self was crucified with Him, that our body of sin might be done away with , that we should no longer be slaves to sin; for he who has died is freed from sin." (Romans 6:6-7)

You see, there were three men who were crucified that day, but the two thieves bore only their physical death on their cross. Jesus, our Messiah, delivered us by bearing the sin of the world and our death to sin upon Him while He was dying a physical death on the cross. In this, in the darkest moments there, at about three o'clock in the afternoon, He cries out, 'My God, My God, why have you forsaken Me?' (Psalm 22:1) The Lord laid on Him the iniquity of us all. (Isaiah 53:6) He experienced the abandonment of God on our behalf. The Holy Presence of God was not present.

Our minds cannot fathom what He did for us that day on the cross. The Holy Spirit, in time, touches our hearts in quiet observation and reveals what we are able to comprehend. It is one thing to hear someone say, 'He takes away our sin and the penalty for it.' And it is an entirely different level of being to be given a spiritual inkling of what that really means.

The depths of your soul are changed into everlasting gratitude and forgiveness for you have been forgiven of all your sin and need to be with Him as a result. We do not understand holy love either until we are touched by the Holy Spirit divine. He made this possible by His death; a vicious, cruel, horrendous physical death and taking our sin upon Him in the spirit to pay the death penalty for us.

December 20th

It is Finished

"And Jesus cried out again with a loud voice, and yielded up His spirit." (Matthew 27:50)

"When Jesus therefore had received the sour wine, He said, 'It is finished!' And He bowed His head, and gave up His spirit." (John 19:30)

My life is poured out like water, and all my bones are out of joint.
My heart is like wax, melting within me.
My strength is dried up like sun baked clay
My tongue sticks to the roof of my mouth.
You have laid me in the dust and left me for dead.
My enemies surround me like a pack of dogs;
An evil gang closes in on me.
They have pierced my hands and feet.
I can count all my bones.
My enemies stare at me and gloat.
They divide my garments among themselves
And throw dice for my clothing.
      (Psalm 22:14-18, NLT)

When Jesus had suffered His final suffering, His last words were, 'It is finished.' His purpose of coming to the earth to die for the sins of the world had been accomplished. As horrible as His death was on that cross, it became a gateway for us into eternal life. He paid that price with His blood. He paved the way for us because He was the Way, the Truth, and the Life and no man gets to the Father except through Him.

It is finished means all is completed. He conquered sin, death, hell, and the grave. He paid the penalty for all our sins, past, present, and future because He paid for all sin for all time. That is the marvelous work He accomplished that day…the destruction of the power of sin. His marvelous grace is so wonderful, so powerful, and so magnificent, that when He said, 'It is finished!' we can catch a glimpse of understanding of just how marvelous His grace is.

His grace is greater than all our sin. His love covers a multitude of sin. His love covers all and by covering all, that is all who live in Him and remain in Him forever. It is for those who are chosen by Him to believe that in believing we receive this marvelous work unto ourselves.

He has done the work, now it is up to us to abide and remain in Him and allow Him to live His wonderful life-giving life through us to a world that needs to hear about His Kingdom of love, grace, and mercy. Give God praise! Give God Thanks! Give God honor by honoring Him in His holy love.

December 21st

Kindness and Honor

"And when it was evening, there came a rich man from Arimathea, named Joseph, who himself had also become a disciple of Jesus." (Matthew 27:57)

It is amazing to me that no matter how some people are treated, there are still those who know how to treat people with kindness, honor, and respect. These traits are traits of those who have it in them. It can be taught, but it is mostly nature. The nature to be compassionate and kind is not in many people. It takes a kind nature to see needs in other people and have not only a desire to help, but be gifted with the ability to help. The ability to treat all people with honor and respect whether they deserve it, or not, is not in most people, but in the ones that it is in, it is what makes life bearable for the ones needing the most kindness offered.

I have seen some men be kind and considerate to others, but secretly seek a monetary reward for their 'services'. These men seek 'gifts in kind', that when they display a needed kindness to you, they need that reciprocated by loyalty, allegiance, monetary gain, or power over you somehow, someway. They want the 'payback'. That is not kindness, nor do they understand benevolence. That type of behavior is ultimately a type of malevolence where the intent of the kindness offered is for personal gain and not for the benefit of the needy person. Men of renown consider real kindness and respect as weak which is where a real disciple will find his persecution.

Not so with this Joseph of Arimathea. He was "a prominent member of the Council, who himself was waiting for the kingdom of God; and he gathered up courage and went in before Pilate, and asked for the body of Jesus…and Joseph brought linen cloth, took Him down, wrapped Him in the linen cloth, and laid Him in a tomb which had been hewn out in the rock; and he rolled a stone against the entrance of the tomb." (Mark 15:43, 46)

Joseph of Arimathea treated the body of Jesus with the utmost of respect, honor, and dignity. And, he expected no payback for his behavior. His testimony is in all four Gospels. He was a disciple of Jesus Christ who believed in Jesus and trusted in His words. He had in him the nature that God had placed inside of him and that was to treat Jesus with the most dignity he was able to do. After Jesus' resurrection, that tomb that had been given for Jesus' rest was never used again.

Why do you do what you do? What is in you in the deepest crevices of your heart that motivates you to do what you do when it comes to helping another person? The Holy Spirit knows for certain, even though you may not know at times, and, at times, you deceive even yourself. Measure the outflow by the subsequent desire. Get to the point that when you are called on to be kind, honorable, and compassionate that there is ne'er no inkling of the desire for reciprocation, in this life or beyond.

December 22nd

He Is Risen

"And behold, a severe earthquake had occurred, for an angel of the Lord had descended from heaven and came and rolled away the stone and sat upon it."
(Matthew 28:2)

There are two perspectives given in chapter 28 about this particular event in time. The first is the Truth and the other was the religious cover-up. The first perspective is the Truth and not a perspective at all. Truth is. Truth is one; all other perspectives are mis-truths and are not truth at all. What happened that morning is that a severe earthquake occurred at the behest of our Father in heaven. An angel of the Lord rolled the stone away and sat upon it. This sequence of events frightened the guards so severely that they ran to the chief priests to tell them what they believed had happened. The subsequent meeting that takes place with the soldiers, the chief priests and the assembly of elders results in a bribe, a payoff, and a web of lies in order to perpetuate their version of the events to protect their image and create doubt among any who might believe the Truth. As was typical in the events of Jesus Christ, for every Holy Spirit act, there was an opposite reaction by the evil one to contradict the Truth. It was always the religious rulers that were used as the conduit for the evil one's implementation of his destructive, distracting, and debilitating propaganda.

In this event, the angel of the Lord speaks to Mary Magdalene and the other Mary, the mother of James (Jacob) and Joses, the wife of Cleophas, and Salome, the mother of James and John. (Mark 16:1-8) The angel's appearance was like lightning and his garments as white as snow to the guards, but to the women he was in the form of a young man (Mark). He tells the women, "Do not be afraid; for I know that you are looking for Jesus who has been crucified. He is not here, for He is risen, just as He said. Come, see the place where He was lying. And go quickly and tell His disciples that He has risen from the dead; and, behold, He is going before you into Galilee, there you will see Him…" (Matthew 28:5-7)

Jesus, the Christ, has done just as He said. All that He had said about Himself regarding the road to Jerusalem of being betrayed, beaten, scourged, crucified, and resurrected was all true and it has come to pass just as He said. He is still risen. That is the glory of God in the testimony of the believer. This faith fact you either believe, or you don't. It is the work of the Holy Spirit now to convict the world of sin, of judgment, and of righteousness. It is the Holy Spirit that draws men unto Himself. Our responsibility in all of this is to allow Him to speak through us these faith facts that as we believe, He speaks through us to a lost and dying world that desperately needs Him. He has risen from the grave and He dwells within the hearts and lives of every true disciple of Christ Jesus. It is His Kingdom that has come by the preaching of Him into the hearts of men and men and women everywhere who hear His call by His Spirit. We are brought into His Kingdom Light by that same power of the Holy One of God, Christ Jesus who reigns forever. Shout hallelujah!

December 23rd

Seeing the Resurrection

"Then Jesus said to them, 'Do not be afraid; go and take word to My brethren to leave for Galilee, and there they shall see Me.'"   (Matthew 28:10)

If seeing is believing, then what of the myriads of peoples throughout time who have believed without seeing? It is one thing to see the resurrection first hand and believe, but as the disciples proved themselves, they didn't believe until they saw Him in His resurrected state for themselves. Mark 16:9-14, gives Marks perspective on the disciples that even when Jesus appeared to Mary Magadalene and subsequently reported to the disciples of His appearance, they didn't believe her. Neither did they believe the two disciples that walked along the roadside with Jesus. The eleven disciples didn't believe until they saw Him face to face with Thomas having to literally touch Him in order to believe. (John 20:24-29) Jesus responded to Thomas, "Have you believed because you have seen me? Blessed are those who have not seen and yet believe."

This presents our present predicament. In order for us to further the Gospel, we have to tell the whole story in order for people to really believe wholly and truly. There are those evangelists and preachers who give a shortened synopsis of Jesus and then offer an eight second prayer and say, 'Believe!' My question to that is, "Believe what? Believe the Christ story in the Kingdom of God, or believe the preacher man when he hasn't even faithfully told the Gospel?"

Again, it is easy for us to look in hindsight and reprove the disciples for their unbelief, but that reproof would be unwarranted and judgmental. The only One who had the right to reprove the disciples was Jesus and He did so. Their testimony isn't there for us to judge them for unbelief for they eventually did believe. Their testimony is there to prove that it is not an easy task to believe this Christ story and it takes a power greater than ourselves for us to truly believe in the resurrection. No man can make another man believe. That is the work of the Holy Spirit. The Holy Spirit works through the preaching and testifying of the Gospel of Jesus Christ; He works through us to speak the real Truth in conviction of sin, judgment, and righteousness. The Holy Spirit does the work of faith and the giving and growing of faith. This is beyond any man's work or abilities.

Our responsibility is to be the epistle written for others to read. Other people who do not know Jesus Christ and His Gospel of the Kingdom need to receive a testimony that is God-breathed. Our lives are that testimony. The words of our testimony allow the fruit of the Holy Spirit to speak to the hearts of people who are available to listen, really hear, and believe in Him…not in us.

His Gospel is not about us, but is all about Him. People need to see the resurrection in us, because we are resurrected into new life in Him. The new birth is the seeing and the believing. Faithfulness to His heart and nature is the key. Otherwise, what people will see is hypocrisy and a lack of consistency to what they think is Holy. We are made righteous because He is righteous. We are made holy because He is Holy, not because of anything that we could ever do. The moment we start doing the work for Him is the moment the consistency of His Spirit lies waiting for us to submit onces again. Dwell in Him and let Him do His work in you and through you and the work of His resurrection will be seen in your very life.

December 24th

Back in the Boat

"After these things Jesus manifested Himself again to the disciples at the Sea of Tiberias, and He manifested Himself in this way."   (John 21:1)

Christ Jesus manifested in His resurrected body on numerous occasions. We have spoken of a few occasions of His appearances and here in John 21, He appears to the disciples on the shore of the Sea of Tiberias after they had spent all night fishing and, once again, have caught nothing.

Luke chapter 5, tells the story of how Jesus got into one the boats to present His Gospel to the people standing on the shore. After the verbal teaching, He implores the disciples to go out further into the deep. It is here that Jesus was illustrating to them what He had been teaching. He wanted to get into their boat, their work, into them, into what they saw themselves as…fishermen; but, the point was that He wanted to get 'into' them in order for His purposes to come to pass in them. He was saying, "You are your boat, your body, your life, your hands, your mind… now let Me have My way with all of that and trust Me to take you out into the deep where the big fish are."

It takes a bigger boat to go into the deeps; a bigger boat is a bigger faith; a bigger faith is a deeper possession of Jesus, a trust of Him that He is in you and is with you. The deeper the possession He has in you is where He speaks and uses your boat, your life, for His purposes for the more or the bigger.

Another episode of Jesus in the boat is in Luke 8:22-25. Again, Jesus' desire is to be in the boat and He asks them in the midst of the storm, "Where is your faith?" The answer was asking the question. He is our faith. He desires to be in us, in our boat, where He is the constant, the Master and Commander. In Him, there is no fear!

This brings us to John 21, where, again, the disciples have gotten back into 'their boat', which is really Jesus' boat, but when they get back into it alone, they fish all night, again, catching nothing. The resurrected Jesus is on the shore and tells them to 'cast the net on the right side, and you will find some. So, they cast it, and now they were not able to haul it in, for the quantity of fish. That disciple whom Jesus loved said to Peter, 'It is the Lord!'" (John 21:6b-7a, RSV)

Again and again, Jesus is teaching His disciples of the power that dwells in Him and would soon dwell in them in the form of the Holy Spirit. It is the infilling of the Holy Spirit into our lives where Jesus abides in Spirit and in Truth. The same Jesus that wanted to get into their boat to show them the way, The Way, is still waiting on the shore of your life, saying, 'Let Me into your boat!' He isn't just a better way; He is The Way into life, and into being fishers of men. He will draw men unto Himself in us by being in our boat. It is here that we get to dine with Him with the fish that He catches; the everlasting life of Him. There's nothing like dining with Jesus. He is here waiting on you to eat with Him in His Kingdom. Come and eat!

December 25th

Follow Me!

"Peter therefore seeing him said to Jesus, 'Lord, and what about this man?' Jesus said to him, If I want him to remain until I come, what is that to you? You follow Me!'" (John 21:21-22)

It seems that in the whole of life, people tend to constantly compare their walks, their finances, their families, homes, cars, and jobs with other people and their possessions. In our self-indulgences, we compare ourselves with others in order to maintain appearances, get ahead of the neighbor, get ahead of ourselves, or get ahead of God. Comparing what we have been given or our specific purpose in life primarily leads to deprivation of the Spirit because we are no longer looking to Him with our focus on Him, but on our fellow man or his things. Is it possible to not compare ourselves with others as long as we live on this earth? If it is possible, how is it accomplished?

As always, every problem that we have ultimately is a spiritual problem. Every question that we have eventually leads us to deeper and more profound questions that ultimately end in Jesus Christ. He is the author and finisher of our faith. He is our Lord Creator. There is no thing that He does not know. In this, the answer to the question of 'is it possible to not compare ourselves with others' is found in Christ Jesus. Focus the faith that He has given you and just as He told Peter, 'You, you follow Me!' Focus your faith in Jesus and follow Him and no one else.

We can be taught by others for certain, but no man should ever take the place of the Father in your life. There is only One who is good. There is only One who is Father. There is only One who leads us to the Father, one way, one gate, one narrow way, one door, and only one cross of the truth in Jesus Christ.

"Let this mind be in you, which was in Christ Jesus: Who, being in the form of God, thought it not robbery to be equal with God: but made Himself of no reputation, and took upon Him the form of a servant, and was made in the likeness of men: and being found in fashion as a man, he humbled himself, and became obedient unto death, even the death of the cross." (Phil. 2:5-8, KJV) Jesus told Peter, "You, you follow Me!"

In submission to Him, allow Him to live His life through you. Then, the things of this world and the people with all their shortcomings will not matter in the Light of His grace. You will be able to see others, and not their things, as Christ Jesus sees them for you will be seeing with spiritual eyes. See Jesus and focus the faith He has given you on Him.

The spiritual world of the Kingdom of God is far more than you could ever imagine. In Him, you move and have your being. Remain in Him and the following will take your breath away as you go through Bethlehem to Calvary and beyond. *Merry Christmas!*

December 26th

The Kingdom of God Continues

"To these He also presented Himself alive, after His suffering, by many convincing proofs, appearing to them over a period of forty days, and speaking of the things concerning the kingdom of God." (Acts 1:3)

All that Jesus taught was not fully written in the annals of the Gospels, just as John says, "And there are also many other things which Jesus did, which if they were written in detail, I suppose that even the world itself would not contain the books which were written." (John 21:25) So, when Luke writes in the book of the Acts of the Apostles, he states that Jesus continued "speaking of the things concerning the kingdom of God." Not all that He said is recorded, but what we do have, we have what we need in order to understand the spiritual Kingdom of God.

He tells them to wait in Jerusalem together for what the Father had promised. "… for John baptized with water, but you shall be baptized with the Holy Spirit not many days from now." (v.5) But the disciples, who could not help themselves from thinking in the natural realm, asked Him, "Lord, is it at this time You are restoring the kingdom to Israel?" (v.6) Jesus responds firmly in the midst of their lack of discernment of spiritual things and says, "It is not for you to know times or epochs which the Father has fixed by His own authority." (v.7) These times and epochs 'in time' are the things of the natural, the things that will take place in time, but do not have to do with the spiritual kingdom of God. "But you shall receive power when the Holy Spirit has come upon you; and you shall be My witnesses…" (v. 8a) The spiritual kingdom of God is furthered in this time frame by the introduction of the Holy Spirit Who will baptize them and us into Him. This took place in the upper room days later, "And they were all filled with the Holy Spirit and began to speak with other tongues, as the Spirit was giving them utterance." (Acts 2:4)

Subsequently, Peter preaches to the multitudes that day and quotes the prophet Joel, "'And it shall be in the last days,' God says, 'that I will pour forth of My Spirit upon all mankind; and your sons and your daughters shall prophesy.'" (Acts 2:17; Joel 2:28, 32)

This is how the Kingdom of God is exponentially expanded in just a matter of two different moments in time. The coming of the Holy Spirit to the 120 disciples in the upper room and the subsequent preaching of the Gospel to the masses resulted in over 3000 souls receiving the gift of the Holy Spirit that day. (Acts 2:37-41)

The baptism that Jesus talked about was the baptism of the Holy Spirit. When we are baptized of His Holy Spirit, we are simultaneously regenerated into the new birth. He comes into us and we go into Him; just like the full immersion into water and yet even that picture doesn't do justice to the baptism of the Holy Spirit because we are baptized into Him and He is indwelling in us…at the same time. This is regeneration. This is the new birth, being born again in His Spirit, the mystery of the Gospel, the Christ in you, the hope of glory. (Colossians 1:27) This is the place and person of the Kingdom of God, Jesus Christ.

December 27th

His Command

"And Jesus came up and spoke to them, saying, 'All authority has been given to Me in heaven and on earth. Go therefore and make disciples of all the nations, baptizing them in the name of the Father, and the Son and the Holy Spirit, teaching them to observe all that I commanded you; and, lo, I am with you always, even to the end of the age." (Matthew 28:18-20)

This verse, perhaps, has been the most misunderstood of the directives of Jesus Christ. Depending on how one might interpret religion in general and the Gospel of Jesus Christ, specifically, this verse has become the launching point of many a false doctrine and millions upon millions of deaths in the crusades of the middle ages. If men perceive that the kingdom of God is a natural phenomenon on the earth where men are to take over land, nations, and peoples, then one would easily presume that the Gospel demands that that command be carried out in the natural realm by armies and scores of armies. However, that was never Christ Jesus' intent, but was the very doctrine He preached against. He stated explicitly that His Kingdom was not of this world. His Kingdom is a Holy Spirit kingdom of God that dwells within the hearts of people.

According to Jesus' Gospel, which was and still is the Kingdom of God, the charge for His disciples was as they went into the world, they were to make disciples. The Holy Spirit is the One who leads men unto conviction of sin, not men. The Holy Spirit is the One who leads men into judgment, not men. Men are to present the

Gospel of Jesus Christ and when He is lifted up, He draws men unto Himself. The religious structure and system since it was created by men has, for the most part, drawn men to themselves out of greed, ignorance, false doctrine and error filled teachings. Manipulative ploys, coercive influences, money driven evangelism, and power driven abusers have attempted to control the Gospel through religion for the last two thousand years. Jesus did not tell His disciples to go and 'save' people. That is His work that He accomplished on the cross. Our work is to pray and allow His Spirit to move about in the earth through us. Men do not and cannot save other men.

Making a disciple is teaching them all the things that Jesus talked about, which is the Kingdom of God. If a disciple is not teaching about the Kingdom of God, they are not making disciples of Jesus Christ, but disciples of religious exercise, works, and a myriad of other cultic maladies that have plagued man for almost two thousand years. The religious spirit is the anti-christ spirit, the substitute for the real thing.

This is the time of the Kingdom of God. These writings have been a treatise, of sort, to propel an understanding into Jesus' Gospel of the Kingdom. It was His message and it still is. Blood atonement, grace, the cross, holy love, and mercy are all a part of the Kingdom of God Gospel, but, alone to stand they cannot. Together, united and entwined in His Holy Spirit, they are the revelation of the Gospel. This is and always has been His work. We are blessed to have our names written in the Lamb's book of Life and our names only get there by His work and His work alone. He is that great that He can do that. It is a joy to be a part of His Kingdom work and a joy that will last forever. Amen!

December 28th

Paul Preached the Kingdom of God

"And he stayed two full years in his own rented quarters, and was welcoming all who came to him, preaching the kingdom of God, and teaching concerning the Lord Jesus Christ with all openness, unhindered." (Acts 28:30-31)

I find it amazing at how men have taught their own versions of the gospel and called it The Gospel. Traditional church thought, for more than a thousand years now, has taught that the kingdom of God is eschatological; it is something that it is to come in the end of time and for the future of heaven. That is not what Jesus taught. "But if I cast out demons by the Spirit of God, then the kingdom of God has come upon you." (Matthew 12:28) Over and over again, John the Baptist's message and Jesus' message was the same, "Repent, for the kingdom of God is at hand." Jesus explicitly stated that the kingdom of God does not come with observation, but is within you. Paul preached the same message of the kingdom of God. The Word of God says so.

There isn't another Gospel other than the Kingdom of God. There are other false teachings and interpretations such as saying that the gospel is 'Jesus Christ and Him crucified', but that is only a part of the whole Gospel, not the Gospel itself. And, this is not just semantics, as one might say, "Well, you're just saying it differently than what I'm saying and we're both right." Not true! To preach a facet of the Word and say that what you say is totality is to say an incomplete truth. Anything short of the whole Truth is a lie and is no truth. There is no such thing as a 'half-truth'. What people have been hearing is an incomplete gospel. There are those who preach the whole Gospel, but, by far the majority of the mainline churches for centuries have presented portions of the gospel and it has led to many a sin and a downfall.

This is a correction and rebuke to those, who for centuries have preached their convenient truths to the masses of peoples and have led in error what the True Gospel actually is. The Gospel of Jesus Christ is the Kingdom of God and is the only gospel with the promise that when it is preached to the ends of the earth, then the end will come.

"And this gospel of the kingdom shall be preached in the whole world for a witness to all the nations, and then the end shall come." (Matthew 24:14)

"For as in Adam all die, so also in Christ all shall be made alive. But each in his own order: Christ the first fruits, after that those who are Christ's at His coming, then comes the end, when He delivers up the kingdom to the God and Father, when He has abolished all rule and authority and power." (1 Corinthians 15:22-24)

Those who are 'in Christ" are in the kingdom. The kingdom of God is here and now and we are the first fruits. He will present His kingdom, we who dwell in Him, to the God and Father at the end. Believe 'in' Him. Remain 'in' Him. Rest 'in' Him.

December 29th

The Spiritual Kingdom

"Now I say this, brethren, that flesh and blood cannot inherit the kingdom of God; nor does the perishable inherit the imperishable." (1 Corinthians 15:50)

The Kingdom of God is a spiritual kingdom. It is not made of flesh and blood, nor is it a place on earth as some men have thought to be the holy city of Jerusalem. Jesus' kingdom has always been a spiritual kingdom and is received as a spiritual kingdom. Just as in Matthew 16:17, when Jesus said to Peter, "…Blessed are you Simon, Barjona, because flesh and blood did not reveal this to you, but My Father who is in heaven….I will give you the keys of the kingdom of heaven; and whatever you bind on earth shall be bound in heaven, and whatever you loose on earth shall be loosed in heaven." (v.19) The Kingdom is given as a spiritual domain and the idea of it is only given by our spiritual heavenly Father. Man did not conjure up the Kingdom, nor can he comprehend it without the revelation of the Father revealing it to him. Flesh and blood, man's thoughts, deeds, and works cannot create the Kingdom in himself or in any other man. It is a gift from God and that, a spiritual gift indeed.

The fact that the 'keys to the kingdom of heaven' were given to Peter in the spiritual binding and loosing on earth meant that whatever the Kingdom was in them in the earth, it was in heaven, because it is purely spiritual in the heart of man. The Holy Spirit is our connection in this spiritual kingdom. You cannot buy, barter, trade, or sell the Kingdom of God. It is only given by the Spirit of God and only understood with His revelation. It is His work and His choice to give to whom He gives. Flesh and blood corrupts everything it touches and has no inheritance in the Kingdom of God.

Just as the Spirit of God dwells in us now for those who name the name of Jesus Christ, so is the conviction, judgment, and righteousness abiding in us only by the power of His Holy Spirit. We have no righteousness of our own. Even the best of us is as filthy rags according to God. Our bodies will all die and then the corruptible will put on the incorruptible which is totally wholly spiritual. The seed of that which dwells within us is the incorruptible seed, the seed of righteousness that is the Holy Spirit of God in faith. We cannot corrupt Him dwelling within us because we have been born again of His Spirit and the power of His Spirit is greater in you than the spirit of the world.

It is in this that the eternal life is not just for eternity, but is in us for here and now. What you say is eternal life is also the Kingdom of God. He is His life; He is His Kingdom.

"The saying is trustworthy, for if we have died with him, we shall also live with him; if we endure, we will also reign with him; if we deny him, he will also deny us; if we are faithless, he remains faithful for he cannot deny himself."
(2 Timothy 2:11-13, ESV)

December 30th

Delivered into His Kingdom

"For He delivered us from the domain of darkness, and transferred us to the kingdom of His beloved Son, in whom we have redemption, the forgiveness of sins."   (Colossians 1:13-14)

Praise the Lord and bless His holy Name! He did for us what we could not do ourselves. He delivered us from the dark domain and brought us into His glorious light, the Light of His Son and His kingdom, the Kingdom of God. It is in Him that we have the forgiveness of sins. It is in Him we have redemption, the payment for our sins being made and paid for by His blood. If we live in Him, we abide in Him…we are partakers in His kingdom, the kingdom of grace.

Note that it was He who did the work and there is nothing that we could ever do to deserve His grace. He delivered us from sin and the domain, the dwelling place of darkness and transferred us to the kingdom of His Son where we dwell and remain in Him. This is the 'hallelujah' place, the place of rejoicing, the place of deliverance, and the place of eternal peace. He who is our peace allows us to abide in Him. That fact should put a great smile on your face and help you to breathe easier and rest in His Presence.

He wants you to rest in Him through faithfully trusting in Him. His Kingdom is the most wonderful place to be. It is the place where Paul was able to say, "Not that I am speaking of being in need, for I have learned in whatever situation I am to be content. I know how to be brought low and I know how to abound. In any and every circumstance, I have learned the secret of facing plenty and hunger, abundance and need. I can do all things through him who strengthens me." (Philippians 4:11-12, ESV)

This spiritual transference is accomplished because of what He did for us on the cross. But what He did for us on the cross is just the beginning of this new life in Him. He is the Deliverer, the Redeemer, and the Transferrer. He transfers us into Himself at the point of regeneration as we are baptized into His Holy Spirit. His

Holy Spirit gets into us as we receive Him and He receives us. It is simultaneous transference from one spiritual domain to another. "Therefore consider the members of your body as dead to immorality, impurity, passion, evil desire, and greed, which amounts to idolatry…put aside: anger, wrath, malice, slander, and abusive speech from your mouth. Do not lie to one another, since you laid aside the old self with its evil practices, and have put on the new self who is being renewed to a true knowledge according to the image of the One who created him – a renewal in which there is not distinction between Greek and Jew, circumcised and uncircumcised, barbarian, Scythian, slave and freeman, but Christ is all, and in all." (Colossians 3:5, 8-11)

If you have been born of His Spirit, walk in His Spirit and allow His Holy Spirit's power to rule and reign in you and you will not fulfill the desires of the flesh. Amen and Amen!

December 31st

Christ in You, the Hope of Glory

"…that I might carry out the preaching of the word of God, that is, the mystery which has been hidden from the past ages and generations; but has now been manifested to His saints, to whom God willed to make known what is the riches of the glory of this mystery among the Gentiles, which is Christ in you, the hope of glory." (Colossians 1:25b-27)

The tremendous blessing of Jesus Christ is Himself. It's not a vague promise nor is it a financial proposition. The blessing of Jesus Christ is the joy of Him being in you! Happy are you when whatever happens to you on account of Him. The Holy Lord is in our midst and even now speaking in the still, small voice saying, "Come, follow Me!" He is with me now, this I know, for His word has become evident. The rough places have been made plain. The crooked paths have been made straight. For some, this is still an untold story, but for you and for me, He has become the mystery of the ages dwelling in all the fullness of the Godhead, He is the Christ in you, the hope of glory.

"Now we see things imperfectly, like puzzling reflections in a mirror, but then we will see everything with perfect clarity. All that I know now is partial and incomplete, but then I will know everything completely, just as God knows me completely." (1 Cor. 13:12, NLT)

We cannot pretend to understand His mysteries, particularly all that there is to know of the Kingdom of God. What we know we have been given to know only by His Spirit. He is the gospel revelation and anything that we come to know will be revealed to us in His time and in accordance to our belief and our obedience. He will not reveal beyond your obedience. He will not reveal beyond the holy love within you. Men of all intelligence and educational statuses can attain all knowledge within the book, but the revelation of His Spirit only comes from Him.

He is His Spirit. He is His Holy Love. He is the indwelling One, the Redeemer, the Messiah, and the Prince of Peace. He is the Author and Finisher of our faith and in Him we move and have our being. In Him, there is life and that more abundantly. In Him, there is faith, hope, and love.

"These things I have written to you who believe in the name of the Son of God, in order that you may know that you have eternal life. And this is the confidence which we have before Him, that if we ask anything according to His will, He hears us. And if we know that He hears us in whatever we ask, we know that we have the requests which we have asked from Him...we know that no one who is born of God sins; but He who was born of God keeps him and the evil one does not touch him. We know that we are of God, and the whole world lies in the power of the evil one. And we know that the Son of God has come, and has given us understanding, in order that we might know Him who is true, and we are in Him who is true, in His Son Jesus Christ. This is the true God and eternal life."
(1 John 5:13-15, 18-20)

Amen.

Bible Translations

New Living Translation (Wheaton, Illinois: Tyndale House Publishers, Inc., 1996)
The English-Greek Reverse Interlinear New Testament, English Standard Version (Wheaton, Illinois: Crossway Books, 2006)
The Guideposts Parallel Bible, The King James Version, The New International Version, The Living Bible, The Revised Standard Version (Carmel, New York: Guideposts, 1981)
The Interlinear Greek-English New Testament, King James Version (New York: The Iverson-Norman Associates, 1975)
The New American Standard Bible (Nashville, Tennessee: Holman Bible Publishers, 1985)
The New King James Version (Nashville, Tennessee: Thomas Nelson Publishers, 1982)
The New Testament An Expanded Translation by Kenneth S. Wuest (Grand Rapids, Michigan: William B. Eerdmans Publishing Company, 1989)

General Bibliography For Reference and Further Reading

Aland, Kurt, ed., *Synopsis of the Four Gospels* (USA: United Bible Societies, 1982)
Bonhoeffer, Dietrich, *The Cost of Discipleship* (Scribner Paper Fiction, 1963)
Bonhoeffer, Dietrich, *A Testament To Freedom* (New York, New York: Harper Collins Publishers, 1995)
Chambers, Oswald, *The Complete Works of Oswald Chambers* (Grand Rapids, Michigan: Discovery House Publishers, 2000)
Henry, Matthew *Concise Commentary on the Whole Bible* (Chicago, Ill.: Moody Press, 1983)
Latourette, Kenneth Scott, *A History of Christianity* (New York: Harper & Brothers, 1953)
Selby, Donald J., *Introduction to the New Testament* (New York: Macmillan Publishing Company, Inc., 1971)
Strong, James, S.T.D., L.T.D., *The Exhaustive Concordance of the Bible Authorized and Revised Versions* (Nashville, New York: Abingdon Press, 1975)
Tenney, Merrill C., General ed., *Pictorial Bible Dictionary* © 1975, Zondervan Publishing, www.zondervan.com
Tolstoy, Leo, *The Gospel in Brief The Life of Jesus* (New York: Harper Perennial, 2011)
Tolstoy, Leo, *The Kingdom of God is Within You* (Wildside Press, LLC: 2006, written in 1893)
Webster's New Collegiate Dictionary (Springfield, Mass.: G.& C. Merriam Company, 1974)
Wuest, Kenneth S., *Word Studies in the Greek New Testament Vols. I-III* (Grand Rapids, Michigan: William B. Eerdman's Publishing Company, 1989)
Zodhiates, Spiros, Th.D., *The Complete Word Study New Testament King James Version* (Chattanooga, Tennessee, 1992)

NOTES and REFERENCES

Preface
[1]Taken from *The Complete Works of Oswald Chambers* © 2000 by the Oswald Chambers Publications Assn., Ltd. Used by permission of Discovery House Publishers, Grand Rapids, MI 49501. All rights reserved, p. 27.
January 12th
Dietrich Bonhoeffer, A Testament to Freedom, The Essential Writings of Dietrich Bonhoeffer (New York, New York: Harper Collins Publishers) p. 308.
January 13th
Dietrich Bonhoeffer, p. 313.
March 31st
Oswald Chambers, p. 605.
April 6th
Oswald Chambers, p. 106.
April 15th
Leo Tolstoy, The Kingdom of God is Within You (Wildside Press: www.wildsidepress.com, 2006), p. 10.
May 11th
Oswald Chambers, p. 793.
May 12th
Oswald Chambers, p. 177.
June 22
James Strong, The Exhaustive Concordance of the Bible Authorized and Revised Versions (Nashville, New York: Abingdon Press, 1975) The Greek Dictionary of the N.T., p. 29.
August 7th
Oswald Chambers, p. 386.
August 16th
Kenneth S. Wuest, Word Studies in the Greek New Testament Vol. I (Grand Rapids: William B. Eerdman's Publishing Company, 1989), p.85.
August 19th
Taken from *The Zondervan Pictorial Bible Dictionary* by Merrill C. Tenney, General Ed. © 1975 by Zondervan Publishing. Use by permission of Zondervan. www.zondervan.com p. 668.
Ibid., p. 669.
August 24th
Donald J. Selby, Introduction to the New Testament (New York: Macmillan Publishing Company, Inc., 1971) p. 90.
September 5th
"Stadia" The New American Standard Bible (Nashville: Holman Bible Publishers, 1985) Commentary Notes, p. 849.
September 23rd
Oswald Chambers, p. 220.
October 2nd
Merrill C. Tenney, p. 846.
October 6th
Merrill C. Tenney, p. 553.
October 9th
Spiros Zodhiates, ed., The Complete Word Study New Testament King James Version (Chattanooga: AMG International, 1992) p. 65.

October 18th
Merrill C. Tenney, p. 554.
October 19th
Ibid., p. 554.
October 21st
Spiros Zodhiates, pp. 68-69.
October 24th
Oswald Chambers, p. 547.
November 3rd
Merrill C. Tenney[1,2,3], p. 555.
Kenneth S. Wuest[4], Vol. 1, p. 221.
November 4th
Merrill C. Tenney, p. 361
November 5th
Matthew Henry, Concise Commentary on the Whole Bible (Chicago: Moody Press, 1983), p. 708
November 20th
[1]Matthew Henry, Concise Commentary on the Whole Bible (Chicago: Moody Press, 1983), p. 711.
[2]Flavius Josephus, The War of the Jews. History of the Destruction of Jerusalem, Book VI. Chapters 1.1 and 9.3, Taken from Wikipedia – The Destruction of the Temple of Jerusalem in 70 A.D.
November 23rd
[1]Kenneth Scott Latourette, A History of Christianity (New York: Harper & Brothers, 1953), pp. 129-131.
[2]Ibid., p. 130.
December 15th - Oswald Chambers, p. 106

Index to Biblical References

January 1 – Jn. 3:34-36, 6:63
    2 - Col. 1:25b-27, Jn. 17:23
    3 - Gen. 2:7, Jn. 10:10b
    4 - Eph. 2:4-7, 3:12
    5 - Phil. 3:7-9
    6 - Jn. 14:23
    7 - Jn. 14:6
    8 - Ps. 104:34
    9 - Jn. 10:7, 9
    10- Jn. 10:14-15
    11- Jn. 10:27-28
    12 - Jn. 11:25-26
    13 - Jn. 12:24-25, 32
    14 - Jn. 12:36
    15 - Jn. 13:12-14, 17
    16 - Jn. 13:35
    17 - Jn. 14:15
    18 - Jn. 14:16-17
    19 - Jn. 15:2, Gal. 5:22
    20 - Jn. 15:4
    21 - Jn. 16:33
    22 - Jn. 17:1-3
    23 - Jn. 17:23, 14:23, Gal. 1:27b
    24- Jn. 18:37
    25 - Ps. 34:1-3
    26 - Ps. 37:3-4
    27 - Ps. 16:1-2
    28 - 2 Cor. 5:17
    29 - 2 Cor. 6:5
    30 - Ps. 46:10a
    31 - Lk.17:20b-21, Jn. 14:20, Jn. 17:23
February 1 - Ps. 139:23-24
    2 - Mk. 4:39, Ps. 65:7, Ps. 89:5
    3 - Jer. 19:25-27
    4 - Jn. 4:23-24
    5 - Phil. 4:8
    6 - Lk. 6:37, 39, 40
    7 - Rom. 12:2
    8 - Ps. 84:1-2, Eph. 2:6, Matt. 6:6
    9 - Pr. 19:21-22
    10 - Pr. 19:20
    11 – Acts 3:16
    12 – Acts 19:13
    13 – Mt. 1:1
    14 - Mt. 1:2a, 2 Sam. 7:17
    15 - Matt. 1:6b, 1 Sam. 15:14,
    16 - Mt. 1:12a, 16; Lam. 1:5, Mic. 5:4a
    17 - Mt. 1:17, Gen. 12:3, Ps. 89:3
    18 - Mt. 1:18, Lk. 1:35, 37; Jn. 3:11, Luke 11:13
    19 - Mt. 1:19
    20 - Mt. 1:20b, Is. 7:14
    21 - Mt. 2:1a
    22 - Mt. 2:1b-2
    23 - Mt. 2:6b
    24 - Mt. 2:11a
    25 - Mt. 2:11b, Mt. 6:21
    26 - Mt. 2:13a, Mt. 13:14b, Jn. 10:34
    27 - Mt. 2:15b
    28 - Mt. 2:19-20, Jn. 16:13b-14
    29 - Mt. 2:22b-23, Pr. 3:5-6
March 1 - Mt. 3:1-2
    2 - Mt. 3:3, Is. 40:1-2, 4
    3 - Mt. 3:4, Lk.1:66-68, 76-77, 80
    4 - Mt. 3:5-6
    5 - Mt. 3:10b
    6 - Mt. 3:11
    7 - Mt. 3:11, Lk.7:28
    8 - Mt. 3:12b, Jn. 15:11
    9 - Mt. 3:13
    10 - Mt. 3:16-17
    11 - Mt. 4:1
    12 - Mt. 4:2, 1 Cor. 9:27, Rom. 12:1
    13 - Mt. 4:3, Gen. 34:1, 4, 5; Lk.9:23
    14 - Mt. 4:4
    15 - Mt. 4:6a-7
    16 - Mt. 4:8-9
    17 - Mt. 4:10, Deut. 5:7-9a, 11; Lk.9:23-25
    18 - Mt. 4:11, Rom. 8:26-27, 2 Cor.12:9
    19 - Mt. 4:14, Is. 9:1-2, Jn. 1:1, 4, 5
    20 - Mt. 4:17, Lk. 9:23
    21 - Mt. 4:17
    22 - Mt. 4:19-20, Jn. 3:17
    23 - Mt. 4:21
    24 - Mt. 4:23, Mk. 1:15
    25 - Mt. 4:24b
    26 - Mt. 5:1-2
    27 - Mt. 5:3-4
    28 - Mt. 5:5
    29 - Mt. 5:6, Rom. 5:17
    30 - Mt. 5:7
    31 - Mt. 5:8
April 1 - Mt. 5:9, Rom. 5:1
    2 - Mt. 5:10, Rom. 3:10-11, Phil. 3:9
    3 - Mt. 5:10-12
    4 - Mt. 5:13
    5 - Mt. 5:14-16
    6 - Mt. 5:17-18b, Gal. 3:23-25,

	Rom. 8:4	26	- Mt. 8:5-6, Ps. 103:1-5
	7 - Mt. 5:20	27	- Lk. 17:20-21, 4:43
	8 - Mt. 5:22a, Is. 55:8a, Pr. 4:23	28	- Mt. 8:13, 16:13
	9 - Mt. 5:22b, Eph. 4:26, Jn. 4:23	29	- Mt. 8:14-15, 21:22
	10 - Mt. 5:27-28, Ex. 20:14	30	- Mt. 8:16-17, 2 Cor. 10:3-4
April	11 - Mt. 5:29, Jn. 18:36	31	- Mt. 8:18-20, 3:10
	12 - Mt. 5:30	June 1	- Mt. 8:23, Lk. 9:23
	13 - Mt. 5:31-32, Mal. 2:6	2	- Mt. 8:24-25
	14 - Mt. 5:33-34a, Ps. 101:7, Jn. 17:18	3	- Mt. 8:28, Ps. 46:10, 1 Jn. 4:4
	15 - Mt. 5:38-39, 1 Jn. 4:4, Heb. 10:30	4	- Mt. 8:34, Lk. 6:23-24
	16 - Mt. 5:40, Js. 1:17, Lk. 12:14, 42-44	5	- Mt. 9:2
		6	- Mt. 9:2b, 5-6
	17 - Mt. 5:41-41, Lk. 6:38	7	- Mt. 9:6
	18 - Mt. 5:43-45	8	- Mt. 9:9
	19 - Mt. 5:48, 1 Jn. 3:11, 23; 4:11	9	- Mt. 9:10
	20 - Mt. 6:1	10	- Mt. 9:11-12, Rom. 3:10, Is. 64:6
	21 - Mt. 6:3-4	11	- Mt. 9:12-13
	22 - Mt. 6:5	12	- Mt. 9:17, 4:17, Jn. 3:3
	23 - Mt. 6:6	13	- Mt. 9:21-22
	24 - Mt. 6:7-8	14	- Mt. 9:24-25
	25 - Mt. 6:9, Is. 6:36b, Lev. 19:2, Ps. 42:2	15	- Mt. 9:28-30a
		16	- Mt. 9:32, Eph. 6:12-13
	26 - Mt. 6:10, 10:7, 11:12; Col. 1:13, Lk. 4:43	17	- Mt. 9:35, 3:2, 4:17, Jn. 3:3
		18	- Mt. 9:36, 25:35-36, 40b
	27 - Mt. 6:11	19	- Mt. 9:37-38
	28 - Mt. 6:12, 14-15	20	- Mt. 10:1-2a
	29 - Mt. 6:13	21	- Mt. 10:6-7
	30 - Mt. 6:14-15, 18:27	22	- Mt. 10:7b-8
May	1 - Mt. 6:16	23	- Mt. 10:9-10
	2 - Mt. 6:21, 33	24	- Mt. 10:12-13
	3 - Mt. 6:22-23	25	- Mt. 10:14
	4 - Mt. 6:24	26	- Mt. 10:16
	5 - Mt. 6:25, Rom. 8:28	27	- Mt. 10:17-18
	6 - Mt. 6:26	28	- Mt. 10:19-20, Jn. 16:13
	7 - Mt. 6:28	29	- Mt. 10:21-22
	8 - Mt. 6:31, 32b	30	- Mt. 10:23
	9 - Mt. 6:33	July 1	- Mt. 10:24-26
	10 - Mt. 6:34	2	- Mt. 10:27-28, Is. 30:21
	11 - Mt. 7:1-2	3	- Mt. 10:30-31, Eph. 3:17-19, Ps. 139:13-18
	12 - Mt. 7:3, Phil. 12:12-15a		
	13 - Mt. 7:6	4	- Mt. 10:32-33, Jn. 1:17
	14 - Mt. 7:7-8, 6:6	5	- Mt. 10:34, Mk. 12:30
	15 - Mt. 7:9-11, Mk. 8:24b	6	- Mt. 10:38-39, Mk. 8:37, Ps. 139:15-16
	16 - Mt. 7:12, 5:17		
	17 - Mt. 7:13-14, Lk. 9:62	7	- Mt. 10:40-41
	18 - Mt. 7:17-18, 19:17b	8	- Mt. 10:42, 25:35-36
	19 - Mt. 7:21, 23b	9	- Mt. 11:1, 4:17, 23; Mk. 4:14-15
	20 - Mt. 7:24-25, 11:15	10	- Mt. 11:2-4a
	21 - Mt. 7:26-27	11	- Mt. 11:7, Mal. 3:1, Rev. 2:10
	22 - Is. 66:1-2	12	- Mt. 11:11, Lk. 1:15-17, 76-77
	23 - Mt. 7:28-29	13	- Mt. 11:12
	24 - Mt. 8:1	14	- Mt. 11:13-14, Mal. 4:5-6, Rev. 13:8, Eph. 1:4
	25 - Mt. 8:2-3		

July 15 - Mt. 11:15, Mk. 4:10-12,
           2 Pet. 3:19
      16 - Mt. 11:19b, 1 Cor. 2:11
      17 - Mt. 11:20
      18 - Mt. 11:25, 1 Cor. 12:3b
      19 - Mt. 11:26-27,
           2 Pet. 1:20, Ecc. 8:1
      20 - Mt. 11:28
      21 - Mt. 11:29
      22 - Mt. 12:1
      23 - Mt. 12:7-8, 11:29b
      24 - Mt. 12:10
      25 - Mt. 12:13-14
      26 - Mt. 12:15-16, Prov. 3:5-6
      27 - Mt. 12:18, 3:16a, 17; 4:1a;
           1 Pet. 2:9
      28 - Mt. 12:19, 20b-21
      29 - Mt. 12:12:22, Eph. 6:12,
           1 Jn. 4:4, 1 Jn. 5:5
      30 - Mt. 12:23, 2 Sam. 7:12-13
      31 - Mt. 12:25
August 1 - Mt. 12:28-29, 1 Jn. 4:1
       2 - Mt. 12:30
       3 - Mt. 12:32, Jn. 3:16
       4 - Mt. 12:33
       5 - Mt. 12:34, Gal. 5:19-23
       6 - Mt. 12:36-37
       7 - Mt. 12:38-39
       8 - Mt. 12:43-44
       9 - Mt. 12:49b-50
      10 - Mt. 13:2
      11 - Mt. 13:3, 13, 18-19a; Ps. 147:11
      12 - Mt. 13:4, 19b; Rom. 10:14-15;
           Ps. 115:1
      13 - Mt. 13:5-6, 20b-21
      14 - Mt. 13:7, 22
      15 - Mt. 13:8-9, 23
      16 - Mt. 13:11-12, Mk. 4:13
      17 - Mt. 13:13-15, Is. 6:10
      18 - Mt. 13:16
      19 - Mt. 13:24-25, Gal. 5:19-21
      20 - Mt. 13:37-39, 1 Jn. 1:7, Jn. 3:36
      21 - Mt. 13:41-42
      22 - Mt. 13:31; Eph. 4:15-16
      23 - Mt. 13:33
      24 - Ps. 78:1-3, Lk. 18:17
      25 - Mt. 13:44, 7:7
      26 - Mt. 13:45-46; Mk. 8:34
      27 - Mt. 13:47-48
      28 - Mt. 13:52
      29 - Mt. 13:58
      30 - Mt. 14:1-2
      31 - Mt. 14:13a

Sept. 1 - Mt. 14:13b-14
       2 - Mt. 14:16, 18, 21
       3 - Mt. 14:22-23
       4 - Mt. 14:23, Mk. 6:46, Lk. 6:12
       5 - Mt. 14:24-25, 27
       6 - Mt. 14:28-29
       7 - Mt. 14:30-31; Jn. 3:8
       8 - Mt. 14:33
       9 - Mt. 14:35-36
      10 - Mt. 15:1-2; Jn. 15:21; Lk. 17:20
      11 - Mt. 15:8-9; Is. 29:13
      12 - Mt. 15:10b-11, 18-19
      13 - Mt. 15:18; Titus 3:4-7
      14 - Mt. 15:28
      15 - Mt. 15:31
      16 - Mt. 15:32
      17 - Mt. 16:5-6
      18 - Mt. 16:13, 1 Cor. 12:3, 1 Jn. 3:2-3
      19 - Mt. 16:18
      20 - Mt. 16:19, Rom. 14:17, Jn. 8:36
      21 - Mt. 16:21, Rev. 13:8, Mt. 12:40,
           Rom. 6:11
      22 - Mt. 16:23, 1 Jn. 2:27
      23 - Mt. 16:24
      24 - Mt. 16:24
      25 - Mt. 16:25; Eph. 1:3-4
      26 - Mt. 16:26
      27 - Mt. 16:25-26
      28 - Mt. 16:27, Lk. 13:28
      29 - Mt. 16:28
      30 - Mt. 17:2-3, Is. 60:1, Ez. 3:23
Oct.   1 - Mt. 17:4-6
       2 - Mt. 17:7, 9
       3 - Mt. 17:11-12
       4 - Mt. 17:19-20
       5 - Mt. 17:22-23
       6 - Mt. 17:27
       7 - Mt. 18:1-2
       8 - Mt. 18:6
       9 - Mt. 18:7
      10 - Mt. 18:10
      11 - Mt. 18:7b
      12 - Mt. 18:14
      13 - Mt. 18:15
      14 - Mt. 18:16a
      15 - Mt. 18:18-19
      16 - Mt. 18:20
      17 - Mt. 18:21-22
      18 - Mt. 18:23
      19 - Mt. 18:34-35
      20 - Mt. 19:5-6
      21 - Mt. 19:8
      22 - Mt. 19:14

- 23- Mt. 19:21; Mt. 16:24
- 24- Mt. 19:23, 26
- 25- Mt. 19:29, 1 Jn. 5:11-12
- 26- Mt. 20:15-16; Is. 55:8-9
- 27- Mt. 20:18-19, Jn. 1:14
- 28- Mt. 20:20-21, Phil. 4:8
- 29- Mt. 20:22a, 25b-27
- 30- Mt. 20:28
- 31- Mt. 20:29-30

Nov.
- 1 - Mt. 21:1b-3
- 2 - Mt. 21:9-11
- 3 - Mt. 21:12; Mk. 11:17
- 4 - Mt. 21:14-17
- 5 - Mt. 21:21; Acts 17:28
- 6 - Mt. 21:22; Lk. 17:5; 1 Thess. 3:42
- 7 - Mt. 21:24; Rom. 6:5
- 8 - Mt. 21:31b-32
- 9 - Mt. 21:43; Eph. 6:12; 1 Jn. 4:4
- 10- Mt. 22:2
- 11- Mt. 22:21-22
- 12- Mt. 22:29-30; 1 Cor. 15:49-51; Lk. 17:21
- 13- Mt. 22:37-40
- 14- Mt. 22:46
- 15- Mt. 23:1-3
- 16- Mt. 23:8-12
- 17- Mt. 23:13; Lk. 17:21
- 18- Mt. 23:26; Jn. 14:11-12, 23-24; 15:4
- 19- Mt. 23:37-38; Lk. 4:17b-21
- 20- Mt. 24:2
- 21- Mt. 24:4, 11
- 22- Mt. 24:13
- 23- Mt. 24:14
- 24- Mt. 24:36
- 25- Mt. 24:42, 44
- 26- Mt. 24:45-46
- 27- Mt. 25:10
- 28- Mt. 25:11-12
- 29- Mt. 25:21
- 30- Mt. 25:29-30

Dec.
- 1 - Mt. 25:34
- 2 - Mt. 25:45-46
- 3 - Mt. 26:1-2; Rev. 13:8; Is. 53:11-12; Ps. 22:1, 7-18; Deut. 21:22-23a
- 4 - Mt. 26:6, 12
- 5 - Mt. 26:14-15; 1 Thess. 5:2-6
- 6 - Mt. 26:26-28; Lk. 17:20b-21; Jn. 14:11, 23; Jn. 15:5; Col. 1:27
- 7 - Mt. 26:35; Rev. 2:10
- 8 - Mt. 26:40-41
- 9 - Mt. 26:42; Jn. 14:31; Jn. 14:9
- 10- Mt. 26:55-56, 25; Zech. 13:6-7, Zech. 11:12; Ps. 41:9; Is. 53:7-9

Dec.
- 11- Mt. 26:63-64, 66b-67
- 12- Mt. 26:75; 1 Cor. 6:19
- 13- Mt. 27:1-2
- 14- Mt. 27:12-14
- 15- Mt. 27:20
- 16- Mt. 27:29-30; Lk. 23:20-23; Jn. 19:1-3; Is. 53:5, 10-11
- 17- Mt. 27:33-35; Jn. 19:23
- 18- Mt. 27:38; Lk. 23:39-43
- 19- Mt. 27:45-46; Jn. 1:29; 2 Cor. 5:19, 21; Rom. 6:6-7; Is. 53:6
- 20- Mt. 27:50; Jn. 19:30; Ps. 22:14-18
- 21- Mt. 27:57; Mk.15:43, 46
- 22- Mt. 28:2, 5-7
- 23- Mt. 28:10
- 24- Jn. 21:1; Jn. 1:66-67a
- 25- Jn. 21:21-22; Phil. 2:5-8
- 26- Acts 1:3; Jn. 21:25; Acts 1:5-8a, Acts 2:4, 17; Col. 1:27b
- 27- Mt. 28:18-20
- 28- Acts 28:30-31; Mt. 12:28; Mt. 24:14; 1 Cor. 15:22-24
- 29- 1 Cor. 15:50; Mt. 16:17, 19; 2 Tim. 2:11-13
- 30- Col. 1:13-14; Phil. 4:11-12; Col. 3:5, 8-11
- 31- Col. 1:25b-27; 1 Cor. 13:12; 1 Jn. 5:13-15, 18-20

www.ingramcontent.com/pod-product-compliance
Lightning Source LLC
Chambersburg PA
CBHW031402290426
44110CB00011B/235